Anton Chekhov
The Island: A Journey to Sakhalin

"A man of letters is a responsible person, under contract to his conscience and the consciousness of his duty . . . bound to battle with his fastidiousness and soil his imagination with the grime of life."
—*from a letter of 1887*

His health impaired by tuberculosis, Anton Chekhov undertook the arduous journey across Siberia and the Tatar Strait to study conditions in the tsarist penal colonies on Sakhalin Island. Briefing himself with every pertinent book and report, he arrived armed with letters of introduction and an exhaustive series of printed questionnaires, unaware that a secret memorandum prohibiting contact with political prisoners had preceded his arrival. Ostensibly conducting a census, he received splendid cooperation from many administrative heads. His interviews were met with frankness, contributing greatly to the richness of the data he acquired. After months of tireless work, he returned home announcing that he had spoken "with every man, woman, and child on the island."

These experiences were to become the substance of the only work of nonfiction by Russia's greatest dramatis

"*The Island of Sakhalin* . . . superb as a as reportage, and merciless in its objecti

— Marc Slonim in *Modern Russian Literature from Chekhov to the Present*

D1213060

THE RUSSIAN LIBRARY

General Editor ROBERT PAYNE

TITLES IN PRINT, FALL, 1967

The Island

A Journey to Sakhalin

ANTON CHEKHOV

The Island
A Journey to Sakhalin

Translated by LUBA *and* MICHAEL TERPAK

With an Introduction by ROBERT PAYNE

WASHINGTON SQUARE PRESS, INC., *New York, 1967*

LIBRARY OF CONGRESS CATALOG CARD NUMBER: 67–10299

PUBLISHED SIMULTANEOUSLY IN THE UNITED STATES AND CANADA BY WASHINGTON SQUARE PRESS, INC.

PRINTED IN THE UNITED STATES OF AMERICA.

Contents

Introduction

I

ON JANUARY 16, 1890, his thirtieth birthday, Anton Chekhov was at the height of his fame. Astonishingly handsome, quiet-mannered, gentle, ironical, in full enjoyment of his genius and with no trace of arrogance, he seemed to be one of those men who are especially favored by the gods to accomplish everything they set out to do. In five years he had reached a dazzling position in Russian literature as the acknowledged master of the short story and as a playwright of indisputable power. He had already written most of the short stories for which he would be remembered, and many of the plays, and there was no indication that the tide was ebbing. On the contrary, he was in the full possession of the marvelous instrument he had created, and knew exactly how to play it. He had received the Pushkin Prize from the Imperial Academy of Sciences, and he had been elected a member of the Society of Lovers of Russian Literature. These were rare honors, and although he half despised his growing fame, he derived pleasure from them. It was not only that he was at the height of his fame and of his powers, but he was aware of being loved as few writers are ever loved. People were happy in his presence, and there appeared to be no dark shadows.

To have known Chekhov in those days was to have known genius robed in the garments of an extraordinary humanity. Over six feet tall, and so slender that he seemed taller, with a mane of thick brown hair, fine eyes, a straight nose, a sensual mouth and a well-trimmed beard, he looked like a young Viking. There was nothing in the least melancholy and abstracted about his appearance. He enjoyed life passionately, entertained his friends continually, never happier than when he collected flocks of actors, actresses, circus clowns, professional men and vagabonds of all kinds in his country house, where he regaled them with a running fire of jokes and ludicrous improvisations, treating them with princely hospitality. He enjoyed a number of liaisons with young women, who did not always write their memoirs. He had a steady income, and if it should ever happen that the vein of literature should dry up, he could always return to his medical practice. He was, and knew himself to be, the darling of the gods. Nevertheless, wherever he looked, the dark shadows were pressing in on him.

Although outwardly gay and carefree, confident of his powers and generous with his gifts of friendship and compassion, he was strangely restless. There was no single name for this form of restlessness which increasingly took hold of him, like a fever. From time to time he would examine it, like a doctor examining a clinical chart, and he would offer himself or his close friends elaborate explanations of the nature of the disease, but nearly always mockingly, with happy improvisations, as though it would go away if he laughed at it. He was too sensible, too down-to-earth, to take himself or his moods seriously. He was profoundly dissatisfied with his art, his fame and Russian society. At the same time he enjoyed his art, relished his fame and found himself at ease on all levels of Russian society, although he was oppressed by the poverty and ignorance of the Russian peasants and by the stupidity of their masters and of all bureaucrats. This was a dissatisfaction he shared with nearly all the educated men of his time, and though it weighed heavily on him, he found it no more oppressive on the eve of his thirtieth birthday than at any other period of his life.

What did oppress him more than he ever dared to admit was the death of his brother Nikolay the previous June. Nikolay was a gifted painter who had thrown his talents away, a wastrel with a common-law wife, a drunkard who deliberately set himself to live like a bohemian. Charming, stupid and uncultivated, Nikolay was continually borrowing money from his brother, spending it on women and drink. He was already dying of typhoid fever and tuberculosis when Chekhov brought him to a rented estate in the Ukraine, hoping his diseases would be cured or alleviated in the dry summer air. He kept watch by the bedside, hoping against hope, reminding himself that miracles had happened before and might happen again, his affection at war with his medical knowledge, for he knew the diseases were incurable. Most of the Chekhov family gathered on the small estate and Alexey Suvorin, the publisher, came down from St. Petersburg to share the long vigil. When at last Nikolay died, Chekhov's grief shocked his friends. "Poor Nikolay is dead," he wrote. "I am stupid, extinguished. I am bored to death, and there is not a penny-worth of poetry in life, and I have no desires." Quite suddenly he seemed to be drifting aimlessly in a sea of uncertainties. There was nothing he wanted to do, nowhere he wanted to go. Nikolay was the first of the large family to die, and he seemed to feel that his family, which gave meaning to his life, was in some curious way threatened. The "vagabond artist" had gone, and left a gaping hole in their lives.

It was about this time, when he was still recovering from the shock of grief, that he chanced upon a copy of the penal code and observed to his brother Mikhail that when a criminal is arrested and placed on trial, everyone is interested, but when he is sentenced to imprisonment no one cares about his fate. He suffers hunger and cold, leads a life of desolate privation, and no one cares. He is made to perform absurd and useless labors, brutal guards have him at their mercy, but it is as though he had completely vanished from the world. According to Mikhail it was this chance reading of the penal code which set him off on his journey to the island of Sakhalin, that cold and barren island which the Russian government had chosen as the place of exile for its most dangerous prisoners. Sakhalin lay at the farthest limits of the Russian empire, and could be reached only by a long and difficult journey across the whole length of Siberia. Even to Mikhail the motives for the journey remained mysterious. "Anton Pavlovich," he wrote, "began making preparations for the journey to the Far East so suddenly and unexpectedly that at first we scarcely knew whether he was serious, or only joking."

Chekhov himself scarcely knew why he was going there; he knew only that he had to go there, that some impulse stronger than himself was driving him to it. At various times he would offer explanations to his friends, who were anxious for his health and disturbed by the prospect of his long absence. He would turn their questions into a joke, saying he needed "a good shaking-up," or he would explain patiently that he owed a debt to medicine and proposed to write a carefully documented dissertation on the medical aspects of the penal colony. To others he would say that he was bored, and an arduous journey relentlessly pursued would give him two or three days which he would remember with gratitude for the rest of his life. Or else he would explain that he had grown lazy and needed six months of uninterrupted physical and mental work to keep himself in training. He had so many explanations that the real one eventually vanished in a cocoon of myths, exaggerations and inventive half-truths, for it amused him to see the bewilderment of his friends and he could deploy whole armies of reasons whenever they were required. It became a kind of game. It was a dangerous game, and he may have known that his life was at stake.

To those who were especially close to him he would hint that there were more serious reasons for the journey. To one he hinted darkly that he did not expect to return, to another he spoke of the need for a Russian writer to venture into the forbidding landscape of imprisonment for his soul's sake, while to a third he spoke of a restlessness which had gripped him by the throat and would not give him any rest—only a long journey would quieten him. But even when he spoke in this way we are made aware of evasions and circumlocutions. These statements were perhaps closer to the truth, but they were not the whole truth.

When the time came for him to make formal application to the authorities for permission to visit Sakhalin, which was under the administration of the Office of Prisons in St. Petersburg, Chekhov explained that he had only "scientific and literary purposes" in view, and those colorless words appear to have been designed to put the authorities off the scent. The head of the Office of Prisons was a pompous and much-decorated official called Mikhail Galkin-Vrasky, and to this elderly nobleman Chekhov accordingly wrote a humble letter of petition:

20 January 1890

> Your Excellency,
>   Mikhail Nikolayevich!
> Proposing in the spring of the present year to journey to the Far East for scientific and literary purposes, and desiring among other things to visit the island of Sakhalin both in its central and southern parts, I make bold to present this humble petition to Your Excellency for any assistance it may be possible for you to give me toward the fulfillment of the above-mentioned aims.
> With sincere devotion and respect I have the honor to be Your Excellency's most humble servant,
>
> Anton Chekhov

It was the kind of letter one writes with the sweat of one's brow, hoping for the precise degree of required flattery, the proper subservience, the necessary bureaucratic tone. The head of the Office of Prisons was suitably impressed by the letter and Chekhov was granted an audience, where he explained at some length exactly what he intended to accomplish during the journey. He especially wanted to see the inside of the prisons and to study the industries which were being established on Sakhalin. Galkin-Vrasky could not have been more agreeable and polite, and when Chekhov left the Office of Prisons he was under the impression that all doors would be open to him. The nobleman understood thoroughly the purpose of the journey, congratulated Chekhov on his laudable desire to study the prison system, and immediately sent off a letter to Sakhalin, warning the authorities against the forthcoming visit of "the noted writer Anton Chekhov," who must on no account be allowed to have any contact with political prisoners and certain specified categories of prisoners.

Meanwhile Chekhov was spending every available moment studying the history of Sakhalin, the geology, geography, meteorology, the flora and fauna, the habits of the primitive tribes which still maintained an existence on the island. He pored over maps, and consulted obscure articles in magazines and newspapers, collecting so many books and articles that his rooms were piled high with them. He became an avid collector of statistics, which he copied out in his notebooks, and sketched out whole sections of the book he proposed to write—all those sections which did not depend on direct observation—and already the shape of the book was clear in his mind. What particularly distressed him was the discovery that most of the articles published on Sakhalin were written by people who had never been there, had not the least idea of the problems faced by the prisoners on the island, and were interested only in making pontifical statements on the virtues of the penal system and the high moral attitude of the government which kindly offered them a suitable method of expiating their crimes. Such men would enjoy a good meal and then sit down to write a learned discussion on some subject like "The Problems of Prison Management in Sakhalin," and an hour later they would have completed a formidable inquiry into a subject they knew nothing about. To his astonishment Chekhov discovered that there was very little worth reading about Sakhalin, and he had to piece together his knowledge of the island from hundreds of books and articles, finding a fact here and a description there, juxtaposing the impressions of a visitor recorded in some out-of-the-way magazine article with a set of official statistics. He was in no mood to suffer fools gently, and in his letters he railed against the idiocy of the bureaucrats who wrote out of insolence and ignorance on matters which were desperately serious.

He worked in the libraries of St. Petersburg and Moscow, and set his friends working for him. His brother

Alexander was made to work through the old files of the Petersburg newspaper, while his sister Maria went to work in the Rumyantsev library in Moscow, copying out long articles with the help of her girl friends. Chekhov was an exacting taskmaster, for he demanded to see everything that had been written about Sakhalin, and every map, however ancient, which showed the island. "Day after day I read and write, write and read," he wrote to Suvorin in the second half of February. "The more I read, the stronger grows my conviction that in my two months on Sakhalin I shall not be able to accomplish more than a quarter of what I had hoped to accomplish." He had become, he said, "such a scholarly son of a bitch" that everyone will be surprised out of their wits, and he added that he had stolen a multitude of ideas from other people which he would later claim as his own. "In a practical age like ours, it is impossible to do otherwise," he wrote, and there was something in his letter which suggested that he was about to write the book to end all books on Sakhalin, a compilation of every known fact and surmise about the island with a twenty-page bibliography. With such a large volume, with so many authorities quoted in so many footnotes, he hinted that he would become what he always hoped to become— a real writer.

Chekhov was perfectly serious in his desire to write an authoritative work on Sakhalin, and he was only half joking when he spoke of becoming a real writer after writing his account of the penal colony. He had a great affection for the still unwritten book; it was his "brain-child," the fruit of interminable labors and many furious contemplations; and he was determined in those early days that it should have an impact on society. When the book was finally written he was less hopeful about the impact on society.

As the winter gave way to spring, his friends became understandably more nervous about the journey. Now at last it became clear that he must be taken seriously. He was telling his friends that he would leave Moscow as soon as the ice melted on the Kama River, so that he could make part of the journey by river. The ice melted shortly after Easter, and now Easter was approaching. Suvorin came to the conclusion that Chekhov was deadly serious and one last effort must be made to dissuade him. He listed all the dangers and inconveniences of the journey, doubted whether there could be any fruitful result, wondered whether Sakhalin had the slightest interest for anybody, and advanced the claims of Chekhov's friends, who were entitled to know that he was in good health, not risking his life in some godforsaken island on the other end of the earth. The journey could be postponed; better still, it could be abandoned. Chekhov replied good-humoredly, prefacing the letter, as he often did, with the saint's day and a general indication of the weather he was enjoying in Moscow—by "10,000 skylarks" he meant that spring had already come. He wrote:

March 9. The Forty Martyrs
and 10,000 skylarks

Dear Alexey Sergeyevich,

We are both mistaken about Sakhalin, but you probably more than I. I am leaving in the firm conviction that my expedition will not yield anything valuable in the way of literature or science; for this I have not enough knowledge or time or ambition. I have not carefully worked out plans like Humboldt or Kennan.[1] I want to write a couple of hundred pages, and in this way repay in some small part the debt I owe to medicine, which, as you know, I have neglected like a swine.

Perhaps I shall not be able to write anything worthwhile, but the journey does not lose its glamour for me; by reading, observing, listening I shall discover and learn much. Although I have not yet left, thanks to the books I have gone through I have learned many things which everyone ought to know under a penalty of forty lashes, things which in my ignorance were hitherto unknown to me. Moreover I believe the journey will be an uninterrupted

---

[1] Alexander von Humboldt (1769–1859) at the age of sixty made a famous journey across Asiatic Russia in search of geological data. George Kennan (1845–1924), the American explorer, studied the Siberian prisons in 1886 and wrote his classic work *Siberia and the Exile System.*

six months of physical and mental labor, and for me this is necessary because I am a Little Russian and I have already grown lazy. I have to discipline myself. Granting that my journey may be the purest nonsense, a mere whim, an act of stubbornness—think it over and tell me, what do I lose by going? Time? Money? Shall I have to undergo hardships? My time isn't worth anything, I'll never have any money anyway, as for hardships I'll be traveling by horse for twenty-five or thirty days, no longer, and for the rest of the time I shall be sitting on deck in a steamer or in a room, and I'll be bombarding you incessantly with letters.

Even if the journey turns out to be absolutely unrewarding, there are still bound to be two or three days in the course of the entire journey which I will remember for the rest of my life with joy or poignancy, surely? Etc., etc. That's how it is, my dear sir. You will say that this is not convincing, but what you write is equally unconvincing. For example, you write that Sakhalin is no use to anybody, and no one has the slightest interest in the place. Is this really true? Sakhalin may be useless and uninteresting only to a society that does not exile thousands of people to it and does not spend millions maintaining it. Except for Australia in the old days and Cayenne, Sakhalin is the only place left where it is possible to study colonization by criminals: all Europe is interested in it, and we pay no attention to it.

Not more than twenty-five or thirty years ago our Russian people, while exploring Sakhalin, performed wonderful exploits, for which one could believe men were gods, but we have no use for this sort of thing, we don't want to know what kind of people they were, and so we sit comfortably surrounded by our four walls and complain that God created man to no good purpose. Sakhalin is a place of intolerable sufferings, and man alone, whether free or enslaved, is capable of making such a place. Those who work near the island or on it have solved terrible and responsible problems, and are doing so now. I am sorry I am not sentimental: otherwise I would say we ought to go on pilgrimage to Sakhalin as the Turks go to Mecca, while seamen and criminologists in particular should regard Sakhalin as military men look upon Sebastopol. From the books I have read and am reading, it is clear that we have sent *millions* of people to rot in prison, we have let them rot casually, barbarously, without giving it a thought, we have driven people in chains for thousands of miles through the cold, infected them with syphilis, made them depraved, multiplied criminals, and we have thrust the blame for all this on red-nosed jail-keepers.

Today all of educated Europe knows that it is not the fault of the jailers, but rather of all of us—and this is none of our concern, this is not interesting! The celebrated '60s did *nothing* for the sick and imprisoned, thus breaking the most important commandment of Christian civilization. In our time something is being done for the sick, but nothing for prisoners: the study of prison conditions does not interest our jurists in the least. No, I assure you, Sakhalin is of use, and it is interesting, and my sole regret is that it is I who am going there, and not someone else more capable of arousing public interest. I personally am going after the merest trifles. . . .

So Chekhov wrote in the longest and most carefully considered defense of his quixotic journey, when it became clear that some kind of explanation to his friends could no longer be avoided. But the explanation is not wholly convincing, and he was a little more convincing when he wrote a few days later to his friend Ivan Leontiev-Shcheglov:

I am not going in order to observe or get impressions, but simply so that I can live for half a year as I have never lived up to this time. So don't expect anything from me, old fellow; if I have the time and ability to achieve anything, then glory be to God; if not, don't find fault with me. I shall be going after Easter week. . . .

II

When Chekhov left Moscow on April 21 on the first stage of his journey to the Far East, he believed he had made all the proper arrangements and taken all the proper precautions. He was armed with a bottle of cognac, top boots, a sheepskin, a waterproof leather coat, a knife "useful for cutting sausages and killing tigers," as he explained to Suvorin, and a revolver, which proved to be an unnecessary luxury, for it was never used. He was in good spirits, although in the excitement of preparing for the journey he had been spitting blood. He had been spitting blood at intervals since the previous December; he had succeeded in convincing himself that it came from his throat and not from his lungs.

He had made his plans carefully and sensibly, and from conversations with people who had made the journey across Siberia he thought there would be no difficulties until he reached Sakhalin. In fact many things went wrong. Most of the time he was lonely, miserable, in a state of settled melancholy. If there had been a companion he liked, if the painter Isaac Levitan had accompanied him as he had once hoped, it might have been more endurable. The journey by train to Yaroslavl was uneventful, but traveling by boat along the Volga and Kama rivers shocked him because he seemed to be sinking into hitherto unknown regions of boredom. His first glimpse of the Volga was spoiled by rain, and when the sun came out he was delighted by the sight of the white churches and monasteries along the banks and by the water meadows, but afterward when the sun lay hidden behind the clouds, the gray river became a torment. The Kama was no better, and besides, it grew colder the farther they traveled eastward. There were patches of snow on the banks; ice floes floated down the river. The towns on the Kama seemed to be inhabited by people "who manufactured clouds, boredom, wet fences and garbage." He reached Perm at two o'clock in the morning, coughing and spitting blood. It was raining and bitterly cold. He took the train to Tyumen, where he discovered that the first boat did not leave for Tomsk for another two weeks, and so he arranged to hire a coach, a decision which he later regretted. He wore two pairs of trousers, a sheepskin jacket, a leather coat, and still he felt cold. Sometimes he saw straggling files of prisoners, and the sight of those tragic figures making their way to their place of exile in Siberia only filled him with greater uneasiness, a more intolerable melancholy.

Still, there were some things he enjoyed or found amusing during the long journey from Tyumen to Tomsk. At first he enjoyed the sensation of spinning along at great speed in his small coach, a small springless carriage called a *tarantass,* drawn by a pair of horses. It resembled a wicker basket on wheels, and he liked "to look out on God's earth like a bird in a cage without a thought in the world." But soon the horses wearied and the coachman no longer shouted at them or whipped them. He found himself "groaning and moaning like an Egyptian pigeon."

Chekhov enjoyed the villages they passed through, and he had pleasant things to say about their sweet-smelling cleanliness, the soft beds with feather mattresses and huge pillows, the kindness of the villagers, who were well-mannered and as clean as their huts. People did not belch or scratch or put their fingers in the glass when they were offering you milk. He liked the white bread, and ate so much of it that "for some days I made a pig of myself." He was entranced by the dignity and good sense of these people. "My God," he exclaimed, "how rich Russia is in good people! If it were not for the cold which deprives Siberia of any summer, and the officials who corrupt the peasants and the exiles, Siberia would be the richest and happiest place on earth."

One day not long after he set out from Tyumen he was nearly killed in a fantastic collision, which he related in one of those long letters he wrote regularly to his sister Maria:

> During the night of May 6th, before dawn, I was being driven by a charming old man in a little tarantass with a pair of horses. I was drowsy, and having nothing more important to do, I watched the gleaming, snakelike flames darting about in the fields and the birchwoods. This is the way people here burn the last year's grass. Suddenly I heard the broken sound of wheels. Coming toward us at full tilt like a bird, hurtling along, was a troika belonging to the mail service. The old fellow quickly turned to the right, the troika flew past, and then I saw in the shadows an enormous, heavy three-horse post wagon with the coachman making the return trip. Behind this wagon I saw another tearing along, also at full speed. We hurriedly turned right, and then to my great amazement and horror this

troika turned not to the right, but to the left. I scarcely had time to think: "Good God, we're colliding!" when there was a horrible crash, the horses becoming entangled in a dark mass, the yokes fell away, my tarantass rose up in the air, and I lay on the road with all my trunks on top of me. But that was not the end. A third troika came dashing up. This last troika should really have reduced me and my trunks to pulp, but thank God I was not asleep and had not broken any bones in my fall, and so I was able to jump up quickly and run to one side. "Stop!" I yelled to the third troika. "Stop!" The third troika hurled itself on the second and came to a stop. Of course if I had been able to sleep in the tarantass, or if the third troika had flung itself immediately on the second, I would have returned home a cripple or a headless horseman. Results of the collision: broken shafts, torn harness, yokes and baggage on the ground, frightened and exhausted horses, and the terror of having experienced extreme danger. It appears that the first driver had been whipping up his horses, while the coachmen of the other two troikas were fast asleep, with no one in command. After recovering from the excitement, my old driver and the drivers of the other three mail coaches began swearing furiously at each other. How they cursed! I thought it would end up in a wild battle. You cannot imagine how lonely I felt amid that wild, blaspheming horde, in the open country, at dawn, beside the flames far and near which were devouring the grass without making the cold night air any warmer. And my soul was heavy within me! You listen to the curses, gaze down at the broken shafts and your own littered luggage, and you cannot help feeling you are in another world and at any moment you will be trampled to death. . . .

It was a landscape which seemed to have sprung straight out of Chekhov's short stories, at once commonplace and fantastical, where nothing of importance ever happened although at any moment there might be a strange gathering of forces, a lonely death, flames running along the grass. The road between Tyumen and Tomsk was a nightmare, full of ruts, so that he was always being jolted, yet flat and straight, seeming to go on forever. After five or six days the rains began, and then there was no end to them. It rained all day and all night, the bridges were washed away, the mud clung to the wheels, the cold wind froze him. The Irtysh was in flood, making strange hollow sounds as though thousands of coffins on the bed of the river were jostling together, lapping against the banks and then withdrawing quickly as though it could not tolerate a land inhabited only by toads and the souls of murderers. The ferrymen were insolent, the ferryboats terrifying with their long sweeps like the pincers of crabs, and there was something about the swollen rivers which was like death on the soul.

When he reached Tomsk it was still pouring with rain, and the town was so uninviting, so dreary, so unbelievably without any redeeming features that he found himself willingly surrendering to the good offices of an assistant chief of police, who wrote plays and was having an affair with a married woman, on whose behalf he had written a petition to the Tsar pleading for a divorce. Chekhov read the petition, and was solemnly rewarded with an invitation to tour the local brothels. He returned to his lodging at two o'clock in the morning, more miserable and disgusted than ever.

The journey went better after Tomsk. He bought a light carriage for 130 rubles, expecting to sell it later at a profit. In fact he sold it at a loss, and indeed all his financial arrangements during his travels across Siberia were disastrous, because he was continually bribing his drivers to make up for lost time, paying them twice or three times the proper fee and feeling a great sorrow for them, for their work was as arduous as penal servitude. At intervals the carriage broke down, and in a mood of towering frustration he would have to wait until it was mended. But when he reached Krasnoyarsk on the river Yenisei his spirits revived, for the majestic river was like "a mighty warrior," far more powerful than the Volga and spectacularly beautiful, and Krasnoyarsk with its clean streets and white churches was like paradise after the muddy villages he had passed through. He felt better, no longer spitting blood. The rain had stopped, the birds were singing, the carriage thundered along well-made roads; he could even sleep in the carriage at night. After Krasnoyarsk came the *taiga*, the mysterious haunted forests of firs, larches and birch trees, and he would muse for hours on the little pathways leading to forgotten villages, secret stills, perhaps gold mines, lost in the immensity of the silent forests. He delighted in the odor of resin, the blue, pink and yellow flowers bordering the road, the fuming mountains beyond. Lake Baikal, too, enchanted him, and he wrote to his mother that he would never forget his journey across the vast mirror-smooth surface of the lake on a clear sunny day, looking down two-thirds of a mile into the crystal-clear depths of turquoise blue and seeing the rock formations on the bottom. The wooded heights around the lake teemed with bears, sables and wild goats, and he so delighted in the lake and these mysterious mountainous forests that he spent two days on the shore, wildly content with a landscape which reminded him of Finland, Switzerland and the banks of the Don. His spirits revived during these last days of the journey, and he was able to forget the horrors of the earlier days. "God grant that everyone make as good a journey as mine," he wrote, and he evidently meant it.

At Sretensk he boarded a river steamer for the thousand-mile journey on the Amur to the Pacific. He had a first-class cabin to himself, and now at last he could enjoy the companionship of his fellow travelers or lose himself in solitary dreams as he pleased. Summer had come, the heat and the wild shores stimulated him, and he was delighted with the frankness of speech of the people on the boat, now so far from St. Petersburg that they could say anything that came into their heads without fear of punishment. For hours he gazed through his binoculars at the wild duck, wild geese, loons and herons. For the first time he met the Chinese, for the Amur was the frontier between China and Russia. He thought them a good-humored and happy people, and speaks about them with a kind of envy. But it was the landscape which absorbed him, all cliffs and crags and a wilderness of forests, and he confessed that he was awestruck before its beauty and could not even begin to describe it. He had the feeling that he had escaped from Russia altogether: it was like being in Texas or Patagonia.

When he reached Nikolayevsk, there remained only the short passage to Alexandrovsk, the administrative capital of Sakhalin Island. On July 10, on a brilliant sunny day, he set sail on the S.S. *Baikal* across the Gulf of Tartary. On that day the real torment began, for there were chained convicts on the ship and he saw the five-year-old daughter of a convict helping her father by holding up his chains, while she climbed the gangway.

When Sakhalin came in sight, it looked like Hell, for five enormous forest fires were burning, and there were more fires reddening the sky from behind the mountains. That flame-lit inferno seemed to be ideally chosen for a prison colony. It was evening, there were flames everywhere, and no people in sight—only the belching flames and the dark clouds of smoke over an inhospitable island. He spent the night on board ship, and the next morning, July 11, he was taken by cutter to the port of Alexandrovsk.

Altogether he had spent nearly three months—exactly eighty-two days—on the journey from Moscow, and now he felt like someone who had passed an examination and could go on to better things. He was elated with all the vast prospects which now opened out to him, and ready for the hardest work he had ever done in his life.

III

It is a mistake to believe that a writer cannot come to grips with a small country in a short space of time. In three months he may learn more than he will learn in three years. He comes with eyes which are not dulled with familiarity, with a sense of passionate involvement, with a devotion which remains intense even when he works calmly and systematically. The antennae of his mind spread out to capture the urgent and important, and skillfully avoid the transitory and impermanent. Chekhov spent only three months on Sakhalin, and wrote a four-hundred-page book on his observations. Most of the time he was like .a harpooner poised for the kill.

Although he had feared that the authorities might prove to be unsympathetic and uncooperative, he was pleasantly surprised by the assistance they gave him. They permitted him to go nearly everywhere he wanted to go and to see nearly everyone he wanted to see. He was not permitted to meet political prisoners. The officials sometimes told lies, but they were palpable lies. They lied mechanically, systematically and senselessly, like bureaucrats everywhere, and Chekhov came in time to regard them as well-meaning people who seemed not to realize the intolerable stupidity of their actions. He was permitted to quote from their official documents and did so with a fine relish: some of the more fantastic passages in the book come from the official documents quoted without comment.

Chekhov spent the first days in Alexandrovsk as the guest of a bewhiskered doctor who bore a curious resemblance to Henrik Ibsen. He was a cantankerous man, always fighting against the administration, and he had in fact sent in his resignation only a few hours before Chekhov's arrival on the island. The doctor painted an alarming picture of the administration, and said the authorities would not be particularly pleased to learn that Chekhov was staying with him. But a visit with General Kononovich, the commandant of the island, proved on the contrary that the authorities were mildly amused by the presence of two unruly doctors in their midst. When Chekhov paid his courtesy call on General Kononovich, he was told: "I'm glad you are staying with our enemy. You will be able to learn our shortcomings." The general was very suave, very kind, very intelligent, and totally inefficient.

General Kononovich was an experienced administrator who performed the rituals of government in a polite vacuum. Like Baron Korf, the Governor-General, he spoke about "the civilizing mission" of the penal colony as though these words possessed an independent existence of their own. In fact, as Chekhov soon learned, the colony was an inferno and every prison was a shambles. "The civilizing mission" consisted of reducing the prisoners to the lowest common denominator of human indignity. Prisoners were flogged for no reason at all, or because it amused the guards, or because they had committed some minor infraction of the rule book. Those who were not sent out in working parties lived in loathsome squalor, guarded by ignorant and sadistic guards. Some prisoners amassed small fortunes through the institution of the *maidanshchik,* a kind of pawnbroker's shop which was tolerated and even encouraged by the administration, and sometimes these rich prisoners became the real rulers of the prison. The most terrible fate of all was reserved for the "free" women who accompanied their husbands to Sakhalin. They received no assistance from the government and could only survive by selling themselves or their young daughters. Thirteen-year-old prostitutes were common. Any warden or government official could obtain a woman simply by requisitioning one. In the same way he could requisition a whole flock of servants, and Chekhov mentions a warden who acquired a seamstress, a chambermaid, a children's nurse, a laundress and a scrubwoman, and in addition to these five female servants he acquired a footman, a shoemaker and a chef. In 1872 the use of convicts as servants was expressly forbidden by the Governor-General, but General Kononovich on his own authority permitted their employment in order to maintain the supervision and upkeep of government property. "This is not penal servitude," Chekhov commented. "It is serfdom."

The evils of the system were inherent in the theory of prison colonization, which involves the exploitation of natural resources by the use of forced labor and arbitrary standards of punishment. The prisoner becomes a statistic in the ill-kept books of statistics, and it is his fate to become totally demoralized, stupefied by the bureaucracy, and reduced to a state of imbecility. Again and again, as Chekhov talked with the prisoners, he seemed to be in the presence of madmen. They were no longer men, but witless caricatures; and the prison officials were also witless caricatures of humanity, although they talked suavely and grammatically about their "civilizing mission." Madmen were exploiting madmen, but two entirely different kinds of madness were involved; and sometimes, as he attempts to describe the two opposing forms of madness, Chekhov seems to lose heart, abandoning all hope of a society in which bureaucrats reign over prisoners. He had no particular sympathy for the prisoners: they were murderers, cutthroats and arsonists, the dregs of Russia, but he had less sympathy for their guards and the officials who saw themselves as virtuous champions of the oppressed. Toward the end of the book he indicates that the only solution lay in the abandonment of the penal colony, with settlers from Russia taking over the colonization of the island.

While the evils of the system were obvious, it was far more difficult to suggest any workable palliatives. Since the books of statistics were ill-kept, he decided to carry out his own census. Perhaps on the basis of these new statistics—for the census was intended to include an abbreviated biography of each prisoner and settler on the island—a more liberal policy might be worked out by the authorities in St. Petersburg. General Kononovich had no objection to the census. Cards were printed on the government printing press, so designed that many questions could be answered by simply striking out a word or inserting a single letter in the appropriate column. It was a peculiarly modern method of inquiry and Chekhov went to great pains to devise a suitable list of questions. Apparently he was not permitted to make a census of the prisoners in confinement, but only of the settlers who worked in gangs as forced laborers or who lived in the settlements dotted all over the island, eking out a small living from the hard soil while attempting to open out the virgin land. There were various categories of settlers, most of them being prisoners. The category of "peasants-formerly-exiles" referred to peasants who enjoyed considerable freedom but were not yet permitted to leave the island; to them went the least onerous tasks, although they still remained under supervision. The card devised by Chekhov had twelve entries:

```
Settlement  ......................
No. of house  ....................
Status  ..........................
Name  ...........................
Age  ............................
Religion  .......................
Birthplace  ..................
Year of arrival  .................
Principal occupation  .............
Literate, illiterate, educated  ........
Married in homeland, in Sakhalin, wid-
    ower, bachelor  ..............
Does he receive assistance from the
    prison?  Yes.  No.
```

Chekhov claimed that in three months he filled out 10,000 of these census cards, a claim which has been regarded with reserve by his biographers. Yet it was not an impossible number. He would go through a settlement house by house, quickly interviewing everyone he met. He rose at five o'clock in the morning and worked till late in the night, wholly immersed in his task, driven by the need to explore deeper and deeper into the heart of the mystery. The census was intended to provide necessary sociological data, but it had other uses. Armed with his census cards, he entered the huts like a man with a well-defined purpose and a semiofficial status; he was treated with respect and sometimes with awe; and to this extent the census cards constituted his disguise. What he really wanted was an excuse to enter the huts without incurring suspicion. He would ask all manner of questions, not only the questions on the card. Late at night he would record what they said to him in his notebooks, trying to catch the exact tone of voice, the expressions on the faces of these people who had become the playthings of an inefficient and ludicrously in-effective administration.

In this way he spent his days, going from one hut to another, often alone, but sometimes accompanied by a prison guard with a revolver or by a prison attendant. The presence of the guard or the attendant made him important in the eyes of the prisoners, and he did nothing to dispel the impression that he was in some way connected with the administration. Sometimes he thought of himself as an impostor, gathering information under false pretenses. At other times he regarded himself as a man with a load of mischief and did not know what dangerous stratagems he might find himself contemplating. He was working so hard that his eyelids developed a tic and he blinked continually, and there were ominous headaches.

The census cards, on which he worked so carefully, have survived, and are now preserved in the Lenin Library in Moscow. His method of filling in the cards was a very simple one. He would write as little as possible, simply underlining the appropriate words on the card, entering the names of the settlers carefully, and the rest hurriedly. It could not have taken him more than a few minutes to ask the questions, and it would take only a few seconds to complete the cards.

The journeys from one settlement to another were often nightmares. He would come at the end of the day to some godforsaken settlement in the backwoods, only to be de-voured by insects in some wretched prison house, the only place where he could be put up for the night. He speaks of whole walls covered with dark crepe, which stirred as if blown by a wind, boiling and seething with the energies of beetles, cockroaches and other insects; the loud rustling and whispering would keep him awake all night. Usually it was bitterly cold, and he was often drenched by the rain and had to sleep in his damp clothes. He was already suffering from tuberculosis, and these months on Sakhalin were at least partly responsible for his premature death.

It was not only the sounds of the insects which dis-turbed him at night. Sometimes he heard the prisoners moaning in their sleep, the endless litany of lament which ended only with the cold dawn, and at such times the full horror of the prison system would come to him out of the darkness. At Derbinskoye, which he reached after a miserable journey through the rain, he was given lodging in a warehouse incomprehensibly filled with Viennese furniture. It was clean, there were no insects, and after visiting some huts he spent many hours poring over the official records before turning to bed. He wrote about that night and the next morning:

> The rain fell continually, rattling on the roof, and once in a while a belated prisoner or soldier passed by, slopping through the mud. It was quiet in the warehouse and in my soul, but I had scarcely put out the candle and gone to bed when I heard a rustling, whispering, knocking, splashing sound, and deep sighs. Raindrops fell from the ceiling onto the latticework of the Viennese chairs and made a hollow, ringing sound, and after each such sound someone whispered in despair: "Oh, my God, my God!" Next to the warehouse was the prison. Were the convicts coming at me through an underground passage? But then there came a gust of wind, the rain rattled even more strongly, somewhere a tree rustled—and again, a deep, despairing sigh: "Oh, my God, my God!"
>
> In the morning I went out on the steps. The sky was gray and overcast, the rain continued to fall, and it was muddy. The warden walked hurriedly from door to door with his keys.
>
> "I'll give you such a ticket you'll be scratching yourself for a week," he shouted. "I'll show you what kind of ticket you'll get!"
>
> These words were intended for a group of twenty prisoners who, from the phrases I overheard, were pleading to be sent to the hospital. They were ragged, soaked by the rain, covered with mud and shivering. They wanted to demonstrate in mime exactly what ailed them, but on their pinched, frozen faces it somehow came out false and crooked, though they were probably not lying at all. "Oh, my God, my God!" someone sighed, and my nightmare seemed to be continuing. The word "pariah" comes to mind, meaning that a person can fall no lower. . . . I felt that I saw before me the extreme limits of man's degradation, lower than which he cannot go.

The sight of the prisoners miming their illnesses on that rainy morning afflicted Chekhov more deeply than any act of physical brutality he saw on the island. He saw men being flogged within an inch of their lives, he saw prisoners chained to wheelbarrows, but a man in chains can possess a human dignity, and a man who is flogged and drenched in his own blood also possesses dignity; but the poor devils miming their illnesses had none. They were whining silently, begging the merciless to give them mercy, more like dogs than human beings. Chekhov was not revolted by them. He was revolted by the machine which inevitably produced them.

He had studied human degradation and knew it well. Acutely sensitive to suffering, he was equally sensitive to the degradation of the human spirit. In his book he describes a flogging with an almost clinical detachment, but there was no detachment when he spoke about the strange miming in the rain-swept courtyard. Only a few years before he had written his credo in a letter to his friend Alexey Pleshcheyev: "My Holy of Holies are the human body, health, intelligence, inspiration, love and the most absolute freedom from violence and lying in whatever forms they may manifest themselves." Against those who degraded men, he was prepared to wage implacable war.

So he spent his days on the island, looking keenly at the evidence of a degradation so complete that he sometimes hoped the whole island would be swept off the face of the earth. He spent two months in the central part of the island and another month of exploring in the southern part, which was to belong to Russia for a few more years, coming under Japanese domination at the conclusion of the Russo-Japanese War. Having visited all the prisons and settlements except a few very small and isolated communities, he would claim that he had talked to every settler and convict, studied all the church records, all the regulations and all the laws, and there was no aspect of life on Sakhalin which was foreign to him. The claim was very nearly true, and it only remained to put all his notes in order and write the book.

On October 13, on a cold, blustery day, he was rowed from the Korsakov landing to the S.S. *Petersburg* anchored in the Tatar Strait, and a few hours later he saw the mountains of Sakhalin sinking below the horizon. The ship was bound for Odessa with ports of call at Hong Kong, Singapore and Ceylon, where there was time to make a journey into the interior. Ceylon was paradise; he enjoyed the palm groves and the sight of the bronze-hued women walking in the paddy fields, and in later years he liked to remember a brief romance with a Ceylonese girl in the moonlight. It was here in Ceylon that the journey really came to an end. He wrote to his friend Leontiev-Shcheglov in December when he reached Moscow: "I am so filled with joy and satisfaction that it would not bother me in the least if I succumbed to paralysis or departed this world by way of dysentery. I can say: *I have lived! I have had everything I want!* I have been in Hell, which is Sakhalin, and in Paradise, which is the island of Ceylon!"

IV

Chekhov was never a social reformer, and had no interest in revolutionary theories. While he hoped to be instrumental in changing the penal system in Sakhalin, he had no illusions about the difficulties and dangers of the enterprise. The roots of the system lay deep in Russian history, in the peculiar forms of brutality which had been encouraged by generations of autocrats for their own protection. Not only the monarchy and the bureaucracy were implicated; the Russian character and the Russian people were equally responsible. There were no easy panaceas, and soon Chekhov resigned himself to the knowledge that at the very best he could only help to change the situation a little. If he had lived to see the Bolsheviks come to power, he would have learned that the system was virtually unchangeable.

Because the system was evil, and because he was determined to fight it with all his available energy, he gave himself up to the book with passionate absorption. But the form escaped him. He complained that he had seen so much, and had so much to say, that it was difficult to know how to begin. The truth was that he was never quite sure whether he was writing a treatise or a book for popular consumption, and until the end he hovered uncertainly between two entirely different kinds of book. In May, 1891, when he was engrossed in the early chapters, he wrote to Suvorin that he was having difficulties. "Still, I was able to get the devil by the tail. I have described the climate so well that you will shiver with cold when you are reading it. How unpleasant it is to have to give statistics." Unpleasant or not, Chekhov insisted on giving them in abundance. He offers the reader every statistic he can lay his hands on, compares them, adds them up, and not having a mind which moves easily among numbers, he sometimes reduced them to bathos. Writing again a few days later to Suvorin, he said he had discovered the main cause of the trouble. "I had the illusion that my Sakhalin book was intended to teach certain things," he wrote. "I realized I was holding something back, not letting myself go. But no sooner had I begun to recount the funny things I saw on Sakhalin—the pigs, too—the work went splendidly." He added regretfully that he found some difficulty in getting any humor into the book.

He planned to complete the book and see it through the press by the autumn of 1891, but fate was against him. There were stories to be written, and there were delays caused by the purchase of a small estate in Melikhovo, fifty miles south of Moscow. Then he fell ill. In 1892 there was a cholera epidemic, and he became a doctor superintending relief work in an entire district. Sakhalin was forgotten in the presence of an even more dangerous tribulation, and since the epidemic continued well into the following year, many months passed before he could return to his manuscript. Chapters from the book appeared in a volume of essays and stories called *Help for the Starving*, published in aid of victims of the famine which followed the cholera epidemic, and in the magazine *Russian Thought,* but the complete work was not published until the summer of 1895. Writing to Suvorin in the spring when the last pages were being written, he said: "Well, it turns out to be a very fat book, with a lot of notes, anecdotes, statistics, etc. Perhaps it will do well. And if not, it's nothing to worry about —death will come anyway."

In this mood, half hopeful, wholly detached, Chekhov gave his book to a world which preferred his short stories. It is a strange work, brilliant and wayward, scrupulously honest and unpretentious, lit by a flame of quiet indignation and furious sorrow. The horror is made all the more credible because he refuses to dramatize it. This is how it is, he says, leaving to the reader the task of changing the conditions on the island, for he has presented all the evidence—the geography, the geology, the ecology, all the statistics in the prison records and the very souls of the people suffering under a ferocious administration—and there is nothing left for him to do. It was perhaps his greatest work, and certainly he expended more energy and affection on it than on any other. "It gives me joy," he wrote, "that this harsh convict's robe shall have a place in my literary wardrobe."

So he wrote long before the book was completed, knowing that it would rank among the best, and certain that in this quiet contemplative account of a prison colony there were the seeds of a future revolution which would eventually bring about the end of prison colonies in Russia. The book had no immediate effect. It did not change the Tsarist prison system, and it had no effect on the altogether more terrible prison systems of the Bolsheviks. Yet he had lit the fuse, and it is still burning.

In a story written a few weeks after leaving Sakhalin, Chekhov spoke of "the huge bull without eyes," the ultimate horror, the symbol of all that was powerful, degrading and meaningless in life. *The Island* describes his deliberate confrontation with the bull and his attempt to tame it and reduce it to human proportions. The bullring was an obscure wind-swept island in the north Pacific; the bull-fighter had no weapons except his bare hands and his native intelligence. He fought because he had to fight, and it never occurred to him that his health or his reputation might suffer. What concerned him was the act of protest, the need to protect the humiliated and degraded, the slow burning of the fuse. In this sense he was a greater revolutionary than many of those who came after him.

Robert Payne

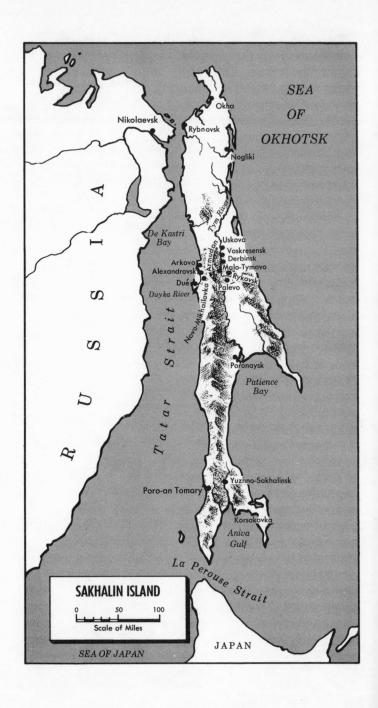

SEA
OF
OKHOTSK

Nikolaevsk

Okha

Rybnovsk

Nogliki

Tym River

De Kastri Bay

Uskovo

Voskresensk

Derbinsk

Arkovo

Malo-Tymovo

Alexandrovsk

Rykovsk

Dué

Palevo

Duyka River

Novo-Mikhailovka

Armudan

R U S S I A

T a t a r   S t r a i t

Poronaysk

Patience Bay

Poro-an Tomary

Yuzhno-Sakhalinsk

Korsakovka

Aniva Gulf

La Perouse Strait

SAKHALIN ISLAND

0   50   100

Scale of Miles

SEA OF JAPAN   JAPAN

The Island

A Journey to Sakhalin

WEIGHTS AND MEASURES USED IN TEXT

1 verst	=	0.66	mile
1 sazhen	=	7	feet
1 vershok	=	1.75	inches
1 arshin	=	28	inches
1 desyatin	=	2.7	acres
1 pood	=	40	pounds

Temperatures are given in Centigrade°.

I

Nikolayevsk-on-the-Amur - The Steamship
Baikal - *Cape Pronge and the Estuary Inlet - The
Sakhalin Peninsula - La Pérouse, Broughton,
Krusenstern and Nevelskoy - Japanese Explorers -
Cape Dzhaore - The Tatar Coast - De Kastri*

ON JULY 5, 1890, I arrived by ship at Nikolayevsk, one
of the easternmost outposts of our Fatherland. Here the
Amur is very wide and the sea is only 27 *versts* away. It is
a majestic and beautiful place. Stories told about the past,
the tales told by my companions about the vicious winters
and the no less vicious local pastimes, the proximity of the
convict camps and the very aspect of the filthy, dying town
completely banished any desire to enjoy the landscape.

Nikolayevsk was founded not too long ago, in 1850, by
the famous Gennady Nevelskoy: this was probably the only
bright spot in the town's history. In the '50s and '60s,
when, sparing neither soldiers, prisoners nor emigrants,
civilization was being planted along the Amur, residences
were maintained in Nikolayevsk by the governing officials
of the region. Many Russian and foreign adventurers came
here, and colonists settled here, attracted by the abundance
of fish and game, and so the town was obviously not devoid
of human interest; this was illustrated by the fact that a
visiting scholar found it necessary and possible to give a
public lecture at the club.

Now almost half of the houses have been abandoned by
their owners. They stand dilapidated, the dark frameless
windows staring like the eye sockets of a skull. The inhabitants pursue a somnolent, drunken existence and generally live hand to mouth on whatever God has provided.
They subsist by supplying fish to Sakhalin, stealing gold,
exploiting non-Russians and selling deer antlers, from
which the Chinese make stimulating medicines. On the

way from Khabarovka to Nikolayevsk I met a number of smugglers. They do not conceal their profession. Showing me gold dust and a pair of antlers, one of them proudly told me, "My father was also a smuggler!" The exploitation of non-Russians, in addition to customarily turning them into drunkards, hoaxing them and the like, is occasionally quite original. Thus the now deceased Nikolayevsk trader Ivanov yearly took a trip to Sakhalin and exacted tribute from the Gilyaks. He tortured and hanged those who did not pay up promptly.

There is no hotel in the town. At the club permission was granted me to rest after dinner in a low-ceilinged room where, they told me, balls were given during the winter. They only shrugged their shoulders when I asked where I could spend the night. There is nothing one can do. I was obliged to spend two nights on the boat. When it departed on the return voyage to Khabarovka, I found myself stranded like a crayfish on the sand. Where should I go? My baggage was on the pier. I walked along the shore and did not know what to do. Exactly opposite the town, some two or three versts away, lay the *Baikal,* the boat on which I would voyage down the Tatar Strait, but they said it would not sail for four or five days, although the departure flag already waved from the mast. Perhaps I should go on board the *Baikal?* But that is awkward; suppose they don't allow it—they'll say it is too early.

The wind began to blow. The Amur turned dark and threatening, like the sea. I became melancholy. I went to the club and took a long time over my dinner and listened to people at the neighboring table talking about gold and antlers, about a juggler who had arrived in Nikolayevsk, and about a Japanese who does not pull teeth with pliers but with his fingers. If one listens carefully and long, then, O my God, how remote is this life from that of Russia!

Everything here, from the cured back of salmon which is taken with vodka to the quality of the conversation, is native to the place, not Russian. While sailing along the Amur I had the distinct impression that I was not in Russia at all but somewhere in Patagonia or Texas. Without even

2

considering the strange, non-Russian aspects of my surroundings, it constantly seemed to me that the composition of our Russian life was alien to the native Amurians, that here Pushkin and Gogol were incomprehensible and therefore unnecessary, that our history was boring, and that we who came from Russia were indeed foreigners. I noted complete indifference to religion and politics.

The priests I saw on the Amur eat meat during Lent. I was told that one who was dressed in a white silk cassock was a gold smuggler who competes with his spiritual charges. If you want to bore an Amurian and start him yawning, talk to him of politics, the Russian government or Russian art. Moreover, morality here is quite peculiar, unlike our own. Chivalrous behavior toward women has become a cult, but at the same time it is not considered reprehensible to relinquish one's wife to a friend in exchange for money. Here is an even better illustration: there are no class prejudices, for exiles here are considered equals, but at the same time it is not regarded as a sin to shoot some Chinese beggar met in the forest, killing him like a dog, or to engage in secret hunting parties against escaping convicts.

However, I will continue relating my experiences. Not having found shelter, toward evening I decided to board the *Baikal*. But there was a new problem. A strong swell had developed and the Gilyak boatmen refused to row me over no matter how much money I offered them. I wandered along the shore, and did not know what to do. Meanwhile the sun was setting and the waves of the Amur were darkening. On both banks of the river the Gilyak dogs were howling frantically. "Why have I come here?" I asked myself, and my journey seemed to be utter folly. The knowledge that the convict camps were nearby, that in a few days I would disembark on Sakhalin soil without possessing even a letter of recommendation, and that they might force me to turn back, disturbed me unpleasantly. Finally the Gilyaks agreed to carry me for a ruble and I arrived safely on the *Baikal* in a rowboat constructed of three planks nailed together.

3

This is a seagoing ship of medium size, a trading vessel, which was quite bearable after the Baikal and Amur boats. It travels between Nikolayevsk, Vladivostok and Japanese ports, carries mail, soldiers, convicts, passengers and freight, especially government freight. On contract to the Treasury, which pays it a considerable subsidy, it is obliged to voyage to the island of Sakhalin several times each summer, putting in at the Alexandrovsk and the southern Korsakov posts. The tariff is extremely high and is probably not to be matched anywhere else in the world. It is completely incomprehensible why such high tariffs are exacted when colonization primarily requires freedom and ease of travel.

The wardroom and the cabins on the *Baikal* were small but clean and were completely furnished in European style; there was even a piano. The members of the crew were Chinese, wearing long queues; they are called "boy" in the English manner. The chef is also Chinese but his cuisine is Russian, although all the food is bitter with curry and smells somewhat like *corilopsis*.[1]

Having read a great deal about the storms and ice floes in the Tatar Strait, I expected to meet on the ship hoarse-voiced whalers spitting out tobacco juice as they talked. In fact I met fully cultured people. L., the ship's captain, a native of a western country, has been sailing the northern seas for over thirty years and has crossed them lengthwise and crosswise. During his lifetime he has seen many wonderful things, is very knowledgeable and recounts events interestingly. Having spent half of his life around Kamchatka and the Kurile Islands, he could speak perhaps with greater authority than Othello of barren wastes, terrifying chasms, insurmountable cliffs. I am obliged to him for a great deal of information included in this journal. He had three assistants—the nephew of an eminent astronomer and two Swedes, Ivan Martynich and Ivan Venyaminich, both fine and affable persons.

The *Baikal* got under way on July 8 before dinner. Traveling with us were 300 soldiers under the command of an officer, and several prisoners. One prisoner was accompanied by his five-year-old daughter, who clung to his shackles as he came up the gangway. One woman convict attracted attention because her husband was voluntarily following her into penal servitude.[2]

In addition to myself and the officer there were several first-class passengers of both sexes and even one baroness. The reader should not be amazed at such a number of cultured people here in the wilderness. Along the Amur and in the Primorskaya region the percentage of intellectuals is quite large with respect to the generally small population, and there are relatively more intellectuals here than in any Russian *guberniya*. On the Amur there is one city with sixteen active and inactive generals. Perhaps there are even more today.

The day was calm and bright. It was hot on deck and stuffy in the cabins; the temperature of the water was $+18°$. Such weather would rather be expected on the Black Sea. On the right bank a forest was on fire. The dense green mass belched scarlet flames; clouds of smoke merged into an elongated, black, stationary column which hung over the forest. The conflagration was enormous, but all around was quiet and tranquil; nobody cared that the forests were being destroyed. Obviously the green wealth belongs to God alone.

We arrived at Cape Pronge after dinner, at six o'clock. Asia comes to an end. One could say the Amur flows into the Pacific Ocean here, if Sakhalin Island did not bar its passage. The estuary spreads out broadly before your eyes. Scarcely visible ahead is a hazy strip of land; this is the penal island. To the left, dropping away in its own convolutions, the shore disappears into the haze on its way to the unknown North. This seems to be the end of the world, and there is nowhere else to go. The soul is seized with the same emotion which Odysseus must have experienced when he sailed an unknown sea, filled with melancholy forebodings of encounters with strange creatures. On the right, where the river falls into the estuary and a Gilyak village stands sheltered on the bank, strange creatures were rowing out to us in two boats, yelling in an unknown language and waving something at us. It was difficult to see what they were holding in their hands, but when they approached closer I recognized some gray birds. "They want to sell us live geese," someone said.

We turned to the right. Markers indicated the waterway along the entire course. The captain did not leave the bridge nor did the engineer come up from the engine room. The *Baikal* began to go slower and slower, and practically groped its way forward. Great care was required because it was extremely easy to get caught on a sandbank. The ship drew 12½ feet of water and in some spots it had only 14 feet in which to navigate. There was even a moment when we heard the keel scrape the sand. This shallow waterway and the peculiar contours of the Tatar and Sakhalin coasts were the main reasons for the long-held belief in Europe that Sakhalin was a peninsula.

In June, 1787, the famous French navigator Count de la Pérouse landed on the western bank of Sakhalin, above 48° longitude, and talked with the natives. We learn from his notes that he found not only Ainus but also Gilyaks who came as traders, and they were experienced people well acquainted with Sakhalin and the Tatar shore. Drawing a sketch on the sand, they told him the land where they lived was an island and the island was separated from the mainland and Iesso (Japan) by the straits.[3]

Later, while sailing farther north along the western bank, he expected to find a passage from the North Japanese Sea into the Okhotsk Sea and thus to shorten considerably the distance to Kamchatka. But the farther north he sailed, the more shallow became the strait. The depth decreased by one *sazhen* each mile. He sailed northward as far as the dimensions of his ship permitted and stopped on reaching a depth of 9 sazhens. The gradual rise of the bottom and the almost imperceptible current in the strait convinced him that he was not in a strait but in a bay and that Sakhalin is connected with the mainland by an isthmus.

In De Kastri he again encountered Gilyaks. When he drew a sketch of the island for them on paper, one of them took the pencil and, drawing a line across the strait, ex-

6

plained that at times the Gilyaks must portage their boats across this isthmus and that grass even grows on it: that was La Pérouse' understanding. This made him even more certain that Sakhalin was a peninsula.[4]

The Englishman V. Broughton visited the Tatar Strait nine years after La Pérouse. He had a small ship which drew no more than 9 feet of water, thus enabling him to sail farther north than La Pérouse. Stopping at two sazhens, he sent his assistant to take soundings farther north. On his trip the latter found deep water among the shallows but they gradually decreased and kept leading him alternately, back and forth, to the Sakhalin shore and then to the low sandy shores of the other side. The picture he obtained was that both shores seem to merge. It seemed that the bay ended here and that there was no through passage. Therefore Broughton also was forced to the same conclusion as La Pérouse.

Our own celebrated Krusenstern, who explored the shores of the island in 1805, fell into the same error. He sailed to Sakhalin with a preconceived notion, since he was using La Pérouse' map. He sailed along the eastern coast and, after passing Sakhalin's northern capes, he entered the strait, sailing from north to south. It seemed that he was very close to solving the riddle, but the gradual decrease of soundings to $3\frac{1}{2}$ sazhens, the specific gravity of the water and especially his preconceived notion also forced him to admit the existence of an isthmus which he was unable to find. But his conscience bothered him. He wrote: "It is obvious that Sakhalin was previously an island and perhaps even in not too distant times." He returned with a restless spirit. When he first saw Broughton's notes in China, he was "quite overjoyed."[5]

The error was rectified by Nevelskoy in 1849. The authority of his predecessors was so great, however, that when he reported his discoveries in Petersburg, they did not believe him. They considered his conduct as impertinent and subject to punishment, and they "concluded" that he should be degraded. Nobody knows how this would all have ended if the Tsar himself had not come to his defense. The Tsar decided that Nevelskoy had acted with courage, nobility and patriotism.[6]

Nevelskoy was an energetic, highly temperamental man, well-educated, unselfish, humanitarian, completely permeated with an idea and fanatically devoted to it, and possessing high principles. One of his acquaintances wrote: "I never met a more honorable man." In five years he made a brilliant career for himself on the eastern shore and on Sakhalin, but he lost his daughter, who died of starvation, and he soon grew old. His wife aged and lost her health. She had been "a young, lovely and amiable person," who had borne all her privations heroically.[7]

In order to conclude the discussion on the question of the isthmus and the peninsula, I consider it rather important to note a few more details. In 1710, by order of the Chinese Emperor, missionaries in Peking drew a map of Tatary. The missionaries made use of Japanese maps. This is obvious since at that time the passage through the La Pérouse and Tatar Straits was known only to the Japanese. The map was sent to France and became widely known because it was included in the atlas compiled by the geographer d'Anville.[8]

To a small mistake on this map Sakhalin owes its name. On the western bank of Sakhalin, exactly across from the mouth of the Amur, the map includes a name given by the missionaries: "Saghalien-angahata," which means "The Cliffs of the Black River" in Mongolian. This name probably refers to some crag or cape at the mouth of the Amur. In France it was understood differently, and believed to be the name of the island. Hence the name Sakhalin, which was retained by Krusenstern on Russian maps. The Japanese called Sakhalin Karafto or Karaftu, which means "Chinese Island."

The works of the Japanese either reached Europe very late when they were no longer needed or they were subjected to erroneous corrections. On the missionaries' map, Sakhalin was an island, but d'Anville, who mistrusted their map, placed an isthmus between the island and the mainland.

8

The Japanese were the first to explore Sakhalin, beginning in 1613, but so little significance was attached to their explorations in Europe that when the Russians and the Japanese attempted to decide who owned Sakhalin, only the Russians wrote and spoke about the rights deriving from this first expedition.[9]

A new survey containing all possible details of the Tatar and Sakhalin shores has long been necessary. The present maps are unsatisfactory, as we know from the fact that both naval and commercial vessels often run aground on sand and rocks, and this occurs much more frequently than reported in the newspapers. Due chiefly to the inaccuracy of existing maps, the ships' captains here are very cautious, overanxious and nervous. The captain of the *Baikal* does not believe the official maps and follows his own map, which he draws and corrects each trip.

To avoid being stranded on the sand, the captain decided not to sail that night and after sunset we anchored off Cape Dzhaore. On the cape itself there was a lone cabin inhabited by the naval officer in charge of placing and maintaining markers along the waterway. Behind the cabin lay the impassable, somnolent *taiga*. The captain sent him some fresh meat. I took advantage of the situation and went to shore with the launch. Instead of a pier there were only large slippery rocks, and it was necessary to jump over them. There were steps to the cabin, made of timber struck almost perpendicularly into the ground, so that in climbing it was necessary to take strong handholds. It was awful! By the time I climbed the hill and reached the cabin I was surrounded with swarms of mosquitoes; the air was black with them. My hands and face smarted and there was no way to defend myself. I believe that if one had to sleep here under the bare sky without being surrounded with bonfires, one would perish or at the very least go insane.

The cabin was cut in half by a hallway. To the left lived the sailors; to the right, the officer and his family. The master was not at home. I met an elegantly gowned, cultured lady, his wife, and his two little daughters, who were covered with mosquito bites. All the walls of the rooms

9

were festooned with fir branches, gauze was stretched over the windows, there was a strong odor of smoke, yet the mosquitoes were oblivious to all these precautions, and hovered over everything, and stung the poor little girls. The furniture of the room was poor, composed only of camp equipment, but the decorations were charming and tasteful. There were sketches on the wall, among them one of a woman's head done in pencil. It appeared that the lieutenant was an artist.

"Do you live well here?" I asked the lady.

"We live well, except for the mosquitoes."

She was not pleased with the gift of fresh meat. She said that she and the children had grown accustomed to salted meat long ago, and they did not like fresh meat.

"However, I did cook trout yesterday," she added.

A sullen sailor accompanied me to the launch. As though he had guessed the question I proposed to ask him, he sighed and said, "One doesn't come here voluntarily!"

The next morning we resumed the journey in complete calm. The weather was warm. The Tatar shore was mountainous, and there were many sharp, conical peaks. The coast was lightly covered with a bluish haze, the smoke from distant forest fires. They say the haze is sometimes so thick here that it is just as dangerous as sea mist to the sailors. If a bird should fly straight from the sea over the mountains, it would probably not encounter a single house or a single living person within 500 versts and more. The green shore glistens merrily in the sunshine and is obviously quite content to be uninhabited.

At six o'clock we were in the narrowest part of the strait, between Capes Pogobi and Lazarev, and we saw both banks at close hand. At eight o'clock, we passed near Nevelskoy Head, a mountain with a kind of protuberance on the top like a little hat. The morning was clear and sparkling, and my pleasure was enhanced by the proud knowledge that I was gazing on these shores.

At two o'clock we entered De Kastri Bay. This is the only place where ships sailing the strait can gain shelter during a storm. Without this bay, it would be impossible to sail along the completely inhospitable Sakhalin shore.[10] There is even an expression: "to scamper into De Kastri." The bay is beautiful, a made-to-order natural phenomenon. It is a round lake, three versts in diameter, with high banks which give shelter from the winds and form a wide outlet to the sea. If one judges from outward appearances, this bay is ideal—but, alas, it only seems so. Seven months of the year it is covered with ice, is barely sheltered from the eastern winds and is so shallow that ships must cast anchor some two versts from the shore. The outlet to the sea is guarded by three islands, or, more accurately, reefs, which endow the bay with an original beauty. One of them is named Oyster Reef from the very large, plump oysters which abound on it.

On the shore there were several small houses and a church. This is the Alexandrovsk command post. The commandant, his factor and the telegraph operators live here. One of the local officials who came to dine on board, a boring and bored man, talked constantly at the table, drank a great deal and related the old anecdote about the geese who, having eaten berries used in making liqueur, became drunk, were taken for dead, plucked and thrown outside, and later, after sleeping off the effects of the alcohol, returned home completely nude. The official swore that the event with the geese took place at De Kastri, in his own home.

There is no resident priest at the church; when one is required, a priest comes from Mariinsk. Good weather is as rare here as in Nikolayevsk. They say that a surveying commission worked here this past spring and that there were only three sunny days during all of May. How can anyone work without the sun!

At sea we passed the naval vessels *Borb* and *Tunnis* and two torpedo boats.

I recall still another detail. We had scarcely dropped anchor when the sky darkened, thunder clouds gathered and the water turned an unusual, bright green. The *Baikal* had to unload 4,000 *poods* of government cargo and therefore we remained at De Kastri overnight. To pass the time more quickly, the machinist and I fished from the deck and we caught some very large, fat-headed gobies, the like of which I had never caught either in the Black Sea or in the Sea of Azov. We also caught some plaice.

The unloading of cargo from ships is always tiresomely slow, accompanied by exasperation and bad blood. Furthermore, this is the bitter lot of all our eastern ports. At De Kastri the cargo is unloaded on small barges which can only reach the shore during high tide and therefore the loaded barges often run aground on the sand. Sometimes because of this the ship must sit and wait out the tide for the sake of a few hundred pounds of flour.

In Nikolayevsk everything was even more inefficient. While standing on the deck of the *Baikal,* I saw a tugboat, which was towing a large barge with 200 soldiers, lose its tow rope. The barge floated out with the tide and headed straight for the anchor chain of a steamship which was anchored close to us. With sinking hearts we awaited the next moment, when the barge would be cut in half by the chain, but, fortunately, some good people caught the tow rope in time and the soldiers only suffered from severe fright.

[1] A flower of the aster family with a distinctive odor—TRANS.

[2] On the *Baikal* and on the Amur ships the prisoners generally stay on deck with third-class passengers. Once when I went up on the forecastle at dawn to stretch my legs I saw soldiers, women, children, two Chinese and convicts in shackles sleeping soundly, all huddled together; dew fell on them and it was chilly. The guard was standing amid the heap of bodies, asleep and holding his rifle in his hands.

[3] La Pérouse wrote that they called their island Choko, but the Gilyaks were probably referring to another place with this name and he did not understand them. On a map drawn by our Krashcheninnikov (1752) the Chukha River is shown on the western coast of Sakhalin. Chukha appears to be quite similar to Choko. Le Pérouse says that when the Gilyak drew the island and called it Choko, he also drew a small river. Choko means "we."

⁴   Regarding this, I would like to cite Nevelskoy's observation:
the natives usually draw a line between the shores to show that
the opposite shores can be reached by boat—in other words, that
a strait actually exists between the shores.

⁵   The fact that three serious explorers made exactly the same
mistake speaks for itself. If they did not find the entrance to the
Amur, it is because they had the most meager means for exploration at their disposal and also because they were talented people
who had certain misgivings and almost guessed at the truth, while
failing to reckon with all the evidence. The fact that the isthmus
and the Sakhalin peninsula are not myths, but at one time actually existed, has now been proved.

A detailed history on the exploration of Sakhalin is contained
in A. M. Nikolsky, *Sakhalin Island and Its Fauna of Vertebrate
Animals.* This book also contains an extensive bibliography on
Sakhalin.

⁶   The details can be found in Nevelskoy's book: *The Exploits of
Russian Naval Officers in the Easternmost Part of Russia* (1849–
55).

⁷   On her journey from Russia to join her husband, although ill,
Nevelskoy's wife, Ekaterina Ivanovna, rode 1,100 versts on horseback in 23 days over swamps, through wild, mountainous taigas,
and over the glaciers of the Okhotsk route. The most capable of
Nevelskoy's associates, N. K. Boshnyak, who discovered Imperial
Harbor [a town on the mainland opposite Uglegorsk, now known
as Soviet Harbor—TRANS.] when he was only 20 years old, "a
dreamer and a child"—as he is called by one of his colleagues—
related in his notes: "We all went together to Ayan on the transport *Baikal,* and there we transferred to the decrepit barque
Shelekhov. When the barque started to sink, nobody could convince Mme. Nevelskaya to be the first to leave the barque. 'The
commander and the officers are the last to leave,' she said. 'I too
will leave the ship only when there isn't a single woman or child
left on board.' And that's exactly what she did. The barque was
already lying on its side. . . ." Boshnyak writes further that although they were often in Mme. Nevelskaya's company, he and
his friends "never heard a word of complaint or reproach—on the
contrary, there was often observed a calm and proud awareness of
that bitter but lofty position which was predestined for her by
Providence." She usually passed the winter alone since the men
were out on various missions. The temperature in her quarters was
5°. When provision ships did not arrive from Kamchatka in 1852,
they were all in a desperate position. There was no milk for nursing babies, there was no fresh food for the sick, and several per-

13

sons died of scurvy. Nevelskaya arranged that milk from her cow should be given to all of them. She conducted herself toward the natives with such simplicity and paid so much attention to them that even the uncouth savages noticed it. And she was then only 19 years old" (Lieutenant Boshnyak, "Expedition into the Amur Countryside," *Naval Collection*, 1859, II). Her husband also mentions her touching treatment of the Gilyaks in his notes. He writes: "Ekaterina Ivanovna sat them [the Gilyaks] down on the floor in a circle near a large urn filled with gruel or tea in the one room in our quarters which served as reception room, sitting room and dining room combined. Enjoying more of the same hospitality, they very often slapped their hostess on the back, sending her to get *tamcha* [tobacco] or tea."

8   *Nouvel Atlas de la Chine, de la Tartaire, Chinoise et de Thibet* (1737).

9   In 1808, when the Japanese surveyor Mamia-Rinzo sailed along the western bank of the island, he reached the Tatar shore at the very mouth of the Amur and made the journey from the island to the mainland and back many times. He was the first to prove that Sakhalin is an island. The Russian naturalist F. Shmidt praised his map highly, saying it was "altogether admirable since it was obviously based on independent surveys."

10 The present and future importance of this bay is described in K. Skalkovskoy, *Russkaya Torgovlya v Tikhom Okeane* [Russian Commerce in the Pacific Ocean], p. 75.

II   *A Short Geography - Arrival in Northern Sakhalin - Fire - The Pier - In the Village - Dinner with Mr. L. - Acquaintances - General Kononovich - The Arrival of the Governor-General - Dinner and the Illumination*

SAKHALIN lies in the Okhotsk Sea, protecting almost a thousand versts of eastern Siberian shoreline as well as the entrance into the mouth of the Amur from the ocean. It is long in form, running from north to south; its shape in the opinion of one author suggests a sturgeon. Its geographic location is from 45°54′ to 54°53′ latitude and from 141°40′ to 144°53′ longitude. The northern section of Sakhalin, which is crossed by a belt of permafrost, can be compared with Ryazan *guberniya,* the southern section with the Crimea. The island is 900 versts long, its widest portion measuring 125 versts and its narrowest 25 versts. It is twice as large as Greece and one and a half times the size of Denmark.

The former division of Sakhalin into northern, central and southern districts was impracticable, and it is now divided only into northern and southern. The upper third of the island precludes colonization due to its climatic and soil conditions. The central section is called Northern Sakhalin and the lower, Southern Sakhalin. There are no rigid boundaries between them. At the present time convicts inhabit the northern section along the Duyka and Tym Rivers; the Duyka falls into the Tatar Strait and the Tym into the Okhotsk Sea; both rivers meet at their source according to the map. Convicts also live along the western bank in a small area above and below the Duyka estuary. Administratively, Northern Sakhalin is composed of two districts: Alexandrovsk and Tymovsk.

After spending the night at De Kastri, we sailed at

noon on the next day, July 10, across the Tatar Strait to the mouth of the Duyka, where the Alexandrovsk command post is situated. The weather again was calm and bright, a rare phenomenon here. On the completely becalmed sea whales swam past in pairs, shooting fountains into the air. This lovely and unusual spectacle amused us the entire trip. But I must admit my spirits were depressed and the closer I got to Sakhalin the more uncomfortable I became. The officer in charge of the soldiers, learning of my mission in Sakhalin, was greatly amazed and began to argue that I had absolutely no right to visit the penal settlement and the colony since I was not a government official. Naturally I knew he was wrong. Nevertheless, I was greatly troubled by his words and feared that I would probably encounter the same point of view on Sakhalin.

When we cast anchor at nine o'clock, huge fires were burning at five different places on the Sakhalin taiga. I could not see the wharf and buildings through the darkness and the smoke drifting across the sea, and could barely distinguish dim lights at the post, two of which were red. The horrifying scene, compounded of darkness, the silhouettes of mountains, smoke, flames and fiery sparks, was fantastic. On my left monstrous fires were burning, above them the mountains, and beyond the mountains a red glow rose to the sky from remote conflagrations. It seemed that all of Sakhalin was on fire.

To the right, Cape Zhonkiyer reached out to sea, a long, heavy shoulder similar to the Crimean Ayu-Dag. A lighthouse shone brightly on the summit, while below in the water between us and the shore rose the three sharp reefs—"The Three Brothers." And all were covered with smoke, as in hell.

A cutter with a barge in tow approached the ship. Convicts were being brought to unload the freight. We could hear Tatar being spoken, and curses in Russian.

"Don't let them come on board," someone shouted. "Don't let them! At night they will steal everything on the boat."

"Here in Alexandrovsk it is not so bad," said the engineer, as he saw how depressed I was while gazing to shore. "Wait until you see Dué! The cliffs are completely vertical, with dark canyons and layers of coal; fog everywhere! Sometimes we carried two to three hundred prisoners on the *Baikal* to Dué and many burst into tears when they saw the shore!"

"We are the prisoners, not the convicts," said the captain. "It is calm here now, but you should see it in the fall: wind, snow, storms, cold, the waves dash over the side of the ship—and that's the end of you!"

I spent the night on board. At five o'clock in the morning I was noisily awakened with, "Hurry, hurry! The cutter is making its last trip to shore! We are leaving at once!" A moment later I was sitting in the cutter. Next to me was a young official with an angry, sleepy face. The cutter sounded its whistle and we left for the shore towing two barges full of convicts. Sleepy and exhausted by their night's labor, the prisoners were limp and sullen, completely silent. Their faces were covered with dew. I now recall several Caucasians with sharp features, wearing fur hats pulled down to their eyebrows.

"Permit me to introduce myself," said an official. "I am the college registrar D."

He was my first Sakhalin acquaintance, a poet, author of a denunciatory poem entitled "Sakhalinó," which begins: "Tell me, Doctor, was it not in vain. . . ." Later he often visited me and accompanied me around Alexandrovsk and nearby places, relating anecdotes and endlessly reading his own compositions. During the long winter nights he writes progressive stories. On occasion he enjoys informing people that he is the college registrar and is in charge of the tenth grade. When a woman who had visited him on business called him Mr. D., he was insulted and angrily screamed, "I'm not Mr. D. to you, but 'your worship.'" While strolling along the shore I questioned him about life on Sakhalin, about what was happening, but he only sighed ominously and said, "You will see!"

The sun was high. Yesterday's fog and darkness, which had so terrified me, vanished in the brilliance of the early

17

morning. The dense, clumsy Zhonkiyer with its lighthouse, "The Three Brothers" and the high, craggy shores which were visible for tens of versts on both sides, the transparent mist on the mountains and the smoke from the fires did not present such a horrifying scene in the bright sunlight.

There is no harbor here, and the coast is dangerous. This fact was impressively demonstrated by the presence of the Swedish ship *Atlas,* which was wrecked shortly before my arrival and now lay broken on the shore. Boats usually anchor a verst from shore and rarely any nearer. There is a pier, but it is only usable by cutters and barges. It is a large pier, several sazhens long, and T-shaped. Thick log piles had been securely driven into the sea bottom, in the form of squares, which were filled with stone. The top was covered with planking, and there were freight-car rails running the length of the pier. A charming building, the pier office, sits on the wide end of the T; here also stands a tall black mast. The construction is solid, but not permanent. I was told that during a heavy storm the waves sometimes reach the windows of the building and the spray even reaches the yardarm of the mast; the entire pier trembles.

Along the shore near the pier some 50 convicts were wandering, obviously idle; some were in overalls, others in jackets or gray cloth coats. When I approached, they all removed their caps. It is possible that no writer has ever previously received such an honor. Somebody's horse was standing on shore harnessed to a springless carriage. The convicts loaded my luggage in the carriage; a black-bearded man in a coat with his shirt tail hanging got up on the box. We took off.

"Where do you wish to go, your worship?" he asked, turning around and removing his cap.

I asked him if it would be possible to rent lodgings here, even if it was only one room.

"Certainly, your worship, rooms can be rented."

For the two versts from the pier to the Alexandrovsk Post I traveled along an excellent highway. In comparison to the Siberian roads this is a clean, smooth road with gutters and street lights; it is absolutely luxurious. Adjacent to it runs a railway. However, the scenery along the way is depressing in its barrenness. Along the tops of the mountains and hills encircling the Alexandrovsk valley, through which the River Duyka flows, charred stumps and trunks of larch trees, dried out by fire and wind, project like porcupine quills, while in the valley below there are hillocks covered with sorrel—the remains of swamps which until recently were impassable. The fresh slashes in the earth made by the gutters reveal the complete barrenness of the swampy scorched earth with its half-*vershok* layer of poor soil. There are no spruce trees, no oaks, no maples —only larches, gaunt, pitiful, fretted in precise shapes, and they do not beautify the forests and parklands as they do in Russia, but serve only to emphasize the poor marshy soil and the severe climate.

The Alexandrovsk Post, or Alexandrovsk for short, is a small, pretty Siberian-type town with 3,000 inhabitants. It does not contain even one stone building. Everything is built of wood, chiefly of larch—the church, the houses and the sidewalks. Here is located the residence of the island's commandant, the center of Sakhalin civilization. The prison is situated near the main street. Its exterior is quite similar to an army barracks, and as a result Alexandrovsk is completely free of the dismal prison atmosphere which I had expected.

The driver took me to the Alexandrovsk residential district in the suburbs, to the home of one of the peasant exiles. Here I was shown my lodgings. There was a small yard, paved Siberian fashion with timbers and surrounded with awnings. The house contained five spacious, clean rooms and a kitchen, but not a stick of furniture. The landlady, a young peasant woman, brought out a table, and a chair came about five minutes later. "With firewood the price is 25 rubles; without firewood, 15," she said.

About an hour later, she brought a samovar and said with a sigh:

"So you have come to visit this godforsaken hole!"

She had come as a little child with her mother, following her father, a convict who has not yet served out his sentence. Now she is married to one of the exiled peasants, a gloomy old man whom I glimpsed crossing the yard. He had some sort of sickness and spent his time lying under the awning and groaning.

"At home in Tambovsk *guberniya* they are probably reaping," she said. "Here there is nothing to look at."

And truly there is nothing interesting to look at. Through the window you could see rows of cabbage plants, and some ugly ditches nearby, and beyond these a gaunt larch tree withering away.

Groaning and holding his side, the landlord entered and began complaining of crop failure, the cold climate, the poor soil. He had completed his prison term and exile, and now owned two houses, some horses and a cow. He employed many workmen and did nothing himself. He had married a young woman and, most important, he had long since been granted permission to return to the mainland—but still he complained.

At noon I sauntered in the suburbs. On the edge of the suburbs there was a pretty little house with a little garden in front and a brass nameplate on the door. Near the house in the same yard was a small shop. I entered to buy something to eat. "Commerce" and "Trade Commission Warehouse" was the description of this modest shop on a printed and handwritten price list which I saved. It was owned by a settler, a former officer of the guard who had been sentenced to penal servitude for murder by the Petersburg Regional Court twelve years ago. He had completed his sentence and was now engaged in business and he also fulfilled various commissions for road-making and other matters. For this he received a senior supervisor's salary. His wife was a free woman, belonging to the nobility, and worked as a doctor's assistant in the prison hospital. The shop sold the little stars which go on epaulets, Turkish delight, crosscut saws, sickles and "most up-to-date ladies' summer hats, very fashionable, from 4 rubles 50 kopecks to 12 rubles each." While I was speaking with the clerk, the owner entered the shop. He was dressed in a silk jacket and bright tie. We introduced ourselves.

"Won't you be so kind as to have dinner with me?" he asked.

I agreed and we entered the house. His home is comfortable, with Viennese furniture, flowers, an American Ariston musical box and a rocking chair on which he rocks after dinner. In addition to the housewife there were other guests in the dining room—four officials. One of them, an old man without a mustache but wearing gray whiskers and resembling the dramatist Ibsen, proved to be the junior physician at the local hospital. Another, also an old man, introduced himself as a staff officer of the Orenburg Cossack Army. From his very first words this officer impressed me as a very good man and a great patriot. He is meek and good-naturedly judicious, but when politics are discussed he comes out of his shell and begins a serious exposition of Russian military power and speaks scornfully of the Germans and the English, whom he has never seen in his life. The story is told that when he was in Singapore en route to Sakhalin he wanted to buy his wife a silk shawl. He was told to exchange his Russian money for dollars, and became grossly insulted. "How do you like that!" he said. "Do I have to exchange my Orthodox money for some kind of Ethiopian money?" And the shawl was not purchased.

At dinner they served soup, chickens and ice cream. Wine was also served.

"When, roughly, was the last snowfall?" I asked.

"In May," the shopkeeper replied.

"That's a lie, it was in June," said the doctor who resembled Ibsen.

"I know a settler," said the shopkeeper, "who had a twenty-fold yield from California wheat."

And again there was an objection from the doctor: "That's a lie! Your Sakhalin gives nothing. It is a cursed land."

"However, permit me," said one of the officials. "In

'82 there was a forty-fold wheat yield. I know this personally."

"Don't believe it," said the doctor. "They're pulling wool over your eyes."

At dinner the following legend was related. When the Russians occupied the island and began to offend the Gilyaks, the Gilyak shaman cursed Sakhalin and predicted that no good would ever come of it.

"So it has come to pass," sighed the doctor.

After dinner, the shopkeeper played the music box. The doctor invited me to stay with him and that very evening I moved to the post's main street. It was one of the houses close to the business district. That evening began my initiation into the mysteries of Sakhalin. The doctor told me that just before my arrival, during a medical inspection of livestock at the pier, there had been a serious misunderstanding between him and the island's commandant, and the general had even raised his stick against him. The following day his resignation was accepted, although he had not tendered it. The doctor showed me a huge pile of papers written by him, evidence of how he had spoken in defense of truth and humanity. There were copies of requests, complaints, reports and denunciations.[1]

"The general won't be pleased at your staying with me," said the doctor, winking at me knowingly.

The following day I paid a visit to the commandant of the island, V. O. Kononovich. Notwithstanding his fatigue and lack of time, the general greeted me most courteously and conversed with me for almost an hour. He is cultured, well read, and in addition has a great deal of practical experience, since he was the prison commandant at Kara for eighteen years before being appointed to Sakhalin. He speaks and writes beautifully and gives the impression of being a sincere man with benevolent aspirations. I cannot forget how satisfied I was with our conversation and how favorably I was impressed by his aversion to corporal punishment, a subject to which he referred many times. George Kennan describes him glowingly in his famous book.

Learning that I planned to spend several months on Sakhalin, the general warned me that life here was difficult and boring.

"Everyone tries to escape from this place—the convicts, the settlers and the officials," he said. "I have no desire to escape yet, but already I am exhausted by the great amount of mental exertion demanded of me, chiefly because there are so many matters to attend to."

He promised me full cooperation but asked that I wait a few days, because Sakhalin was preparing for the forthcoming visit of the Governor-General and everyone was busy.

"I'm glad you are staying with our enemy," he said, as we parted. "You will learn our weak points."

Up to the time of the Governor-General's arrival I lived in the doctor's apartment in Alexandrovsk. Life was not completely normal. When I awoke in the morning the very diversity of sounds reminded me where I was. Under my windows the convicts passed along the street to the measured clanging of their irons. Opposite the apartment, in the military barracks, musicians were learning the marches with which they would greet the Governor-General. The flute played passages from one song, the trombone from another, and the bassoon from still another, and the result was inconceivable cacophony. In our rooms the canaries whistled continually and my doctor host paced from corner to corner, thumbing through lawbooks and thinking out loud.

"If on the basis of this particular section I submit a request to the department . . ." and so on.

Or he sat with his son and labored over more pettifogging statements.

It was unbearably hot in the street. They were complaining about the drought, and the officers were walking about in their single-breasted jackets. But this was not true of every summer. The traffic on the streets was much greater than in our provincial towns. This could be explained by the preparations for welcoming the Governor-General, and also by the preponderance of people of working age, who spent most of the day out of doors. The prison, with over 1,000 inhabitants, and the barracks, with 500 soldiers, were grouped together in a very small area. Workmen were rapidly building a bridge over the Dukya, they were constructing archways, cleaning, painting, sweeping, marching. Troikas and two-horsed carriages with bells were driving along the streets; these horses were being made ready for the Governor-General. They were all in such a hurry to be ready that they were even working on holidays.

Along the street a group of Gilyaks, the native aborigines, were being taken to the police station. They were being angrily barked at by the meek Sakhalin mongrels, who for some reason only bark at the Gilyaks. And there was another group: fettered prisoners, some wearing hats, some bareheaded, clanging their chains, dragging a heavy barrow filled with sand. Little boys latched on to the back of the barrow; sweaty, red-faced guards strode along with rifles on their shoulders. After pouring out the sand on the little square in front of the general's residence, the convicts returned along the same road, the clang of chains never stopping. A prisoner in overalls, with diamond-shaped markings on the back to indicate that he was a convict, went from courtyard to courtyard selling blueberries. When you go down the street, everyone who is sitting stands up and everyone you meet doffs his hat.

The prisoners and the exiles, with some exceptions, walk the streets freely, without chains and without guards; you meet them in groups and singly every step of the way. They are everywhere, in the streets and in the houses. They serve as drivers, watchmen, chefs, cooks and nurse-maids. I was not accustomed to seeing so many convicts, and at first their proximity was disturbing and perplexing. You walk past a construction site and you see convicts with axes, saws and hammers. "Well," you think, "they are going to haul off and murder me!" Or else you are visiting an acquaintance and, not finding him at home, you sit down to write a note, while his convict servant stands waiting behind you, holding the knife with which he has been peeling potatoes in the kitchen. Or it may happen that at about four o'clock in the morning you will wake up and hear a rustling sound, and you look and see a convict approaching the bed on tiptoe, scarcely breathing.

"What's the matter? What do you want?"

"To clean your shoes, your worship."

Soon I became accustomed to this. Everyone becomes accustomed to it, even women and children. The local ladies think nothing of permitting their children to go out and play in the care of nursemaids sentenced to exile for life.

One correspondent writes that at first he was terrified of every bush, and groped for the revolver under his coat at every encounter with a prisoner on the roads and pathways. Later he calmed down, having come to the conclusion that "the prisoners are generally nothing more than a herd of sheep, cowardly, lazy, half-starved and servile." To believe that Russian prisoners do not murder and rob a passerby merely out of cowardice and laziness, one must be either a very poor judge of men or not know them at all.

The Governor-General of the Amur region, Baron Korf, arrived on Sakhalin on July 19 on the warship *Bobr*. He was formally received in the square which lies between the commandant's house and the church. There was an honor guard, many officials and a crowd of exiles and prisoners. The same band played which I described a little while ago. A handsome old man, Potemkin by name, a former convict who had grown rich on Sakhalin, presented bread and salt on a silver platter of local workmanship. My doctor host was present. He wore a black swallowtail coat and a cap, and held a petition in his hand. Here I saw the Sakhalin crowd for the first time, and its mournful character made a deep impression on me. There were men and women of working age, old folks and children, but there were absolutely no young people. It seemed that there was nobody on Sakhalin between thirteen and twenty years of age. And I reluctantly asked myself, "Doesn't this mean that when the young people are old enough they leave the island at the first opportunity?"

The day following his arrival, the Governor-General

began to inspect the prisons and the settlements of the exiles. Everywhere the exiles, who had awaited him with the greatest impatience, presented him with petitions and made oral requests. Everyone spoke for himself or one spoke for the entire settlement. Since oratorical art flourishes on Sakhalin, there were not a few speeches. At Derbinsk, the settler Maslov several times in his speech referred to the officials as "our most gracious governors." Unfortunately, almost none of those who approached Baron Korf made sensible requests. Here, as in similar situations in Russia, the intolerable ignorance of the peasants was revealed. They did not ask for schools, or justice, or wages. Instead they asked for trifles. Some asked for more rations, some asked that their children be adopted; in other words, they presented petitions which could have been granted by the local authorities. Baron Korf listened to their petitions with complete attention and goodwill. Deeply moved by their poverty-stricken circumstances, he made promises and raised their hopes for a better life.[2]

When the assistant superintendent at the Arkovo prison reported that all was well in the Arkovo settlement, the baron mentioned the winter and summer grain yields and said, "All is well except there is no bread in Arkovo."

In honor of his arrival the Alexandrovsk prison inmates were fed fresh meat and even venison. He visited all the cells, accepted petitions and ordered the chains removed from many of the convicts.

On July 22, after the *Te Deum* and a parade (it was a holiday), the superintendent hastened to my lodging and announced that the Governor-General wished to see me. I went to meet him. Baron Korf received me most graciously and spoke with me for about half an hour. Our conversation took place in the presence of General Kononovich. Incidentally, he asked whether I had some sort of official assignment. I said, "No!"

"Do you not at least have an assignment from some scientific society or newspaper?" the baron asked.

I had a correspondent's card in my pocket, but since I had no intention of printing anything about Sakhalin in the press and did not wish to delude the persons dealing with me, I naturally answered with complete honesty, "No!"

"I permit you to visit anywhere and anyone you wish," the baron said. "We have nothing to hide. You can examine everything. You will be given free access to all the prisons and settlements, you may make use of any documents needed for your work. In other words, all doors will be open to you everywhere. There is but one permission which I cannot grant. I have no right to allow you to have any communication whatsoever with political prisoners."

In dismissing me, the baron said:

"We will talk again tomorrow. Bring some writing paper."

On the same day I attended a gala dinner at the home of the island commandant. I met almost the entire Sakhalin administrative staff. Music was played during dinner, and there were speeches. When they toasted his good health, Baron Korf made a short speech, the words of which I still recall.

"I am convinced that the 'unfortunates' live better on Sakhalin than in any other place in Russia or even in Europe. In conjunction with this, much still remains to be done, and we are confronted with an endless road leading to their welfare."

He had visited Sakhalin five years earlier and now found significant progress surpassing all his expectations. His words of praise omitted any reference to hunger, habitual prostitution by women exiles, and terrible corporal punishments, but the audience was forced to believe him. In comparison with what had transpired five years ago, the present situation was almost the beginning of a golden age.

There were illuminations during the evening. Until late at night soldiers, settlers and prisoners milled around in throngs along the streets lit with lamps and Bengal lights. The prison was open. The Duyka River, always pitiful and dirty with its bleak and barren banks, was now decorated on both sides with multicolored lanterns and

Bengal lights, and their reflections in the water were lovely that evening, majestic and ludicrous, like a cook's daughter dressed up in the gown of a baroness. Music was being played in the general's garden, and there were singers. They even shot off the cannon, and the cannon burst.

In spite of all this gaiety, it was dull on the streets. There were no songs, no accordions, not even one drunkard. The people wandered around like shadows and were as silent as shadows. Convict life, even with Bengal lights, remains convict life; and music which is heard from afar by a person who will never return to his homeland only evokes deadly melancholy.

When I arrived with my writing paper to keep my appointment with the Governor-General, he gave me his opinions on penal servitude in Sakhalin and on the colony, and suggested that I record everything he said. I agreed most willingly. He suggested that I entitle my inquiry: "A Record of the Life of the Unfortunates." From our previous conversation and from his dictation I received the impression that he was a magnanimous and honorable man, but that the "life of the unfortunates" was not as well known to him as he thought. Here are several sentences which he dictated to me:

"Nobody is bereft of the hope of enjoying his full rights; there is no such thing as perpetual punishment. Penal servitude for an indefinite period is limited to twenty years. Convict hard labor is not onerous. Forced labor gives no personal gain to the workers; herein lies its burden, and not in physical oppression. There are no chains, no guards, no shaved heads."

The days were beautiful with a bright sky and clear air, reminiscent of fall in Russia. The evenings were magnificent. I remember the glowing western sky, the dark-blue sea and a completely white moon rising over the mountains. On such evenings I enjoyed driving along the valley between the post and the village of Novo-Mikhaylovka; the road is smooth, straight; alongside is a railway and a telegraph line. The further we drove from Alexandrovsk, the more the valley narrowed, the shadows deepened; there were giant burdocks in tropical luxuriance; dark mountains rose on all sides. In the distance we could see the flames from coke fires, and there were more flames from a forest fire. The moon rose. Suddenly a fantastic scene. Coming toward us along the railway was a convict, riding in a small cart, dressed in white and leaning on a pole. He stopped abruptly.

"Isn't it time to turn back?" asked my convict driver. Then he turned the horses, and glancing up at the mountains and the fires, he said:

"It is lonesome here, your worship. It is much better at home in Russia."

1   Following is a sample of a denunciation via telegraph: "It is my bounden duty, according to the seven hundred and twelfth article of volume three of the criminal code, to trouble your honor to come to the defense of justice against impunity for extortion, forgery and torture perpetrated by X."

2   The hopes were not unattainable. At one settlement, speaking of the fact that peasant exiles were now permitted to move to the mainland, he said, "And later you can go back to your homeland, to Russia."

III
The Census - Contents of the Statistical Form - My Questions and the Answers Received - The Huts and Their Inhabitants - The Exiles' Opinions of the Census

IN ORDER to be able to visit all the settlements possible and to become intimately acquainted with the majority of the exiles, I devised a method which seemed the only possible one for achieving my purpose. I took a census. In the settlements I went into each hut and recorded the names of the owners, the members of their families, and who lodged with them and worked with them. I was graciously offered assistance to lighten my work and save time, but since my chief aim in taking the census was not to produce a final record but to gain impressions through the recording process itself, I used help only on the rarest occasions. All this was done by one man in three months, and cannot really be called a census. The record cannot be considered accurate and complete. However, since more competent data does not exist either in literature or in the Sakhalin administrative offices, it is possible that my figures may be useful.

To record the census I used forms printed for me at the printing shop of the police department. The arrangement was as follows. On the first line of each form I noted the name of the post or settlement. On the second line was the number of the house according to the prison list of homesteads. The third line noted the status of the person interviewed: convict, settler, peasant formerly exiled, free person. I recorded free persons only if they directly participated in an exile's household—for example, if they were married, legally or illegally, and generally belonged to his family, or lived in his house as workers, lodgers, etc.

Great significance is attached to status according to Sakhalin customs. A convict is unquestionably ashamed of his status. To the question "What is your status?" he answers, "I am a worker." If he had been a soldier before his imprisonment, he always adds, "A soldier, your worship." Having completed, or as he himself expresses it, served his term, he becomes a forced settler. This new status is not considered lowly because the term used for a settler is not too dissimilar to the term for a peasant, but does not possess, naturally, the rights which go with being a peasant.

Asked "What are you?" a settler always answers, "A free man." After ten years, or, under favorable circumstances provided by the laws of exile, after six years, the settler gains the status of "peasant formerly exiled." When asked his status, the peasant answers with dignity, as if he should not be included with the others and is in some way remarkably different from them, "I am a peasant." But he does not add "formerly exiled."

I did not question the exiles on their former status since the administrative offices have sufficient information on this. They themselves, except for the soldiers, never mention their lost status, as if it were something they had already forgotten. There was not one among the lower-middle-class people, those town people, tradesmen and priests, who did not describe his former state as "freedom." If someone starts a conversation about his past, he always begins, "When I was free. . . ."

The fourth line contains the given name, the patronymic and the surname. As to names, I can only recall that it appears that I did not record even one female Tatar name correctly. In a Tatar family with many daughters and the father and mother scarcely understanding Russian, it is difficult to make sense and I had to make my records by guesswork. Tatar names are also incorrectly written in the prison records.

When I asked an Orthodox Russian peasant his name, he answered, "Karl." He was not being facetious. He was a vagrant who had borrowed his name from a German. I remember that I recorded two of those: Karl Langer and Karl Karlov. One convict was called Napoleon. There was a female vagrant Praskovya, although her real name was Maria. As to surnames, for some strange reason there were many Bogdanovs [God-given] and Bespalovs [Without Fingers] on Sakhalin. There were many curious names: Shkandyba [Limper], Zheludok [Stomach], Bezbozhny [Godless] and Zevaka [Yawner].

I am told that Tatar titles are still retained in Sakhalin, disregarding the fact that everyone has forfeited all rights to status, prefixes and particles which denote high status. I don't know how correct this is, but I recorded many khans, sultans and oglis. The most common name among the vagrants is Ivan, and the most common surname is Nepomnyashchy [Unremembered]. Here are some of the vagrants' names: Mustafa Nepomnyashchy, Vasily Bezotechestva [Countryless], Franz Nepomnyashchy, Ivan Nepomnyashchy 20 Years, Yakov Besprozvaniya [Nameless], Vagrant Ivan 35 Years[1] and Chelovek Neizvestnovo Zvaniya [Man with Unknown Name].

On the same line I noted the relationship of those I interviewed to the master of the house: wife, son, mistress, worker, lodger, son of lodger, etc. In recording children I noted the legal and illegal offspring, their own and adopted. Adopted children are frequently encountered on Sakhalin and I was not only obliged to record adopted children, but also foster parents.

The relationship of many of those living in the huts toward the master of the house was that of co-owner or half-owner. In both of the northern districts there were two or even three proprietors to a land allotment and so it was in more than half of the households. A settler takes possession of a piece of land, builds a house and starts farming. In two or three years the authorities assign a co-owner, or they give one plot to two settlers at the same time. A convict who has served his term sometimes requests that he be permitted to settle at a certain post or settlement where there is no more room available for settlement, and they are forced to assign him to an already existing homestead. The number of co-owners especially rises after the announcement of an imperial edict. At such times the administration is forced to find places immediately for several hundred persons.

The fifth line notes age. Women who have passed forty do not easily remember their age and must think before answering the question. The Armenians from Erivan *guberniya* never know their age. One answered, "Maybe thirty, maybe I'm even fifty." In such instances there had to be an approximation to the age, which was later verified by the records. Usually youngsters of fifteen and older decrease their age. Some who are already married or who have been prostitutes for a long time say they are thirteen or fourteen. The reason for this is that infants and children in the poorest families receive food from the prison, which is distributed only to those below fifteen years of age, and thus the young people and their parents are forced to tell lies.

The sixth line pertains to religion.

The seventh: "Where were you born?" This question was answered without difficulty and only the vagrants answered with a quip or merely "I don't remember." When I asked a girl, Natalya Nepomnyashchaya, from which *guberniya* she had come, she told me, "A bit from all of them."

Fellow countrymen usually stay together, they pass the time together, and when they escape, they also escape together. A Tulyak prefers to become a co-owner with a Tulyak; a Bakinets with another Bakinets. Obviously societies of fellow countrymen exist. When questions had to be asked about an absentee, his fellow countrymen gave the most detailed information about him.

The eighth line asked: "Which year did you arrive on Sakhalin?" Very few of the Sakhalin dwellers answered this question immediately, without strain. The year he arrived on Sakhalin was the year of dire misfortune. Furthermore, they don't even know the year, or have forgotten it. I asked an old convict woman when she had arrived on Sakhalin and she answered dully, without thinking, "Who

33

knows? Maybe in '83." Either her husband or her lover interrupts, "So why do you wag your tongue for nothing? You came in '85." "Maybe in '85," she agrees with a sigh. We begin counting, and the peasant is correct. Men are not as listless as the women, but they do not answer immediately. They ponder and discuss.

"When did they send you to Sakhalin?" I asked a settler.

"I came in the same group with Gladky," he answers uncertainly, looking at his friends.

Gladky came in the first group, and the first group— i.e., the first "volunteers"—came to Sakhalin in 1879. Thus I record it. Or they say, "I was in prison for six years, but I have been a settler for three years. So figure it out." "That means you have been on Sakhalin nine years?" "Not at all! Before Sakhalin I was in the central prison for two years." And so forth. Or they say, "I came in the year when they killed Derbin," or "Mitsul died that year."

It was extremely important that I should receive correct answers from those who had come in the '60s and '70s. I did not want to miss a single one. In all probability I was unsuccessful. How many have survived of those who came here twenty to twenty-five years ago is a question which can be said to be fateful for Sakhalin colonization.

On the ninth line I recorded the main occupation and trade.

On the tenth: literacy. Usually the question is phrased in the form: "Are you literate?" Instead I asked: "Can you read?" which often saved me from incorrect answers because peasants who cannot write and can only read printed words say they are illiterate. There are even those who from modesty say rudely, "What's the use of reading? What is literacy?" and only after the question is repeated, they say, "I was able to read print at one time, but now, you know, I've forgotten. We are a stupid people—we are only peasants." Those who are blind or see only with difficulty also call themselves illiterate.

The eleventh line pertained to family status: married, widowed or single. If married, where: in the homeland or on Sakhalin? The words "married, widowed, single" do not define family status on Sakhalin. Here very frequently married men are doomed to a solitary, unmarried life because their wives live back home and refuse to give them a divorce, while single men and widows live a family life together and have half a dozen children. Therefore, even though they did not live alone and even though they considered themselves married, I did not consider it superfluous to describe them as "single."

Nowhere else in Russia is illicit marriage so widely and notoriously prevalent, and nowhere else does it take the peculiar form it does on Sakhalin. Illicit marriage or, as it is called here, free cohabitation does not find objectors among either the officials or the priesthood, but, on the contrary, it receives encouragement and is sanctioned. There are settlements where not even one legal marriage is encountered. Free couples form a household under the same conditions as legally married couples. They beget children for the colony and therefore there are no reasons to pass separate laws for them at registration.

Finally, the twelfth line: "Does he receive assistance from the prison?" Based on the answers received to this question, I wanted to find out which portion of the population was unable to exist without material aid from the prison, or, in other words, who feeds the colony? Does it feed itself or does the prison feed it? Assistance is received from the prison in the shape of food, equipment or money by all the convicts, by the settlers in the first years after serving their sentence, by paupers and by children of the poorer families. In addition to these officially recognized pensioners, I noted those exiles living at the expense of the prison who receive wages from the prison for the services they rendered as teachers, clerks, jailers, etc. However, the answers were not quite complete. In addition to the customary allotments, i.e., food and wages, another widespread practice is the distribution of assistance which could not always be recorded on the form. For example: assistance given to couples when they marry, the purchase of grains from the settlers at deliberately high prices, and, chiefly, the distribution of seeds, livestock and the like on credit. A settler might be in debt to the prison for several hundred rubles which he will never repay, but I was forced to record him as not receiving aid.

I drew a red pencil line along the bottom of each form involving a female and found this to be more convenient than a special heading indicating sex. I only recorded the people who were actually living with the family. If they said that their oldest son had gone to work in Vladivostok and the second son is a laborer in the Rykovsk settlement, I did not record the first at all, and the latter I recorded at his present residence.

I went alone from one hut to the next. Sometimes I was accompanied by a convict or a settler who had taken upon himself the role of guide only to relieve his boredom. Sometimes a guard armed with a revolver followed me like a shadow, keeping close to me or keeping his distance. If I wanted him to, he would come and clarify their answers for me. When I did ask him about anything, his forehead was immediately covered with sweat, and he said, "I couldn't possibly know, your worship!" Usually my barefoot and hatless companion, bearing my inkstand in his hands, would go running out in front of me, loudly banging open the doors, and then taking the opportunity to whisper something to the master of the house inside the doorway: probably his opinions of my census. Then I entered the house.

On Sakhalin there are all types of huts, depending on who built them—a Siberian, a Khokhol [Ukrainian] or a Chukhonets [Finn]. Most frequently it was a small frame box 14 feet by 14 feet, having two or three windows, without any exterior decorations, the roofs covered with straw or bark, and occasionally some thin planks. There is no courtyard, and there are no trees. Shacks and Siberian-type bathhouses are rare. If there are dogs, they are gentle, not vicious, and, as I have already stated, they only bark at the Gilyaks—probably because their footwear is made of dog fur. Therefore these tame, harmless dogs are not tied up. If these people own a pig, it has a lock and chain around its neck. A rooster is also tied up by its leg.

"Why are your pig and rooster tied up?" I asked a householder.

"In our Sakhalin everything is chained," he replied jokingly. "That's the kind of land it is."

The hut consists of one room with a Russian stove. The floor is of wood. There is a table, two or three stools, a bench, a bed with bedding, or the bedding is placed directly on the floor. Sometimes there is absolutely no furniture and only a featherbed lies in the middle of the floor, and it is obvious that it has just been slept on. A cup with remnants of food stands on the windowsill. The conditions are such that it is not a home, not a room, but, more accurately, a cell for solitary confinement.

Where there are women and children, no matter how impoverished, the hut does resemble a household full of peasant life. Nevertheless there is a persistent feeling that something important is missing; no grandmother, no grandfather, no old paintings, no inherited furniture; consequently, the household contains nothing from the past, nothing traditional. There is no beautiful icon corner, or if there is, it is very barren and dreary, without a lamp or any decorations. Here normal customs no longer exist. The furnishings are haphazard and it seems that the family is not living in its own home but in someone else's, or it has just arrived and has not yet had the opportunity to settle down. There is no cat, and on cold evenings no crickets can be heard. And this is all due to the fact that we are no longer in Russia.

The scenes which I ordinarily observed did not indicate good housekeeping, comfort and stability in the households. Most frequently I found a single inhabitant, lonesome and forlorn, who seems to have grown numb from forced idleness and boredom. He is dressed as a free man, but from habit his coat is thrown over his shoulders in prison fashion and if he has recently been released from prison, his peaked prison cap, minus its peak, has been tossed on the table. His stove is not lit; his only kitchenware consists of a small

37

pot and a bottle stopped with paper. He reacts scornfully, with icy contempt, concerning his own life and his household. He says that he has tried everything but nothing makes sense. There's but one thing left: ignore everything. While I am speaking with him his neighbors gather in the house and a conversation commences on various subjects: about the administration, the climate, women. . . . From boredom they are all willing to talk and listen endlessly.

Occasionally, in addition to the householder, you find a whole crowd of lodgers and workmen in the hut. On one threshold sits a convict-lodger with a ribbon tied around his hair, sewing shoes; a strong odor of leather and cobbler's wax permeates the air. In the doorway his children lie on rags. Here also in a dark, tight corner his wife, who had voluntarily accompanied him, is making *vareniky* [Ukrainian dumplings] from blueberries, while working on a tiny table. This family had just recently arrived from Russia.

Further, in the house itself are five men who call themselves a lodger, a worker or a cohabitant. One stands near the stove. With cheeks puffed out, eyes popping, he is soldering something. Another, obviously a buffoon with a deliberately moronic expression, is muttering something while the rest are laughing boisterously into their hands. On the bed sits a Babylonian whore, the mistress of the house herself, Lukerya Nepomnyashchaya, tousled, emaciated, covered with freckles. She attempts to answer my questions flippantly while swinging her legs. Her lackluster eyes are not pretty, and from her hollow-cheeked, apathetic face I can imagine how much she has suffered during her short life in prisons and convict stations, and from her many illnesses. This Lukerya sets the tone of life in the house, and because of her the entire atmosphere reveals the close proximity of an insane, debauched vagabond. There is no possibility of a normal household here.

Occasionally I came upon a group of people in a hut who had been playing cards before I arrived. Their faces show confusion, boredom and expectation; perhaps they are anxious to return to their cards as soon as I leave? At other times I walk into a cabin completely devoid of furnishings; the stove is bare, and on the floor, along the wall, Cherkess men sit in a row, some wearing hats, others with bare, shaven, rigid heads, who stare at me without blinking. If there was only one woman in the hut, she was always lying in bed; and she would answer questions while yawning and stretching herself, and when I left she would lay down again.

The convict population regarded me as an official and thought the census was just one more of the many formal inquisitions which never lead to anything. However, the fact that I was not a local man, not an official of the Sakhalin government, awakened some curiosity among the convicts, and they would ask me, "Why are you taking a census of all of us?"

And then there would be various conjectures. Some said that the high authorities probably wanted to distribute aid among the convicts, others that the authorities had probably finally decided to resettle everyone on the mainland. It is generally believed that sooner or later the prison and the settlers will be moved to the mainland. A third group, pretending skepticism, said they never expected anything because God Himself has abandoned them, and they would say this in order to force me to raise an objection to their theory. And then, from either the doorway or the top of the stove, as if mocking all our hopes and conjectures, there could be heard a voice, full of fatigue, boredom and annoyance at being disturbed, saying, "They keep writing, they keep writing, they keep writing, Oh, Queen of Heaven!"

I did not suffer hunger or any inconvenience during my travels round Sakhalin. I had read that supposedly the agronomist Mitsul suffered terrible privations while surveying the island, and was even forced to eat his dog. Since then the situation has changed considerably. Your present-day agronomist rides on good roads, and even in the very poorest settlements there are guardhouses, or so-called quarters, where a warm lodging, a samovar and a bed can always be found.

When explorers set out for the interior of the island,

into the taiga, they take with them American canned goods, red wine, plates, forks, pillows and anything else they can pack on the backs of convicts, who are used on Sakhalin in place of draft animals. Some people still eat rotten wood with salt, and even practice cannibalism, but this does not apply to tourists or officials.

In the following chapters I will describe the posts and the settlements and will acquaint the reader with the various types of convict labor and the prisons to the extent that I was able to know them in a short time. Convict labor on Sakhalin is extremely varied. The labor is not specialized; it does not depend on coal- or gold-mining, but encompasses the entire range of Sakhalin life and is spread throughout the populated areas of the island. Digging out stumps in the forest, building houses, draining swamps, fishing, mowing, loading and unloading cargo on ships are all types of convict labor which have necessarily merged with the life of the colony to such a degree that they cannot be isolated. Convict labor can be discussed as something existing independently on the island only if we embark on a precise survey of the location of mines and the organization of factory work.

I will commence with the Alexandrovsk valley and the settlements along the Duyka River. This valley was first chosen for settlement in Northern Sakhalin not because it had been explored better than all the others or because it satisfied the aims of colonization, but purely by chance, because it was closest to Dué, where penal servitude was first established on Sakhalin.

1 The length of the sentence was added to his name. He was actually 48 years old.

IV
The Duyka River - The Alexandrovsk Valley - The Alexandrovka Slobodka - Vagrant Krasivy - The Alexandrovsk Post - Its Past - Yunts - The Sakhalin Paris

WHEN THE DUYKA RIVER, also called the Alexandrovka, was charted by the zoologist Polyakov, it was some 70 feet wide in its lower reaches. Its banks were luxuriant with tremendous stands of trees reaching down to the water; the lowlands were covered with forests of fir, larch, alder and willows, and surrounded by impassable swamps. Now the river is only a long, narrow puddle. In its width, barren shores and slow current it resembles the Moscow canal.

It is only necessary to read Polyakov's account of the Alexandrovsk valley and then glance at it today to understand what a tremendous amount of hard and forced labor has already been expended on cultivating this area. "From the heights of neighboring mountains," writes Polyakov, "the Alexandrovsk valley is stifling, dark and heavily forested . . . a tremendous fir and pine forest covers a significant portion of the valley bottom."

He writes of swamps, impassable marshes, forbidding quagmires and forests where "in addition to tremendous trees standing in their bare roots, the ground is often covered with huge, half-rotten trunks fallen from age or storms. Moss-covered hillocks often protrude amid the roots of the fallen trees, beside the gulleys and ravines."

Now an entire city stands on the former taiga with its swamps and ravines; roads have been built, there are green meadows, rye fields and market gardens are harvested, and already complaints are heard of the scarcity of trees.

The appalling labor and struggle of the convicts who

worked in waist-high swamps, in freezing cold, in icy rain, lonely for home, suffering all manner of indignities, beaten by birch rods—all this makes a horrifying impression. It is not surprising that one kindly Sakhalin official always reads aloud to me from Nekrasov's sad poem "The Railroad" while we are driving to some destination.

A small stream, called the Malaya Alexandrovka, falls into the Duyka on the right side, at its very mouth. On both sides of the stream lies the Alexandrovka settlement, or the Slobodka, which I have already mentioned. It lies in the suburbs of the post and has already merged with it. However, since it differs from the post in a number of peculiar ways and has an independent life, it must be described separately.

This is one of the oldest settlements. Colonization began here soon after penal servitude was instituted in Dué. This area was chosen, as Mitsul writes, because of its luxurious meadows, good timber, navigable river and rich soil. "Obviously," writes this fanatic who considered Sakhalin the promised land, "it was impossible even to doubt that colonization could be successful; however, of the eight men who were sent for this purpose to Sakhalin in 1862, only four settled near the Duyka River." And what could those four possibly do? They worked the soil with pickaxes and spades, sowed winter grain in the spring rather than summer grain, and the result was that they were soon pleading to return to the mainland. In 1869 an agricultural farm was organized on the present site of Slobodka. A very important question was to be resolved here: Could forced labor by convicts be successfully used in agriculture?

For three years the convicts dug out stumps, built cabins, drained the swamps, made roads and plowed the soil. At the end of their term none wished to remain, and they petitioned the Governor-General to be allowed to return to the mainland because agriculture was unproductive and there was no way to make a living. Their petition was granted. However, the so-called farm continued to exist. In time the Dué convicts became settlers. Convicts arrived from Russia with their families and had to be placed on the land. Orders were issued that Sakhalin was to be regarded as a fertile land and suitable for agriculture. Wherever life could not be maintained by natural resources, it slowly but surely expanded artificially, through coercion, at the cost of a vast expenditure of money and human labor.

In 1879, Dr. Augustinovich found 28 cabins in Slobodka.[1]

At the present time there are 15 households in Slobodka. The houses are covered with planks, are spacious, and sometimes contain several rooms. The outbuildings are solid and each household has its own vegetable garden. There is one bathhouse for each two dwellings.

My census revealed 39¾ *desyatins* of land under tillage and 24½ *desyatins* in hay, 23 horses, and 47 head of livestock, including horned cattle, oxen, sheep, goats and pigs.

Owing to the status of the householders, Slobodka is considered an aristocratic settlement. One of the householders is a court councillor married to a settler's daughter, another is a free man who followed his convict mother to the island, seven are peasants formerly exiled, four are settlers, and only two are convicts.

Of the 24 families residing there, only 4 are illegal.

The age groups of Slobodka are almost normal; the working age is not so sharply predominant as in other settlements. There are children, young people and old people over sixty-five and even over seventy-five.

The question is, how can one explain the comparatively prosperous standing of Slobodka even in the light of statements made by the local homesteaders, who say it is impossible to make a living there by farming. It is, however, possible to indicate some of the factors which under ordinary circumstances would be conducive to a normal, settled and prosperous life. For example, Slobodka contains a large percentage of older inhabitants who arrived on Sakhalin prior to 1880 and have already grown accustomed to this land and feel at home. It is also very important that wives followed 19 of the men and almost everyone who settled on a plot already had a family. There are enough women, and only nine of the men are bachelors, though none is living in solitude. Generally speaking, Slobodka was lucky, one of the fortunate circumstances being that a large percentage of the inhabitants was literate: 26 men and 11 women.

Excluding the court councillor, who is working as a surveyor on Sakhalin, why are the homesteaders with a free status and the peasants formerly exiled not departing for the homeland when they have the right to do so? They say they are remaining in Slobodka because they are successful farmers, but this does not apply to everyone. Not all, but only some of the homesteaders use the meadows and plowland in Slobodka. Only 8 homesteaders have meadows and cattle, 12 work the soil, and no matter how you look at it, the amount of farming here is not extensive enough to explain its exceptionally fine economic position. There are no ways to earn money on the side, they do not engage in trade, and only one man, a former officer, keeps a small shop. There is no official data which would reveal why the inhabitants of Slobodka are rich and the only way to solve the problem is to consider the one remaining factor—its bad reputation.

Formerly there was widespread bootlegging of alcohol in Slobodka. The import and sale of alcohol are strictly forbidden on Sakhalin, and these prohibitions gave rise to peculiar methods of acquiring contraband. The alcohol was smuggled into the island in tin cans meant to hold sugar loaves and in samovars, and the smugglers were very nearly carrying it in their belts, but most frequently it was delivered in barrels and in the usual bottles since the lower officials were bribed and the higher officials looked the other way.

In Slobodka a bottle of cheap vodka was sold for six and even ten rubles. It was from here that all the prisons of Northern Sakhalin obtained their vodka. Even the drunkards among the officials were not squeamish about it. I know one official who was on a drinking spree and gave all the money he had to some prisoners for a bottle of spirits.

At the present time the illicit traffic in alcohol has

considerably subsided. Now they gossip about another enterprise—trade in prisoners' used clothing, which is called *barakhlo*. They buy dressing gowns, shirts and jackets for a pittance and dispose of all these rags in Nikolayevsk. They also maintain clandestine pawnshops.

Baron Korf once called the Alexandrovsk Post "The Sakhalin Paris." Everything that exists in this noisy and famished Paris—fornication, drunkenness, gambling, sickness, the buying of spirits and the sale of stolen goods, or selling one's soul to the devil—all this leads directly to Slobodka.

In the area between the seashore and the post, in addition to Slobodka and the railroad, there was still another curiosity. This was the ferry across the Duyka. Instead of a rowboat or ferryboat, there was a large, completely square box. The captain of this unique craft was convict Krasivy Family-forgotten. He was already seventy-one years old. Hunchbacked, shoulder blades protruding, one rib broken, a thumb missing, his whole body was covered with scars from lashings and beatings suffered a long time ago. He had almost no gray hair; his hair seemed faded, his eyes were blue, sparkling, and he wore a happy, good-natured expression. He was dressed in rags and was barefoot. Very lively and talkative, he enjoyed laughter.

In 1855 he had deserted from the army "out of foolishness" and had become a vagabond, calling himself "Family-forgotten." He was captured and sent to Zabaikal, or, as he says, "into Cossack country." He said:

"At that time I imagined that people lived underground in Siberia," he told me. "I took off and fled down the road from Tyumen. I reached Kamyshlov, where I was captured and sentenced, your worship, to twenty years of hard labor and ninety lashes. They sent me to Kara, gave me the ninety lashes, and then sent me to Korsakov on Sakhalin. I escaped from Korsakov with a friend, but I only got as far as Dué. I became ill and couldn't go any farther. My friend reached Blagoveshchensk. Now I am serving my second term and have been living on Sakhalin twenty-two years. My only crime was that I deserted from the army."

"Why do you still hide your real name? Why do you have to do it?"

"I told my real name to an official last year."

"What happened?"

"Nothing! The official said, 'Before we make the correction you'll be dead. Just live as you have been living. Why do you want to change now?' And it's true, that's no mistake. . . . I don't have long to live anyway. But still, my good sir, my family would at least know where I am."

"What do they call you?"

"My name here is Vasily Ignatyev, your worship."

"And your real name?"

Krasivy pondered and said:

"Nikita Trofimov. I come from Skopinsky district, Ryazan *guberniya*."

I began crossing the river in the box. Krasivy pushed against a long pole along the river bottom, straining his whole emaciated bony body. The work was not easy.

"Isn't it too difficult for you?"

"That's all right, your worship. Nobody is rushing me. I take my time."

He told me that in his twenty-two years on Sakhalin he has never been beaten, nor has he been imprisoned.

"That's because when they send me to saw wood, I go. When they give me this pole in my hand, I take it. When they order me to fire up the office stove, I fire up. One must obey. To tell the truth and not anger God, life is good! Glory to Thee, O Lord!"

In the summer he lives in a *yurt* near the crossing. In his yurt are rags, a loaf of bread, a rifle and a stuffy, sour odor. When I asked him why he needs a rifle, he said, "To defend myself from thieves, and to shoot snipe," and laughed. The rifle is broken and is only for show. In winter he reverts to being a wood carrier and lives in the office at the pier. One day I saw him, trousers rolled high, displaying his veined, pale white feet. With a Chinaman he was pulling a net filled with sparkling humpbacked salmon, each the size of our perch. I shouted to him and he answered me joyfully.

46

The Alexandrovsk Post was founded in 1881. One official who has been living on Sakhalin for ten years told me that when he first came he almost drowned in the mud. The priest-monk Irakly, who lived in Alexandrovsk until 1886, said that at first there were only three houses. The small barracks where the musicians now live was the prison. The street was filled with tree stumps. Where the brickyard now stands they used to hunt sables in 1882. The sentry booth was offered to Father Irakly as a church, but he declined, pleading lack of space. In good weather he celebrated Mass in the open on the square; in bad weather, he celebrated Mass in prison or wherever possible.

"You are conducting services, and suddenly you hear the clanging of chains," he said. "It's noisy and hot from the boiler. Here I'm saying, 'Glory to the Holy Consubstantial,' and next to you someone yells, 'I'll break your. . . .'"

The actual growth of Alexandrovsk stems from the time when new regulations were made regarding Sakhalin, and many new official posts were designated, including that of a general. New accommodation was required for the new people and their offices since Dué, which to that time housed the prison administration, was very crowded and gloomy. Six versts from Dué, Slobodka already existed in a cleared area, a prison already stood along the Duyka, and then slowly a residential section began to grow in the neighborhood: houses for officials and offices, a church, warehouses, shops and other buildings. With these arose something without which Sakhalin could not live—a town, the Sakhalin Paris, where congenial company, atmosphere and a piece of bread could be found by town folk who could only survive when they breathed town air and engaged in town enterprises.

The building of the town, the clearing of stumps and the draining of the soil were done by the convicts. Until 1888, before the present prison was built, they lived in yurt dugouts. These were made of boards dug into the ground two or two-and-a-half *arshins* deep with double-pitched clay roofs. The windows were small and narrow, level with the ground. It was dark, especially in winter when the yurts were covered with snow. As a result of water rising from the soil to the floor and the perpetual moisture in the clay roofs and the crumbling, rotting walls, the dampness in these graves was wretched. The people slept in their sheepskin coats. The surrounding ground and the well water were always filthy with human excrement and all kinds of garbage because there were neither privies nor rubbish pits. The convicts lived with their wives and children in these yurts.

At the present time Alexandrovsk covers an area of some two square versts. However, since it has merged with Slobodka and since one of its streets has already extended almost to Korsakov, the aim being to merge with it in the not too distant future, its measurements can only be suggested. It has several straight, wide streets which are called not streets but *slobodkas,* the name used in ancient times. In Sakhalin the custom is to name streets in honor of living officials. They do not use only the surname, but the Christian name and the patronymic are also used.[2]

By some happy chance, however, Alexandrovsk has not yet immortalized even one official and its streets have to date retained the names of the *slobodkas* from which they developed: Kirpichnaya [*kirpich* = brick], Peysikovskaya, Kasyanovskaya [Kasyan = a man's name], Pisarskaya [*pisar* = clerk], Soldatskaya [*soldat* = soldier]. The derivation of all these names except Peysikovskaya can easily be understood. They say that it was so named by convicts in honor of the ringlets of hair worn by a Jew who traded here when the *slobodka* was still in the taiga. Another version is that a woman settler named Peysikova lived and traded there.

Wooden sidewalks line the streets. Everything is very clean and orderly. Even in the farthest streets where the poor huddle together there are no puddles or rubbish heaps.

The main part of the post comprises the official district: the church, the residence of the island commandant, his office, the mail and telegraph offices, the police department with its printing shop, the home of the district commander of the area, the store run by the Colonial Fund, the military barracks, the prison hospital, the military infirmary, a mosque with a minaret under construction, government buildings in which officials are housed, and the penal-servitude prison with its numerous warehouses and workshops. The majority of the houses are new, built in the European style, roofed with iron, and often painted on the exterior. There is no lime or good stone on Sakhalin, and therefore there are no stone buildings.

If we exclude the officials' and officers' quarters as well as the Soldatskaya Slobodka—their inhabitants, being transient, are changed almost yearly—there is a total of 298 households in Alexandrovsk. There are 1,499 inhabitants, 923 of whom are men, and 576 women. If we include the free population, the military and the convicts who sleep in the prison and do not participate in households, we obtain a total figure of 3,000.

In comparison with Slobodka, Alexandrovsk contains very few peasants. The prisoners comprise one-third of the entire population. Convict regulations permit convicts to live outside the prison, but these regulations apparently apply only to reformed prisoners, who are permitted to settle in households. However, this law is regularly ignored because of its impracticability. The huts are not only inhabited by reformed criminals but by probationers, long-term and even life-term convicts. In addition to the clerks, draftsmen and skilled artisans who cannot live in prison because of their work, there are many convicts with families on Sakhalin, husbands and fathers, whom it would be impractical to confine in prisons without their families. This would make for severe confusion in the life of the colony. Families would also have to be detained in prisons, or they would have to be provided with living quarters and food at prison expense, or they would have to be maintained in their homeland during the entire prison term served by the father of the family.

Convict probationers live in huts and therefore often have lighter punishments than reformed prisoners. Here the concept of proportionality of punishment is grossly violated. However, this irregularity finds justification in the

49

conditions implicit in the life of the colony, and so proportionality of punishment is easily set aside. All that remains is to move the rest of the convicts from prisons into huts. Referring to convicts with families, it is impossible to become reconciled to another muddle: the wastefulness of the administration when it permits tens of families to settle where there is neither a homestead nor arable land nor hayfields, while other district settlements, which have more favorable conditions, are inhabited by single men and the farmsteads are completely barren because of the lack of women. In Southern Sakhalin, where there are yearly harvests, there are some settlements without even one woman, while 158 free women, who have followed their husbands into exile voluntarily, live in the Sakhalin Paris.

There is no more arable land in Alexandrovsk. Formerly, when it was still spacious, 100 to 200 and even 500 square sazhens were allocated per family; now only 12 sazhens or even 9 or 8. I counted 161 homesteads which are nestled together, buildings and gardens, on lots no larger than 20 square sazhens each. The main fault lies in the natural conditions of the Alexandrovsk valley: it is impossible to move back toward the sea because of the unfertile soil, while mountains rise on both sides of the post, and it can only grow in one direction, beside the Duyka River along the Korsakov road. Here the huddled homesteads stretch in a long line.

According to data on the homestead list, only 36 homesteaders work arable land and 9 work hayfields. The size of the plots of arable land varies between 300 sazhens and 1 desyatin. Almost everyone plants potatoes. Only 16 homesteaders have horses, 38 have cows. Furthermore, the livestock is owned by peasants and settlers who do not engage in farming but practice trades.

It must be concluded from these few figures that the Alexandrovsk homesteads are not supported by agriculture. The poor soil has so little attraction that there are practically no older settlers here. None remain of those who settled on a plot in 1881; only 6 remain of those settled since 1882; four since 1883; thirteen since 1884; sixty-eight since 1885. This means that the remaining 207 came after 1885. Judging by the small number of peasants, only 19, the conclusion is that each householder stays on his plot only so long as it is necessary for him to acquire peasant rights—that is, the right to abandon the homestead and leave for the mainland.

I have still not fully resolved the question as to how the Alexandrovsk population survives. Let us assume that the householders, their wives and children, eat only potatoes, like the Irish, and that they have enough to last the whole year. But what do the 241 inhabitants and 358 convicts of both sexes eat who live in the huts as cohabitants, male and female, lodgers and workers? It is true that almost half of the population receives aid from the prison in the form of prison rations and children's food allotments. They also earn something. More than one hundred persons work in government workshops and offices. I have many artisans listed on my forms without whom a city could not exist: cabinetmakers, upholsterers, jewelers, watchmakers, tailors, etc. Articles made of wood and metal are very expensive in Alexandrovsk and it is customary to tip nothing less than a ruble.

But are prison rations and meager earnings sufficient for daily life in the town? The artisans' earnings far exceed their needs, but unskilled laborers, as, for example, ordinary carpenters, earn ten kopecks a day for food. The population exists haphazardly; nevertheless they still drink tea daily, smoke Turkish tobacco, wear the clothes worn by free men and pay for their living quarters. They purchase houses from peasants who are leaving for the mainland and build new ones. Shops carry on a brisk business, and various kulaks who have emerged from prison make profits in the tens of thousands.

Much is murky here, and I have reached the conclusion that Alexandrovsk is settled in the main by those who arrived from Russia with money and that the largest portion of the livelihood of the population is gained by illegal means.

The purchase of prisoners' personal possessions and their sale in large quantities in Nikolayevsk, the exploitation of foreigners and newly arrived convicts, whiskey smuggling, lending money at high interest, gambling at cards for high stakes—these are the men's occupations. The women, on the other hand, both the exiles and the free women who voluntarily followed their husbands, earn money by prostitution. When a free woman was asked at a hearing where she obtained her money, she answered, "I earned it with my body."

There is a total of 332 families: 185 are legally married, 147 are cohabitants. The comparatively large number of families is not explained by any exceptional qualities of the homesteads being conducive to good home and family life, but to the following circumstances: the foolishness of the local administration which settles families on plots in Alexandrovsk and not in more suitable areas; and, owing to his proximity to the authorities and the prison, the comparative ease with which a local settler can procure a woman.

When life arises and flows along artificial channels rather than normal ones, and when its growth depends not so much on natural and economic conditions as on the theory and the arbitrary behavior of individuals, then it is forced to accept these circumstances as essential and inevitable, and these circumstances acting on an artificial life assume the aspects of laws.

1   Augustinovich, "Several Accounts of Sakhalin." Extracted from the travel journal *Sovremennost* [The Contemporary] (1880), No. 1. He also wrote the article "Prebyvaniye na o. Sakhaline" [A Sojourn on Sakhalin Island] in the *Pravitelstvenny Vestnik* [Government Herald] (1879), No. 276.

2   If an official's name is Ivan Petrovich Kuznetsov, then one street will be named Kuznetsova Street, another Ivanova Street, and a third Ivanovo-Petrovska Street.

V

The Alexandrovsk Penal Servitude Prison -
The Prison Wards - Convicts in Chains - The
Golden Hand - The Latrines - The Maidan -
Convict Labor in Alexandrovsk - Servants -
Workshops

I VISITED the penal servitude prison in Alexandrovsk soon after my arrival.[1] It is a large four-cornered courtyard enclosed by six wooden prison-type barracks and connecting walls. The gates are always open, with a sentry pacing nearby. The courtyard is swept clean; there is no rubbish, no garbage, no puddles or slops. This exemplary cleanliness gives a good impression.

The doors of all the buildings are wide open. I enter one of the doors into a small corridor. To the right and left are doors leading to prison wards. Over the doorways hang black placards with white lettering: CELL NO. ———. CUBIC VOLUME OF AIR ———. NUMBER OF PRISONERS ———. At the end of the corridor there is another door leading into a small cell which holds two political prisoners in unbuttoned waistcoats, shoes over stockingless feet, who are hastily plumping up their straw-filled mattresses. A book and a piece of black bread lie on the windowsill. The district commander who acted as my guide informed me that these two prisoners had been given permission to live outside the prison, but having no desire to be different from the other convicts, they refused to take advantage of this permission.

"Attention! Stand up!" shouted the guard.

We enter a ward. The premises seem quite large, measuring some 200 cubic sazhens [1,400 cubic feet]. It is very light; the windows are open. The walls are dark and unpainted, full of splinters, with tow between the logs; only the tiles of the Dutch stoves are white. The floor is wood, unpainted, completely dried out. Down the center of the entire ward runs one long continuous plank bed, sloped on either side, so that the convicts sleep in a double row, head to head.

The convicts' places are not numbered and do not differ from one another, so that 70 or even 170 people can sleep on one plank bed. There is no bedding. They sleep on the bare boards or lie down on old torn sacks, on their own clothing and on all sorts of rotten rags, and it is all horrible to look at. The plank bed is covered with hats, footwear, bits of bread, empty milk bottles stoppered with paper or rags, boot trees; under the plank bed lie trunks, dirty sacks, bundles, instruments and old rags. A well-fed cat wanders near the plank bed. The walls are hung with clothing, pots and instruments, and on the shelves there are teapots, bread and boxes filled with all kinds of things.

On Sakhalin free men do not remove their hats on entering a prison. This courtesy is only obligatory for prisoners. We walk along the plank bed wearing our hats while the prisoners stand, hands at their sides, and gaze silently at us. We also remain silent and observe them and the impression is that we have come to buy them. We go to another ward. Here again is that horrible misery which can no more be hidden under all these rags than a fly can be hidden under a magnifying glass. It is a beastly existence, it is nihilistic, a negation of proprietary rights, privacy, comfort and restful sleep.

Prisoners in the Alexandrovsk prison enjoy relative freedom. They do not wear fetters, they can leave the prison during the day and go wherever they please, without guards, and they do not wear uniforms, but wear whatever they possess, depending on weather and their work. Persons under investigation who have recently been returned after attempting to escape and those who for some reason are under temporary arrest are held under lock and key in a separate building which is called "The Irons." The most frequently used threat on Sakhalin is: "I'll put you in The Irons." The entrance to this terrifying place is guarded by sentries and one of them reported to us that all was well in The Irons.

There is the rattling of a huge, awkward padlock, certainly bought from an antique dealer, and we enter a small cell where at present twenty men are incarcerated. They have recently been caught attempting to escape. They are bedraggled, unwashed, in chains, in hideous foot coverings made of rags and rope. One half of their heads displays a disheveled mass of hair; the other half is shaven, and already the hair is beginning to sprout. All are emaciated and shabby, but their gaze is courageous.

There is no bedding. They sleep on the bare floor. In the corner stands a chamber pot. Each prisoner must take care of his natural needs in the presence of twenty witnesses. One begs to be released and vows he will never again attempt an escape. Another begs to have his irons removed. A third complains that he does not get enough bread.

There are cells occupied by two or three prisoners, as well as cells for solitary confinement. There are many interesting people to be found here.

Of the prisoners in solitary, one who evokes special attention is the notorious Sophia Bluvshtein, "The Golden Hand," who was sentenced to three years' hard labor for escaping from Siberia. She is a small, thin, already graying woman, with a crumpled, aging face. Her hands are fettered. On her plank bed there is a gray sheepskin jacket which serves as both warm clothing and bedding. She paces her cell from corner to corner, and seems to be constantly sniffing the air, like a mouse in a mousetrap, and even her facial expression seems mouselike. Looking at her, one finds it unbelievable that not long ago she was still beautiful and could charm her jailers, as she did in Smolensk, when a guard aided her to escape and even accompanied her on her flight. On Sakhalin she lived outside the prison at first, like all the other women prisoners, in free living quarters. Dressed as a soldier, she attempted to escape again, and was caught.

While she was at liberty, several crimes were committed

55

in Alexandrovsk. The shopkeeper Nikitin was murdered, and the Jewish settler Yurkovsky was robbed of fifty-six thousand rubles. The Golden Hand was suspected and accused of these crimes, as either a direct participant or an accessory. The local investigating authorities have entangled her and themselves in such a thick mesh of incongruities and errors that it is impossible to learn anything definite. Nevertheless, the 56,000 rubles have not been found and the most extraordinary tales are told about the money.

I will describe the kitchen where dinner was prepared in my presence for 900 persons, and I will describe the food and how the prisoners eat, in a separate chapter. I will now devote a few words to the latrines.

As everyone knows, this accommodation is located in full sight of the overwhelming majority of Russian houses. In villages there are no privies. At monasteries, fairs, inns and at all kinds of industries where sanitary inspections have not yet been established, they are absolutely disgusting. Disdain for privies has also been carried to Siberia by the Russians. From a study of prison history it is obvious that these latrines were the cause of nauseating stenches and of diseases, and it is equally obvious that the prisoners and the prison administrators became easily reconciled to this.

In 1872, as Vlasov wrote in his report, one of the prisons at Kara had no latrine whatsoever and the prisoners were led out to relieve themselves in the square. Furthermore, this was not done according to their individual needs but only when several persons had been gathered together for this purpose. I could cite a hundred such cases.

In Alexandrovsk the latrine is an ordinary cesspool located in the prison yard in a separate outhouse between the prison buildings. During its construction the primary concern, evidently, was to build it as cheaply as possible, but in comparison to the past it represents significant progress. At least it is not disgusting. The latrine is unheated and is ventilated by wooden pipes. The toilets line the side. They cannot be stood upon but must be sat on, which is what saves this outhouse from filth and damp. It is malodorous but not too much so, since the odor is masked by the usual treatment of tar and carbolic acid. This latrine is open at night as well as during the day, thus obviating the need for a chamber pot, the latter only being used in The Irons.

Outside the prison there is a well by which the depth of the water level can be ascertained. Owing to the peculiar composition of the local soil, the water level rises in the cemetery, which is located on a mountain overlooking the sea. The water rises so high that during a dry spell I saw graves half filled with water. The soil around the prison and throughout the post is drained by canals which are not sufficiently deep, and the prison is not at all free of damp.

On sunny warm days, which are rare, the prison is well ventilated. The windows and doors are thrown wide open, and the prisoners for the most part spend their time outdoors or far away from the prison. In winter and in bad weather, which averages ten months of the year, they must be satisfied with only small ventilating windows and stoves. Larch and fir are used in the construction of the prison and its foundations, and these give good but unreliable natural ventilation. As a result of the high humidity of the Sakhalin climate and the abundance of rain as well as of interior evaporation, the water accumulated in the wood freezes during the winter. The prison is poorly ventilated, and there is insufficient air per inmate.

In my diary I noted: "Ward No. 9. Cubic volume of air—187 sazhens [1,309 cubic feet]. Contains 65 prisoners." This applies to summertime, when only half the prisoners sleep in the prison. Here are the figures from the 1888 medical report: "The total cubic capacity of air for the prisoners in the Alexandrovsk prison is 970 sazhens [6,790 cubic feet]; the largest number of prisoners is 1,950, the smallest number is 1,623 and the average is 1,785. 740 were in the prison during the night, giving a total of 1.31 sazhens [9.17 cubic feet] of air per person."

During the summer there are comparatively few prisoners in the prison, for they are commandeered to work on the roads and in the fields. The largest number is to be found in the fall, when they return from their work and the "volunteer" ship brings new convicts, totaling from 400 to 500 persons. These are always held in the Alexandrovsk prison before being assigned to other prisons. This means that there is less air per inmate when there is the least amount of ventilation.

The convict returns to the prison to sleep after his work, which is most frequently performed in bad weather. His clothing is soaked and his footwear filthy; there is no place to dry anything. He hangs some of his clothing near the plank bed, and uses the rest, when it is still wet, for bedding. His sheepskin coat smells of sheep and his footwear smells of leather and tar. His underwear, completely saturated with excretions from his skin, is wet and has not been washed for a long time. The smelly, sweaty rags from his feet are jumbled up with old sacks and rotten old clothing. He has not had a bath for a long time, is full of lice, smokes cheap tobacco and constantly suffers from flatulence. Bread, meat and salted fish—which he often cures right here in the prison—crumbs, bones, oddments and leavings are all piled together in his kettle. He squashes the bugs on the plank bed with his fingers. All this makes the prison air fetid, foul and acid. The air becomes permeated with a very high degree of water vapor, so that during extreme frosts the windows are covered with ice on the inside and the prison grows warm. Hydrogen sulphide, ammonia and other gases mix in the air with the water vapor and then, as one observer said, "Your soul curdles."

Under the system of communal wards it is impossible to maintain cleanliness in the prison, and hygiene can never break through the bounds set by the Sakhalin climate and the convicts' working conditions. Notwithstanding the fine intentions of the administration, they will always be powerless and they will never be rid of unfavorable criticism. Either we must condemn the communal wards as being obsolete and exchange them for another kind of living space—and this is in fact being partially brought about, since many convicts do not live in prison but in huts—or else we must reconcile ourselves to the unavoidable and necessary evil of filth, and leave the measuring of foul air by cubic sazhens to those who regard hygiene only as an empty formality.

It is very nearly impossible, I believe, to say anything good about the communal system. The people living in a communal ward are neither a community nor an association, where the individual members have responsibilities: they are nothing more than a crowd exempt from any responsibility toward their living space, their neighbors or the surrounding objects. It is impossible to order a convict not to bring in dirt and muck on his feet, not to spit on the floor and not to carry lice. If the cell is smelly and thievery is rampant and they sing filthy songs, then everybody is guilty, or, in other words, nobody is guilty.

I ask a convict, a former respectable citizen, "Why are you so slovenly?" He answers, "Because here it would be useless to be neat." And, indeed, of what value is personal cleanliness to a convict if tomorrow they bring in a new group of prisoners and give him a neighbor smelling to high heaven, with insects crawling out of him in all directions?

The communal ward allows no privacy to the prisoner —that privacy which is so necessary for prayer, for reflection and for that self-analysis which is considered obligatory by all the advocates of reform. They play violent card games with the consent of bribed guards, employ foul language, laugh boisterously, and there is always a clatter and banging of doors, and the night-long clanging of chains from The Irons, and all these things prevent the fatigued prisoner from sleeping and make him irritable. Naturally his stomach and his soul are not left without any ill effects.

That gregarious, animal-like existence with its gross amusements, and the inevitable influence of the evil on the good, has long been acknowledged to affect the morals of the criminal in the most corrupt fashion. It slowly forces him to lose the habits of domesticity, those very qualities which must be preserved above all by a convict who on his release from prison becomes a self-sufficient member of a colony, where from the very first day he is obliged by law and under threat of punishment to become a good householder and a good family man.

These communal wards are places where slander, murder, informing on prisoners and peculation are tolerated and excused. *Kulachestvo* [peculation by rich peasants] is the term employed to describe the phenomenon of the *maidan*,[2] which was introduced to Sakhalin from Siberia. A prisoner who possesses and loves money and has been convicted because he loves it too much, being a rich peasant, a miser and a swindler, arranges to pay his fellow convicts for a monopoly on supplying provisions to the prisoners, and if the prison is large and well populated, the profits can be on the order of several hundred rubles a year.

The man who owns the maidan is officially called the *parashechnik* [*parashka* = chamber pot], since he takes upon himself the duty of emptying the chamber pots, if any, and keeping the place clean. On his plank bed there can usually be found a small trunk about 1½ arshins [42 inches] square, either green or brown; near it and under it are displayed small pieces of sugar, small loaves of white bread about the size of a fist, cigarettes, bottles of milk, and other products wrapped in paper and dirty rags.[3]

Concealed behind these humble pieces of sugar and loaves of white bread is an evil which exerts its influence far beyond the limits of the prison. The maidan is a gambling house, a tiny Monte Carlo, which engenders in the prisoners a contagious passion for faro and other gambling games. The maidan and the card players employ the willing services of brutal and implacable pawnbrokers. Prison pawnbrokers demand 10 percent interest per day and even per hour; if a pawn ticket is not redeemed in a day, the property becomes the possession of the pawnbroker. After completing their terms, the *maidanshchiks* and the pawnbrokers are assigned to settlements, where they continue their profitable activities, and it is no wonder that there are settlers on Sakhalin who have had 56,000 rubles stolen from them.

In the summer of 1890, during my sojourn on Sakhalin,

there were some 2,000 convicts in the Alexandrovsk prison, only 900 of whom lived in the prison. Here are some chance figures: on May 3, 1890, at the beginning of the summer, 1,279 prisoners were being fed and housed in the prison; on September 29, at the end of the summer, there were only 675 prisoners.

As to the work done by the prisoners in Alexandrovsk, this was observed to consist of building and various public works: new houses were put up, others were altered, and they maintained the streets and public squares. Carpentry was considered the most difficult work. A prisoner who had been a carpenter in his homeland really suffers here, and in this respect he is far worse off than a painter or a roofer. The difficulty does not lie with carpentering so much as in the fact that every piece of lumber must be hauled out of the forest by the carpenter himself.

At the present time the logging area is about five miles from the post. During the summer the people are harnessed to logs by chains and they have to haul these logs, which are a foot wide and several feet long, and it is horrible to watch; their faces become contorted, and this is especially true of natives of the Caucasus. It is said that in winter their hands and feet are frozen stiff, and some freeze to death before they have accomplished the grueling task of hauling the logs to the post.

Carpentry also presents difficulties to the administration because there are very few people available on Sakhalin for systematic hard labor, and there is always an insufficient supply of labor, although there are thousands of convicts. General Kononovich told me that it is very difficult to undertake new construction and to erect new buildings. There are just not enough people. If there are enough carpenters, there are not enough people to haul the logs. If they send people out for logs, there are not enough carpenters. The woodmen who cut wood every day, stack it and light the stoves before dawn when everyone is still asleep, also have to work excessively hard.

In order to judge the intensity of the labor and its difficulty, it is necessary to consider not only the physical effort expended, but also the working conditions and the character of the work as it arises from these conditions. The extreme cold in the winter and the humidity at Alexandrovsk—and it is humid throughout the year—place the worker in a very nearly unbearable position. A woodcutter in Russia experiences nothing like this.

The law prescribes "working conditions" for convicts similar to those of an ordinary farm or factory worker.[4] It permits the burden to be eased in various ways for convicts who have reformed. Practice, however, does not always conform to the law, especially in view of local conditions and the peculiarities of the work. You cannot determine how many hours a convict must haul logs during a snowstorm, you cannot release him from night work when he is indispensable, you cannot excuse a reformed prisoner from working on a holiday if he is working in a coal pit with a probationer, because then it would be necessary to excuse both of them and stop the work.

As a result of the incompetent, stupid and coarse people placed in charge of these projects, much more effort is expended than is necessary. For example, the loading and unloading of ships, which does not require exceptional physical strength on the part of laborers in Russia, is virtually a form of martyrdom for the people in Alexandrovsk. There is no specially trained force to work on ships. Every time new people are taken for the job, and as a result there is often terrible confusion in a heavy sea. On the ships the convicts lose their tempers and break out in wild curses, and all the time the barges bump against the ship's sides, and the people stand or lie down, their faces green and distorted. They are all seasick, and meanwhile the oars they have relinquished are floating around the barges. For this reason the work takes a long time, much time is lost and the people suffer unnecessarily. One day during the unloading of a ship I heard a prison overseer say, "My people have not eaten all day."

Much convict labor is expended on required work in prisons. Daily work is done by cooks, bakers, tailors, shoemakers, water carriers, floor scrubbers, orderlies, herdsmen, etc. The military, telegraph and geodetic offices also use convict labor. Some fifty persons have been commandeered for the prison infirmary, but it is uncertain in what capacity and for what reason. I do not know how many are used as servants by the officials.

As far as I was able to discover, every official, even those who are only office workers, can obtain an unlimited number of servants. The doctor with whom I was quartered lived alone with his son; he had a chef, a yard man, a cook and a chambermaid. This is extremely luxurious for a junior prison doctor. One prison warden had eight servants on his staff: a seamstress, a shoemaker, a chambermaid, a footman who delivered messages, a children's nurse, a laundress, a chef and a scrubwoman. The problem of servants on Sakhalin is an offensive and grievous one. It is probably the same wherever there is penal servitude, and it is not new. In "A Short Description of the Disorganization Existing in Penal Servitude," Vlasov describes how when he arrived on the island in 1871 he "was astounded above all by the fact that, with the permission of the former Governor-General, convicts were being used as servants for the commandant and the officers." In his words, women were assigned as servants to members of the administration, not even excluding bachelor guards.

In 1872, Sinelnikov, the Governor-General of Eastern Siberia, forbade the use of convicts as servants. But this prohibition, which is still law here, is bypassed in the most flagrant manner. The college registrar assigns half a dozen servants to himself, and when he goes out on a picnic, he sends scores of convicts ahead with the provisions. General Gintse and General Kononovich, the commandants of the island, fought against the evil, but not energetically enough. At any rate, I found only three orders regarding the question of servants, these being such that an interested person could interpret them as he pleased. Apparently abolishing the Governor-General's order, General Gintse in 1885 permitted officials to employ convict women as servants if they paid them two rubles a month, the money to be returned to the treasury (Order No. 95). In 1888, General

Kononovich annulled his predecessor's order and wrote: "Convict males, as well as females, are not to be assigned as servants to officials, and no money is to be paid to the women. Since the government buildings and the services connected with them cannot remain without supervision and upkeep, I permit the necessary number of men and women to be assigned to each building, their duties to be properly indicated, i.e., guards, wood carriers, floor scrubbers, etc., following the requirements" (Order No. 276). But since the government buildings and services connected with them related to the official quarters, this order was interpreted as a permit to employ convict servants at no cost at all. At any rate, when I was on Sakhalin in 1890, all the officials, even those who had no connection whatever with the prison administration (for example, the manager of the post and telegraph office), employed convicts to take care of their private needs in the most blatant manner. Furthermore, they paid no salary to these servants, who were fed at the expense of the treasury.

Permitting convicts to be used as servants by private persons is in complete contradiction with the point of view of a legislator concerned with evaluating punishment. This is not penal servitude, it is serfdom, since the convict does not serve the government but is in the employ of a private individual who has no connection whatsoever with corrective measures or with the concept of proportionality of punishment. He is not sentenced to penal servitude but to slavery, subordinated to the will of the head of the household and his family, gratifying their whims and participating in kitchen squabbles.

On becoming a settler, he is nothing more than a servant on a country estate, who knows how to clean boots and fry cutlets but is incapable of working the soil and therefore goes hungry, at the mercy of fate. Permitting convict women to go into domestic service has its own special drawbacks in addition to all the others. This is aside from the fact that within the environment of forced labor, favorites and kept women always give rise to a rottenness which is utterly degrading to human dignity; in particular, they completely distort discipline. One of the priests told me that there were instances on Sakhalin when free women or soldiers in service were forced, under well-known circumstances, to clean up and carry out the mess left by a convict woman.[5]

What is grandly called the "factory industry" in Alexandrovsk is well organized in its outward aspects, but to date has been of no serious significance. In the foundry, which is run by a self-taught mechanic, I saw bells, wheels for carriages and wheelbarrows, a hand mill, a lace-making machine, faucets, stove appliances, etc., but all of these gave the impression of being playthings. The articles are excellent but there is no market for them. It would certainly be more advantageous to procure them for local consumption from the mainland or from Odessa than to set up their own steam engines and hire a complete staff of paid employees.

Naturally, there would be no regret at such expenditures if the shops were schools where the convicts could learn trades. In fact, it is not the convicts who work in the foundry and machine shops but experienced settler artisans who are junior supervisors with a salary of eighteen rubles per month. Enthusiasm over an article is very evident here. The wheels go round and the hammers pound and the steam whistles blow in honor of the quality and salability of their work. Commercial and artistic considerations have no connection whatsoever with punishment. Meanwhile, on Sakhalin, as well as everywhere else where there is penal servitude, every undertaking should be directed toward the immediate and long-term consideration of criminal reform. Local factories should not strive to market stove doors and faucets on the mainland, but should attempt to develop useful and well-trained artisans.

The steam mill, the lumberyard and the blacksmith's shop are kept in excellent order. The people work happily, probably because they recognize the usefulness of their work. But even here the work is mainly carried out by specialists who were millers, blacksmiths and so on in private life, and not by those who did not know how to work before they came here. They knew nothing then, and now,

65

more than others, they require experience in the mills and at the blacksmith's forges, where they could be trained to develop their skills.[6]

1   A very fine description of Russian prisons in general was given by N. V. Muravyev in his article "Our Prisons and the Penal Question," *Russky Vestnik* 1878, Vol. IV. To learn about the Siberian prisons which were the prototypes of those on Sakhalin, see the report by S. V. Maximov, "Siberia and Penal Servitude."

2   *Maidan,* from a Persian word meaning a public square or market place. In Russia it meant a privately owned and semi-clandestine commissary patronized by prisoners.—TRANS.

3   A package of nine or ten cigarettes costs one kopeck; a small loaf of white bread, two kopecks; a bottle of milk, eight to ten kopecks; a piece of sugar, two kopecks. The sale is made for cash, or on credit, or by barter. The maidan also sells vodka, cards and candle ends for playing cards secretly at night. It also rents cards.

4   "Working Conditions for Construction Work, According to the Imperial Edict of April 17, 1869" (Petersburg, 1887). When assignments are given for various types of work, the following must be considered: the physical strength of the laborer, and his experience. The law gives the number of working hours per day, conforming to the time of year and the region of Russia. Sakhalin is regarded as being equivalent to the central part of Russia. The maximum working hours are twelve and a half hours per day in May, June and July; the minimum, seven hours in December and January.

5   Vlasov writes in his report: "The strange relationship between an officer, a convict woman who is his mistress, and a soldier who acts as her coachman, cannot but evoke astonishment and regret." They say that this evil is permitted only because it is impossible to obtain servants from among those who are free. But this is not true. First, the number of servants can be limited; officers find that it is quite possible to get along with the services of only one orderly. Second, the officials here on Sakhalin receive a good salary and can hire servants from among the settlers, from peasants who were formerly convicts, and from free women, the majority of whom are impoverished and would therefore not refuse to earn some money. This thought probably occurred to the administration, for there is an order which permitted one woman

settler, since she was incapable of farming, "to obtain means of livelihood by entering the service of officials" (Order No. 44, 1889).

6 The mill and the locksmith shop are housed in one building and the machinery is driven by a single steam engine. The mill contains four sets of millstones with a production of 1,500 poods of grist a day. An old steam engine brought here by Prince Shakhovskoy is in operation in the lumberyard. It is fired by sawdust. The blacksmith shop works night and day; six forges operate in two shifts. A total of 105 workers are employed in the shop. Convicts in Alexandrovsk also work in the coal mines, but it is doubtful whether this undertaking will ever be successful. The coal from local mines is far worse than the coal in Dué. It looks dirtier and is mixed with slate. It is not inexpensive since a permanent staff of miners works the mine under the supervision of a mining engineer. The local mines are scarcely necessary, since Dué is not far away and excellent coal can be obtained from there at any time. However, the local mines were opened up with the beneficent aim of providing jobs for future settlers.

VI *Yegor's Story*

THE DOCTOR with whom I had been lodging left for the mainland soon after being retired from service, and I took lodgings with a young and very decent official. He had only one servant, an old Ukrainian woman, and once a day a convict named Yegor came by. He hauled the fire-wood, but was not considered to be the official's servant; he brought the wood "out of respect," removed the kitchen slops and did all the chores which were too difficult for the old woman. Sometimes when I was reading or writing something, I suddenly heard a rustling and panting noise, and felt something heavy moving under the table at my feet. It was Yegor, barefoot, picking up scraps of newspaper from the floor or dusting it.

He was about forty years old, a clumsy, doltish fellow, with a simple and at first glance stupid face, and with a mouth as wide as an eelpout's. His hair was red, his beard scanty, his eyes small. He did not answer questions immediately, but first squinted at you sideways and said, "What?" or "Who do you want?" He called me "your worship," and addressed me in the second person singular. He could not sit still for a minute without doing something, and he always found work to do. He would be talking to you, and all the time his eyes would be wandering around looking for something to clean or tidy up. He took catnaps two or three times a day, because he never had time for sleep. On holidays he usually stood on a street corner, wearing a jacket over a red shirt, his stomach pushed out, his feet wide apart. He called this "having a good time."

Here, in penal servitude, he built his own cabin, made buckets, tables and crude cupboards. He could make all sorts of furniture, but only "for his own pleasure," that is, for his own use. He was never in a fight and had never been thrashed except in his childhood when his father punished him because he let the rooster into the pea patch when he was supposed to be guarding it.

One day I had the following conversation with him:

"Why were you sent here?" I asked him.

"What's that, your worship?"

"Why were you sent to Sakhalin?"

"For murder!"

"Tell me what happened, from the very beginning."

Yegor leaned against the doorjamb, hands behind his back, and began:

"We worked for Baron Vladimir Mikhailich as wood-cutters, and we sawed the wood and delivered it to the station. Good. We finished and went home. We hadn't gone far from the village when they sent me to the office to witness the paper. I was on horseback. On the way to the office Andryukha turned me back: there was a flood, it was impossible to get through. He said, 'Tomorrow I shall be riding to the office about my lease rent and I will have the paper witnessed.' Good. Then we went on together, I on horseback and the others on foot. We reached Para-khino. The muzhiks went to the tavern for a smoke and Andryukha and I lagged behind on the sidewalk nearby. Then he says, 'Say, my friend, you wouldn't have a five-kopeck piece on you, would you? I'd like a drink.' And I said, 'Well, friend, you're the kind of man who will go in for a five-kopeck drink and come out drunk.' And he answered, 'No, I won't get drunk; I'll have my drink and go home.' We went to the crowd, agreed on a quart, collected enough money all round, went to the tavern and bought a quart of vodka. We all sat down at a table to drink."

"Make it shorter," I said.

"Wait a minute, don't interrupt, your worship. So then we drank the vodka and he, that's Andryukha, bought a half-pint of pepper brandy. He poured a glass for himself and for me. We drank the glass together. Then all the people left the tavern and went home, and we left, following them. I got tired of riding horseback, got off, and sat

69

down near the riverbank. I sang songs and told jokes. There were no disagreements between us. Then we got up and left."

"Tell me about the murder," I interrupted him.

"Wait a minute! At home I went to bed and slept until morning, when they awakened me: 'Get up. Which one of you beat up Andrey?' They had already brought Andrey home, and an official had arrived. The official began questioning everyone; nobody admitted he had done it. But Andrey was still alive and said, 'You, Sergukha, you hit me with a club and I don't remember anything else.' Sergukha didn't confess. We all thought it was Sergukha and began to watch him so he would not harm himself. Andrey died the next day.

"Sergey's family, his sister and father-in-law all advised him, 'Don't deny it, Sergey, it doesn't make any difference. Confess, and implicate everyone, anyone who was around. You'll be let off!' As soon as Andrey died, all of us went to the village elder and denounced Sergey. We interrogated him, but he wouldn't admit anything. Later they let him go home for the night. Some men stood guard so he wouldn't harm himself. He owned a gun. It wasn't safe.

"In the morning they discovered he was gone. We made up a search party; we searched the village and ran around the fields looking for him. Then someone came from the police station and said Sergey was already there. They began to pull us in at the station. Sergey threw himself on his knees before the district police officer and the constable and began to inform against us, saying the Yefremov boys had been planning to beat up Andryukha for the past three years. 'We were walking along the road together, the three of us, Ivan, Yegor and I, and we all of us agreed to beat him up.' He said, 'I hit him with a stick and then Ivan and Yegor started beating him.' And then he said, 'I got frightened and ran back to join the rest.' After that they took us to jail in the town—Ivan, Kirsha, Sergey and me."

"And who are Ivan and Kirsha?"

"My own brothers. Pyotr Mikhailich, the merchant, came to the jail and went bail for us. We stayed with him on bail until the Feast of Our Lady of Perpetual Succor. We lived well, safe and sound. On the second day of the Feast we were tried in the town. Kirsha had witnesses—the men who had brought up the rear testified for him. As for me, my friend, I really got it. I told the court exactly what I just told you, but the court didn't believe me. 'Everyone says they're innocent and they cross their hearts, but it's all lies.' So they sentenced us and sent us to jail. We lived under lock and key in jail, but I was in charge of the chamber pot, swept the cells and served the dinners. For this service each prisoner gave me a portion of bread a month. It was about three pounds per person. When we heard we were about to leave, we sent a telegram home. It was just before the Feast of St. Nicholas. My wife and my brother Kirsha came to visit us and brought some clothing and other things. My wife howled, but nothing could be done. When she left I gave her two portions of bread as a gift. We cried and sent our greetings to the children and to all Christian people.

"On the way we were handcuffed together. We walked two by two. I walked with Ivan. In Novgorod they took our pictures, put us in irons and shaved our heads. Then on to Moscow. While we were in prison in Moscow we kept sending out petitions for a pardon. I don't remember how we got to Odessa. The trip was uneventful. In Odessa we were taken to a doctor, stripped bare and examined. Later they got us together and herded us on a ship. Cossacks and soldiers accompanied us up the gangway and put us below. We sat down on the bunks and that was that. Each person had his own place. Five of us sat on the top bunk. At first we didn't understand, and then they said, 'We've started, we've started!' We sailed on and on and then it began to roll. The heat was so intense, the people stripped off their clothing. Some vomited, others were quiet. Naturally, almost everyone was lying down. It was a real storm. It threw us in all directions. We sailed and sailed and then we struck something. Something banged into us. The day was foggy. It turned dark. When we were hit, the ship stopped and rolled on the rocks. We thought a big fish was rolling under

71

us, turning the boat over.[1] The engines jerked forward, and kept jerking, but it wouldn't move. Then they tried moving backward. Then they jerked backward and there was a hole in the ship's bottom. They tried to stuff the hole with sailcloth; they stuffed and stuffed, but it was useless. The water rose up to the floor of the hold where the people were sitting, and then it came through the ship's plates.

"They were saying, 'Don't let us perish, your worship!' At first he said, 'Don't try to break loose, don't beg, I won't let anyone perish.' The water reached the lower bunks. The Christian folk were pleading and struggling to get away. The master said, 'Well, boys, I'll let you out, but don't riot or I'll shoot all of you!' They let us out. We prayed to God that He would make the sea quiet and not permit us to perish. We prayed on our knees. After we prayed, they issued biscuits and sugar, and the sea grew quiet. The next day they began taking the people to shore on barges. We again prayed on the shore. Later they transferred us to another ship of the Voluntary Fleet, a Turkish ship,[2] and brought us here to Alexandrovsk.

"They took us to the dock before nightfall, but kept us there a long time and we left the pier in pitch dark. The Christian folk staggered out one after another, and to make matters worse, some suffered from night blindness. We clung to one another. Some could see, others could not— and so we held on to one another. I had dozens of Christian folk following me. They brought us to the prison yard and began to assign us to the barracks. They placed us in any old order, and we ate the food we had with us before going to sleep, and the next day they gave us our due. We rested two days, had a bath on the third, and on the fourth they marched us off to work.

"The very first thing, we dug ditches for a building where the hospital now stands. We rooted out stumps, dragged them away, dug holes, and so it went on for a week or two, or maybe a month. Then we carried logs from near Mikhailovka. We dragged them for maybe three versts and dumped them in piles at the bridge. Then they sent us into the kitchen gardens to dig for water. When hay-cutting time came, they began gathering the Christian folk, asking who knew how to mow hay; whoever admitted he could do it would be sent out to mow. They issued bread, groats and meat to the whole group, and sent us with a guard to mow hay at Armudan. I was living all right, God gave me health and I mowed well. The guards thrashed some of the fellows, but I didn't get one bad word. The fellows kept arguing with me, asking why I was walking so briskly; so, what's the difference!

"During my free time or when it rained I wove bast sandals for myself. Folks would lie down and sleep, while I sat over my weaving. I sold the sandals for two rations of beef a pair, worth four kopecks. When the mowing was over, we went home. On reaching home we were put in jail again. Later I was sent to work for the settler Sashka in Mikhailovka. There I did all kinds of farm work: I sowed, reaped, threshed, dug potatoes, and in return Sashka hauled the logs for making traps. We ate everything we trapped. I worked two months and four days. Sashka promised to pay me, but gave me nothing. He did give me 40 pounds of potatoes. Sashka brought me back to the prison. They gave me an ax and a rope for hauling firewood. I took care of seven stoves. I lived in a yurt and did the jailer's work, carrying the water and sweeping. I guarded the maidan for the Tatar called Magzy.[3]

"When I returned from work he turned his maidan over to me. I was the salesman and he paid me 15 kopecks a day. In the spring, when the days were longer, I started to weave bast sandals. I charged 10 kopecks. In the summer I fished wood out of the river. I amassed a large pile and sold it to the Jewish bathhouse keeper. I also cut up 60 logs and sold them at 15 kopecks each. And so I've lived tolerably well, with God's help. But, your worship, I have no time to talk with you. I must fetch some water."

"Will you become a settler soon?"

"In five years."

"Do you miss your home?"

"No! I'm only sorry for the children. They are stupid children."

"Tell me, Yegor, what were you thinking about when they were taking you to the ship in Odessa?"

"I was praying to God."

"For what?"

"That He should put sense in the children's heads."

"Why didn't you bring your wife and children to Sakhalin?"

"Because they're well off at home."

---

[1] The reference is to the shipwreck of the *Kostroma* on the western coast of Sakhalin in 1886.

[2] The steamer *Vladivostok* of the Voluntary Fleet.

[3] In Chinese, *Manza*.

VII
The Lighthouse - Korsakovskoye -
The Collection of Dr. P. I. Suprunenko - The
Meteorological Station - The Climate of the
Alexandrovsk Region - Novo-Mikhaylovka -
Potemkin - Ex-executioner Tersky - Krasny Yar -
Butakovo

MY STROLLS around Alexandrovsk and its environs with the postmaster, the author of "Sakhalinó," left a pleasant impression.

Our favorite stroll was up to the lighthouse which stands high above the valley on Cape Zhonkiyer. When you gaze up at the lighthouse during the day, you see a tiny white house with a mast and lantern. In the dark of night it shines brilliantly, and it seems then that penal servitude peers at the world with its beautiful eye. The road to the lighthouse is steep, running in a spiral around the mountain amid ancient larches and firs. The higher you climb, the freer you breath. The sea spreads out before your eyes, and slowly thoughts come into your mind which have nothing in common with the prison, nor with penal servitude, nor with the exile colony, and only here do you recognize how boring and difficult is life below.

The convicts and settlers bear their punishment from day to day while free people talk from morning to night about who was flogged, who escaped, who was caught and who will be flogged. And it is strange that in a week one grows accustomed to these conversations and preoccupations, and on waking in the morning the first thing you do is to read avidly the general orders—the local daily newspaper—and then all day long you listen to and speak about who escaped, who was shot, etc. But on the mountain, in sight of the sea and the beautiful ravines, all this becomes utterly trivial and vulgar, as indeed it is.

They say that at one time there were benches on the

road to the lighthouse, but they had to remove them because convicts and settlers wandering along the path took to writing on them or carving lampoons and obscenities. There are many fanciers of smut living in freedom, but the cynicism of people sentenced to penal servitude is incomparable. There are disgusting scribbles on benches and backyard walls, and there are also love letters. It is remarkable that a man should write and carve all kinds of nasty things on benches while feeling that he is abandoned by the world, an outcast, and extremely unfortunate. An old man declares that he is tired of the world and it is time for him to die, he has severe rheumatism and cannot see very well, but with what gusto he employs endless gutter talk with long strings of choice invectives and highfalutin nonsense, including incantations against fevers. If he is literate and living in an isolated place, he has difficulty in stifling the urge or resisting the temptation to scratch dirty words with his fingernails.

A vicious dog is struggling against his chain near the little house. A cannon and a bell are nearby. They say that a foghorn will soon be installed, and the inhabitants of Alexandrovsk will be filled with melancholy. If you stand under the lantern of the lighthouse and look down to the sea and on "The Three Brothers," where the waves break in shimmering foam, your head begins to spin and you are terror-stricken. The Tatar Strait can barely be seen from the lighthouse and even the entrance to De Kastri Bay is scarcely visible. The lighthouse keeper says that sometimes he can see ships entering and leaving De Kastri. The wide, sun-drenched, shimmering sea roars dully below; and the far shore tempts you away, and you become overwhelmed with melancholy and anxiety, feeling that you will never be able to get away from Sakhalin. Gazing at the opposite shore, I feel that if I were a convict, I would escape immediately, whatever the consequences.

Behind Alexandrovsk, along the Duyka River, lies the Korsakovskoye settlement, founded in 1881 and named after the former Governor-General of Eastern Siberia, M. S. Korsakov. It is interesting to learn that in Sakhalin they name settlements after the governors of Siberia, prison guards and assistant surgeons, but completely forget such explorers as Nevelskoy, the sea captain Korsakov, Boshnyak, Polyakov and many others whose memory has earned greater respect and regard than, for example, a jailer like Derbin, who was murdered for his cruelty.[1]

Korsakovskoye has 272 inhabitants, 153 male and 119 female. A total of 58 households. In the composition of its householders, 26 of whom are called peasants and only 9 convicts, and in the number of females, meadowland, livestock, etc., Korsakovskoye differs little from the prosperous Alexandrovsk suburb. Eight householders own 2 homes each, and there is 1 bathhouse for every 9 houses. Horses are kept by 45 householders, who have between 4 and 9 cows. Many have 2 horses and 3 or 4 cows. In Eastern Sakhalin it has the largest number of old inhabitants, 43 having lived there since the founding of the settlement. During my census I found 8 who came to Sakhalin in 1870, and 1 back in 1866. A large percentage of old inhabitants is a good sign.

Externally Korsakovskoye gives the illusion of a charming Russian village, but a completely backward one, which has not yet been touched by civilization.

I came here for the first time after dinner on Sunday. The weather was calm and warm, and the people seemed to be taking a holiday. The peasants were either sleeping in the shade or drinking tea. At the gates and under the windows the women searched each other's heads for lice. Flowers grew profusely in the small front yards and in the gardens; geraniums bloomed in the windows. There were many children playing soldiers or horses on the street, or riding on well-fed dogs who would rather have been sleeping. When a herdsman, an old vagrant, drove in a herd of more than 150 head of cattle and the air became filled with summer sounds, the lowing of cattle, the cracking of whips, the shouts of women and children who were driving the calves, the solid smack of bare feet and hoofs along the dusty dung-filled road, and when the smell of milk filled the air, the illusion was complete. Even the Duyka is lovely here. In places it flows along the backyards near the gardens; its banks are green, overgrown with willows and sedge. When I saw it, evening shadows were falling upon the completely smooth surface. The river was calm and seemed to be dozing.

Here, as in the wealthy Alexandrovsk Slobodka, we find a high percentage of old inhabitants, women and literate people. A large number of the women are free and it has almost the same "past history," with its clandestine sale of alcohol, thieving by rich peasants, etc. They explain that in former times favoritism played an important role in setting down homesteads here. In those days the administration readily gave cattle, seeds and even alcohol on credit. This was all the easier because the inhabitants of Korsakovskoye were always clever politicians and carefully arranged that the smallest officials should be greeted as "your worship." However, in contrast to the Alexandrovsk Slobodka, the main reason for its prosperity is neither the sale of alcohol, nor favoritism, nor its proximity to the Sakhalin Paris, but the undoubted success it has achieved in farming. While a fourth of the homesteaders in Slobodka have no arable land and another fourth have very little, here in Korsakovskoye all the homesteaders till the soil and sow grain; although half of the homesteaders in Slobodka have no cattle, they are still well fed; and here almost all of the homesteaders consider it necessary to have cattle.

For many reasons Sakhalin agriculture must be viewed with skepticism, but we must also admit that in Korsakovskoye agriculture is taken seriously and gives comparatively good results. It would be unfair to say that Korsakovskoye people plant two thousand poods of grain annually only because they are obstinate or because they desire to please the administration. I have no accurate figures on the yield and one cannot believe the statements of the people themselves, but on the basis of certain signs—as, for example, the large number of cattle, the external appearance of their life and the fact that the local peasants are not anxious to leave for the mainland although they achieved this right a long time ago—you are led to the conclusion that the grain yields not only feed the population but even bring some profits which incline the settler toward a settled life.

It is not difficult to explain why these people are successful farmers, when the inhabitants of neighboring settlements suffer dire privation due to an entire series of crop failures and have despaired of ever eating their own bread. Korsakovskoye lies in a valley, where the Duyka River is at its widest. From the very beginning, when they first settled here, the people of Korsakovskoye had a vast tract of land at their disposal. They were not only able to settle on the land, but even to choose their own plots. At the present time 20 homesteaders have 3 to 6 desyatins of land under tillage; rarely does anyone have less than 2 desyatins. If the reader wishes to compare the local plots with our own peasant plots, he should keep in mind that the local arable land never lies fallow but is yearly sown to the last inch, and therefore their 2 desyatins are equal to our 3 desyatins. The secret of the success of the people of Korsakovskoye lies in their utilizing the exceptionally large plots of land to the utmost.

With the twofold or threefold yield at harvest time on Sakhalin, there is only enough grain if there is enough land. In Korsakovskoye they have a great deal of land, a large reserve of seed and cheap, free labor. During the years when there is no good harvest, the people of Korsakovskoye rely on their produce of fruit and potatoes, which covers a considerable area, some 33 desyatins.

Because the penal colony is so recent and has a small transient population, there has not been time to collect any accurate statistics. The meager figures available to date can only lead to conclusions based on guesswork and conjecture. If one is pardoned for one's haste in drawing up conclusions and applying the facts concerning Korsakovskoye to the entire colony, one may say that as a result of the insignificant yields on Sakhalin, each homesteader must have more than two desyatins of arable land in addition to hayfields and land for orchards and potatoes so that his work will be profitable and he will be able to feed himself. It is impossible to set a more definite norm at this time, but in all probability it should be about four desyatins.

Incidentally, according to the "Report on the Status of Agriculture in 1889," on Sakhalin the average arable land for each householder is only half a desyatin.

In Korsakovskoye there stands a house which in its dimensions, pretty roofwork and charming garden resembles a medium-size landowner's country home. The owner, the director of the medical unit, Dr. P. I. Suprunenko, had departed in the spring to participate in a prison exhibition and remained in Russia. In the abandoned rooms I found only the remnants of a splendid zoological collection amassed by the doctor. I do not know the present whereabouts of this collection, or who is employing it for research on the Sakhalin fauna, but from the few remaining specimens, which are most beautifully mounted, and from what I heard, it is possible to guess the size of the collection and to realize how much knowledge, labor and love went into this useful activity. Dr. Suprunenko began his collection in 1881, and in ten years was able to gather specimens of almost all the vertebrates on Sakhalin as well as a great deal of anthropological and ethnographical material. If his collection had remained on the island, it could have served as the basis for an excellent museum.

Next to his house is a meteorological station. Until recently it was under the supervision of Dr. Suprunenko. Now an agricultural inspector is in charge. Observations made in my presence by a clerk, the convict Golovatsky, a sensible and amiable fellow, provided me with meteorological tables.

Conclusions can already be based on observations made during the past nine years and I will attempt to give some idea of the climate of the Alexandrovsk region. The mayor of Vladivostok once told me that "there is absolutely no climate" in Vladivostok and on the entire eastern seaboard generally. About Sakhalin, they like to say there is no climate; they say there is "bad weather," or the island has the worst weather in all Russia. I do not know how accurate the last statement is. It was a very lovely summer when

I was there, but meteorological tables and the brief reports of other writers present a general picture of exceptionally bad weather.

The Alexandrovsk region has a maritime climate which is distinctive in its capriciousness, that is, in its significant vacillation in the yearly mean temperature,[2] the number of days with precipitation, etc. Its chief peculiarities are its low yearly mean temperature and the large number of days with precipitation and fog. As a comparison I will take the mean monthly temperature of the Alexandrovsk region as against that of the Cherepovetsky district in Novgorodskaya *guberniya,* whose "climate is grim, humid, unstable and unhealthy."[3]

	Alexandrovsk Region	Cherepovetsky District
January	- 18.9	- 11.0
February	- 15.1	- 8.2
March	- 10.1	- 1.8
April	+ 0.1	+ 2.8
May	+ 5.9	+ 12.7
June	+ 11.0	+ 17.5
July	+ 16.3	+ 18.5
August	+ 17.0	+ 13.5
September	+ 11.4	+ 6.8
October	+ 3.7	+ 1.8
November	- 5.5	- 5.7
December	- 13.8	- 12.8

The average mean temperature in the Alexandrovsk region is +0.1°, almost 0°; in the Cherepovetsky district it is +2.7°. The winter in the Alexandrovsk region is more severe than in Arkhangelsk, the spring and summer are like Finland, and autumn is like St. Petersburg. The mean yearly temperature is the same as in the Solovetsky Islands, where it also equals 0°. There is eternal frost in the Duyka valley. Polyakov found it to be three-quarters of an arshin deep [twenty-one inches] on June 20. Even on July 14 he found snow under piles of rubbish and in hollows near the mountains, and the snow only melted at the end of July. On July 24, 1889, snow fell in the mountains, which are low here, and everyone donned a sheepskin coat. In nine years of observation the earliest the ice broke on the Duyka was April 23, and the latest May 6. During the entire nine years there was no thaw. In only one year there are 189 days when it freezes; on 151 days a cold wind blows. All this is of practical importance. In the Cherepovetsky district, where the summer is warmer and longer, according to Chernov, buckwheat, cucumbers and wheat cannot ripen properly, while in the Alexandrovsk region the local agricultural inspector insists that there has never been a year when the temperature was sufficiently high for oats and wheat to ripen.

The local excessive humidity commands the close attention of agronomists and hygienists. Every year there is an average of 189 days with precipitation: 107 days with snow, and 82 days with rain (in the Cherepovetsky district there are 81 days with rain and 82 with snow). For weeks at a time the sky is covered with leaden clouds and the desolate weather which drags on from day to day seems endless to the inhabitants. Such weather causes oppressive thoughts and drunkenness due to despondency. Many people suffering from the cold seem to become brutal, and many a good soul and many with weak spirits forever lose all hope of a better life after failing to see the sun for weeks and months on end.

Polyakov writes that in June, 1881, there were no bright days during the entire month. From the agricultural inspector's report covering a four-year period, it is clear that there are no more than an average of eight bright days between May 18 and September 1. Fogs are a frequent phenomenon here, especially at sea, where they are a real misery for sailors. Salt-laden sea fogs, they tell me, are destructive to all vegetation along the coast, both trees and ground growth. Later I shall describe the settlements which have ceased sowing grain as a result of the fog, and instead they have planted all their arable land with potatoes. One bright sunny day I saw a milky-white fog bank rolling in from the sea. It was like a white curtain dropping from heaven to earth.

The meteorological station is furnished with instruments which have been checked and acquired from the Central Physical Observatory in Petersburg. It has no library. As well as Galovatsky and his wife, whom I have already mentioned, I recorded six male workers and one female. I do not know what they do.

Korsakovskoye has a school and a chapel. It used to have a medical center where fourteen syphilitics and three lunatics were housed together. One of the latter became infected with syphilis. They also tell me that the syphilitics produced hawsers for ships and lint for the surgical department. However, I was not able to visit this medieval establishment because it had been closed in September by a young military doctor. If they made bonfires of lunatics by order of the prison doctors, this would not astonish me: hospital conditions here are at least two hundred years behind civilized times.

In one hut I found a forty-year-old man dressed in a pea jacket, his trousers unbuttoned, his chin clean shaven, wearing a dirty, unstarched shirt and something that looked like a necktie. To all appearances he was one of the privileged class. He sat on a low stool and was eating bacon and potatoes from a clay cup. He gave a surname with a *ky* ending and for some reason I felt I saw before me a former officer, who also had a name ending in *ky,* and who had been sent to penal servitude for some infraction of discipline.

"Are you a former officer?" I asked.

"Not at all, your worship, I am a priest," he said.

I do not know why he was sent to Sakhalin. I did not even ask him. When a man stands before you who until recently was called Father Ioan and *Batiushka* [Little Father], and whose hands had been kissed by the people, when such a man stands before you in a pitifully worn jacket, you do not think of his crime.

In another hut I observed the following scene. A young, dark-complexioned convict, with an unusually sorrowful

83

face, dressed in an immaculate blouse, sits at a table clutching his head in his hands. A convict woman clears the samovar and the cups from the table. When I ask him if he is married, the young man answers that his wife and daughter have voluntarily followed him. However, it is two months since she left with the child for Nikolayevsk and has not returned, although he sent her a number of telegrams. "And she won't come back," says the convict woman maliciously. "What can she do here? Perhaps she hasn't seen your Sakhalin, eh? It's not easy!" He remains silent, and again she says, "She won't come back. She is a young woman, free, why should she? She took off like a bird and flew away, and not a sign of her. She's not like you and me. If I hadn't murdered my husband and if you hadn't been a firebrand, we too would still be free. And now you sit and wait hopelessly for your wife, and your heart is breaking." He is suffering. Obviously his soul is as heavy as lead, but she keeps on nagging and nagging him. I leave the hut and can still hear her voice.

I was accompanied on my visits to the huts in Korsakovskoye by a very strange convict, Kislyakov. The court reporters have probably not forgotten him. This is the same Kislyakov, a military clerk, who battered his wife to death with a hammer on Nikolayevskaya Street in Petersburg and reported his crime to the authorities. He said his wife had been a beauty and he had loved her madly, but once when he quarreled with her, he vowed before the icon that he would kill her. Since that time up to the actual murder an evil spirit seemed to whisper constantly, "Kill, kill!" He was detained in the St. Nikolay Hospital until his trial, which is probably why he considers himself a psychopath and explains why he kept asking me to use my influence with the authorities to have him ruled insane and committed to a monastery.

His only penal work in the prison consists of making wooden pegs for strengthening the brackets for holding loaves of bread. The work is not difficult, but he hires someone else to do it and "gives lessons," which means he does nothing. He is dressed in a canvas suit and presents a pleasant appearance. He is a dim-witted fellow, but loquacious and a philosopher. "Where there are fleas, there are children," he says in a sweet, velvety baritone whenever he sees children. When they asked me in his presence why I am taking a census, he answered, "So they can send us all to the moon. Do you know where the moon is?" During our walk back to Alexandrovsk each evening he often repeated to nobody in particular, "Revenge is the most noble sensation."

Farther along the Duyka lies the Novo-Mikhaylovka settlement, founded in 1872, and so named because Mitsul's first name was Mikhail. Many authors call it Verkhnoye Urochyshche [Upper Boundary], while the settlers call it Pashnya [Plowland]. It contains 520 settlers, 287 males and 233 females. There are 133 households, of which two have cohouseholders. Arable land is possessed by all the householders according to the records; there are eighty-four head of livestock. Nevertheless, with a few exceptions, the huts are depressingly impoverished and the inhabitants unanimously declare "there is no way" to survive on Sakhalin. They told me that in former years when the poverty in Novo-Mikhaylovka was acute, a path was trodden to Dué by the convicts and free women who wanted to sell themselves to the prisoners in Dué and Voyevodsk for copper pennies. I can testify that the path is still not overgrown.

The settlers here, like those of Korsakovskoye, have larger plots of arable land, from three to six and even eight desyatins, and they are not impoverished. However, there are only a few of them and with each passing year they grow fewer. At the present time more than half of the settlers have only one-eighth to one and a half desyatins, which means that agriculture to them is a complete loss. The experienced old settlers only sow barley and plant potatoes on their land.

The land here is discouraging and not conducive to settling. No householders remain of those who were settlers in the first years of the settlement's existence. There are nine who have been here since 1876; seven since 1877; two since 1878; four since 1879. The remainder are newcomers.

Novo-Mikhaylovka contains a telegraph station, a school, a prison for the destitute and the skeleton of an unfinished wooden church. It has a bakery where bread is baked for the convicts building roads in the Novo-Mikhaylovka region. The bread is made without any official supervision and is abominable.

Everyone passing through Novo-Mikhaylovka is bound to meet the local peasant, formerly-an-exile, Potemkin. If any important person comes to Sakhalin, Potemkin presents the traditional bread and salt. When they wish to prove that the agricultural colony is a success, they use Potemkin as an example. The homestead list shows that he owns 20 horses and 9 head of cattle, but people say he has twice as many horses. He owns a store here, and another in Dué which is run by his son. He gives the impression of being a businesslike, intelligent and prosperous sectarian. His chambers are clean, the walls are wallpapered, and on the wall hangs a picture: "Marienbad, Sea Bathing near Libov."

He and his wife are sober, judicious and politically minded. When I was taking tea with them, they told me that it is possible to live on Sakhalin and that the land is fertile. The problem is that the people today are lazy, spoiled and do not work hard enough. I asked him whether it was true that he had served watermelon and muskmelon from his own gardens to an important guest. Without batting an eye he said, "That's true. At times melons ripen here."[4]

There is another Sakhalin celebrity in Novo-Mikhaylovka—the settler Tersky, a former executioner. He coughs, hugs his chest with pale, bony hands and complains that he is ruptured. He began coughing on the day when, by order of the administration, he was flogged by the present executioner, Komelev. Komelev did such a good job that he had "almost knocked the soul out of him." But one day it was Tersky's turn. He gave full rein to his whip and beat his colleague so mercilessly and vengefully that to this day people say his body is still rotting. They say that if you

86

place two venomous executioners together in one room they will devour each other.

Until 1888, Novo-Mikhaylovka was the last settlement along the Duyka, but today we also find Krasny Yar and Butakovo. A road is being built to these settlements from Novo-Mikhaylovka. I traveled half the way to Krasny Yar, three miles, over a smooth new road, straight as a ruler; the second half I rode over a picturesque path cut through the taiga, where the tree stumps had already been removed and the ride was as easy and pleasant as though we were traveling along a good country road. Large construction timbers had already been cut down, but the taiga was still imposing and beautiful. Birches, aspens, poplars, willows, ashes, elders, bird cherries, spiraeas and hawthorns abound. Among them were grasses which grew man-high and higher; gigantic ferns and burdocks, whose leaves were more than an arshin in diameter, merged with the bushes and trees into a dense and impenetrable thicket, a sanctuary for bears, sables and deer. On both sides where the valley ends and the foothills begin, there are coniferous forests of silver firs, pines and larches forming a green wall, while above them again lies a deciduous forest, and the tops of the mountains are bald or covered with bushes. I never saw such enormous burdocks in Russia as those I found here, and it is primarily due to these leaves that the local thickets, the forest glades and the meadows take on a special aspect. I have already written that at night, especially in the moonlight, they look fantastic. This display is supplemented by another magnificent plant of the umbelliferous family which does not seem to have a name in Russian. It has a straight stem some ten feet tall and about three inches thick; it is purple-red in its upper part and carries an umbrella about a foot in diameter. Around this main umbrella are grouped four to six smaller umbrellas which make the plant look like a candelabrum. In Latin this plant is called *Angelophyllum ursinum* [bear root].[5]

Krasny Yar has only been in existence over a year. It has one wide street, still uncleared. The inhabitants go from hut to hut over hillocks, over heaps of clay and wood chips, and jump over logs, stumps and ditches filled with stagnant brown water. The huts are not yet completed. One homesteader makes bricks, another plasters the stove, a third drags a log across the street. It contains a total of 51 householders. Three of them, including a Chinese Pen-Ogi-Tsoy, abandoned their unfinished huts, took off, and nobody knows where they went. The seven local Caucasians have stopped working, and they huddle together in one hut and are already shivering with cold, although it is only August 2.

The figures show that the settlers are young and are barely beginning their life. There are 90 inhabitants, twice as many males as females. Three families are legally married, 20 are living as cohabitants. Nine children are younger than five years of age. Three householders have horses, nine have cows. At present all the householders are receiving prison rations. Nobody knows how they will survive in the future. There is little hope for agriculture. Only 24½ desyatins have been located and cleared for tillage and potatoes, which means that each household gets less than ½ of a desyatin. There are no hayfields. Since the valley is narrow and enclosed on both sides by mountains which are completely barren, and since the administration acts indiscriminately when it must get rid of people, and will probably settle tens of new householders here, the tillable soil will probably remain at ⅛, ¼ and ½ of a desyatin or even less. I do not know who selected the Krasny Yar site, but it is evident that it was entrusted to incompetent people who never saw a village, and had no concept of an agricultural colony. This place does not even have decent water. When I asked where they obtain drinking water, they pointed to the ditch.

All the huts are identical, with two windows, constructed of poor-quality raw timber, the sole aim being to survive the prison term and return to the mainland. The administration has no building code, probably because nobody among the officials knows how to build a hut and make a stove. An architect is listed on the Sakhalin staff, but he was absent during my visit and in any case he is concerned only with prison structures.

The most cheerful and attractive building is the government dwelling which houses the prison warden Ubi-yennykh [the Overwhelmed], a small, puny soldier with an expression which completely matches his surname. This might be caused by his mistress, a tall, plump settler who lives with him in one room and has presented him with numerous offspring. He is now receiving the top supervisory salary. His entire work consists of reporting to visitors that everything is wonderful in this world. But he, too, dislikes Krasny Yar and wants to leave Sakhalin. He asked me whether they would permit his mistress to leave with him when he retires and departs for the mainland. This question is most disquieting to him.

I did not visit Butakovo.[6] From data in the homestead list, a portion of which I was able to check, supplementing the information from the priest's Confessional Book, it contains 39 people, only 4 of whom are adult females. It has 22 homesteaders. Only 4 houses have been completed, while the remainder are still in the framework stage. Only $4\frac{1}{2}$ desyatins of land are under tillage and potatoes. None of the householders have livestock or poultry.

After visiting the Duyka valley I went on to visit the Arkay River. Along this river there are three settlements. The Arkay valley was chosen for settlement not because it was better surveyed than the others nor because it satisfied the colony's needs, but quite arbitrarily, because it was closer to Alexandrovsk than the other valleys.

---

[1] The greatest benefactors in the penal colony so far were two men: M. S. Mitsul and M. N. Galkin-Vrasky, both notable for their constructiveness and attitude of responsibility. A tiny, impoverished temporary settlement of ten households has been named in honor of Mitsul. A settlement which has long since borne the name of Siyantsy appears on some maps as Galkino-Vraskoye. The name of M. S. Korsakov was given to a settlement and a large post, not because of any personal merits or sacrifices he endured, but because he was the Governor-General and could evoke fear.

2   The yearly mean temperature varies between $+1.2°$ and $-1.2°$. The number of days with precipitation varies between 102 and 209. There were only thirty-five calm, windless days in 1881; in 1884, there were three times as many—112.

3   P. Gryaznov, "Results of a Comparative Study of the Hygienic Conditions of Peasant Life and the Medico-Topography of the Cherepovetsky District" (1880). I have transposed the Réaumur readings used by Gryaznov into Centigrade.

4   Potemkin arrived on Sakhalin a wealthy man. Dr. Augustinovich, who saw him three years after his arrival in Sakhalin, writes that "of all the prisoners' homes Potemkin's is the best." If the convict Potemkin was able to build a beautiful home in three years, own horses and marry his daughter off to a Sakhalin official, I believe that agriculture had nothing to do with it.

5   Most writers disapprove of the local scenery. This is because they arrived on Sakhalin still under the influence of the Ceylonese, Japanese or Amur landscapes and because they began their trips from Alexandrovsk and Dué, where nature is indeed pathetic. The local weather is also at fault. No matter how beautiful and original the Sakhalin scenery might be, if it is hidden for weeks at a time by fog or rain, it is difficult to evaluate its worth.

6   This settlement is named in honor of A. M. Butakov, the superintendent of the Tymovsky district.

VIII
The Arkay Stream - Arkovsky Cordon - First, Second and Third Arkovo - The Arkovo Valley - The Western Bank Settlements, Mgachi, Tangi, Khoe, Trambaus, Viakhty and Vangi - The Tunnel - The Cable House - Dué - Barracks for Families - The Dué Prison - Coal Mines - Voyevodsk Prison - Prisoners in Balls and Chains

THE ARKAY STREAM falls into the Tatar Strait some eight to ten versts north of the Duyka. Not long ago it was a real river where humpback salmon were caught. Then as a result of forest fires and deforestation, it became shallow and now it dries up completely in the summer. However, during severe rainstorms it overflows and rages wildly with tremendous noise. Many times the gardens along its banks have been washed away, and all the crops and the hay have been carried down to the sea. It is impossible to prevent this devastation because the valley is narrow and the only escape from the river is up the mountains.[1]

At the very mouth of the Arkay as it turns into the valley there stands the Gilyak village of Arkay-vo, the old name for Arkovsky Cordon, and the three settlements First, Second and Third Arkovo. Two roads lead to the Arkovo valley from Alexandrovsk—the first, a mountain road which I could not use because the bridges had burned during some forest fires, and the second, a road along the seashore which could be used only at low tide. On my first trip I left for Arkovo on July 31 at 8:00 A.M.

The ebb tide had just begun. It smelled of rain. The gloomy sky, the sea empty of sails, and the craggy clay shore were grim; the waves roared thunderously and mournfully. Stunted, sickly trees gazed downward from the high banks. Here in the open they were all waging a fierce battle against frosts and freezing winds. During the long terrible fall and winter nights they sway restlessly from side to side, cringe toward the earth, creak mournfully, and nobody hears their laments.

Arkovsky Cordon is close to a Gilyak village. Previously it was a guard post for the soldiers who hunted escaped prisoners. It now houses a warden who seems to be the supervisor of the settlements. First Arkovo is two versts from the Cordon. It has but one street and can only grow lengthwise, not crosswise, owing to the local conditions. When the three Arkovos at last join together, Sakhalin will have a very large village possessing only one tremendously long street.

First Arkovo was founded in 1883. It has 136 inhabitants, 83 males and 53 females. There are 28 householders, all of whom are married except for the female convict Pavlovska, a Catholic, whose cohabitant, the actual householder, had recently died. She earnestly entreated me, "Find me a master for the house." Three of the homesteaders own two homes each.

Second Arkovo was founded in 1884. It has 92 inhabitants, 46 males and 46 females. It contains 24 households. Everyone is married. Two of them own two houses each. Third Arkovo was founded at the same time as Second Arkovo, which shows how anxious the authorities were to settle the Arkovo valley. It has 41 inhabitants, 19 males and 22 females. There are ten households, one of which has a co-owner. Nine are married.

The arable land held by the homesteaders in the three Arkovos varies between one-half and two desyatins. One owner has three desyatins. They sow small quantities of wheat, barley and rye, and plant potatoes. The majority have cattle and poultry. If one were to judge by the figures given on the homestead list prepared by the settlement supervisor, you would think that all three Arkovos were showing significant improvements in agriculture in a short time. No wonder one anonymous author describes the local farming in this way: "The work is abundantly rewarding, because the local soil is extremely favorable for farming, as may be clearly demonstrated by the luxurious growths of timber and the vegetation."

In fact this is not true. All three Arkovos belong to the poorest settlements in Northern Sakhalin. There is arable land and cattle, but there has never been a harvest. In addition to the unfavorable conditions prevalent throughout Sakhalin, the local homesteaders encounter another strong enemy in the peculiarities of the Arkovo valley, and especially in the soil so highly praised by our anonymous author. The topsoil is humus, the subsoil pebbly. On hot days the earth heats up and the plant roots dry up; in the rainy season moisture cannot seep down because of the clay, and the roots rot. On soil like this the only plants that can be successfully cultivated are those with strong, deep roots such as burdock. Edible roots like turnips and potatoes can also be cultivated, for the soil can be worked better and deeper for them than for cereals. I have already mentioned the disasters caused by the stream. There are no hayfields. Hay is either mown on the patches of taiga, or it is cut with scythes wherever they find it. The more prosperous people buy it in the Tymovsky district. I have been told of families which did not have one piece of bread during the entire winter; they existed on turnips.

Just before my arrival the settler Skorin died of starvation in Second Arkovo. According to his neighbors, he had eaten only a pound of bread during the last three days of his life; this had been going on for a long time. "The same fate awaits all of us," said one of the neighbors, terrified by the man's death. And as I record these things I remember three women weeping.

In one unfurnished hut with a dark dismal stove taking up half the room, children were wailing and chickens cackling around the housewife. She went on the street, and the children and the chickens followed her. Looking at them, she began laughing and crying and apologizing to me for the weeping and the noise of the chickens. She said it was due to hunger, and she was waiting for her husband to return from the city where he had gone to sell blueberries and buy bread. She cut off some cabbage leaves for the chickens. They greedily picked at the leaves, and feeling deceived, they began to cackle even louder.

In one hut there lives a peasant as hairy as a spider, with hanging eyebrows; he is a convict, and very filthy. With him there is another exactly like him, just as hairy and filthy. Both have large families. In the hut, as the saying goes, it is appallingly barren and poverty-stricken; they do not even own a nail. There was all this weeping and clucking, and then there are deaths like Skorin's, and you find yourself thinking about all the various indirect expressions of hunger and want.

In Third Arkovo the hut of the settler Petrov stands closed because he has been confined in the Voyevodsk prison, where he is held for "negligence in homesteading and the willful slaughter of a calf for meat." Obviously the calf was slaughtered because he was poor; and he had sold the meat in Alexandrovsk. The seeds taken on credit from the prison storehouse are recorded as sown in the homestead list, but in fact half of them are eaten: the settlers make no effort to conceal this in their talk. Their cattle, too, has been taken on credit from the prison stockyard, and they are fed in the same way. The farther you go into the forest, the more trees you will find! All the Arkovo people are in debt, and their indebtedness grows with each annual sowing, with every new head of cattle. In some cases it has reached an impossible figure—two and even three hundred rubles per person.

Between Second and Third Arkovo is the Arkovsky Stanok, where horses are changed on the road to the Tymovsky district. It is a postal station and an inn. Measured by our Russian arshins, two or three helpers would be sufficient to take care of the stanok supervisor. However, on Sakhalin people do everything on a grand scale. In addition to the supervisor, the stanok houses a clerk, an errand boy, a stableman, two bakers, three woodsmen and four additional workers who answered my question about what they do by saying, "I carry hay."

If a traveling artist should happen to visit Sakhalin, I would highly recommend a visit to the Arkovsky valley. In addition to its beautiful location, it is so extraordinarily colorful that it is difficult not to compare it with a multi-colored carpet or a kaleidoscope. Here are dense, opulent stretches of greenery with gigantic burdocks glistening with raindrops from the recent rains; nearby in a small area no more than three sazhens wide there is a patch of green rye, then a patch of barley, then again burdocks, followed by some oats, and a row of potatoes and two small sunflowers with drooping heads; and then a patch of thick green hemp; and here and there are umbrella plants like candelabra, towering proudly over all of them; and all this variety is interspersed with touches of rose, bright-red and crimson poppy flowers.

Along the road you see women wearing tremendous burdock leaves like three-cornered neckerchiefs to protect them from the rain. They look like green beetles. Mountains rise above the valley, and although they are not the Caucasus Mountains, still they are mountains.

Six tiny settlements nestle along the western shore above the mouth of the Arkaya. I did not visit any of them, but obtained the pertinent data from the list of homesteads and the Confessional Book. They were situated on capes jutting into the sea or at the mouths of the streams from which they received their names. They began as picket posts, sometimes with four or five men. After a while, it was discovered that these outposts alone were inadequate, and so they decided (in 1882) to settle the largest capes between Dué and Pogobi with reliable settlers, preferably with families. Their aim in founding these settlements and the cordons was: "To permit mail carriers, passengers and men driving dog sleighs from Nikolayevsk to obtain shelter and protection during their journey and to establish police surveillance along the shore line, which is the only (?)[2] possible route for escaped prisoners and for importing contraband alcohol." There is no road yet to these shore settlements. They can only be reached along the coast on foot at ebb tide and by dog sleigh in winter. They can also be reached by rowboats and steam cutters, but only when good weather permits. From south to north, these settlements are as follows:

MGACHI has 38 inhabitants, 20 males and 18 females; 14 homesteaders. Thirteen families are legally married, only two illegally. Each has about 12 desyatins of arable land, but for the last 3 years no grain has been sown and all the land has been planted with potatoes. There are 11 homesteaders who are the original settlers, 5 of them already having gained the status of peasants. Profits are good, which explains their reluctance to leave for the mainland. Seven are engaged in renting dog sleighs, which carry mail and passengers in the winter. One is a professional hunter. As for the fishing mentioned in the central prison administration records for 1889, there is no trace of it.

TANGI. Inhabitants, 19: 11 male and 8 female; homesteaders, 6. There are some three desyatins of arable land, but as in Mgachi, as a result of frequent sea fogs which make grain culture impossible, only potatoes are raised. Two householders have rowboats and engage in fishing.

KHOE is situated on the cape bearing the same name which juts deeply into the sea and is visible from Alexandrovsk. Inhabitants, 34: 19 male and 15 female; householders, 13. Here the people have not yet become disenchanted and they continue to sow wheat and barley. Three are hunters.

TRAMBAUS. Inhabitants, 8: 3 male and 5 female. Happy is the settlement which has more women than men. Householders, 3.

VIAKHTY is on the Viakhty River, which links a lake with the sea and is reminiscent of the Neva. They say that gangfish and sturgeon can be caught in the lake. Inhabitants, 17: 9 male, 8 female; households, 7.

VANGI, the northernmost settlement. Inhabitants, 13: 9 male, 4 female; households, 7.

Scientists and travelers say that the farther north you go, the poorer and more dismal the landscape. Beginning with Trambaus, the entire northern third of the island is a flat tundra on which the main watershed ridge that runs along the entire length of Sakhalin looks like low undulating elevations. Some authors consider it to have arisen from the alluvia of the Amur River. Along the reddish-brown level marshland here and there you can find areas of ragged coniferous trees. The trunk of the larch is not more than a foot tall and its crown lies on the ground like a green pillow, while the stem of the cedar bush lies along the earth, and between the sparse trees grow lichens and mosses. As in the Russian tundra, we find all kinds of coarse berries, tart or extremely astringent in taste: the mossberry, the whortleberry, the *kostenika* and the cranberry. Only at the northernmost section of the plain, where the land again becomes hilly, is there an area where nature seems to desire to smile in farewell at the very brink of the eternally frozen sea. Krusenstern's map of this area shows an excellent larch forest.

Notwithstanding the grimness and paucity of nature here, it is the belief of some authorities that the inhabitants of the shore settlements live comparatively better than the inhabitants of Arkovo or Alexandrovsk.

This is explained by the fact that there are few inhabitants, and the blessings available to them are shared among not too many people. They are not obliged to till the soil and harvest. They are left to their own devices and choose their own occupations and trades. The winter road from Alexandrovsk to Nikolayevsk passes through the settlements. Gilyaks and Yakuts arrive in winter to trade and the settlers sell to and trade with them directly without commissioners acting as middlemen. There are no shopkeepers, no *maidanshchiks,* no Jewish second-hand dealers, and there are no office workers who exchange alcohol for costly furs and later display them with blissful smirks to their guests.

No new settlements are being formed toward the south. There is only one inhabited region along the western shore south of Alexandrovsk. This is Dué, an appallingly ugly and absolutely horrible city where only saints or utterly depraved people could live voluntarily. It is a post, but the inhabitants call it a port. It was founded in 1857. The name Dué, or Dui, has a long history and referred generally to that portion of the shore where the Dué mines are now situated. Through the narrow valley flows a small river, the Khoyndzhi.

Two roads lead to Dué from Alexandrovsk, one over the mountains and the other along the shore. The huge mass of Cape Zhonkiyer covers the entire shoreline, which would be impassable if a tunnel had not been constructed. They drilled the tunnel without any knowledge of engineering and without engineering skills. As a result it is dark, crooked and filthy. This construction was very costly, and as it turned out quite unnecessary, for there were mountain roads already in existence and there was no need to take the shore road, which could be used only at low tide and was useless at high tide. This tunnel is an excellent example of the Russian inclination to expend one's last resources on all kinds of evasions, while the most urgent necessities are ignored. The tunnel was being burrowed, the supervisors of the work rode up and down the rails in a railroad car bearing the sign ALEXANDROVSK—PORT, while the convicts lived in filthy, damp yurts because there were not enough people to build barracks.

At the exit of the tunnel on the shore road there stands a salt works and the little cable house from which the telegraph cable descends, and crosses over the sand to enter the sea. A convict carpenter, a Pole, lives there with his mistress, who, they tell me, gave birth at twelve years of age after having been raped by some prisoner at a convict way station.

Along the entire road to Dué the steep, sheer shore is crumbling away; here and there black blotches and streaks can be seen, an arshin to a sazhen wide. This is coal. These layers of coal, according to the specialists, are compressed by layers of sandstone, shale, slaty clay and clayey sand. They are raised, curved, shifted by, or combined with, layers of basalt, diorite and porphyry, which jut out in large masses in many places. All this may be very beautiful in its own way, but my prejudices were by now so deep-seated that I regarded not only the people but also the plants with

98

sorrow, because they were growing up in this terrible place rather than elsewhere.

Seven versts along the bank there is a ravine. This is the Voyevodsk Gap; and here stands the lone, formidable Voyevodsk prison, in which infamous criminals are incarcerated, among them convicts shackled to iron balls. Sentries guard the prison; and there is no other living creature in sight, so that they seem to be guarding some extraordinary treasure in the desert wastes.

A verst farther the coal breaks begin; you travel another verst along a bare, desolate shore and finally you reach still another gap, where you find Dué, the former capital of penal servitude in Sakhalin. In the first minutes as you drive into the street, Dué gives the impression of a small, antiquated fortress. The street is straight and smooth—a good drill ground; there are clean white cottages, a striped hut, striped posts. All that is lacking to complete the impression is the roll of drums. The military commander, the warden of the Dué prison, a priest, officers and others occupy these houses. A gray wooden church stands across the end of the short street which bars from the viewer the unofficial section of the post. Here the gap divides into two parts resembling a Y, sending out gorges to the right and left.

To the left is a suburb without a name, formerly called Zhydovskaya [Jewtown], and to the right there are all kinds of prison buildings and another nameless suburb. In both, especially in the left, it is crowded, dirty, uncomfortable; here there are no more clean cottages; the little huts are dilapidated, without courtyards, without greenery, without porches; they cling to the road without order, up the mountain and along the mountaintop. In Dué, the plots of arable land, if this is what they can be called, are tiny. In the household census I recorded that four households have only four square sazhens each. It is so packed that an apple can find no place to fall, but still the Dué executioner, Tolstykh, found a small plot in this crowded, stinking place and is building himself a house.

Not counting the officers, the free population and the

99

prison, Dué contains 291 inhabitants, 167 males and 124 females. There are 46 householders and 6 cohouseholders. The majority are convicts. What impels the administration to settle them and their families here in the gap instead of elsewhere is incomprehensible. The household records show that there is only one-eighth of a desyatin of arable land in Dué, and no hayfields whatsoever.

Let us assume that the men are kept busy with hard labor; but what do the eighty adult women do? How do they pass their time when, by reason of poverty, the foul weather, the never-ending clank of chains, the unchanging view of barren mountains, and the roar of the sea, the moaning and wailing often heard from the prison when punishment is meted out with lashes and birch rods, time must seem far longer and more tormenting than in Russia? The women spend their days in total inactivity. In one hut, consisting usually of a single room, you will find a convict family, and with it a soldier's family, two or three convict boarders or guests. You will find some teen-agers, two or three cradles in the corners, chickens and a dog. On the street near the hut there are piles of garbage and puddles from slops. There is nothing to do, they have nothing, they are tired of talking and arguing; it is boring to go out on the street because everything is equally cheerless and dirty. What an agony!

At night the convict husband returns home from work. He wants to eat and sleep, but the wife begins crying and nagging: "You have destroyed us, curse you! Ruined is my little head, ruined are the children!" "She's howling again!" grumbles the soldier on the stove. Everyone has gone to sleep, the children have cried themselves out and they have been asleep for a long time, but the woman does not sleep. She thinks and listens to the roaring of the sea. She feels compassion for her husband and despises herself for not having restrained herself instead of reproaching him. The next day the story is repeated.

If we may judge Dué by only one factor, the agricultural colony on Sakhalin is overburdened by a surplus of women and convict families. Because of insufficient space in the huts, twenty-seven families are living in old structures condemned long ago for demolition, filthy and repulsive in the highest degree. They are called "barracks for families." There are no rooms here, only wards with plank beds and chamber pots. The composition of the inhabitants is extremely diversified.

In the first ward, with the broken windows, there are a convict and his free wife; a convict, his free wife and daughter; another convict, his settler wife and daughter; still another convict and his free wife; a Polish settler and his convict cohabitant; with all of their possessions they live in one ward and sleep in a row on one continuous plank bed.

In the second ward: a convict, his free wife and son; a Tatar convict woman and her daughter; a Tatar convict, his free wife and two little Tatars in skullcaps; a convict, his free wife and son; a settler who spent thirty-five years in penal servitude but is still youthful, with a black mustache; he walks barefoot because he owns no shoes, but is a passionate card player.[3] Next to him on the plank is his convict mistress, a flabby, sleepy and sorry-looking creature; further on, a convict, his free wife and three children; a single convict; a convict, his free wife and two children; a settler; a convict, an immaculate old man with a shaven face. A piglet wanders around the ward and slobbers; the floor is covered with slimy muck, the ward stinks of bedbugs and something sour; they say the bedbugs never give you any rest.

In the third ward: a convict, his free wife and 2 children; a convict, his free wife and daughter; a convict, his free wife and 7 children—one daughter is 16, another 15; a convict, his free wife and son; another convict with his free wife and son; a convict, his free wife and 4 children.

In the fourth ward: a noncommissioned jailer, his eighteen-year-old wife and a daughter; a convict and his free wife; a settler, a convict; etc., etc.

From these barabaric premises and their atmosphere where fifteen- and sixteen-year-old girls are forced to sleep beside convicts, the reader can judge in what disrespect and contempt women and children are held. They voluntarily followed their husbands and fathers into penal servitude, but how cheaply they are valued and how little thought is given to the agricultural colony!

The Dué prison is smaller, older and far dirtier than that of Alexandrovsk. Here also are common wards and continuous plank beds, but the conditions are poorer and the situation is worse. The walls and floors are equally grimy and have become so blackened from time and damp that they could not be cleaned even if they were scrubbed. According to information in the medical report of 1889, there are 1.12 cubic sazhens of air per prisoner. If in the summer, with the doors and windows wide open, it smells of slops and the latrine, then I can imagine what hell it is in winter when every morning they find frost and icicles in the prison.

The prison superintendent here is a former military surgeon's assistant from Poland who had served as an office worker. In addition to the Dué prison, he is also in charge of Voyevodsk prison, the mines and the Dué Post. The distances involved are not at all compatible with his rank.

The Dué cells hold hard-bitten offenders, for the most part habitual criminals, and prisoners under investigation. These were the most unexceptional-looking people, with good-natured, stupid faces expressing only curiosity and the desire to answer me as respectfully as possible. The crimes of most of them were no more intelligent or clever than their faces. They are usually sent here for five or ten years for murder committed during a fight; they escape, are caught, again escape, and so on until they receive life terms as incorrigible convicts. The crimes of almost all of them are terribly dull, ordinary, without interest, and I purposely included "Yegor's Tale" so that the reader may judge how colorless and barren were those hundreds of similar stories, autobiographies and anecdotes which I heard from prisoners and from other people who are intimate with the penal colony.

One gray-haired old man called Terekhov, sixty to sixty-five years old, sat by himself in a dark cell and looked like a real scoundrel. Just before my arrival he had been beaten with lashes and when he spoke of them he showed me his buttocks, livid with bruises. According to stories told by other prisoners, this old man murdered sixty people in his time. This was the way he operated: he sought out newly arrived prisoners who were affluent and he convinced them to escape with him. Then he robbed them and murdered them in the taiga and in order to cover all traces of the crime, he cut up the corpses and threw them in the river. The last time he was caught he defended himself with a cudgel against the guards. Looking at his dull gray eyes and large half-shaven skull, sharp as a cobblestone, I was ready to believe all these stories.

A Ukrainian who was also sitting alone in a dark cell moved me with his frankness. He asked the guard to return the 195 rubles which were taken from him when he was searched. "Where did you get the money?" asked the guard. "I won it at cards," he answered, and took an oath on it. Turning to me, he explained that this is not at all strange, since almost everyone in the prison plays cards and among the card-playing convicts it is not unusual to find some who have 2,000 and 3,000 rubles at their disposal.

In the cells I saw a vagrant who had chopped off two of his fingers. The wounds were wrapped in a filthy rag. Another vagrant had a shotgun wound through his body. The bullet had fortunately entered along the external edge of his seventh rib. His wound was also bandaged with a dirty rag.[4]

It is always quiet in Dué. The ear soon becomes accustomed to the measured clang of chains, the roar of the surf and the hum of the telegraph wires, and because of these sounds the impression of dead silence becomes even stronger. The aspect of grimness is not only due to the striped posts. If someone unexpectedly happened to laugh out loud on the street, it would sound shrill and unnatural. From the very beginning of Dué, local life took on a form which can only be expressed by these inexorably brutal and hopeless sounds and the fiercely bitter wind blowing from the sea into the gap during the cold nights, which alone sings what it must.

It is therefore strange when in the silence you suddenly hear the singing of the Dué eccentric Shkandyba [Limper]. He is a convict, an old man, who from the very first day of his arrival on Sakhalin refused to work and every conceivable measure was used to break his unconquerable, completely untamable spirit. They put him in dark cells, beat him innumerable times, but he stoically endured his punishments and after each flogging he would say, "I still won't work!" They took a lot of trouble to try to change him, and finally abandoned the endeavor. Now he strolls around Dué and sings.[5]

As I already stated, coal is mined one verst from the post. I was in the mine. They led me through dark, damp corridors and courteously informed me about methods of production, but not being a specialist, I find it very difficult to describe them. However, anyone interested can read the special work by Keppen, the mining engineer who formerly supervised the mines here.[6]

At the present time the Dué mines are exclusively owned by a private company called Sakhalin, whose representatives or owners live in St. Petersburg. According to the twenty-four-year contract signed in 1875, the company derives profit from a strip of land two versts long by one verst deep along the western bank of Sakhalin. It is provided without charge with convenient areas for coalyards in the Primorskaya region and on the adjacent islands. The company also receives free of charge all construction material for buildings and labor; the transportation of all articles needed for technical and agricultural work and in the construction of mines is provided duty free. For every pood of coal purchased by the Navy, the company receives fifteen to thirty kopecks.

Every day no less than 400 convicts are commandeered to work for the company's benefit; if less than this number are sent out to work, for each missing worker the treasury pays a fine to the company of one ruble per day. The required number of people can also be supplied to the company for night shifts.

In order to fulfill the agreed obligations and to protect the company's interests, the treasury maintains two prisons near the mines, the Dué and the Voyevodsk, plus a military detachment of 340 soldiers, the annual expenditure on which is 150,000 rubles. If then the owners of the company living in St. Petersburg number only five people, the treasury guarantees them annual profits of 30,000 rubles each. This takes no account of the fact that in order to maintain these profits, putting aside all the problems of the agricultural colony and the complete mockery of ordinary rules of hygiene, the treasury must maintain more than 700 convicts, their families, soldiers and officials in such terrifying holes as the Voyevodsk and Dué gaps. Nor does it take account of the fact that in releasing convicts to serve a private company for financial gain, the administration sacrifices the aims of reform to industrial considerations, which means that it is repeating the old mistake, one which it has always condemned.

The company, on the other hand, must fulfill three chief obligations. It must develop the Dué mines properly and maintain a mining engineer at Dué to supervise their proper exploitation. Twice annually rent must be paid for the coal and for the services of the convicts. In working the mines, convict labor must be used exclusively. These three obligations exist only on paper, and obviously they have long ago been forgotten. The mines are worked unscrupulously, on the kulak or tough peasant-owner principle. "No improvements in production techniques nor modifications for assuring a stable future have been made," we read in the report of one official. "The different kinds of work, insofar as they consist of economic production, have all the earmarks of plunder, and the last report of the regional engineer concurs."

The mining engineer which the company is obliged to furnish does not exist, and the mines are supervised by an ordinary foreman. As to payments, we are reminded of the report I have just mentioned: the official says it has "all the earmarks of plunder." The company profits from the mines without paying anything. It is obliged to pay, but for some reason it does not pay.

The representatives of the other side should have called on the authorities long ago in view of such blatant disregard of the law, but for some reason they have been delaying, and what is worse, they are continuing to expend 150,000 rubles a year to guarantee the company's profits, and both sides conduct themselves in such a manner that it is difficult to say when these abnormal attitudes will terminate. The company has entrenched itself as securely as Foma[7] in the village of Stepanchikovo, and, like Foma, is implacable.

As of January 1, 1890, it owed the treasury 194,337 rubles, 15 kopecks; a tenth of this money by law goes to the convicts as wages. I do not know when and how they pay off the convicts, who pays them or whether they get anything.

Some 350 to 400 convicts are assigned to work every day, while the remaining 350 to 400 living in the Dué and Voyevodsk prisons form a reserve force. There must be a reserve, because the contract calls for convicts "capable of work" to be supplied every day. Assignments for work in the mine are made at five o'clock in the morning at a so-called dispatch meeting. The convicts enter the presence of the mining administration, which consists of a small group of private persons who make up "the office."

On the discretion of "the office" depends their assignment, the daily amount and load of labor for each individual convict. For this reason "the office" is supposed to see that the prisoners' sentences are distributed proportionally. The prison administration itself is only concerned with controlling their behavior and preventing escapes. It washes its hands of everything else.

There are two mines: the old and the new. The convicts work in the new mine, where the height of the coal strip is about two arshins; the width of the shafts is the same. The distance from the mine entrance to the present mining area is about 150 sazhens. A worker dragging a sled weighing a pood crawls up along a dark and dank corridor; this is the most difficult part of the work. Later, after loading his sled, he returns. At the entrance the coal is loaded into coal cars and sent by rail to the coalyards. Each convict must crawl up with his sled not less than thirteen times a day, and here we deduce a lesson. In 1889–90, each convict mined on the average of 10.8 poods a day, 4.2 poods below the norm established by the mining administration. In general the mine production and the results of convict mining are not great; they vary between 1,500 and 3,000 poods daily.

Settlers are also hired for labor in the Dué mines. They work under far worse conditions than the convicts. In the old mine the coal layer is no more than one arshin wide; the working area is now 230 sazhens from the entrance. The upper layer sweats profusely, which forces them to work in a continually damp atmosphere. They live at their own expense, in premises far worse than the prison. In spite of all this, their labor is more productive than that of the convicts by 70 and even 100 percent. So great are the advantages of free hired labor over forced labor! Hired workers are more convenient to the company than those they must maintain under contract, and therefore if, according to the custom here, a convict hires a settler or another convict to take his place at work, the mining administration enthusiastically agrees to such irregularities. Hence the third obligation has long ago split at the seams.

Since Dué's inception it appears that paupers and simple people work for themselves as well as for others, while cheats and loan sharks drink tea during working hours, play cards, or wander around the port clanking their chains and conversing with the guards they have bribed.

Revolting scenes are everlastingly being played here. A week before my arrival a prisoner, a former Petersburg merchant sentenced for arson, was beaten with birch rods for refusing to work. He is a stupid man who does not know how to conceal his money and he has constantly bribed the guards. Finally he grew tired of giving the guard five rubles and the executioner three rubles, and for some reason, choosing the wrong time, he flatly refused to give them any money. The guard complained to the warden that a certain prisoner refused to work, the inspector ordered thirty strokes with birch rods, and the executioner naturally employed his best efforts. When he was being beaten the merchant kept screaming, "I was never beaten before!" After the beating he changed his mind, paid off the guard and the executioner, and as though nothing had happened, he continues to hire a settler to work in his place.

The exceptionally heavy work in the mines is not due to having to work underground in the dark and damp shafts, always crawling and sliding. Construction and road building in raw and powerful winds require far more physical strength. Whoever is acquainted with conditions in the Donets shafts will not consider the Dué mine so terrible. The exceptionally hard labor is not in the work itself, but in the existing conditions and in the stupidity and unscrupulous behavior of all the minor officials, while at every step the convicts must suffer insolence, injustice and arbitrariness. The rich drink tea, while the poor work and the guards openly dupe their superiors. The inevitable quarrels between the mine and prison administrations result in constant mockery, scandal and all sorts of minor disturbances, the burden of which is borne primarily by the forced laborers. According to the proverb, the masters fight and the boys get rapped over the head.

Moreover, no matter how depraved and contemptible the convict is, he loves fairness above all, and if it does not exist among his superiors, then he becomes more and more malevolent and vicious with every passing year. So many of them become pessimistic, morose old men endlessly discussing people, the officials, and a better life with angry, thoughtful faces! The prison listens and bursts into laughter, because it all sounds very funny.

Work in the Dué mines is also difficult because for many long years without interruption the only things the convict sees are the mine, the road to the prison, and the sea. His whole life is confined to this narrow coastline between the marshy shore and the sea.

Near the mine office there is a barracks for settlers who work in the mine. It is a small old barn which has been set up as a dormitory. I was there at five o'clock in the morning when the settlers had just woken up. What a stench, what drabness, what overcrowding! Their heads were disheveled! Brawling had been going on all night and their yellowish-gray sleepy faces looked sick or insane. It was obvious they had slept in their clothes and boots, packed closely together, some on the plank bed, others under it on the filthy sod floor. According to the physician who accompanied me that morning, there is only one cubic sazhen of air for every three or four men. Moreover, it was the time when cholera was expected on Sakhalin and a quarantine had been placed on all vessels.

That same morning I visited the Voyevodsk prison. It was built in the '70s. To acquaint you with the terrain I must explain that it was necessary to level the high banks of the gap over an area of 480 square sazhens. At the present time it is the most infamous of all the Sakhalin prisons. It has completely resisted reforms and can serve as an exact illustration to describe the old order and the old prisons which have so aroused men's loathing and terror.

Voyevodsk prison consists of three main buildings and one small one containing individual cells. Naturally, there is nothing good to say about the cubic content of air or the ventilation. When I entered the prison, they were just finishing washing down the floors, and the humid foul air had not yet dissipated from the night and it hung there heavily. The floors were wet and unpleasant to look at. The first thing I heard was complaints about bugs. You cannot live with them. At one time they were killed with chlorated lime, or they were frozen to death during intensely cold weather, but now nothing helps. The prison guards' quarters smell of latrines and sourness; they also complain about the bugs.

In the Voyevodsk prison convicts are fettered with balls and chains. There are eight fettered convicts here. They live in the common ward with the other prisoners and pass their time in absolute idleness. In any event, in the *Report on Assigning Various Kinds of Work to the Forced Labor Convicts,* those who are kept in balls and chains are numbered among the unemployed. Each is chained with manacles and fetters. From the middle of the manacles there hangs a long chain about three to four arshins long which is attached to the bottom of a small iron ball. The chains and ball constrain the prisoner and he moves as little as possible, which undoubtedly affects his musculature. Their hands become so accustomed to this that each slightest movement is made with a feeling of heaviness and when the prisoner finally is released from his ball and chain his hands retain their clumsiness and he makes excessively strong, sharp movements. When he takes a cup, for example, he spills his tea as though he were suffering from St. Vitus's dance. At night, while sleeping, the prisoners keep the ball under the plank bed. To facilitate this, the prisoner is usually placed at the end of the bed.

All eight men were incorrigible; they had been convicted a number of times during their lives. One of them, an old man of sixty, was chained for trying to escape, or as he himself says, "for stupidity." He is obviously ill, consumptive, and the former prison warden out of compassion ordered him to have a place closer to the stove.

Another, a former railroad conductor, was convicted for sacrilege, and began forging twenty-five-ruble notes on Sakhalin. When someone walking around the ward teased him for robbing a church, he answered, "So what? God doesn't need money!" Noticing that the other prisoners were not laughing and that his words had displeased them, he added, "That's why I didn't murder people."

A third, a former sailor, was sent to Sakhalin for a disciplinary transgression: he attacked an officer with clenched fists. In prison he attacked everyone in the same way. The last time was when he assaulted the prison warden, who ordered him to be beaten with birches. At the court-martial his lawyer explained that he attacked people because he was ill. The court ordered the death sentence, but Baron Korf commuted it to life imprisonment, a flogging and chains. The others were all chained for murder.

The morning was raw, gloomy, cold. The sea roared turbulently. I recall that on the road from the old mine to the new we stopped for a minute near an old Caucasian who lay on the sand in a dead faint. Two of his countrymen held his hands; they kept looking around helplessly and disconcertedly. The old man was pale, his hands icy, his pulse slow. We spoke to them and went our way without giving him any medical aid. When I mentioned to the physician who was with me that it would not harm to give the old man at least some valerian drops, he said that the Voyevodsk prison assistant surgeon had no medicine whatsoever.

1   Five years ago an important official spoke to the settlers about agriculture and offered them advice, saying: "Bear in mind that the Finlanders sow grain on mountain slopes." But Sakhalin is not Finland. The climate and especially the condition of the soil preclude any agriculture on the mountains. The agricultural inspector advised them to raise sheep, which would "easily make use of the sparse but numerous pastures along the slopes, where the cattle cannot graze." This advice is impracticable, however, since sheep could "make use of" the pastures only during the short summer and they would starve to death during the long winter.

2   The question mark is inserted by Chekhov.—TRANS.

3   He told me that when playing faro he "feels electricity in his veins," his hands shake from nervousness. One of his most pleasant memories is of the time when in his youth he stole the watch of a chief of police. He speaks with excitement about playing faro. I remember his words: "You can push it, and it doesn't go in the right place," which he said with the despair of a hunter who has missed a shot. For card lovers I recorded some of his expressions: "The transport is devoured! napé! naperipé! corner! smear the eye with a ruble! in the color and in the suit, artillery!"

4   I met a number of wounded and ulcerated prisoners, but not once did I smell iodoform, although more than twenty pounds of it are dispensed on Sakhalin annually.

5   Dué has an exaggeratedly bad reputation among people. I was told that when the *Baikal* dropped anchor near Dué, one passen-

ger, an older high official, examined the shore for a long time, and finally he said, "Tell me, please, where is the scaffold on which the convicts are hanged, and their corpses thrown into the sea?"

Dué is the cradle of Sakhalin penal servitude. The opinion exists that this particular spot was chosen for a penal colony by the convicts themselves. Supposedly a man called Ivan Lapshin, serving time for patricide in Nikolayevsk, petitioned to be sent to Sakhalin, and in September, 1858, was landed here. Settling not far from Dué, he began raising garden products and grains, and according to Vlasov, he served his sentence here. He was probably not sent to the island alone, because in 1858 coal was being mined by convicts near Dué. (See "From the Amur and the Shores of the Great Ocean" in *Moskovskiye Vedomosti* [Moscow News], 1874, No. 207.) Vysheslavtsen writes in his book *Notes Written with a Pen and Pencil* that in April, 1859, he found some forty men in Dué, with two officers and an engineering officer in charge of the work. "What beautiful gardens," he writes rapturously, "surround these comfortable, clean cottages! Vegetables ripen twice in the summer."

The period of the rise of Sakhalin penal servitude begins with the '60s, when the disorganization in our deportation system was at its highest. The times were such that the officer in charge of a branch of the Police Executive Department, the councillor Vlasov, scandalized by everything he encountered in penal servitude, stated flatly that the regime and the system are actually increasing the number of serious criminal offenses and debasing civic morals. Approximate, on-the-spot investigations of forced labor convinced him that in Russia *it is practically nonexistent* (see his *Short Outline of Disorganization Existing in Penal Servitude*). The Prison Administrative Headquarters, making a critical survey of penal servitude in its ten-year report, notes that in the period under survey, penal servitude ceased being a higher punitive measure. Indeed, it was the gravest possible disorganization ever engendered by ignorance, callousness and brutality.

Here are the main reasons for the disorganization:

a] Neither those who wrote the laws for convicts nor those who enforced them had any clear conception of the meaning of penal servitude, what it should comprise and why it was necessary. And practice, irrespective of its long duration, neither devised a system nor furnished material for a legal definition of penal servitude.

b] Various economic and financial considerations reacted adversely on reformatory and penal aims. A convict was considered a laborer obliged to produce profit for the state treasury. If the work was not gainful or was produced at a loss, they preferred to keep him in prison doing nothing. Unprofitable idleness was given preference over unprofitable labor. It was also necessary to reckon with the aims of colonization.

c] Lack of knowledge of local conditions and therefore the absence of a definite point of view about the character and nature of types of work can be observed from the recently abolished assignment of work in mines, factories and fortresses. In practice, a convict sentenced to an indefinite term in the mines sat idle in the prison, a convict with a four-year sentence was ordered to work in the factories, but in fact went to work in the mines. In the Tobolsk penal prison the convicts were set to work moving stones from one place to another, reshoveling sand, etc. This point of view became predominant in society and to some extent in literature: the severest and most humiliating penal punishment can only be administered in the mines. If Nekrasov's hero in *To a Russian Woman* had caught fish for the prison or was a woodchopper rather than a miner, the reading public would have been left unsatisfied.

d] The backwardness of our criminal code. It does not answer the numerous questions which arise daily and present a broad field for arbitrary interpretations and illegal actions. It is often a completely worthless book when the need arises to solve the most difficult situations, and this is probably one of the reasons why Vlasov failed to find the code book in some administrative offices in the penal prisons.

e] The absence of uniformity in administering penal servitude.

f] The remoteness of penal servitude from St. Petersburg and the complete lack of publicity. Official reports have only been published since the recent establishment of the Prison Administrative Headquarters.

g] The temper of our society was also greatly responsible for hindering the regulation of the practices of exile and penal servitude. When society does not possess a specific viewpoint on something, it is necessary to consider its mood. Society was always indignant about prison regulations, but at the same time it protested at every step taken to improve the lot of the prisoners, saying, for example, "It is not right for a peasant to live better in prison than at home." If a peasant often lives worse off at home than in prison, it follows logically that penal servitude should be hell. When prisoners in trains were given *kvass** instead of water, this was called "coddling murderers and firebrands," etc. However, as though to counterbalance such a mood, it was noted that the better Russian writers tended to idealize convicts, vagrants and escapees.

In 1863 a committee was organized by royal decree with the aim of investigating and suggesting measures for organizing penal labor on a more sensible basis. The committee declared that it

* A sweet-sour drink made of malt and black bread.—TRANS.

was imperative "to exile serious offenders to a distant colony to be employed in forced labor, with the aim of settling them by preference in the place of exile." Choosing among the distant colonies, the eyes of the committee fell on Sakhalin. A priori it defended its choice of Sakhalin with the following:

1) The geographical location safeguards the mainland from escapees;

2) The sentence is endowed with adequate repressive force, since exile to Sakhalin may be considered irrevocable;

3) There is a large enough space for the activities of a prisoner who resolves to begin a new working life;

4) From the point of view of benefiting the country, the concentration of convicts on Sakhalin is a guarantee for strengthening our position as owners of the island;

5) The coal deposits can be easily exploited to satisfy the huge coal requirements. It was also assumed that the concentration of the entire contingent of convict exiles on the island would cut costs for their upkeep.

6 *Sakhalin Island, Its Coal Deposits and Its Developing Coal Industry* (1875). In addition to Keppen, works on coal were written by the mining engineers: I. Nosov, "Notes on Sakhalin Island and the Coal Beds Being Worked," *Mining Journal* (1859), No. 1. I. A. Lopatin, Extract from a letter. A supplement to the Report of the Siberian Division of the Imperial Russian Geographic Society for 1868. *Ibid.,* "Report to the Governor-General of Eastern Siberia," *Mining Journal* (1870), No. 10. Deykhman, "Sakhalin Island with Respect to the Coal Industry," *Mining Journal* (1871), No. 3. Z. K. Skalkovsky, "Russian Trade in the Pacific Ocean" (1883). The quality of Sakhalin coal was described at various times by the commanders of the ships of the Siberian fleet in their reports published in the *Naval Miscellany*. To complete the list I might as well mention the articles by Y. N. Butkovsky: "Sakhalin Island," *Historical News* (1882), X, and "Sakhalin and Its Significance," *Naval Miscellany* (1874), No. 4.

7 A character in Dostoyevsky's novel *The Village of Stepanchikovo and Its Inhabitants.*—TRANS.

IX
Tym or Tymi - Lieutenant Boshnyak - Polyakov - Upper Armudan - Lower Armudan - Derbinskoye - A Journey on the Tym - Uskovo - The Gypsies - A Journey into the Taiga - Voskresenskoye

THE SECOND DISTRICT of Northern Sakhalin is located on the other side of a ridge of the mountain range and is called Tymovsk, because its settlements lie along the Tym River, which falls into the Okhotsk Sea. As you drive from Alexandrovsk to Novo-Mikhaylovka, the mountain ridge rises before you and blocks out the horizon, and what you see from there is called the Pilinga. From the top of the Pilinga a magnificent panorama opens out with the Duyka valley and the sea on one side, and on the other a vast plain which is watered by the Tym and its tributaries for more than 200 versts. This plain is far more interesting than Alexandrovsk. The water, the many kinds of timber forests, the grasses which grow higher than a man, the fabulous abundance of fish and coal deposits suggest the possibility of a satisfying and pleasant life for a million people. That is the way it should be, but the frozen currents of the Okhotsk Sea and the ice floes floating on the eastern shore even in June attest with incontrovertible clarity to the fact that when nature created Sakhalin man and his welfare was the last thing in her mind. If it were not for the mountains, the plain would be a tundra, colder and bleaker than around Viakhty.

The first person to visit the Tym River and describe it was Lieutenant Boshnyak. In 1852 he was sent here by Nevelskoy to verify information obtained from Gilyaks about coal deposits and to cross the island all the way to the shore of the Okhotsk Sea, where there was said to be a beautiful harbor. He was given a dog team, hardtack for thirty-five days, tea and sugar, a small hand compass and a cross. With these came Nevelskoy's parting words of encouragement: "As long as you have hardtack to quieten your hunger and a mug of water to drink, then with God's help you will find it possible to do your job."

Having made his way down the Tym to the eastern shore and back, he somehow reached the western shore, completely worn out and famished, and with abscesses on his legs. The starving dogs refused to go any farther. He spent Easter day huddled in the corner of a Gilyak yurt, utterly exhausted. His hardtack was gone, he could not communicate with the Gilyaks, his leg was giving him agonies of pain. What was most interesting about Boshnyak's explorations was, quite obviously, the explorer himself, his youth—he was only twenty-one years old—and his supremely heroic devotion to his task. At the time the Tym was covered with deep snow, for it was March. Nevertheless, his journey provided some very interesting data which were recorded in his report.[1]

In 1881 the zoologist Polyakov[2] carried out some serious and extensive explorations of the Tym from a scientific and practical point of view. He left Alexandrovsk on July 24, driving oxen, and crossed the Pilinga with the greatest difficulty. There were only footpaths, and these were climbed by convicts carrying provisions on their backs from the Alexandrovsk district to the Tymovsk. The elevation of the ridge is 2,000 feet. On a Tym tributary, the Admvo, close to the Pilinga, stood the Vedernikovsky way station, of which only one position has survived, the office of the station guard.[3]

The Tym tributaries are fast flowing, tortuous and full of rapids. It is impossible to use boats. Therefore it was necessary for Polyakov to go by oxen to the Tym River. From Derbinskoye he and his companion used a boat throughout the whole length of the river.

It is tiresome to read his account of this journey because of the exactitude with which he recorded all the rapids and sandbanks. In the 272 versts from Derbinskoye to the sea he was forced to overcome 110 obstacles: 11 rapids, 89 sandbanks and 10 places where the water was dammed by drifting trees and bushes. This means that on the average of every two miles the river is either shallow or choked up. Near Derbinskoye it is 20–25 sazhens wide: the wider the river, the shallower. The frequent bends and turns, the rapid flow and the shallows offer no hope that it will ever be navigable in the real sense of the word. In Polyakov's opinion it would probably be used only for floating rafts. Only the last 70 to 100 versts from the mouth of the river, where it is least favorable for colonization, are deeper and straighter. Here the flow is slower, and there are no rapids or sandbanks. A steam cutter or even a shallow-draft tugboat could use this part of the river.

When the rich fisheries in the neighborhood fall into the hands of capitalists, serious attempts will probably be made to clear and deepen the waterway. Perhaps a railroad will be built along the river to its mouth, and there is no doubt that the river will repay all these expenditures with interest. But this is far in the future. Under existing conditions, when we consider only the immediate future, the riches of the Tym are almost an illusion. It offers disappointingly little to the penal colony. The Tymovsk settler lives under the same starvation conditions as the Alexandrovsk settler.

According to Polyakov, the Tym River valley is dotted with lakes, bogs, ravines and pits. It has no straight and level expanses overgrown with nutritious fodder grasses, it has no fertile meadows watered by spring floods, and only rarely are sedge-covered meadows found—these are islands overgrown with coarse grass. A thick coniferous forest covers the slopes of the hill. On these slopes we find birches, willows, elms, aspens and entire stands of poplars. The poplars are extremely tall. They are undermined at the banks and fall into the water, where they look like bushes and beaver dams. The bushes here are the bird cherry, the osier, the sweetbrier, the hawthorn. . . . Swarms of mosquitoes are everywhere. There was frost on the morning of August 1.

The closer you get to the sea, the sparser the vegetation.

Slowly the poplar vanishes, the willow tree becomes a bush; the general scene is dominated by the sandy or turfy shore with whortleberries, cloudberries and moss. Gradually the river widens to 75–100 sazhens; now the tundra has taken over, the coastline consists of lowlands and marshes. . . . A freezing wind blows in from the ocean.

The Tym falls into Nyisky Bay, or the Tro, a small watery wasteland which is the doorway to the Okhotsk Sea, or, which is the same thing, into the Pacific Ocean. The first night Polyakov spent on the shores of the bay was bright and chilly, and a small twin-tailed comet glistened in the sky. Polyakov does not describe the thoughts which crowded in upon him as he enjoyed the sight of the comet and listened to the sounds of the night. Sleep overtook him. On the next day fate rewarded him with an unexpected spectacle. At the mouth of the bay stood a dark ship with some white strakes; the rigging and deckhouse were beautiful; a tied live eagle sat on the prow.[4]

The shore of the bay made a dismal impression on Polyakov. He calls it a typically characteristic example of a polar landscape. The vegetation is meager and malformed. The bay is separated from the sea by a long, narrow sandy tongue of land created by dunes, and beyond this slip of land the morose, angry sea has spread itself boundlessly for thousands of versts. When a little boy has been reading Mayne Reid and his blanket falls off during the night, he starts shivering, and it is then that he dreams of such a sea. It is a nightmare! The surface is leaden, over it there hangs a monotonous gray sky, and the savage waves batter the wild treeless shore. The waves roar, and once in a great while the black shape of a whale or a seal flashes through them.[5]

Today there is no need to cross the Pilinga by climbing over steep hills and through gulleys in order to reach the Tymovsk district. I have already stated that people nowadays travel from Alexandrovsk to the Tymovsk district through the Arkovo valley and change horses at the Arkovo way station. The roads here are excellent and the horses can travel swiftly.

The first settlement of the Tymovsk region lies sixteen miles past the Arkovo way station bearing the Oriental-fairy-tale name of Upper Armudan. It was founded in 1884 and consists of two parts which have spread along the slopes of the mountain near the Armudan River, a tributary of the Tym. It has 178 inhabitants: 123 male and 55 female. There are 78 homesteads with 28 co-owners. Settler Vasilyev even has two co-owners. In comparison with Alexandrovsk, the majority of the Tymovsk settlements, as the reader will see, have many co-owners or half-owners, few women and very few legally married families. In Upper Armudan, of 48 families, only 9 are legal. There are only three free women who followed their husbands, and it is the same in Krasny Yar or Butakovo, which are no more than a year old. This insufficiency of women and families in the Tymovsk settlements is often astounding, and does not conform with the average number of women and families on Sakhalin. It cannot be explained by any local or economic conditions, but by the fact that newly arrived prison parties are sorted out in Alexandrovsk, and the local authorities, according to the proverb that "your own shirt is nearest to your body," retain the majority of the women in their own district and "keep the best for themselves; the worst they send to us," as a Tymovsk official told me.

The huts in Upper Armudan are either thatched or covered with tree bark; some windows have no panes or are completely boarded up. The poverty is terrible. Twenty of the men do not live at home. They have gone elsewhere to earn a livelihood. Only 60 desyatins of land have been cultivated for all 75 homesteads and 28 co-owners; 183 poods of grain have been sown, which is less than 2 poods per household. It is beyond my understanding how grain can be grown here, however much is sown. The settlement is high above sea level and is not protected from northern winds; the snow melts two weeks later than in the neighboring settlement of Malo-Tymovo. In order to fish, they travel 20 to 25 versts to the Tym River in the summer. They hunt fur animals more for sport than for gain, and so little accrues to the economy of the settlement that it is scarcely worth talking about.

I found the householders and the members of their households at home; none of them were occupied even though it was not a holiday, and it seemed that during the warm August weather all of them, from the youngest to the oldest, could have found work either in the field or on the Tym, where the periodic fish was running. The householders and their cohabitants were obviously bored and eager to sit down and discuss anything at all. They laughed from boredom and sometimes cried. They are failures, and most of them are neurasthenics and whiners, "alienated persons." Forced idleness has slowly become a habit and they spend their time waiting for good sea weather, become fatigued, have no desire to sleep, do nothing, and are probably no longer capable of doing anything except shuffling cards. It is not strange that card-playing flourishes in Upper Armudan and the local players are famous all over Sakhalin. Because of lack of money they play for small stakes, but make up for this by playing continually, as in the play *Thirty Years, or the Life of a Card Player*.[6] I had a conversation with one of the most impassioned and indefatigable card-players, a settler called Sizov:

"Your worship, why don't they send us to the mainland?" he asked.

"Why do you want to go there?" I asked jokingly. "You'll have no one to play cards with."

"That's where the real games are."

"Do you play faro?" I asked, and held my tongue.

"That's right, your worship, I play faro."

Later, upon leaving Upper Armudan, I asked my convict driver:

"Do they play for winnings?"

"Naturally, for winnings."

"But what do they lose?"

"What do you mean? Why, they lose their government rations, their smoked fish! They lose their food and clothing and sit about in hunger and cold."

"And what do they eat?"

"Why, sir, when they win, they eat; when they lose, they go to sleep hungry."

Along the lower reaches of the same tributary there is a smaller settlement, Lower Armudan. I arrived late at night and slept in a garret in the jail because the jailer did not permit me to stay in a room. "It's impossible to sleep here, your worship; the bugs and cockroaches win all the time!" he said helplessly, spreading his hands wide. "Please go up to the tower." I climbed to the tower on a ladder, which was soaked and slippery from the rain. When I descended to get some tobacco I saw the "winning creatures," and such things are perhaps only possible on Sakhalin. It seemed as though the walls and ceiling were covered with black crepe, which stirred as if blown by a wind. From the rapid and disorderly movements of portions of the crepe you could guess the composition of this boiling, seething mass. You could hear rustling and a loud whispering, as if the insects were hurrying off somewhere and carrying on a conversation.[7]

There are 101 settlers in Lower Armudan: 76 male and 25 female. There are 47 homesteaders with 23 co-owners. Four families are married; 15 live as cohabitants. There are only two free women. There are no inhabitants between 15 and 20 years of age. The people live in dire poverty. Only six of the houses are covered with planking; the rest are covered with tree bark and, as in Upper Armudan, some have no windowpanes or are boarded up. My records include not a single laborer. Obviously the householders do nothing. In order to find work, 21 of them have left. Since 1884, when the settlement was founded, only 37 desyatins of arable land have been cleared—i.e., one-half desyatin per homestead. One hundred eighty-three poods of winter grain and summer corn have been sown. The settlement in no way resembles an agricultural village. The local inhabitants are a disorganized rabble of Russians, Poles, Finns and Georgians, starving and ragged, who came together not of their own volition but by chance, after a shipwreck.

The next settlement along the route lies on the Tym. Founded in 1880, it was named Derbinskoye in honor of the jailer Derbin, who was murdered for his cruelty. He was still young, but a brutish, stern and implacable fellow. The people who knew him recall that he always walked around the prison and on the streets with a stick which he used for beating people. He was murdered in the bakery. He defended himself and fell into the fermenting bread batter, bloodying the dough. His death was greeted with great rejoicing by the convicts, who donated a purse of 60 rubles to the murderer.

There is nothing else amusing in Derbinskoye. It lies on a flat and narrow piece of land, once covered with a thick birch and ash forest. Below, there is a wide stretch of marshland, seemingly unfit for settlement, once thickly covered with fir and deciduous trees. They had scarcely finished cutting down the forest and clearing stumps in order to build the huts, the jail and the government storehouse, and draining the area, when they were forced to battle with a disaster which none of the colonizers had foreseen. During the spring, the high water of the Amga stream flooded the entire settlement. They had to dig another bed and re-channel it. Now Derbinskoye has an area of more than a square verst and resembles a real Russian village.

You enter by a splendid wooden bridge; the stream babbles, the banks are green with willows, the streets are wide, the huts have plank roofs and gardens. There are new prison buildings, all kinds of storehouses and warehouses, and the house of the prison warden stands in the middle of the settlement, reminding you not so much of a prison as of a manorial estate. The warden is continually going from warehouse to warehouse, and he clanks his keys exactly like a landlord in the good old days who guards his stores day and night. His wife sits near the house in the front garden, majestic as a queen, and she sees that order is kept. Right in front of her house, in an open hothouse, she can see her fully ripened watermelons. The convict gardener Karatayev tends them with indulgence and with a slavish diligence. She can see the convicts fishing in the river, bringing back healthy, choice salmon called *sere-bryanka* [silver fish], which are then cured and given to the officials; they are not given to the convicts. Near the garden play little girls dressed like angels. A convict dressmaker, convicted for arson, sews their clothes. There is a feeling of quiet contentment and ease. These people walk softly like cats, and they also express themselves softly, in diminutives: little fish, little cured fish, little prison rations. . . .

There are 739 inhabitants in Derbinskoye, 442 male and 297 female. Altogether, including the prison population, there is a total of about 1,000. There are 250 householders and 58 co-owners. In its outward aspects as well as in the age groups of the inhabitants and, generally, in all the statistics concerning the place, it is one of the few settlements on Sakhalin which can seriously be called a settlement and not a haphazard rabble of people. It has 121 legitimate families. Twelve of them are free, and among the legally married, free women predominate. There are 103 free women. Children comprise one-third of the population.

However, in attempting to understand the economic status of the Derbinskoye inhabitants, you have to confront the various chance circumstances, which play their major and minor roles as they do in other Sakhalin settlements. Here natural law and economic laws appear to take second place, ceding their priority to such accidental variables as the greater or lesser number of unemployables, the number of sick people, the number of robbers, the number of former citizens forced to become farmers, the number of old people, their proximity to the prison, the personality of the warden, etc., etc., and all of these conditions can change every five years or even less than five years. Those who completed their sentences prior to 1881 were the first to settle here, carrying on their backs the bitter past of the settlement, and they suffered, and gradually took over the better land and homesteads. Those who arrived from Russia with money and families are able to live well. The 220 desyatins of land and the yearly production of 3,000 poods of fish, as shown in the records, obviously pertain to the economic position of these homesteaders. The remainder of the inhabitants, more than one-half of the population of

Derbinskoye, are starving, in rags, and give the impression of being useless and superfluous; they are hardly alive, and they prevent others from living. In our own Russian villages even fires produce no such sharp distinctions.

It was raining, cold and muddy when I arrived in Derbinskoye and visited the huts. Because of his own small quarters, the warden gave me lodging in a new, recently completed warehouse, which was stored with Viennese furniture. They gave me a bed and a table, and put a latch on the door so that I could lock myself in from inside.

All evening to two o'clock in the morning I read or copied data from the list of homesteads and the alphabetical list of the inhabitants. The rain fell continually, rattling on the roof, and once in a while a belated prisoner or soldier passed by, slopping through the mud. It was quiet in the warehouse and in my soul, but I had scarcely put out the candle and gone to bed when I heard a rustling, whispering, knocking, splashing sound, and deep sighs. Raindrops fell from the ceiling onto the latticework of the Viennese chairs and made a hollow, ringing sound, and after each such sound someone whispered in despair: "Oh, my God, my God!" Next to the warehouse was the prison. Were the convicts coming at me through an underground passage? But then there came a gust of wind, the rain rattled even more strongly, somewhere a tree rustled—and again, a deep, despairing sigh: "Oh, my God, my God!"

In the morning I went out on the steps. The sky was gray and overcast, the rain continued to fall, and it was muddy. The warden walked hurriedly from door to door with his keys.

"I'll give you such a ticket you'll be scratching yourself for a week," he shouted. "I'll show you what kind of ticket you'll get!"

These words were intended for a group of twenty prisoners who, from the few phrases I overheard, were pleading to be sent to the hospital. They were ragged, soaked by the rain, covered with mud and shivering. They wanted to demonstrate in mime exactly what ailed them, but on their pinched, frozen faces it somehow came out false and crooked, although they were probably not lying at all. "Oh, my God, my God!" someone sighed, and my nightmare seemed to be continuing. The word "pariah" comes to mind, meaning that a person can fall no lower. During my entire sojourn on Sakhalin only in the settlers' barracks near the mine and here, in Derbinskoye, on that rainy, muddy morning, did I live through moments when I felt that I saw before me the extreme limits of man's degradation, lower than which he cannot go.

In Derbinskoye there is a convict, a former baroness, whom the local women call "the working baroness." She lives a simple, laborer's life, and they say she is content with her circumstances. One former Moscow merchant who once had a shop on Tverskaya-Yamskaya told me with a sigh, "The racing season is on in Moscow," and then, turning to the settlers, he began to explain what kind of races they were and how many people go on Sundays to the racecourse along Tverskaya-Yamskaya. "Believe me, your worship," he said, his excitement mounting as he discussed the racecourse, "I would give everything, my whole life, if I could see not Russia, not Moscow, but the Tverskaya!"

In Derbinskoye there live two people called Emelyan Samokhvalov, who are related to one another, and I remember that in the yard of one of them I saw a rooster tied up by its legs. The people of Derbinskoye are amused by the fact that these two Emelyan Samokhvalovs were by a strange and very complex combination of events brought together from the opposite ends of Russia to Derbinskoye, bearing the same name and being related to one another.

On August 27, General Kononovich arrived in Derbinskoye with the commandant of the Tymovsk district, A. M. Butakov, and another young official. All three were intelligent and interesting people. The four of us went on a small trip. From beginning to end we were beset with so much discomfort that it turned out to be not a trip at all; it was a parody of an expedition.

First of all, it was pouring. It was muddy and slippery; everything you touched was soaking wet. Water leaked through our collars after running down our necks; our boots were cold and wet. To smoke a cigarette was a complicated, difficult affair which was accomplished only when we all helped one another. Near Derbinskoye we got into a rowboat and went down the Tym. On the way we stopped to inspect the fisheries, a water mill and plowland belonging to the prison. I will describe the fishing elsewhere; we all agreed the water mill was wonderful; and the fields were nothing special, being interesting only because they were so small; a serious homesteader would regard them as child's play.

The river was swift, and the four rowers and the steersman worked in unison. Because of the speed and frequent bends in the river, the scenery changed every minute. We were floating along a mountain taiga river, but all of its wild charms, the green banks, the steep hills and the lone motionless figures of the fishermen, I would have enthusiastically exchanged for a warm room and dry shoes, especially since the landscape was monotonous, not novel to me, and, furthermore, it was covered with gray, rainy mist. A. M. Butakov sat on the bow with a rifle and shot at wild ducks which were startled at our approach.

Northeast from Derbinskoye along the Tym there are only two settlements to date, Voskresenskoye and Uskovo. To settle the Tym up to its mouth would require at least thirty such settlements with ten versts between each of them. The administration plans to set up one or two every year, connecting them with a road which will eventually span the distance between Derbinskoye and Nyisky Bay. The road will bring life and stand guard over a whole series of settlements. As we came close to Voskresenskoye, a guard stood at attention, obviously expecting us. A. M. Butakov shouted to him that on returning from Uskovo we would spend the night there and that he should prepare more straw.

A little while later, the air was strongly permeated with the stench of rotting fish. We were approaching the Gilyak village of Usk-vo, the former name of the present Uskovo. We were met on shore by Gilyaks, their wives, children and bobtailed dogs, but our coming was not regarded with the same amazement as the coming of the late Polyakov. Even the children and the dogs looked at us calmly.

The Russian colony is two versts from the riverbank. In Uskovo the same conditions exist as in Krasny Yar. The street is wide with many tree trunks still to be uprooted, full of hillocks, covered with forest grass, and on each side stand unfinished huts, felled trees and piles of rubble. All new construction on Sakhalin gives the impression of having been destroyed by an enemy or else of being long since abandoned. Only the fresh, bright colors of the hut frames and the shavings give evidence that something quite opposite to destruction is taking place.

Uskovo has 77 inhabitants, 59 male and 18 female, 33 householders and 20 other persons—in other words, co-owners. Only nine have families. When the people of Uskovo gathered around the jail, where we were taking tea, and when the women and children, being more curious, came up front, the crowd looked like a gypsy camp. Among the women there were actually several dark-skinned gypsies with sly, hypocritically sorrowful faces, and almost all the children were gypsies. Uskovo has a few convict gypsies whose bitter fate is shared by their families, who followed them voluntarily. I was slightly acquainted with two or three of the gypsy women. A week before my arrival at Uskovo I had seen them in Rykovskoye with rucksacks on their backs begging at people's windows.[8]

The Uskovo inhabitants live very poorly. Only eleven desyatins of land are cultivated for grain and kitchen gardens—that is, almost one-fifth of a desyatin per homestead. All live at government expense, receiving prison rations which are not acquired cheaply because they have to carry them on their backs over the roadless taiga from Derbinskoye.

After a rest, we set out at five o'clock in the afternoon on foot for Voskresenskoye. The distance is short, only six versts, but because of my inexperience in walking through the taiga I began to feel tired after the first verst. It was raining heavily. Immediately after leaving Uskovo we had to cross a stream about a sazhen wide on thin, crooked logs.

My companions crossed safely, but I slipped and got my boot full of water. Before us lay a long, straight road cut through the forest for a projected highway. There was literally not one sazhen which you could walk without being thrown off balance or stumbling: hillocks, holes full of water, stiff tangles of bushes or roots treacherously concealed under the water, and against these you stumble as against a doorstep. The most unpleasant of all were the windfalls and the piles of logs cut down in order to carve out the road. You climb up one pile, sweat, and go on walking through the mud, and then you find another pile of logs and there is no way of bypassing it. So you start climbing again, while your companions shout that you are going the wrong way, it should be either left or right of the pile, etc. At the beginning I tried not to get my other boot full of water, but soon I gave up and resigned myself to it. I could hear the labored breathing of the three settlers who were following behind, carrying our belongings. I was fatigued by the oppressive weather, shortness of breath and thirst. We walked without our service caps; it was easier.

The breathless general sat down on a thick log. We sat down beside him. We gave a cigarette to each of the settlers, who dared not sit down.

"Well, it's hard going!"

"How many versts to Voskresenskoye?"

"Three more."

A. M. Butakov walked the most briskly. He had formerly covered tremendous distances over the taiga and tundra, and a six-verst hike was nothing to him. He described his trip along the Poronay River and around Terpeniya Bay. The first day you are exhausted, all your strength gone, the second day your entire body aches but it is already becoming easier to walk; on the third and following days you feel you have sprouted wings, you are not walking but are being carried along by some unknown force, although your legs continue to get entangled in the merciless marsh grass and stuck in swamps.

Halfway it began to grow dark and soon we were surrounded by pitch darkness. I gave up hope that we would ever end our trip, and just groped ahead, splashing in water to my knees, and bumping into logs. Here and there the will-o'-the-wisps gleamed and flickered; entire pools and tremendous rotting trees were lit with phosphorescent colors and my boots were covered with moving sparks which shimmered like the glowworms on a midsummer night.

But, thank God, at last a light shone in front of us, and was not phosphorescent, but a real light. Someone shouted at us, and we answered. The warden appeared with a lantern. Across pools brightly lit by his lantern, he came with large strides to lead us across the whole of Voskresenskoye, which was barely visible in the darkness, until at last we reached his quarters.[9]

My companions had brought with them a change of clothing. When they reached the warden's quarters they hastened to change. But I had nothing with me, although I was literally soaked through. We drank some tea, talked a bit and went to sleep. There was only one bed in the warden's quarters, and this was taken by the general, while we ordinary mortals went to sleep on straw heaped on the floor.

Voskresenskoye is twice as large as Uskovo. Inhabitants, 183: 175 male and 8 female. There are 7 free families but not one legally married. There are few children in the settlement and only one little girl. It has 97 homesteaders and 77 co-owners.

1 Four years later L. I. Shrenk traveled along the Tym to the eastern shore and back. He also journeyed during the winter when the river was covered with snow.

2 He is now dead. He died soon after his tour of Sakhalin. Judging from his hastily written and sketchy notes, he was a talented and erudite person. His articles include: "Journey on Sakhalin Island 1881–1882" (Letters to the Secretary of the Society) included in Vol. XIX of *Reports of the Imperial Russian Geographical Society* (1883); "Report on Explorations on Sakhalin Island and in the Yuzhno-Ussuruysky Kray," Supplement

No. 6, Vol. XLVIII of *Notes of the Imperial Academy of Science* (1884); and "On Sakhalin," *News* (1885), No. 1.

3   With regard to this station, the guard acts somewhat like a former king toward his obligations, having nothing whatsoever to do with them.

4   A two-sazhen pole could not reach bottom at the river's mouth. A large boat could anchor in the bay. If shipping developed on the Okhotsk Sea near Sakhalin, ships would find calm and completely safe anchorage in this bay.

5   Mining Engineer Lopatin saw the sea covered with ice here in the middle of June. The ice remained until July. The water in the teakettle froze on St. Peter's Day [June 29].

6   A novel written by the French novelist Victor Henri Ducange (1783–1853).—TRANS.

7   The people of Sakhalin believe the insects and cockroaches come from the moss, which is brought from the forest and used here to caulk the dwellings. This belief arises from the fact that the insects and cockroaches appear in the chinks when they have barely finished caulking the walls. Obviously it is not due to the moss. The carpenters who sleep in the prison or in the settlers' huts bring the insects with them.

8   A writer who was on Sakhalin two years after me found an entire drove of horses near Uskovo.

9   It took us three hours to walk the six versts from Uskovo to Voskresenskoye. If the reader can imagine a hiker loaded down with flour, bacon and other government stores, or a sick person who must walk from Uskovo to Rykovskoye to the hospital there, he will understand the meaning of the common Sakhalin phrase, "There is simply no road." It is impossible to go by wagon or horseback. There have been occasions when those who attempted to go on horseback failed, because the horses broke their legs.

X *Rykovskoye - The Local Prison - The Meteorological Station of M. N. Galkin-Vrasky - Palevo - Mikryukov - Valzy and Longari - Malo-Tymovo - Andreye-Ivanovskoye*

IN THE UPPER REACHES of the Tym River, especially in its southernmost watershed, we encountered a more developed life. Here, whatever else there is, the climate is warmer, nature's tints are softer, and starving, freezing man finds more favorable natural conditions than in the middle or lower reaches of the river. Here the scenery is reminiscent of Russia. This resemblance, so enchanting and moving to the convict, is especially noticeable in the plain surrounding the Rykovskoye settlement. This is the administrative center of the Tymovsk region, and the plain is about six versts wide. A low mountain range shelters it somewhat from the easternwinds, while in the west the spurs of a tremendous watershed show blue in the distance. There are no hills or elevations. It is a completely flat and familiar Russian plain with plowlands, meadows, pastures and green groves. Polyakov first saw it when the entire valley was covered with hillocks, pits and water-filled hollows, and with little lakes and rivulets flowing into the river Tym. He rode horseback, and his horse floundered through knee-high and breast-high swamps. Now the area has been completely cleared and drained, and from Derbinskoye to Rykovskoye there stretches an exemplary road, 14 versts long, amazing in its smoothness and straightness.

Rykovskoye, or Rykovo, was settled in 1878; it was happily chosen and designated as the site of a settlement by the prison warden, a noncommissioned officer called Rykov. It is distinguished by its rapid growth, unusual even for a Sakhalin settlement. The area and population have quadrupled in the past five years. At present it covers 3 square versts and contains 1,368 inhabitants: 831 male and 537 female. Including the prison and the military detachment, there are over 2,000 people. It does not resemble the Alexandrovsk Post. It is a small town, a small Babylon, containing gambling houses and even family bath houses maintained by a Jew. It is a real, raw Russian village with no pretensions to culture.

As you ride or walk down the street, which stretches for three versts, you soon become bored with its monotonous length. Roads are not called *slobodkas,* Siberian fashion, as in Alexandrovsk, but streets, and the majority retain names given them by the settlers themselves. There is a Sizovskaya Street, so called from the hut of the woman settler Sizovaya which stands on the corner; there is a Khrebtovaya [Backbone] Street, and a Malorossyskaya [Little Russian] Street.

There are many Ukrainians living in Rykovskoye and therefore in no other settlement will you probably come across such exquisite surnames as: Zheltonog [Yellow Foot] and Zheludok [Stomach]. There are nine people called Bezbozhny [Godless]. Also Zaryvay [Buried], Reka [River], Bublyk [Doughnut], Sivokobylka [Gray Filly], Koloda [Fetter], Zamozdrya [Behind Mortared Walls], etc.

In the middle of the settlement there stands a wooden church, surrounded not with shops as in our villages but with prison buildings, offices and the officials' living quarters. As you walk across the square you seem to be on a noisy, happy fairground; you hear the loud voice of the Uskovo gypsies trading horses, you smell tar, manure and smoked fish, you hear lowing cows, and the shrieking of accordions mixed with drunken songs. But the peaceful scene comes to an end when you suddenly hear the clang of chains and the shuffling feet of the prisoners and guards making their way back to prison across the square.

Rykovskoye has 335 householders and 189 half-owners jointly working the homesteads. The half-owners consider themselves householders. There are 195 legally married families, and 91 cohabitants. The majority of the legal wives are free women who followed their husbands. There are 155 of them. These figures are high, but they are no cause for joy or enthusiasm, for they promise little good. The large number of half-owners, those supernumerary householders, indicates the large proportion of deprived people who have no means or possibility to work their own homesteads. It shows how crowded and famished the place is.

The Sakhalin administration sets the people down on small plots of land without any order, giving no consideration to existing conditions and without looking to the future. Their methods of creating new settlements and homesteads are so inefficient that those which are in the comparatively favorable situation of Rykovskoye eventually come to present an appearance of vast poverty, as bad as Upper Armudan. With the existing amount of arable land in Rykovskoye, and under local conditions of productivity, assuming some possible profit, two hundred homesteads would be a magnificent accomplishment. In fact, there are over 500, including the supernumeraries, and yearly the administration continues to add to the number.

The prison in Rykovskoye is new. It is built like all Sakhalin prisons: wooden barracks, cell blocks, filth, dire poverty and discomfort, all those things which are in their very nature inevitable in the gregarious existence within a Sakhalin prison. Recently, for reasons which are quite obvious, the Rykovskoye prison was beginning to be regarded as the best prison in Northern Sakhalin. For my own purposes, too, it was better. I was obtaining information from prison records and employing the services of literate people in all the prisons of the region, and I could not help noticing from the beginning that throughout the entire Tym area, especially in Rykovskoye, there were local clerks who were well trained and disciplined. They worked as though they had all attended a specialized school. The homestead lists and the alphabetical lists of settlers were in exemplary order. Later, when I visited the prison, I found the cooks and bakers and all the rest equally disciplined, and even the older jailers did not seem so satiated, so grossly stupid and so callous as those in Alexandrovsk or Dué.

In the parts of the prison where cleanliness can be maintained, the rule of tidiness was obviously strictly observed. In the kitchen and the bakery, for example, the premises themselves, the very air, the furnishings, dishes and clothing of the employees are so immaculate that they would pass the most rigid sanitary inspection. Quite obviously there is constant supervision for cleanliness, and this is done without any regard for expected visitors.

When I visited the kitchen they were cooking fish soup, a most unhealthy food, for the convicts get bad cases of intestinal flu from the migratory fish caught in the uppermost reaches of the river. Nevertheless, the entire process is so arranged that the convict would appear to receive the full amount of food to which he is entitled by law. Because the work of supervisors, overseers and others inside the prison has attracted privileged exiles responsible for the quantity and quality of the food, I believe that the really terrible features do not arise, and that evil-smelling cabbage soup and bread made from clay are not possible here. I took several loaves of bread from the huge number being prepared and weighed them; and each weighed over three pounds.

The latrine here is constructed in the usual way: it is a cesspool, but it is not maintained in the same way as in other prisons. The demand for cleanliness is so strict that it is probably embarrassing for the prisoners; the latrine is warm, but has no odor. This is achieved by special ventilation described in the famous textbook of Professor Erisman and is brought about by an inverse draft.[1]

The warden of the Rykovskoye prison is Mr. Livin, a talented, experienced man, full of initiative. All the good things at the prison are mainly due to him. Unfortunately he is strongly partial to the use of birch rods, a circumstance which once nearly cost him his life. A convict fell upon him with a knife, as upon a wild beast, with fatal results for the attacker. Mr. Livin's constant concern for the welfare of the people and his simultaneous wielding of birch rods, his ecstatic delight in corporal punishment, and other forms of brutality provide an entirely incongruous and inexplicable combination. Captain Ventzel in Garshin's *Notes of Private Ivanov*[2] was obviously not a fantasy.

Rykovskoye has a school, a telegraph office, a hospital and a meteorological station named after M. N. Galkin-Vrasky, unofficially in the charge of a privileged convict, a former midshipman who is marvelously industrious and kind. He is also the churchwarden. Not too much data has been gathered during the four years of the station's existence, but there is an obvious difference between the two northern districts. While the climate of the Alexandrovsk district is coastal, the Tymovsk climate is continental, although there are only 70 versts between the 2 stations. Temperature changes and the number of days with precipitation are not as marked in Tymovsk. The summer is warmer, the winter more severe; the mean annual temperature is below zero, which is even lower than on Solovetsky Island.

The Tymovsky district is at a greater height above sea level than Alexandrovsk, but because the place is encircled with mountains and lies in a circular valley, it has an average of over 60 calm days and less than 20 days of bitter winds. A small difference is also evident in days with precipitation: Tymovsky has more—116 days of snow and 76 of rain. The amount of precipitation in both regions is quite different, almost by 300 millimeters; however, Alexandrovsk has the greater amount of humidity.

On July 24, 1889, a morning frost killed the Derbinskoye potato blooms. On August 18, all the potato plants in the entire district were killed by frost.

South of Rykovskoye, on the site of a former Gilyak village called Palevo, on a tributary of the Tym bearing the same name, there stands the Palevo settlement, founded in 1886. A good country road leads from Rykovskoye over a flat plain along groves and fields which were very suggestive of Russia, perhaps because I came here during excellent weather. The road is 14 versts long. A telegraph and post road, projected some time ago from Rykovskoye to Palevo, will soon unite Northern and Southern Sakhalin. The road is now under construction.

Palevo has 396 inhabitants, 345 male and 51 female. It has 183 homesteaders and 137 co-owners, although the local conditions warrant no more than 50 homesteaders. It would be difficult to find another such settlement on Sakhalin containing so many varied and unfavorable conditions for an agricultural colony.

The soil is pebbly. According to older people, the Tungus pastured their reindeer at the site of lower Palevo. The settlers also say that in ancient times it was a sea bottom, and the Gilyaks still find parts of ships in the area. Only 108 desyatins of land have been cultivated for pasture, gardens and meadows, while there are over 300 householders. There are only 30 adult females, one for every 10 males, and as though to emphasize the melancholy significance of this proportion with a joke, death recently visited Palevo and struck down 3 females in a few days.

Before their conviction, a third of the convicts were former city dwellers, and did no farming. Unfortunately the list of unfavorable conditions does not end here. For some reason, probably in order to illustrate the old proverb "A really unfortunate man will drown in a teacup," no other Sakhalin settlement has so many thieves as this greatly suffering, unlucky Palevo. Every night there are robberies; on the eve of my arrival three men were put in irons for stealing rye grain. Together with those who steal from hunger, Palevo also has many "mischief makers," who do harm because it amuses them. For no reason at all they will slaughter livestock at night, uproot unripened potatoes and break windowpanes. All this causes severe damage and brings ruin to the wretched, impoverished homesteads. What is even more serious is that it forces the population to live in constant fear.

The living conditions describe poverty and nothing else. The roofs are covered with bark and straw; there are no yards or outbuildings; 49 of the houses are still unfinished and have obviously been abandoned by the owners, 17 of whom have left in search of work.

When I visited the huts in Palevo I was constantly followed by a settler guard named Pskovich. I recall that I asked whether it was Wednesday or Thursday. He answered:

"I can't remember, your worship."

A retired quartermaster, Karp Yerofeyich Mikryukov, the oldest Sakhalin guard, lives in the prison house. He arrived in Sakhalin in 1860, when the Sakhalin penal colony was just being organized. Of all the people on Sakhalin he is the only one who could write its entire history. He is loquacious and answers questions with evident relish and, as is customary with old men, he talks at vast length. His memory is beginning to fail and he can recall accurately only events that happened in the remote past. His furnishings are decent, completely homelike; he even has two oil paintings—one of himself, the other of his deceased wife wearing a flower at her breast. He was born in Vyatskaya *guberniya*. He closely resembles the late writer Fet. He conceals his true age, says he is only sixty-one, but actually is over seventy. He took the daughter of a settler for his second wife; he has six children ranging from one to nine years of age with this young woman. The youngest is still breast-feeding.

My conversation with Karp Yerofeyich lasted past midnight, and all the stories he told me were concerned with penal servitude and its heroes. He told me about the prison superintendent Selivanov who angrily smashed door locks with his fist and was eventually murdered by the convicts for his brutality.

When he went into the half of the house where his wife and children were sleeping, I went out on the street. It was a perfectly quiet, starry night. A watchman was knocking somewhere, and close by, a brook babbled. I stood for a long time and looked at the sky and then at the huts, and it seemed that it was due to some magic that I was 10,000 versts from home, somewhere in Palevo, at the end of the earth where no one can remember the days of the week, and where they really do not have to remember because it makes no difference whether it is Wednesday or Thursday. . . .

Farther south along the projected post road is the Valzy settlement, founded in 1889. It has forty men and not one woman. A week before my arrival in Rykovskoye, three families had been sent farther south to establish the Longari settlement along one of the tributaries of the Poronaya River. I will leave these two settlements which have barely begun to exist to some other writer, who has the opportunity to visit them over a good road and will be able to examine them closely.

To conclude my survey of the Tymovsk district settlements, there remain only two: the Malo-Tymovo and the Andreye-Ivanovsko. Both are situated on the Malo Tym River, which starts near the Pilinga and falls into the Tym near Derbinskoye. The first, the oldest settlement in the Tymovsk district, was founded in 1877. Formerly, when they crossed the Pilinga, the road to the Tym crossed this settlement. It now has 190 inhabitants: 111 male and 79 female. Together with co-owners, there are 67 homesteaders. Previously Malo-Tymovo was the chief settlement and central part of what is now the Tymovsk district; today it has no great importance and resembles an unimportant village where all life has come to a standstill. Its former importance is evident only in the small prison and in the house where the prison warden resides.

At present the post of prison warden is held by K., an intelligent and kindly young man from Petersburg who is obviously pining for Russia. The large prison quarters with their big, high-ceilinged rooms resounding with his solitary footsteps, and the wearisome days with nothing to do, oppress him to the point that he feels that he is himself in prison. Quite deliberately this young man rises early, at four or five o'clock in the morning. Then he drinks some tea and visits the prison—and then, what is there to do? He paces within the labyrinth, gazing at the oakum-packed wooden walls, then he paces some more, and pours out tea, and he hears nothing but his own footsteps and the wailing wind.

Malo-Tymovo has many old inhabitants. Among them I met the Tatar Furazhiyev, who had accompanied Polyakov to Nyisky Bay. He fondly recalls both Polyakov himself and the expedition.

One of the old men, Bogdanov, is probably interesting in the way he lives. He is a sectarian and a pawnbroker. He did not permit me to enter for a long time and after opening the door he expounded on the theme that all kinds of people are walking around—if you let them in they steal anything worthwhile.

The Andreye-Ivanovsko settlement is named after a settler of the same name. It was settled in 1885 on a marsh. It has 382 inhabitants: 277 male and 105 female. Together with co-owners it has 231 homesteaders, although, as in Palevo, 50 would be sufficient. The type of settlers is also unfortunate. As in Palevo there is a surplus of city folk and intelligentsia who have never farmed and there are many who are not of the Orthodox faith: there are 47 Catholics, the same number of Muhammadans and 12 Lutherans. Among the Orthodox are a number of foreigners, including Georgians.[3]

Such a variegated population gives the settlement a riffraff character and prevents it from merging into an agricultural society.

[1] At Rykovskoye prison the draft is achieved in the following way: stoves are lit in the structure over the cesspool, their interior doors hermetically sealed; the air current needed for combustion is obtained from the pit, which is connected to the stoves by a pipe. Thus all fetid gases rise from the pit into the stove and escape by the smokestack. The latrine itself is kept warm by means of the stoves; the air enters the pit through the seat apertures and thence into the smokestack. A match flame held at a toilet seat is noticeably drawn downward.

[2] The story by Vsevolod Mikhailovich Garshin (1855–88) describes the experiences of a young volunteer in an infantry division during the Russo-Turkish war of 1877–78. Captain Ventzel was extremely brutal toward his men.—TRANS.

[3] The former noblemen from Kutais, the brothers Alexey and Teymuras Chikovani, live here. There was a third brother, but he died of consumption. They have no furniture in their hut and only a featherbed lies on the floor. One of them is ill.

XI
*A Projected District - The Stone Age -
Was There Free Colonization? - The Gilyaks -
Their Numerical Composition, Appearance,
Physique, Food, Clothing, Dwellings, Hygiene -
Their Character - Attempts at Their Russification -
Orochi*

BOTH of the northern districts, as the reader may readily
see from my survey of the settlements, cover an area equal
to a small Russian district. It is impossible to compute the
area of both of them because there are no northern and
southern boundaries. Between the administrative centers of
both districts, the Alexandrovsk Post and Rykovskoye, there
is a distance of 60 versts by the shorter route which crosses
the Pilinga, while across the Arkovskaya valley it is 74
versts. In this kind of country these are large distances.
Without considering Tangi and Vangi, even Palevo is considered a distant settlement. Meanwhile the newly founded
settlements to the south of Palevo on the Poronaya tributaries raise the question of whether a new district will
have to be established.

As an administrative unit, a Sakhalin district corresponds to a Russian district. According to the Siberian way
of thinking, this term can only be applied to a postal distance which cannot be traveled in under a month, as for
example the Anadyrsky district. To a Siberian official
working alone in an area of 200 to 300 versts, the breaking up of Sakhalin into small districts would be a luxury.
The Sakhalin population, however, lives under exceptional
conditions and the administrative mechanism is far more
complicated than in the Anadyrsky district. The need to
break up the penal colonies into small administrative units
has been shown by experience, and this has proved, in addition to other matters to be explained later, that the shorter

the distances in the penal colony, the easier and more effective is the administration. Also, a breakup into smaller districts has the effect of enlarging the number of officials, and the result is an influx of new people who inevitably have a beneficial influence on the colony. And so with a quantitative increase of intelligent people on the staff, there occurs a significant increase in quality.

When I arrived in Sakhalin I heard a great deal of talk about a newly projected district. They described it as the Land of Canaan, because the plan called for a road which would cross the entire region southward along the Poronaya River. It was believed that the convicts at Dué and Voyevodsk would be transferred to the new district, and these horrifying places would become nothing more than a memory. Also, the mines would be taken away from the "Sakhalin Company," which had long since broken its contract, and then the mines would be worked by convicts and settlers as a collective enterprise.[1]

Before completing my report on Northern Sakhalin, I feel I should discuss briefly a people who have lived here at different times and continue to live here outside the penal colony.

In the Duyka valley Polyakov found chipped obsidian knives, stone arrows, grinding stones, stone axes and other objects. He came to the conclusion that a people who did not use metal lived in the Dué valley in ancient times; they belonged to the Stone Age. Shards, the bones of dogs and bears, sinkers from large fishing nets, which were found in these formerly inhabited areas, indicate that they made pottery, hunted bear, went fishing and had hunting dogs. Clearly they derived flint from their neighbors on the mainland and on the neighboring islands, because flint does not exist on Sakhalin. Probably the dogs played the same role in their migration as they do now; they are used for drawing sleighs. In the Tym valley Polyakov found the remnants of primitive structures and crude weapons. He concluded that in Northern Sakhalin "it is possible for tribes to survive on a relatively low level of intellectual development; the people who lived here for centuries developed ways to protect themselves from cold, thirst and hunger. In all probability these ancient people lived in relatively small communities and were not a completely settled people."

When sending Boshnyak to Sakhalin, Nevelskoy asked him to verify the rumor about people who had been left on Sakhalin by Lieutenant Khvostov and who had lived, according to the Gilyaks, on the Tym River.[2]

Boshnyak was successful in discovering traces of these people. In one Tym River settlement the Gilyaks exchanged four pages torn from a prayerbook for three arshins of nankeen cloth, saying the prayerbook had been the property of Russians who had once lived there. On the title page, in barely legible script, were the words: "We, Ivan, Danilo, Pyotr, Sergey and Vasily, were landed in the Aniva settlement of Tomari-Aniva by Khvostov on August 17, 1805. We moved to the Tym River in 1810 when the Japanese arrived in Tomari." Later, exploring the area where the Russians had lived, Boshnyak concluded that they had lived in three huts and cultivated gardens. The natives told him that the last of the Russians, Vasily, died recently, that they were fine people, that they went fishing and hunting with the natives and dressed native fashion except for cutting their hair. Elsewhere the natives informed him that two of the Russians had had children with native women. Today the Russians left by Khvostov on Northern Sakhalin have been forgotten and nothing is known of their children.

Boshnyak adds that as a result of his constant inquiries concerning any Russians settled on the island, he learned from natives in the Tangi settlement that some thirty-five or forty years ago there had been a shipwreck, the crew were saved and they built themselves first a house and later a boat. They made their way across La Pérouse to the Tatar Strait by boat and they were again shipwrecked near the village of Mgachi. This time only one man was saved. His name was Kemets. Not long afterward two Russians came from the Amur. Their names were Vasily and Nikita, and they joined Kemets and built themselves a house in

Mgachi. They hunted game professionally and traded with the Manchurians and Japanese.

One Gilyak showed Boshnyak a mirror supposedly given to his father by Kemets. The Gilyak would not sell the mirror at any price, saying that he was keeping it as a precious memento of his father's friend. Vasily and Nikita were terrified of the Tsar, and it is obvious that they had escaped from his prisons. All three died on Sakhalin.

The Japanese Mamia-Rinzo[3] learned in 1808 on Sakhalin that Russian boats often appeared on the western side of the island, and the piracy practiced by the Russians eventually forced the natives to expel one group of Russians and to massacre another. Mamia-Rinzo names these Russians as Kamutsi, Simena, Momu and Vasire. "The last three," says Shrenk, "are easily recognizable as the Russian names Semyon, Foma and Vasily. Kamutsi is quite similar to Kemets," in his opinion.

This short history of eight Sakhalin Robinson Crusoes exhausts all the data concerning the free colonization of Northern Sakhalin. If the extraordinary fate of five of Khvostov's sailors, Kemets and the two refugees from prison resembles an attempt at free colonization, this attempt must be regarded as insignificant and completely unsuccessful. The really important fact is that they all lived on Sakhalin for a long time, and to the end of their lives not one of them engaged in agriculture. They lived by fishing and hunting.

To round out the picture I must mention the local indigenous population—the Gilyaks. They live on the western and eastern banks of Northern Sakhalin and along the rivers, especially the Tym.[4]

The villages are old; their names, mentioned in the writings of old authors, have come down without change. However, their way of life cannot be called completely settled, because a Gilyak feels no ties toward his birthplace or to any particular place. They often leave their yurts to practice their trades, and to wander over Northern Sakhalin with their families and dogs. But as to their wanderings, even when they are forced to take long journeys to the mainland, they remain faithful to the island, and the Sakhalin Gilyak differs in language and customs from the Gilyak living on the mainland no less than the Ukrainian differs from the Muscovite.

In view of this, it seems to me that it would not be very difficult to count the number of Sakhalin Gilyaks without confusing them with those who come for trading purposes from the Tatar shore. There would be no harm in taking a census of them every five to ten years; otherwise the important question of the influence of the penal colony on their numbers will long remain open and will be solved in a quite arbitrary fashion.

According to data gathered by Boshnyak in 1856, there were 3,270 Gilyaks on Sakhalin. Fifteen years later Mitsul found only 1,500, and the latest data which I obtained from the prison copy of *Statistical Records of Foreigners,* 1889, showed there were only 320 Gilyaks in both regions. If these figures hold true, not one Gilyak will remain in ten or fifteen years' time. I cannot judge the correctness of the figures given by Boshnyak and Mitsul, but the official figure of 320 can have no significance whatsoever. There are several reasons for this. Statistics on foreigners are calculated by clerks who have neither the educational background nor the practical knowledge to do it, and they are given no instructions. When they gather information at the Gilyak settlements, they naturally conduct themselves in an overbearing manner. They are rude and disagreeable, in contrast to the polite Gilyaks, who do not permit an arrogant and domineering attitude toward people. Because they are averse to any kind of census or registration, considerable skill is needed in handling them. Also, the data is gathered by the administration without any definite plan, only in passing, and the investigator uses no ethnographic map but works in his own arbitrary fashion. The data on the Alexandrovsk district includes only those Gilyaks who live south of the Vangi settlement, while in the Tymovsky district they counted only those they found near the Rykovskoye settlement. Actually they do not live in this settlement, but pass through it on their way to other places.

Undoubtedly the number of Sakhalin Gilyaks is constantly decreasing, and this judgment can be made simply by eye-count. How large is this decrease? Why is it taking place? Is it because Gilyaks are becoming extinct, or because they are moving to the mainland or farther north on the island? Due to the lack of actual statistics (and our figures on the destructive influence of Russian colonization can be based only on analogies) it is quite possible that up to the present day Russian influence has been insignificant, almost zero, since the Sakhalin Gilyaks live by preference along the Tym and the eastern shores of the island, which the Russian settlements have not yet reached.[5]

The Gilyaks are neither Mongols nor Tungus, but belong to some unknown race which may once have been powerful and ruled all of Asia. Now, living out their last centuries on a small patch of land, they are only a small remnant. Yet they are a wonderful and cheerful people. Because of their unusual sociability and mobility, the Gilyaks long ago succeeded in having relations with all the neighboring peoples, and so it is almost impossible to find a pure-blooded Gilyak without Mongol, Tungus or Ainu elements.

A Gilyak's face is round, flat, moonlike, of yellowish cast, with prominent cheekbones, dirty, with slanting eyes and a barely visible beard. His hair is smooth, black, wiry, gathered into a braid at the nape of the neck. His facial expression is not savage; it is always intelligent, gentle, naïvely attentive; he is either blissfully smiling or thoughtfully mournful, like a widow. When he stands in profile with his sparse beard and braid, with a soft, womanish expression, he could be a model for a picture of Kuteykin,[6] and it becomes almost understandable why some travelers regard the Gilyaks as belonging to the Caucasian race.

Anyone who wants to become thoroughly acquainted with the Gilyaks should consult an ethnographic specialist, L. I. Shrenk.[7] I will limit myself to discussing some of the characteristics of local natural conditions, which may be useful as direct or indirect guidance for new colonists.

The Gilyak has a strong, stocky build, and he is of

medium or short stature. Height would be of no advantage to him in the taiga. His bones are thick and distinguished by the strong development of his limbs from rowing and tramping over the hills. This exercise strengthens the muscles, and they indicate powerful musculature and a perpetual, intense struggle against nature. His body is lean, without fat. There are no stout or corpulent Gilyaks. All his fat is used for the warmth which a man on Sakhalin must generate in his body in order to compensate for the heat loss caused by the low temperature and the excessive humidity. It is understandable that a Gilyak should require a good deal of fat in his diet. He eats fatty seal meat, salmon, sturgeon and whale fat. He also eats rare meat in large quantities in raw, dry and frozen form, and because he eats coarse food his chewing muscles are unusually well-developed and all his teeth are badly worn. His food consists exclusively of meat but on rare occasions, at home or while carousing, they add Manchurian garlic or berries to their menus. According to Nevelskoy, the Gilyaks consider agriculture a grievous transgression; whoever plows the land or plants anything will soon die. But they eat the bread which the Russians introduced to them with relish, as a delicacy, and it is not unusual to see a Gilyak in Alexandrovsk or Rykovskoye carrying a loaf of bread under his arm.

The Gilyak's clothing has been adapted to the cold, damp and rapidly changing climate. In the summer he wears a shirt of blue nankeen or daba cloth with trousers of the same material. Over his back, as insurance against changing weather, he wears either a coat or a jacket made of seal or dog fur. He puts on fur boots. In winter he wears fur trousers. All this warm clothing is cut and sewn so as not to impede his deft and quick movements while hunting or while riding with his dogs. Sometimes, in order to be in fashion, he wears convict overalls. Eighty-five years ago Krusenstern saw a Gilyak dressed in a magnificent silk costume "with many flowers woven into it." Today you will not find such a peacock on Sakhalin if you search with a lamp.

As to Gilyak yurts, these again answer the demands of a damp and cold climate. There are both summer and winter yurts. The first are built on stilts, the second are dugouts with timber walls having the form of a truncated pyramid. The wood outside is covered with sod. These yurts are made of cheap material which is always at hand, and when the necessity arises they have no regret at leaving them. They are warm and dry, and are certainly far superior to the damp and cold huts made of bark in which our convicts live when they are working on roads or in the fields. These summer yurts should positively be recommended for gardeners, charcoal makers, fishermen and all convicts and settlers who work outside the prison and not in their homes.

Gilyaks never wash, with the result that even ethnographers find it difficult to ascertain the color of their skins. They never wash their underclothing, and their furs and boots look exactly as if they had just been stripped off a dead dog. The Gilyaks themselves exude a heavy, sharp odor and the close proximity of their dwellings is indicated by the foul, almost unbearable odor of drying fish and rotting fish wastes. Usually near every yurt there is a drying contrivance which is filled to the top with flattened fish, which from afar, especially in the sunshine, looks like strings of coral. Krusenstern found huge masses of tiny maggots an inch thick on the ground surrounding these fish driers. In the winter the yurts are full of pungent smoke issuing from the hearth. In addition, the Gilyak men, their wives and even the children smoke tobacco.

Nothing is known of the diseases and mortality of the Gilyaks, but it may be supposed that the unhealthy, unhygienic circumstances are detrimental to their health. This may be the cause of their short stature, bloated faces, the sluggishness and laziness of their movements; and this is perhaps why the Gilyaks always have weak resistance to epidemics. The devastation on Sakhalin caused by smallpox is well known.

Krusenstern found twenty-seven houses on Sakhalin's northernmost point, between the Elizaveta and Maria capes.

In 1860, P. P. Glen, a participant in a wonderful Siberian expedition, found only traces of the settlement, while in other parts of the island, he tells us, he found evidence that there was once a considerable population. The Gilyaks told him that during the past ten years—i.e., after 1850— the population had been radically reduced by smallpox. It is certain that the terrible smallpox epidemics which devastated Kamchatka and the Kurile Islands did not bypass Sakhalin. Naturally this was not due to the virulence of the smallpox itself but to the Gilyaks' poor ability to resist it. If typhus or diphtheria are brought into the penal colony and reach the Gilyak yurts, the same effect will be achieved as by the smallpox. I did not hear of any epidemics on Sakhalin; it seems there were none for the past twenty years with the exception of an epidemic of conjunctivitis, which can be observed even now.

General Kononovich gave permission to the regional hospitals to accept non-Russian patients at government expense (Order No. 335, 1890). We have no exact observations of Gilyak diseases, but some inferences can be drawn as to the causes of their diseases: dirtiness, excessive use of alcohol, intercourse with Chinese and Japanese,[8] constant closeness to dogs, traumas, etc., etc.

There is no doubt they have frequent illnesses and require medical assistance, and if circumstances permit them to take advantage of the new order granting them admission to the hospitals, the local doctors will have the opportunity of studying them more closely. Medicine cannot arrest their yearly mortality, but perhaps the doctors may discover the circumstances under which our interference with the lives of these people will be least harmful.

The character of the Gilyaks is described in different ways by different authors, but all agree that they are not aggressive, dislike brawls and quarrels, and live peacefully with their neighbors. When strangers appear, they are always suspicious and apprehensive; nevertheless, they greet them courteously, without any protest, and sometimes they will lie, describing Sakhalin in the worst possible light, hoping in this way to discourage strangers from the island. They embraced Krusenstern's companions, and when L. I. Shrenk became ill, the news quickly spread among the Gilyaks and evoked the deepest sympathy.

They lie only when they are trading or when speaking to someone they look upon with suspicion, who is therefore in their eyes dangerous, but before telling a lie they always look at one another—a distinctive childish trait. All other lying and boasting in daily life, outside of trading, is repugnant to them.

The following incident occurred early one evening. Two Gilyaks, one with a beard and the other with a swollen feminine face, lay on the grass in front of a settler's hut. I was passing by. They called out to me and started begging me to enter the hut and bring out their outer clothing, which they had left at the settler's that morning. They themselves did not dare to go in. I told them I had no right to go into someone's hut in the absence of the owner. They grew silent.

"You are a politician?" asked the feminine-looking Gilyak in bad Russian.

"No."

"That means you are a *pishi-pishi?*" [*pisar* means clerk] he said, seeing some paper in my hands.

"Yes, I write."

"How much salary do you get?"

I was earning about 300 rubles a month. I told them the figure. You should have seen the disagreeable and even painful expressions which my answer produced. Both Gilyaks suddenly grabbed their stomachs, and throwing themselves on the ground, they began rolling around exactly as though they had severe stomach cramps. Their faces expressed despair.

"How can you talk that way?" they said. "Why did you say such an awful thing? That's terrible! You shouldn't do that!"

"What did I say that was bad?" I asked.

"Butakov, the regional superintendent, well, he's a big man, gets 200, while you are not even an official—a clerk

—amounts to nothing, and you get 300! You spoke untruth! You shouldn't do that!"

I tried to explain that a regional superintendent remains in one place and therefore only gets 200 rubles. Although I am just a *"pishi-pishi,"* I have come a long way—10,000 versts away. My expenses are greater than Butakov's and therefore I need more money. This calmed the Gilyaks. They exchanged glances, spoke together in Gilyak, and stopped suffering. Their faces showed that they finally believed me.

"It's true, it's true!" said the bearded Gilyak briskly. "That's fine. You may leave now!"

"It's true," nodded the other. "You may go!"

When a Gilyak accepts an obligation, he fulfills it properly. There has never been a single case of a Gilyak dumping mail along the road or embezzling the property of others. Polyakov, who had dealings with Gilyak boatmen, wrote that they were most punctilious in fulfilling an obligation, and this is characteristic of them today when we find them unloading government freight for the prisons.

They are clever, intelligent, cheerful, brash, and are never shy in the society of strong and rich men. They do not accept authority, and they do not even understand the meaning of "older" and "younger." In *The History of Siberia,* by I. Fisher, we read that the renowned Polyakov visited the Gilyaks, who were then "under no foreign domination." They have a word, *dzhanchin,* which denotes "your excellency," and they use it equally to a general or to a rich trader who has a great deal of nankeen and tobacco. Seeing Nevelskoy's picture of the Tsar, they said he must be a strong man who distributes much nankeen and tobacco.

The commandant of the island possesses vast and terrifying powers. Nevertheless, when I was riding with him from Verkhny Armudan to Arkovo, a Gilyak had no compunction about shouting at us imperiously: "Stop!" Then he asked if we had seen his white dog along the road.

As it is often said and written, Gilyaks have no respect for family seniority. A father does not believe he is senior to his son, and a son does not respect his father, but lives as he pleases. An old mother has no more authority in the yurt than a teen-age daughter. Boshnyak wrote that he often saw a son beat his mother and chase her out of the house and no one dared say a word against him. The male members of a family are equal to one another. If you treat Gilyaks to vodka, it must also be served to the very youngest males.

The females are equally without rights, whether it is a grandmother, mother or breast-fed baby girl. They are treated as domestic animals, as chattels, which can be thrown out, sold or kicked like a dog. The Gilyaks pet their dogs, but women—never. Marriage is considered nonsense— much less important, for example, than a drinking bout. It is not accompanied by any religious or superstitious rites. A Gilyak exchanges a spear, a boat or a dog for a young girl, drives her to his yurt and lies down with her on a bearskin—and that is all there is to it. Polygamy is permitted but is not widespread, although there are obviously more women than men. Contempt for women as for a lower creature or possession has come to such a pass that the Gilyak does not consider slavery, in the exact and coarse meaning of the word, as reprehensible. As Shrenk witnessed, the Gilyaks often bring Ainu women home with them as slaves. Plainly a woman is an object of barter, like tobacco or daba cloth. Strindberg, that famous misogynist, who thought women should be slaves of men's desires, follows the Gilyak pattern. If he happened to visit Northern Sakhalin, they would embrace him warmly.

General Kononovich told me he wants to Russify the Sakhalin Gilyaks. I don't know why this is necessary. Furthermore, Russification had already begun long before the general's arrival. It began when some prison wardens, receiving very small salaries, began acquiring expensive fox and sable cloaks at the same time that Russian water jars appeared in Gilyak yurts.[9]

As time passed, the Gilyaks were hired to help in tracking down prisoners who escaped from the prison. There was a reward for capturing them, dead or alive. General

Kononovich ordered Gilyaks to be hired as jailers. One of his orders says this is being done because of the dire need for people who are well acquainted with the countryside, and to ease relations between the local authorities and the non-Russians. He told me personally that his new ruling is also aimed at their Russification.

The first ones approved as jailers were the Gilyaks Vaska, Ibalka, Orkun and Pavlinka (Order No. 308, 1889). Later, Ibalka and Orkun were discharged "for continuous failure to appear at the administrative office to receive their orders," and they then approved Sofronka (Order No. 426, 1889). I saw these jailers; they wore tin badges and revolvers. The most popular and the one who is seen most often is the Gilyak Vaska, a shrewd, sly drunkard. One day I went to the shop supported by the colonization fund and met a large group of the intelligentsia. Someone, pointing at a shelf full of bottles, said that if you drank them all down you would really get drunk, and Vaska smirked fawningly, glowing with the wild joy of a tippler. Just before my arrival a Gilyak jailer on duty killed a convict and the local sages were concerned with only one question: whether he was shot in the chest or in the back—that is, whether to arrest the Gilyak or not.

That their proximity to the prison will not Russify but eventually alienate the Gilyaks does not have to be proved. They are far from understanding our requirements, and there is scarcely any opportunity to explain to them that convicts are caught, deprived of their freedom, wounded and killed not because of caprice, but in the interests of justice. They regard this as coercion, a display of bestiality, and probably consider themselves as hired killers.[10]

If it is absolutely necessary to Russify them and if it cannot be avoided, I believe that when we choose our methods, our primary concern should not be our own needs, but theirs. The order permitting them to become patients in our hospitals, the distribution of aid in the form of flour and groats, as was done in 1886 when the Gilyaks were starving, and the order not to confiscate their property for debt, and the remission of their debts (Order No. 204,

1890), and all similar measures will probably achieve this aim more quickly than tin badges and revolvers.

In addition to the Gilyaks, there are a small number of Oroki, or Orochi, of the Tungus tribe living in Northern Sakhalin. Since they are barely heard of in the colony and since no Russian settlements exist in this area, I merely mention them here.

[1] Among the orders issued by General Kononovich there is one which refers to the long-desired abolition of the Dué and Voyevodsk prisons:

"After inspecting the Voyevodsk prison I became personally convinced that neither the location nor the significance to be attached to the prisoners who are held in it—most of them are long-term convicts or else they are recidivists—can justify the conditions at the prison, or, more accurately, the complete lack of supervision which has been characteristic of the prison from the beginning. The present situation is as follows: the prison stands in a narrow valley one and a half versts north of the Dué Post. Communication with the post exists only along a shore road which is drowned by the tide twice every twenty-four hours, while communication over the mountains is difficult in the summer, and impossible in the winter. The prison warden lives in Dué; so does his assistant. The local garrison supplies the sentries and a number of convoy guards, and they are sent out on various jobs by arrangement with the "Sakhalin Company," which is stationed at the post. Meanwhile there are only a few jailers in the prison, and there is one guard, who is changed daily; the military authorities do not supervise him closely or over a long period of time. Without entering into a discussion of the circumstances which brought about the construction of a prison in such an unlikely locality, where there is no possibility of direct supervision, and before raising the question of whether the Dué and Voyevodsk prisons should be abolished and moving them elsewhere, I must at least partially correct the existing deficiencies," etc. (Order No. 348, 1888).

[2] See Davydov's *The Twofold Journey to America of the Naval Officers Khvostov and Davydov, Written by the Latter. With a Foreword by Shishkov* (1810). In his foreword, Admiral Shishkov states that "Khvostov combined two opposed traits within his soul: the gentleness of a lamb and the ferocity of a lion." He says that Davydov "was more hot-tempered than Khvostov, but was his inferior in toughness and courage." This lamblike gentleness did not prevent Khvostov in 1806 from devastating Japanese ware-

houses and capturing four Japanese on the shore of the Aniva in Southern Sakhalin. In 1807, together with his friend Davydov, he destroyed Japanese factories on the Kurile Islands and again pillaged Southern Sakhalin. These valiant officers fought against Japan without the government's knowledge and with full confidence in their impunity. They ended their lives in an unusual fashion. They were hurrying across a bridge in St. Petersburg at the moment when it was being raised, and they were drowned in the river Neva. Their exploits, which caused quite a sensation at the time, stimulated interest in Sakhalin society; it was discussed and, who knows, perhaps the destiny of this afflicted, terrifying island was even then predetermined. In his foreword Shishkov offers his unfounded belief that the Russians wanted to take possession of the island in the previous century and had actually organized a colony to achieve that purpose.

3 His work is called *To-tats Ki Ko*. I did not read it myself but used the quotations of L. I. Shrenk, the author of *Non-Russians in the Amur Region*.

4 The Gilyaks live in small tribes on both banks of the lower Amur, beginning with Sofyska, then along the Liman, and along the adjacent bank of the Okhotsk Sea and in the northern section of Sakhalin. Existing historical records, dating back two hundred years, show no significant change in their boundaries. The presumption is that Sakhalin was the Gilyak homeland and they later migrated to the nearest part of the mainland, neighboring the Ainu to the south, who were struggling against the Japanese, and also living close to the Japanese.

5 Sakhalin has an official Gilyak and Ainu translator. Since the translator does not know one word of Gilyak or Ainu, and most of the Gilyaks and Ainu do not understand Russian, this unnecessary official may serve as a useful adjunct to the aforementioned inspector of the nonexistent Vedernikovsky way station. If there were an official who knew something about ethnography and statistics instead of a translator, the matter would be handled far better.

6 Kuteykin was a character in the comedy *The Semiliterate*, by Denis Fonvizin (1745–92).—TRANS.

7 His excellent work *Non-Russians in the Amur Region* contains an ethnographic map and two drawings by Mr. Dmitriyev-Orenburgsky. One of them depicts a Gilyak.

8 Our Amur non-Russians and those on Kamchatka were infected with syphilis by the Chinese and Japanese. It was not the fault of

the Russians. One Chinese merchant, a great devotee of opium, told me he has one *babushka,* or wife, living at home in China and another Gilyak *babushka* near Nikolayevsk. Under such conditions it is not difficult to infect the whole of the Amur and Sakhalin region.

9 The warden of the Dué Post, Major Nikolayev, told a correspondent in 1866: "I don't have dealings with them in the summer, but in the winter I often buy furs from them and buy them quite cheaply. You can obtain a fine pair of sables for a bottle of vodka or a loaf of bread."

A correspondent was amazed at the huge number of furs he saw at the home of the major (see Lukashevich, "My Acquaintances in Dué, on Sakhalin," *The Kronstadt News,* 1868, Nos. 47, 49). I will speak of this legendary major on a later occasion.

10 They have no court and do not know the meaning of justice. How difficult it is for them to understand our way of life may be seen from the fact that they have not yet completely understood the purpose of roads. Even where roads have already been built, they continue to travel over the taiga. Often you will see them, their families and dogs laboriously making their way in single file through the marshes beside the road.

XII
My Departure for the South - A Jovial Lady - The Western Shore - The Flux - Mauka - Krilon - Aniva - The Korsakov Post - New Acquaintances - A Northeaster - The Climate of Southern Sakhalin - The Korsakov Prison - The Fire Wagons

ON SEPTEMBER 10 I sailed on the *Baikal,* already familiar to the reader, for Southern Sakhalin. I departed with the greatest pleasure, because I was weary of the North and eager for new impressions. The *Baikal* cast anchor at ten o'clock at night. It was very dark. I stood alone on the stern, looking back and bidding farewell to that gloomy little world guarded from the sea by The Three Brothers, which could scarcely be discerned above the water, resembling in the darkness three black monks. Over the noise of the ship I could hear the waves smashing against the reefs.

Soon Zhonkiyer and The Three Brothers were left far behind, vanishing in the gloom, and I would never see them again. The roar of the breaking waves, expressing an impotent, evil yearning, slowly stilled. We had sailed eight versts when we saw fires gleaming. We were passing the dreadful Voyevodsk prison; a little farther on we saw the fires of Dué. But soon all this vanished, and all we could see was the darkness, and there was a horrible feeling as though we had come out of a terrifying nightmare.

Below deck I came upon a cheerful company. There were several passengers in the wardroom as well as the ship's commander and the officers. These were a lady, a young Japanese, a commissary official, the priest-monk Irakly, a Sakhalin missionary who was following me south so that we could travel to Russia together. The lady was the wife of a naval officer. She had fled from Vladivostok in fear of the cholera, and now, somewhat calmer, she was going back. She possessed an enviable character. For the simplest reason she would break out in the most sincere, joyful gales of lively laughter, leading to exhaustion, to tears. She starts explaining something in a guttural voice and suddenly she laughs, her joy bursting like a fountain, and, looking at her, I too begin laughing, and then Father Irakly laughs, and then it is the turn of the Japanese. Finally the commander says, "Well, now," and he also breaks out into laughter. Probably there has never been as much laughter on the normally angry Tatar Strait. The next morning we met on deck for conversation, the priest-monk, the lady, the Japanese and I. And again laughter; all that was needed was that the whales with their heads in the air should laugh when they saw us.

As though on purpose, the weather turned warm, calm and bright. To our left Sakhalin showed green, like a wilderness in this primitive region not yet touched by the penal colony. On the right, in the clear, transparent air the Tatar shore could be dimly seen. Here the strait is more like a sea and the water is not so muddy as it is near Dué. Here everything was more spacious and it was easier to breathe.

The lower third of Sakhalin corresponds geographically to France, and if it were not for the freezing currents, it would be a delightful country where others besides Shkandybas and Bezbozhnys would live.

The cold currents which wash both sides of Sakhalin flow down from the northern islands, where even at the end of summer there are ice floes. The eastern bank, being more open to the currents and the icy winds, takes the full brunt of the buffeting. Here nature is absolutely grim; the flora is polar. The western bank is more fortunate, for the influence of the cold current is softened by the warm Japanese current known as the Kuro-Sivo. There is no doubt that the farther south you go, the warmer it is, and the southern section of the western coast has comparatively far richer flora. Nevertheless, it is far from being like France or Japan.[1]

It is remarkable that while the Sakhalin colonizers have been sowing wheat in the tundra for the past thirty-five years and building fine roads to places where only the lowest species of mollusks can survive, the warmest area of the island, the southern part of the western shore, is completely disregarded. With or without binoculars you can see from the ship the fine timber forests and the sloping shores covered with bright-green grass, probably succulent, but there are no dwellings, and not a living soul in sight. On our second day out the commander called my attention to a small group of huts and sheds and said, "That is Mauka."

In Mauka the sea cabbage, which is eagerly bought by the Chinese, has been harvested for a long time. Since this is a serious business venture and has been profitable for many Russians and non-Russians, the location is very popular on Sakhalin. It is 400 versts south of Dué at 47° latitude and enjoys a comparatively good climate. At one time the enterprise was in Japanese hands. In Mitsul's day there were 30 Japanese houses occupied by 40 inhabitants of both sexes. In the spring, another 300 persons arrived from Japan. They worked with the Ainus, who made up the main working population. Today the cabbage business is owned by a Russian trader, Semenov, whose son resides permanently in Mauka. The work is supervised by a Scotsman, Demby, an older man and obviously knowledgeable. He has a house in Nagasaki, Japan, and when I made his acquaintance and said I would probably be in Japan in the autumn, he kindly invited me to be his house guest.

Semenov employs Chinese, Koreans and Russians. It was only in 1886 that our settlers began to make a living here. They probably came on their own initiative, because the prison supervisors were more interested in sauerkraut than in sea cabbage. The first attempts were not very successful. The Russians had little experience from the technical point of view. Now they have become used to the work and although Demby is not as satisfied with them as with the Chinese, it is reasonably certain that in time some hundreds of settlers will be able to earn bread here.

Mauka is in the Korsakov district. At present 38 people live here: 33 male and 5 female. All 33 have homesteads. Three have already achieved peasant status. The women are all convicts and live as cohabitants. There are no children and there is no church. The tedium must be overwhelming in winter when the workers go home. The civil administration consists of one jailer, and there is a military detachment composed of a corporal and three soldiers.[2]

The comparison of Sakhalin to a sturgeon is most apt in the southern part, which resembles a fish tail. The left half of the tail is called Cape Krilon, the right, Cape Anivsky, and the semicircular bay between them, Aniva. Krilon, around which the ship makes a sharp turn to the northeast, looks like an attractive town in the sunlight and the solitary red lighthouse resembles an aristocratic villa. The large headland juts into the sea, which is green and smooth as a lovely water meadow. The earth is covered with velvety grass, and to someone on a sentimental journey all it seems to lack is a herd of cattle wandering under the shade trees on the edge of the forest. But they say the grasses here are poor and that agriculture is barely possible because Krilon is hidden in salt-laden fog for most of the summer, and the fog is destructive to vegetation.[3]

We passed Krilon and entered Aniva Bay before noon on September 12. The entire shoreline was visible from one cape to the other, although the diameter of the bay is 80 to 90 versts.[4]

Practically in the center of the semicircular shore is a small hollow called Lasosey [Salmon] Bay. Here lies the Korsakov Post, the administrative center of the Southern region.

A most pleasant chance meeting awaited our shipmate the happy lady. On the Korsakov waterfront lay the *Vladivostok,* a ship of the Voluntary Fleet, which had just arrived from Kamchatka. The lady's officer husband was on board.

So many cries of joy, so much uncontrollable laughter, such a tremendous fuss!

From the sea the post looks like a charming town, not at all Siberian, possessing a distinctive character of its own which I cannot put into words. It was settled almost forty years ago, when Japanese homes and sheds were scattered here and there along the south shore, and it is quite possible that these Japanese buildings influenced it and gave it some characteristic features.

We are told that Korsakov was founded in 1869, but this is correct only for the penal colony. Actually the first Russian post on Lasosey Bay dates from 1853–54. It lies on an incline which even today bears the Japanese name Khakhka-Tomari. Only the main street is visible from the sea, and from afar the road and the two rows of houses seem to drop sharply to the shore, but this is only in perspective, for in reality the slope is not very deep. New wooden buildings shine and shimmer in the sun. A plain church, old and therefore of beautiful architecture, gleams whitely. There are tall poles on all the houses, probably for flags, and they give the town an unpleasant aspect, as though it bristled.

As on the northern routes, the ship drops anchor a verst or two from the shore, and the pier is used only by cutters and barges. A cutter came out to our ship. It had officials on board, and immediately there were joyful cries: "Boy, some beer! Boy, a jigger of cognac!" Later a whaleboat came up, rowed by convicts dressed as sailors. At the prow sat the district commander, I. I. Bely, who, when the whaleboat reached the ladder, gave out the order in naval fashion: "Lift up oars!"

Within a few minutes Mr. Bely and I became acquainted. We went ashore together and I dined with him. From our conversation I learned that he had just returned on the *Vladivostok* from the so-called Tarayka, where convicts are now building a road. The Tarayka lies on the shore of the Okhotsk Sea.

His quarters are small, but pleasant and luxurious. He loves comfort and a good cuisine, and this is obvious from the nature of the entire region under his supervision. Traveling over it later I found not only knives, forks and wineglasses in the jailers' quarters and at way stations, but there were even clean napkins. I found guards who knew how to make a tasty soup. There are fewer fleas and cockroaches here than in the North. According to Mr. Bely, when he was working at the road-construction site in Tarayka he lived in comfort in a small mansion, had his own chef and read French novels in his free time.[5]

By origin he is a Ukrainian, by education a former law student. He is young, not over forty, which is about average for a Sakhalin official.

Times have changed. Young officials are now more common than old ones, and should an artist portray a scene showing a prisoner being flogged, the painting would depict an intelligent young man in a smart new uniform instead of the former old drunken captain with a purple nose.

We talked on and on. Evening came and the lamp was lit. I bade farewell to the hospitable Mr. Bely and went to the quarters of the secretary of the police administration, where lodgings had been prepared for me. It was dark and quiet, the sea murmured dully and the starry sky seemed gloomy, as if it knew that nature was preparing something evil.

I had walked down the street almost to the sea, and saw the ships at anchor, and when I turned to the right, I heard loud voices and boisterous laughter. Brightly lit windows glowed in the darkness. I seemed to be approaching a provincial club on an autumn evening. These were the quarters of the secretary. I climbed the ancient, creaking stairs to the veranda and entered the house. In the parlor, through the fog and tobacco smoke usually found in taverns and damp premises, I saw military men and officials gliding like gods walking on clouds. I was already acquainted with one of them, Mr. von F., the agricultural inspector, whom I had met previously in Alexandrovsk. I saw the rest for the first time, although all greeted my appearance with such complacency that they gave the impression they had known me for a long time. They led me to the table and compelled me to drink vodka, half diluted with water, and some very bad cognac. I was served some tough fried meat served by the convict Khomenko, a Ukrainian with a black mustache. Another visitor at the party was the director of the Irkutsk magneto-meteorological observatory, E. V. Shtelling, who had arrived on the *Vladivostok* from Kamchatka and Okhotsk, where he was trying to obtain instruments for the meteorological station.

Here I also met Major S., the warden of the Korsakov prison, who had formerly served under General Greser in the Petersburg police. He is a tall, stout man with that solid, impressive carriage which I have found only in private and police officials. Recounting his brief meetings with many famous Petersburg writers, he called them by their first names, Misha and Vanya. And when he invited me to lunch and dinner, he twice addressed me familiarly as *ty* [thou].[6]

When the guests departed at 2 A.M., I went to bed. Suddenly I heard a roaring and a whistling sound. It was the northeaster. Now I knew why the sky had been lowering all evening. Khomenko came in from outside and told us the ships had sailed and a tremendous storm was raging on the sea. "But don't worry, they'll come back," he said and laughed. "How can they fight it?"

The room became cold and damp. It was probably no more than six or seven degrees. Poor F., the young secretary of the police department, could not get any sleep; he had a severe cold and racking cough. Captain K., who shared his quarters, also could not sleep. He came out of his room and spoke through the partition:

"I get the *Nedelya*.[7] Would you like to have it?"

In the morning it was cold in bed, in the room, in the town. When I went out of doors a cold rain was falling, a strong wind bent the trees, and the sea roared. The gusts of wind and rain were hurled against your face and they drummed against the roofs like bird shot. The *Vladivostok* and *Baikal*, unable to battle the storm, had returned and now lay at anchor, shrouded in mist. I took a walk along the streets and along the shore near the jetty. The grass was soaked, the trees showered water.

Near the guardhouse on the jetty there lies the skeleton of a young whale. Once it was happy, playful, roaming the expanses of the northern seas. Now the white bones of the giant lie in the mud, pounded by rain.

The main street is paved and well maintained, with sidewalks, street lamps and trees. It is swept daily by an old man bearing the brand of a criminal. In the street there are only the offices and homes of the officials, and not one convict is housed there. Most of the houses are new and pleasant looking. The heavy prison atmosphere, which is so obvious in Dué, is missing. In those four streets of Korsakov, there are more old buildings than new, and there is no lack of houses which are twenty or thirty years old. In Korsakov we find more old buildings and more old officials than in the North, indicating perhaps that the South is more conducive to a settled and peaceful life than the two Northern districts. I observed that life was more patriarchal here, the people were more conservative, and even the very worst customs were observed more carefully.

Corporal punishment is administered more frequently than in the North; they have been known to beat fifty men at a time. In the South a stupid custom initiated long ago by a forgotten colonel has survived. When a group of prisoners on the street or along the shore moves in the direction of a free citizen, then from 50 feet away you hear the guard shouting, "Attention! Caps off!" And so, sunk in misery, with bared heads, the prisoners scowl at you as though they feared that if they had taken off their caps at 20 or 30 feet, rather than 50, you would have beaten them with a stick. This is what Mr. Z. and Mr. N. do.

I am sorry I did not meet the oldest Sakhalin officer, Second Captain Shishmarev. At his age and as an old inhabitant he could have argued with old Mikryukov, who lives in Palensk. He died several months before my arrival, and all I saw was the house where he lived. He settled on Sakhalin in prehistoric times when there was no penal servitude, so long ago that a legend grew up concerning the origin of Sakhalin. In this legend the officer's name is closely connected with a geological cataclysm.

Once upon a time, in a remote age, Sakhalin did not exist. Suddenly a submerged cliff rose above sea level, and on the cliff there sat two creatures—a gray stallion and Second Captain Shishmarev. We are told that he wore a woolen frock coat with epaulets, and in his official reports he described non-Russians as "barbaric forest dwellers." He had taken part in several expeditions. Once he went down the Tym River with Polyakov and quarreled with him. We can read all this in the expedition's reports.

Korsakov Post has 163 inhabitants, 93 male and 70 female. Including the free men, soldiers, their wives and children, and the prisoners sleeping in the prison, the population is a little over 1,000.

There are 56 homesteads. None of these are rural, but rather urban and bourgeois. From the agricultural point of view they are completely meaningless. There are only 3 desyatins of arable land and only 18 desyatins of meadow-land, also used by the prison. It is necessary to see how close the houses are to each other and how they cling picturesquely to the slope and along the bottom of a valley-like ravine to understand how whoever chose the site failed to realize that homesteaders would come to live here as well as soldiers.

The homesteaders answered the question about what work they do and how they supported themselves by saying: "A little work, a little trade. . . ." As to additional earnings, as the reader will see below, the inhabitant of Southern Sakhalin finds himself in a better position than one in the North. If he wants to, he can earn extra money during the spring and summer, but the Korsakov people are not particularly interested, for they rarely try to earn extra money. They are citizens who live by uncertain means —uncertain because they are fortuitous and haphazard. Some live on money brought from Russia, and these are in the majority; another is a scribe; a third is a clerk; a fourth runs a store, although by law he has no right to do so; a fifth exchanges odds and ends from prisoners for Japanese vodka, which he sells, etc. The women, even the free women, engage in prostitution, and this includes a woman of the privileged class, of whom it is said that she completed her course at an institute. It is not so cold and people are less hungry here than in the North. The convicts whose wives sell their bodies smoke Turkish tobacco at 50 kopecks a quarter-pound. Prostitution appears to be more malignant here than in the North, although in fact there is probably very little difference.

There are 41 families. Of these, there are 21 couples who are not legally married. There are only 10 free women, which is 16 times less than in Rykovskoye and 4 times less than in a hole-in-the-wall like Dué.

There are some interesting characters among the Korsakov convicts. I will mention Pishchikov, a convict with an indefinite term, whose crime provided the material for G. I. Uspensky's "One on One." This man flogged his wife to death. She was an intelligent woman, and nine months pregnant. He flogged her for six hours. He did this because he was jealous of some things that had happened to her before their marriage. During the recent war she had fallen in love with a captured Turk. Pishchikov carried letters to the Turk, invited him to meet the young woman, and generally helped both parties. When the Turk left the town, the girl fell in love with Pishchikov because he had been so kind to her. Pishchikov married her, and had already sired four children when he was troubled with a fit of jealousy.

He is a tall, thin, handsome man with a huge beard, a secretary in the police department, and consequently he wears the clothes of a free man. He is most industrious, extremely courteous, and judging from his expression, he has withdrawn into himself and locked the door. I visited his quarters, but he was not at home. He has a small room in a hut. His immaculate bed is covered with a red woolen blanket, and on the wall near the bed there hangs a framed portrait of a lady, who is probably his wife.

The Zhakomin family is also interesting. It consists of

the father, a former skipper who served on the Black Sea, his wife and son. In 1878 all three were tried at a Nikolayevsk court-martial for murder and sentenced. They assure you they were innocent. The old lady and the son have served their terms, but the old man, Karp Nikolayevich, remains a convict. They operate a small store and their rooms are very well furnished, even better than those of rich Potemkin in Novo-Mikhaylovka. The old Zhakomins traveled to Siberia on foot; their son came by sea. The son arrived three years before his parents, and there is an immense difference between the two methods of travel. When you listen to the old man you are petrified. He speaks of the horrors he saw and suffered before his trial, the agonies in various prisons, and the three-year march across Siberia. His young daughter, who voluntarily followed her father and mother, died of exhaustion. The boat which brought them to Korsakov was shipwrecked near Mayka. So the old man tells the story, and the old woman weeps. "Well, so what?" says the old man, waving his hand. "This is how God wanted it!"

Culturally Korsakov is obviously behind the districts in the North. It has no telegraph or meteorological station.[8] The climate of Sakhalin can be judged only by the fragmentary, chance reports of various authors who served here or, like me, had visited for short periods. According to these data, taking mean temperatures, summer, autumn and spring are warmer by 2° in Korsakov Post than in Dué, and winter is less severe by 5°. However, on the Aniva River, which is not far east of Korsakov, the temperature in the Muravyevsky settlement is significantly lower, closer to that of Dué than of Korsakov. In Naybuchi, which is some 88 versts north of Korsakov Post, the commander of the *Vsadnik* recorded a temperature of 2° of frost on the morning of May 11, 1870, when it snowed. As the reader can see, the South here has nothing in common with the usual idea of a southern climate. The winter is as severe as in Olonetskaya *guberniya,* the summer is like summer in Arkhangelsk. Krusenstern saw snow in the middle of May on the western bank of the Aniva. In the northern part of the Korsakov region, in Kusunnay, where sea cabbage is harvested, there were 149 rainy days, while in the Muravyevsky Post in the south there were 130. Nevertheless, the climate is still more favorable in the Southern region than in the two regions of the North, and life should be better here. In the South, thaws occur in the middle of winter. None such have ever been seen near Dué and Rykovskoye. Ice breaks in the rivers sooner and the sun shines through the clouds more frequently.

The Korsakov prison stands on the highest point of the post and is probably the healthiest place in the neighborhood. The modest prison gates are located where the main street runs into the prison enclosure. That these are not ordinary gates is evident only from the sign posted outside and from the crowd of convicts who mill around each evening before being permitted to enter the wicket gate one at a time to be searched. The prison yard is located on a slope. Although it is enclosed and there are buildings all around, the blue sea and the far horizon can be seen from inside the prison, and there would appear to be fresh air within the prison walls.

When I inspected the prison, it became obvious to me from the beginning that the local administration tried to isolate the convicts from the settlers. In Alexandrovsk the prison shops and the living quarters of several hundred convicts are spread all over the post; here, however, all the workshops and even the firehouse are located within the prison compound. With rare exceptions, even reformed prisoners are not allowed to live outside the prison. The post is self-contained. You can live for a long time at the post and never notice that the prison lies at the end of the street.

The barracks are old, the air in the wards is fetid, the latrine is far worse than in the northern prisons, the bakery is dark, the solitary cells are dark, unventilated and cold. Sometimes I saw prisoners in the solitary cells shivering from the cold and dampness. Only one thing is better here than in the North. The cell where the prisoners are shackled is much larger and the number of convicts in chains is comparatively smaller. Of those in the wards, former sailors are the cleanest; even their clothing is cleaner.[9]

While I was there, only 450 persons slept in the prison, the remainder having been commandeered for outside work, especially road-building. The total number of convicts in the district is 1,205.

The local prison warden delights in showing visitors the fire trucks. These trucks are well-made and in this respect Korsakov surpasses many large cities. The barrels, water pumps and axes in their cases all glisten like toys, as though they had been specially prepared for exhibition. The fire alarm sounded. At once the convicts dashed out of the workshops coatless and hatless, exactly as they were. In a minute everything was ready and they were rolling thunderously down the main street. The spectacle was impressive, and Major S., the creator of the fire trucks, was completely satisfied. He asked me many times if I liked them. It was regrettable that old men were forced to participate in the game, dragging the fire trucks into the street and running with them. They were not well enough for it, and should have stayed behind.

[1] Someone suggested a project: to construct a dike at the narrowest part of the strait to hold back the cold currents. This project is naturally and historically justifiable. It is known that when the isthmus existed, the climate of Sakhalin was remarkably mild. Nevertheless, the construction of the dike would bring few benefits. The flora of the southern part of the western shore would be enriched by many new species, but the climate of the lower part of the island would hardly change for the better. The entire southern part lies close to the Okhotsk Sea, where ice floes and even icebergs float in the middle of summer. The Korsakov region is separated from this sea only by a low mountain range, and then, near the sea, lie the lowlands, full of lakes and open to the cold winds.

[2] Semenov runs a store in Mauka which is very expensive. The prices on food staples are high so that the settlers must spend half their wages to feed themselves. The commander of the clipper ship *Vsadnik* reported in 1870 that the clipper intended to land ten people near Mauka to prepare the land for cultivation because a new post was being planned in this location during the summer.

Let me add that all this took place at a time when there were some slight misunderstandings between the Russians and the Japanese. I have found further information in the *Kronstadt News* (1880), No. 112, in an article entitled "Sakhalin Island. Some Interesting Information Regarding Mauka-Koyuv [Mauka-Cove]." According to the article Mauka is the headquarters of a company which has received the right from the Russian government to harvest sea plants for 10 years and the population consists of 3 Europeans, 7 Russian soldiers and 700 Koreans, Ainus and Chinese laborers.

That the cabbage business is profitable and is expanding can be seen from the fact that Semenov and Demby already have imitators. A settler named Birich, a former instructor and steward for Semenov, borrowed money, constructed all the necessary buildings for the industry near Kusunnay, and began inviting settlers to work for him. He has some 30 employees. This is an unofficial undertaking, and there is no jailer. The Kusunnay Post, abandoned long ago, is one hundred versts south of Mauka at the mouth of the Kusunnay River, which was once the boundary between the island's Russian and Japanese administrations.

3   North of Krilon I saw the rocks into which the *Kostroma* crashed and settled after being lost in the fog. Dr. A. V. Shcherbak, who was escorting the convicts on the *Kostroma,* set off signal rockets after the shipwreck. He told me later that he lived through three prolonged emotional experiences. During the first, which was the longest and most excruciating, he believed they would inevitably sink; the convicts were screaming with panic; the women and children were taken off on a lifeboat under the command of an officer; they headed toward where they thought the shore would be, and soon disappeared in the fog. The second experience came when they hoped they might be rescued; a gun was heard booming from the Krilon lighthouse, this being a sign that the women and children had reached the shore safely. The third experience came when the air was suddenly filled with the music of the cornet being played by the returning officer, and then he felt complete confidence in being rescued.

4   N. V. Rudanovsky, a Russian officer and one of G. I. Nevelskoy's fellow adventurers, was the first to investigate and describe the Aniva shore. The details are available in the diary of N. V. Bussé, who participated in the Amur expedition. The diary is called "Sakhalin Island and Its Expedition of 1853–54." There is also the article by G. I. Nevelskoy and Rudanovsky: "In Connection with the Memoirs of N. V. Bussé" in *Vestnik Evropy* [News of Europe] (1872), VIII, and Nevelskoy's notes. Major N. V. Bussé, a nervous and quarrelsome man, wrote that "Nevelskoy's

attitude in the preparation and spirit of his papers is not sufficiently serious," and about Rudanovsky he said: "he is difficult as a subordinate and an intolerable companion." He said that Rudanovsky "made obtuse remarks," while Boshnyak was described as "a dreamer and a child." He was irritated when Nevelskoy lit his pipe slowly. While spending the winter in Aniva with Rudanovsky, senior officer Bussé tiresomely demanded all the honors due his rank and the observance of all minor conventions. All this occurred in the wilderness, when they were living "eye to eye," and when the young man was completely immersed in important scientific work.

5 Men have almost forgotten the time when officers and officials serving on Sakhalin suffered any privations. In 1876 they paid four rubles for a pood of white flour, three rubles for a bottle of vodka, and "practically no one ever saw fresh meat." (*Russky Mir* [Russian World], 1877, No. 7.) Nothing is said about how the common people lived. In fact, they suffered dire poverty. Only five years ago the correspondent of *Vladivostok* wrote that "nobody could put his hands on half a jigger of vodka, while Manchurian tobacco (similar to our *makhorka*) cost 2 rubles 50 kopecks per pound. The settlers and some guards smoked Bohea tea leaves and brick tea" (1886, No. 22).

6 In all fairness I must admit that Major S. was most respectful of my profession of letters, and during my entire stay in Korsakov he went to great lengths to keep me from getting bored. Several weeks before my arrival he was just as solicitous about the Englishman Howard, also a writer seeking adventure. Howard had been shipwrecked in a Japanese junk on the Aniva. He later wrote some absolute nonsense about the Ainus in his book *Life with Trans-Siberian Savages.*

7 *Nedelya* [The Week] was a Sunday newspaper.—TRANS.

8 In my presence E. V. Shtelling expressed the desire to build a meteorological station, and he was strongly supported by the military doctor, an old inhabitant of Korsakov and a very fine man. But I see no reason why the station should be built in Korsakov, which is open to the east winds. It should be built in some more central location, such as the Vladimirovka settlement. Moreover, in Southern Sakhalin, where each locale has its own climate, it would be more efficient to establish meteorological observation points in several places simultaneously: in Bussé Bay, Korsakov, Krilon, Mayka, Vladimirovka, Naybuchi and Tarayka. This will not be easy, but the problems are not insuperable. The services of educated convicts could be employed. As experience has shown,

they quickly learn to conduct observations on their own, and all that is needed is someone to supervise them.

9   I. I. Bely was successful in organizing naval convicts into an expert crew for work at sea. The senior man among them is a convict called Golitsyn, a little man with whiskers. When he sits at the rudder and bellows his command "Cut the spar," or "Oars in the water," he acts with typical authoritative severity. Notwithstanding his commanding appearance and seniority, I saw him beaten two or three times for drunkenness and coarse language.

After him, the most expert seaman is convict Medvedev, an intelligent and courageous man. When the Japanese consul, Mr. Kuze, was returning from Tarayka, Medvedev was at the helm. A guard was with them in the whaleboat. Toward evening the wind freshened and it turned dark. When they were near Naybuchi, the entrance to the Nayba River could not be seen and it was dangerous to land. Medvedev decided to spend the night at sea in spite of the storm. Mr. Kuze sharply commanded him to stay close to shore, but Medvedev disobeyed and kept taking the boat farther and farther out to sea. The storm raged all night. The waves hammered at the boat, and every moment they were in danger of being swamped and overturned. The consul later told me it was the most terrifying night of his life. When Medvedev sailed into the mouth of the little river at dawn, the whaleboat was still shipping water while crossing the bar. Nowadays when Mr. Bely sends anyone with Medvedev, he always says, "No matter what he does, please be quiet and don't protest."

Two brothers attract attention in the prison. They are former Persian princes who are addressed in letters from Persia by their full titles. They were sentenced for murder in the Caucasus. They dress in Persian clothing, in tall lambskin hats with foreheads bare. They are still probationers and are not permitted to carry money. One of them complained that he has no money for tobacco, and he thinks that if he could smoke his cough would get better. He glues envelopes for the office very clumsily. After watching him work, I said, "Very good!" Obviously this praise was received with great satisfaction by the former prince.

The secretary at the prison is a convict called Heyman, a stout, handsome, dark-haired man, formerly a Moscow police officer sentenced for corruption. While I was at the prison he dogged my heels. Each time I turned around, he respectfully removed his hat.

The local executioner is called Minayev. A merchant's son, he is still quite a young man. The day I saw him he told me he had just flogged eight men with birch rods.

XIII

Poro-an-Tomari, Muravyevsky Post - First, Second and Third Drop - Solovyevka - Lyutoga - Goly Mys - Mitsulka - Listvenichnoye - Khomutovka - Bolshaya Yelan - Vladimirovka - The Farm, or Firm - Lugovoye - Popovskiye Yurty - Berezniki - Kresty - Bolshoye and Maloye Takoe - Galkino-Vraskoye - Dubky - Naybuchi - The Sea

I WILL BEGIN THE SURVEY of the Korsakov district with the populated areas lying along the banks of the Aniva. The first settlement, four versts southeast of the post, bears the Japanese name of *Poro-an-Tomari*. It was settled in 1882 on the site of a former Ainu village. It has 72 inhabitants, 53 male and 19 female. There are 47 home-steaders, of whom 38 live alone. Although the area around the settlement seems spacious, each homesteader has only one-quarter of a desyatin of arable land and less than one-half desyatin of meadowland. This indicates either that no more can be obtained or that it is extremely difficult to clear more land. Nevertheless, if Poro-an-Tomari were located in the North it would long since have had 200 homesteaders and 150 co-owners. In this respect the Southern administration is more moderate and prefers to found new settlements rather than expand the old.

I recorded nine old men from sixty-five to eighty-five years of age here. One of them, Yan Rytseborsky, who looked like one of those soldiers of Ochakiv days,[1] was 75 and so old that he has probably forgotten whether he was guilty of any crime. It is strange to learn that they have all been sentenced to life terms for robbery. Baron Korf transferred them to the status of settler because of their advanced age.

Settler Kostin lives in a dugout. He never comes outside, permits no one to visit him, and prays continually. They call the settler Gorbunov "the slave of God," because he wandered about the land when he was free. By profession he was an artist, but now he is a shepherd in Third Drop, probably because he loves solitude and contemplation.

Some 40 versts eastward is the *Muravyevsky Post,* which exists only on the map. It was founded a comparatively long while ago, in 1853, on the shore of Lasosey Cove. When there were rumors of war in 1854, it was razed to the ground and rebuilt 12 years later on the banks of Bussé Bay, or the Twelvefoot Harbor, which is the name of a shallow lake which joins the sea by a canal. Only small boats drawing a few feet of water can pass through the canal. In Mitsul's time it held 300 soldiers, who suffered from severe scurvy. The post was founded in order to consolidate Russian influence on Southern Sakhalin. After the treaty of 1875 it was abandoned as useless, and they say that the abandoned huts were burned by escaped prisoners.[2]

A charming shore road leads to the settlements west of Korsakov Post. On the right are steep clay hills and ravines thick with greenery. To the left is the clamorous sea. On the sand, where the waves burst into foam and roll back as though overcome with weariness, the seaweed poured out by the ocean lies along the coast in green ribbons, exuding the sweet but not unpleasant odor of rotting sea plants. The smell is just as typical in the southern area as the wild ducks always rising, which are a source of amusement during the entire journey along the coast. Steamboats and sailing vessels are rare visitors here. There is nothing to see on the horizon or closer to shore, and therefore the sea looks deserted. Occasionally you see a clumsy hay raft which barely moves, and sometimes it will have a dark, ugly sail, or you will see a convict wading through knee-high water and dragging a roped log behind him. You never see anything else.

The steep coast is broken by a long, deep valley, through which there flows the little Untanay or Unta River. At one time this was the site of the Untovsk farm, which the convicts called Dranka [Bedraggled], for obvious reasons. At the moment this is the site of the prison vegetable garden and only three settlers' huts remain. This is known as *First Drop*.

There follows *Second Drop,* which has six homesteaders. An old man, a peasant formerly exiled, lives here with an old woman, the maid Ulyana. Very long ago she killed her baby and buried him, but in court it was stated that she had not killed him but buried him alive, and thought she would be acquitted. The court sentenced her to 20 years. Telling me about this, Ulyana cried bitterly, then she dried her eyes and asked, "Won't you buy some sauerkraut?"

There are 17 homesteads at *Third Drop*. It contains 46 inhabitants, 17 of whom are women. There are 26 homesteaders. All the people here are substantial and prosperous. They have a large number of livestock and some even earn their living raising and selling livestock. I must admit that in all probability the chief reasons for such prosperity are good climate and excellent soil. However, I also think that if the Alexandrovsk or Dué officials were invited to take charge here, there would be 300, not 26, homesteaders within a year, not counting co-owners, and all of them would prove to be negligent and self-willed householders, and would languish without a piece of bread. I believe the example set by these three tiny settlements enables us to establish the rule that when a colony is still young and unstable, the fewer the homesteaders the better. The longer the street, the greater the poverty.

Four versts from the post lies *Solovyevka,* founded in 1882. It has the most convenient location of all the Sakhalin settlements. It is near the sea and close to the mouth of the Susui, a fine fishing stream. The inhabitants raise cattle and sell milk. They also engage in agriculture. It has 74 inhabitants, 37 male and 37 female, with 26 householders. They all have arable meadowlands on an average of one desyatin per person. The soil is only good along the slopes near the sea and further inland it is quite poor, having formerly been covered with fir trees.

There is one more remote settlement along the Aniva River. It is 25 versts from the post, or 14 if you travel by sea. It is called Lyutoga. It is 5 versts from the mouth of the Lyutoga River and was founded in 1886. Communication with the post is extremely difficult. One must travel along the coast or by cutter; the settlers use hay rafts. It has 53 inhabitants, 37 male and 16 female, and 33 homesteaders.

The road past Solovyevka turns sharply to the right at the mouth of the Susui and then runs northward. The map shows that the upper reaches of the Susui are close to the Nayba River, which falls into the Okhotsk Sea. A long line of settlements lies along both of these rivers. These are connected by a single road 88 versts long. This row of settlements is wholly characteristic of the Southern region, its very essence, while the road is the beginning of the post road with which they want to unite Northern Sakhalin with the South.

I had become fatigued, or lazy, and did not work as zealously in the South as I had in the North. Often I spent entire days on outings and picnics and had no desire to continue visiting the huts. When help was graciously offered, I did not refuse it.

My first trip to and from the Okhotsk Sea was in the company of Mr. Bely, who wanted to show me the entire region. Later, while continuing my census, I was always accompanied by the settlement inspector N. N. Yartsev.[3]

The settlements of the Southern district have their own peculiarities, and a person who recently arrived from the North cannot fail to observe them. First, here there is considerably less poverty. I did not see any unfinished or abandoned huts, and plank roofs are as commonplace and normal here as thatched and bark roofs in the North. The people look younger, healthier and more cheerful than their Northern counterparts, and this, as well as the comparative prosperity of the district, can probably be explained by the fact that the main contingent of prisoners living in the

South comprises short-term convicts, which means that for the most part they are young and are less exhausted by penal servitude. You meet some who are only twenty to twenty-five years old, have already served their sentences, and are homesteaders. There are quite a number of peasants-formerly-exiles who are between thirty and forty years old.[4]

Another favorable aspect of the Southern settlements is that the local peasants are not anxious to leave for the mainland. For example, of the 26 homesteaders in the above-mentioned Solovyevka, sixteen have achieved peasant status. There are very few women. Some settlements do not have even one woman. In comparison to the men, the majority of the women look ill and old. One is compelled to believe the local officials and settlers who complain that only "useless" women are sent to them from the North while the Northerners retain the young and healthy for themselves. Dr. Z. told me that in performing his duties as the prison doctor, he decided to examine a group of newly arrived women and found all of them suffering from female illnesses.

The terms co-owner and half-owner are not used at all in the South, since each plot of land is assigned to only one homesteader. However, there are homesteaders who are assigned to settlements but have no homes, exactly as in the North. There are no Jews in the post nor in the settlements. Japanese prints hang on the walls of some of the huts. I also saw some Japanese silver coins.

The first settlement on the Susui is *Goly Mys*. It has only been in existence since last year and the huts are still unfinished. It has 24 men but not a single woman. The settlement stands on a hill which was formerly called "Bald Cape." The stream is quite a distance from the houses and is reached by going downhill. There is no well.

The second settlement is *Mitsulka,* named in honor of M. S. Mitsul.[5]

In the days when there was no road, there was a way station at Mitsulka, where horses were kept for officials traveling on government business. The grooms and laborers were permitted to remain for the duration of their terms;

they settled near the station and set up their own home-steads. There are only 10 holdings with 25 inhabitants, 16 male and 9 female. After 1886 the regional commander refused to permit any more settlers in Mitsulka, and he was right, because the land is poor and there is only enough meadowland for ten homesteads. Now the settlement has 17 cows and 13 horses in addition to sheep, goats and swine, and the treasury data also show 64 chickens. However, this number would not be doubled if the number of households were doubled.

In speaking of the peculiarities of the Southern district, I forgot to mention one thing: very often people are poisoned by wolfsbane (*Aconitum napellus*). In Mitsulka the settler Takovy's pig died of wolfsbane poisoning. Takovy greedily ate the liver and almost died himself. When I was in his hut he could barely stand and scarcely speak, but he recalled the liver with a smile. One could see by his swollen, bluish face how dearly he had paid for it. Somewhat earlier an old man called Konkov was poisoned by wolfsbane and died. His house stands empty.

This house is one of Mitsulka's sights. Several years ago the prison warden L., mistaking a climbing plant for a grapevine, notified General Gintse that there are grapevines in Southern Sakhalin which could be successfully cultivated. General Gintse immediately instituted a search for a prisoner who had formerly labored in a vineyard. They soon found the settler Rayevsky, an extremely tall man, who said he was an expert. They believed him and give him an official document before sending him by the first ship from Alexandrovsk Post to Korsakov. Then they asked him, "Why have you come?" and he answered, "To grow grapes." They looked at him, read the document and shrugged their shoulders. The vine dresser went wandering around the district, his cap tilted debonairly. Since he had been sent out by the island commandant, he did not feel it necessary to report to the inspector of the settlements. A misunderstanding occurred. In Mitsulka his extreme height and the dignity with which he carried on his pursuits aroused suspicion. They thought he was a vagrant, bound him and sent him to the post. There he was held in prison for a long time while the investigations continued. Finally he was released, and eventually he settled in Mitsulka, where he died, and Sakhalin was left without vineyards. Rayevsky's house reverted to the government for debts unpaid and was sold to Konkov for 15 rubles. When paying his money, old Konkov winked slyly and said to the district commander, "Well, wait a bit, I'll die, and then you'll have more trouble with the house." And sure enough, soon afterward he was poisoned by wolfsbane and the government again has the house on its hands.[6]

In Mitsulka lives the Sakhalin Gretchen, the daughter of the settler Nikolayev. Tanya, born in Pskov *guberniya,* is sixteen years old. She is blond and slender; her features are fine, soft and delicate. She has been promised in marriage to a guard. When passing through Mitsulka I always saw her sitting at her window and dreaming. God knows what this young and lovely girl, whom fate has brought to Sakhalin, is dreaming about!

The new settlement of Listvenichnoye [The Larches] is five versts from Mitsulka. The road here cuts through a larch forest. It is also called Khristoforovka, because a long time ago a Gilyak named Khristofor used to set sable traps here. It is not a good site for a settlement, because the soil is very poor and unfavorable for cultivation.[7] It has fifteen inhabitants, no women.

A bit farther along the Khristoforovka River, a few convicts previously made various wooden objects. They were permitted to settle there to serve out their sentences. However, the site was found to be unfavorable and in 1886 their four huts were moved to another location four versts north of Listvenichnoye, and this became the foundation of the Khomutovka settlement. It is thus called because a free settler, the peasant Khomutov, at one time used this as a hunting site. It has 38 inhabitants, 25 males and 13 females. This is one of the most uninteresting settlements, although it can pride itself on having one specialty. Here lives the settler Bronovsky, who is known throughout the Southern district as a passionate and insatiable thief.

Three versts farther on there is the Bolshaya Yelan settlement, founded two years ago. The river valleys covered with elms, oak, hawthorn, elder, ash and birch are here called *yelan*. They are usually protected from cold winds. While the vegetation on the neighboring hills and marshes is unpleasantly sparse and differs little from that of polar regions, we find luxurious vegetation and grasses twice as tall as a man in the *yelan*. On sunny summery days the whole place steams, the air grows sultry as in a bathhouse, and the warmed soil turns all grasses into hay, with the result that in one month rye grows almost a sazhen high. The *yelan* reminds a Ukrainian of his native tree-encircled grasslands, where meadows alternate with orchards and groves, and these are the best sites for settlements.[8]

There are forty inhabitants in Bolshaya Yelan, 32 male and 8 female. There are 30 homesteaders. When the settlers cleared land for their homesteads, they were ordered to save as many old trees as possible. Thanks to this, the settlement does not look new. In the courtyards and along the streets stand stately broad-leafed elms, so old that they might have been planted by their grandfathers.

Among the local inhabitants the Babich brothers of Kiev *guberniya* are interesting. At first they lived in one hut, later they began quarreling and begged the administration to separate them. One of the Babich brothers complained of the other and said, "I'm just as afraid of him as of a snake."

Five miles farther is Vladimirovka, settled in 1881, and named in honor of a major named Vladimir, who was in charge of penal work. The settlers also call it Chernaya Rechka [Black Stream]. Inhabitants, 91: 55 male and 36 female. It has 46 homesteaders, 19 of whom are bachelors, and they milk their cows themselves. Only 6 of the 27 families are legally married.

As an agricultural colony this settlement is worth as much as both the Northern districts put together. However, of the great number of women who have followed their convict husbands to Sakhalin, those women who are free and untouched by prison and the most valuable to a colony, only one has been settled here, and even she was recently imprisoned on suspicion of having murdered her husband. The unfortunate free women who are forced to languish in Dué by the Northern officials in family barracks would be of inestimable value here. In Vladimirovka there are over 100 head of horned cattle, 40 horses, fine meadowland, but there are no housewives, and therefore no true homesteads.[9]

In Vladimirovka the settlement inspector, Mr. Y., lives in a government house with his wife, who practices as a midwife. Here there is an agricultural farm known by the settlers as "the firm." Mr. Y. is interested in the natural sciences and especially in botany, and he calls plants by their Latin names. When beans are served at his table, he will say, "This is *Phaseolus.*" He calls his nasty little black dog Favus. Of all the Sakhalin officials he is the most knowledgeable in agronomy and he goes about his work lovingly and conscientiously, but the yield on his model farm is often poorer than that of a settler, a state of affairs which evokes surprise and derision.

In my opinion this accidental difference in crop yields is no more due to Mr. Y. than to any other official. A farm which has no meteorological station or cattle, no manure, no decent building, no agricultural expert who will work from morning to night, is not a farm, but rather a "firm"; it is an empty plaything pretending to be a model agricultural station. It cannot even be called a research station because there are only five desyatins of land. As to quality, there exists an official document stating that an average plot was purposely chosen "with the aim of demonstrating by example to the settlers that with known methods and with the best kind of cultivation even an average plot can successfully yield a satisfactory result."

A love story took place here in Vladimirovka. A certain Vukol Popov, a peasant, caught his wife in bed with his own father, pulled up his sleeves, and murdered the old man. He was sentenced to penal servitude, sent to the Korsakov district and then assigned to the firm of Mr. Y. as a coachman. He was young, handsome and athletically built, and he had a mild and earnest character. He was always silent and thinking about something, and from the start the settlers trusted him. When they left home they were sure that Vukol would not steal the money in the chest and would not drink the alcohol in the pantry. He could not marry in Sakhalin because his wife was still living back home and would not give him a divorce. Such, very roughly, was our hero.

The heroine was a convict, Yelena Tertyshnaya, cohabitating with a settler called Koshelev. She was an absurd, stupid and homely woman, and she began arguing with her lover, who complained to the district commander. As a punishment she was assigned to work at the firm, and here Vukol saw her and fell in love with her. She also fell in love with him. Koshelev obviously noticed this, because he began to beg her passionately to return to him.

"Well, that's fine, but I know you well enough," she said. "Marry me, and then I'll come back."

Koshelev presented a petition to marry the maid Tertyshnaya, and this was granted by the administration. Meanwhile Vukol declared his love and begged her to live with him. She also declared her love for him, saying:

"I can come and see you, but I can't live with you! You are married, while I am a woman and must think of myself. I must marry a good man."

When Vukol learned that she was going to marry Koshelev, he became despondent and poisoned himself with wolfsbane. The woman was questioned, and she admitted she had spent four nights with him. They say that two weeks before his death, watching her scrub the floor, Vukol said:

"Women, women! I went to prison over one woman and I'll probably have to die for another!"

In Vladimirovka I met the convict Vasily Smirnov, who was sentenced for forging credit notes. He had completed his sentence and his settler's term and was now engaged in hunting sables. This was something he obviously enjoyed very much. He told me that the forged credit notes netted him 300 rubles a day, and he was caught after he had abandoned forgery and was living honestly. He spoke about forging notes like a specialist. In his opinion present-day credit notes could be forged by any woman. He spoke calmly of the past, not without irony, and was very proud that he was defended in court by the lawyer Plevako.

Just outside Vladimirovka you come upon a vast stretch of meadowland covering an area of several hundred desyatins, in a semicircle four versts in diameter. On the road where the meadow ends there is the Lugovoye settlement, or Luzhki, founded in 1888. It has 69 men and only 5 women.

Four versts farther on, you arrive at Popovskiye Yurty, which was settled in 1884. They wanted to name it Novo-Alexandrovsk, but this name was later abandoned. Father Simeon Kazansky, known as Pop Simeon, rode on a dog sleigh to Naybuchi to "place a fast" on the soldiers, but was caught in a raging snowstorm and became seriously ill (others say he was returning from Alexandrovsk). Luckily there were Ainu fishing yurts nearby, where he found shelter. His driver went to Vladimirovka, where free settlers were living at the time. They came for him and brought him to Korsakov Post. He was barely alive. After this the place where the Ainu yurts had been was called Popovskiye, and the name was given to the whole district.

The settlers also call their settlement Warsaw because it contains many Catholics. There are 111 inhabitants, 95 males and 16 females. Of the 42 homesteaders, only 10 are married.

Popovskiye Yurty stands exactly in the middle between Korsakov Post and Naybuchi. Here ends the basin of the Susui River, and after crossing the slight, almost imperceptible ridge of the watershed we descended into the valley watered by the Nayba.

The first settlement of this basin is eight versts from the Yurty and is called Berezniki, because at one time it was full of birch trees. This is the largest of the Southern settlements. It has 159 inhabitants, 142 male and 17 female; 140 homesteaders. There are already four streets and a cleared area, where it is planned to build a church, a telegraph station and a house for the settlement inspector. If the colonization is successful, they also propose to make Berezniki the small district center of several villages. But the site is very boring and the people are bored. They are not keen on the new district and think only of serving their sentences as soon as possible and leaving for the mainland. When I asked one settler if he was married, he answered in a bored tone, "I was married. I murdered my wife." Another man, who was spitting blood, followed me around when he heard I was a doctor. He kept asking me if he had consumption and gazed searchingly into my eyes. He was terrified of the thought that he might not live long enough to obtain his peasant rights and would die on Sakhalin.

Kresty [The Crosses], founded in 1885, lies five versts farther on. Some while ago two vagrants were murdered here and over their graves there once stood crosses, which have now vanished. There is another version: a coniferous forest, which was cut down long ago, formed a cross over the Yelan. Both explanations are poetic; obviously the name Kresty was given by the settlers themselves.

Kresty stands on the Takoe River right at the mouth of a tributary. The earth is clay with a good silt topsoil. There are almost yearly harvests. There are many meadows, and fortunately the people turned out to be good farmers. However, during the first years the settlement differed little from Verkhny Armudan and almost perished. Thirty men were assigned simultaneously to the area, but the tools did not arrive from Alexandrovsk for a long time and the settlers were left bare-handed. In pity for them, the prison officers gave them some axes so that they could cut down trees. Then for three whole years no livestock was given to them, for the same reason that Alexandrovsk failed to send any tools.

It has 90 inhabitants, 63 males and 27 females; 52 homesteaders.

In Kresty there is a shop run by a retired sergeant major who was formerly the inspector of the Tymovsky district. He sells groceries, bracelets and sardines. When I entered the shop he obviously took me for a very important official, because he immediately, and without any reason, began explaining to me that at one time he had been involved in something but had been put right, and hurriedly showed me various official documents attesting to his services. Among others, he showed me a letter from a Mr. Schneider, which ended, as I recall, with the following words: "And when it gets warm, then ardor thaws." Desiring to show me that he was no longer indebted to anybody, the sergeant major began burrowing among his papers to find some receipts, which he never found, and I left the shop with the firm belief that he was completely innocent, and also with a pound of ordinary peasant candies. He soaked me for the candies, charging fifty kopecks.

The settlement after Kresty is on a river which falls into the Nayba. The river bears the Japanese name of Takoe, and the settlement is called Takoyskaya. It is well known because free settlers formerly lived there. Bolshoye Takoe has officially existed since 1884, but was founded much earlier. They wanted to call it Vlasovskoye in honor of Vlasov, but the name did not take. It has 71 inhabitants, 56 male and 15 female; 47 householders. A man who was formerly a surgeon's assistant at a medical school resides here permanently and the settlers regard him as a first-rate doctor. A week before my arrival his young wife poisoned herself with wolfsbane.

Close to the settlement, especially along the road to Kresty, there are some magnificent elms. There is a good deal of greenery, succulent and dazzling, as though it had been just washed. The Takoyskaya valley flora is incomparably richer than in the North, but the northern scenery is more vivid and often reminded me of Russia. True, nature in Russia is mournful and grim, but it is grim in a Russian way. Here it smiles and grieves, perhaps in the Ainu fashion, and it arouses an indefinable sadness in the Russian soul.[10]

In the Takoyskaya valley, 4½ versts from Bolshoye Takoe, lies Maloye Takoe, on a stream which flows into the Takoe.[11] It was founded in 1885. It has 52 inhabitants, 37 male and 15 female. It contains 35 homesteads. Only 9 have "wives" and none are legally married.

Some eight versts farther on there is a district which the Japanese and Ainus called Siyancha. Formerly a Japanese fishing shed was located here, and this became the settlement of Galkino-Vraskoye or Siyantsy, founded in 1884. This site, at the fall of the Takoe River into the Nayba River, is lovely but most impractical. In the spring and autumn, and even during the summer rains, the Nayba, which is capricious like all mountain rivers, overflows and floods Siyantsy. The strong Nayba current closes off the inlet of the Takoe and that, too, overflows its banks. The same occurs with the small tributaries of the Takoe. During that period Galkino-Vraskoye resembles Venice and they row about in Ainu boats. The floors of the huts which are built on low-lying plots are usually flooded. The site was chosen by a certain Ivanov, who understood as much about the matter as he knows about the Gilyak and Ainu languages, of which he is the official translator. At that time he was the assistant to the prison warden and he discharged the duties which are today discharged by the inspector of settlements. The Ainus and the settlers warned him that the site was swampy, but he paid no attention to them. Whoever complained was beaten. In one flood an ox was lost, in another a horse.

The fall of the Takoe into the Nayba creates a peninsula which is reached by a high bridge. It is quite beautiful here. The area is enchanting. The inspector's house is well-lit and clean; it even has a fireplace. A terrace overlooks the river and an orchard blooms in the garden. The watchman is an old convict named Savelyev, who serves as a manservant and cook when officials spend the night here. When he was serving dinner to me and another official, he served something incorrectly and the official shouted angrily, "Fool!" I glanced at the timid old man and I remember thinking that all the Russian intelligentsia had been able to accomplish with penal servitude merely served to debase it to serfdom in the most vulgar manner.

Galkino-Vraskoye has 74 inhabitants, 50 males and 24 females. There are 45 householders, 24 of whom have peasant status.

The last settlement on that road is Dubky [The Oaks], founded in 1886 on the site of a former oak forest. In the eight versts between Siyantsy and Dubky you see burned-out forests, and between them cultivated land where they say kapor tea grows. As you ride along, you are shown the stream where the settler Malovechkin used to fish: now the stream bears his name. Dubky has 44 inhabitants, 31 male and 13 female. It has 30 householders. The site is considered good, on the principle that where there are oaks, the land is good for wheat. A large part of the land which is now under tillage and hay was swamp land until recently. On the advice of Mr. Y. the settlers dug a canal a sazhen deep to the Nayba and now it has good soil.

Possibly because this is the last settlement and is practically isolated, card-playing and tenacity are highly developed. In June the local settler Lifanov lost everything and poisoned himself with wolfsbane.

It is only four versts from Dubky to the mouth of the Nayba, but this area is impossible to settle because the mouth of the river is marshy, the seashore is sandy and the vegetation is of the sand and sea variety, sweetbrier with very large berries, and so on. The road leads to the sea but you can also go downriver on an Ainu rowboat.

Once the Naybuchi Post stood at the mouth of the river. It was established in 1866. Mitsul found 18 buildings and dwelling places, a chapel and a supply depot. One correspondent who visited Naybuchi in 1871 wrote that it had 20 soldiers commanded by a cadet. In one hut he found a tall, beautiful woman, the wife of a soldier, and she served him fresh eggs and black bread. She praised the local life, and only complained that sugar was very expensive.[12]

Today there is no trace of these huts, and as you glance around the wilderness the beautiful woman seems to be a myth. They are building a house which will either be the living quarters of an inspector or a way station, and that is all. The sea looks cold and troubled. It seethes with fury, and the high gray waves smash down on the sand as though shouting in despair, "God, why did you create us?"

This is the Pacific Ocean. On this bank of the Naybuchi there can be heard the sound of convicts hacking away with their axes at a new building site, and far away there lies the coast of America. To the left through the fog you can see the headlands of Sakhalin, to the right more cliffs . . . and not a single living soul around you, not a bird, not a fly. You ask yourself for whom do these waves roar, who hears them during the night, what are they calling for, and for whom they will roar when you have gone away. Here on these coasts you are gripped not by thoughts but by meditations. It is terrible, but at the same time I want to stand there forever and gaze at the monotonous waves and listen to their thunderous roar.

[1]   In the sixteenth and seventeenth centuries the Dnieper Cossacks constantly harassed the Turks, whose main seaport was Ochakiv, on the Black Sea.—TRANS.

[2]   At one time the Muravyevsky mines were located here. They were worked by post soldiers under arrest, which means that the post had its own small penal prison. The local administrators assigned them to work as punishment "for insignificant transgressions" (Mitsul). No one knows who would have benefited from the coal if it had been sold, since it was all burned together with the buildings.

Before 1870 the military authorities founded the posts of Chibisansky, Ochekhpoksky, Manuysky, Malkovsky and many others. All of these have been abandoned and forgotten.

[3]   In September and the beginning of October, excluding those days when a northeaster blew, the weather was marvelously warm. Riding along with me, Mr. Bely complained that he was very lonesome for the Ukraine and there was nothing he wanted so much as to see a cherry tree heavy with fruit. While spending the night at guardhouses, he always rose very early. When I awoke at dawn, I saw him standing at the window reciting in a low voice: "A white light rises over the city, a young woman sleeps a deep sleep. . . ." Mr. Yartsev also constantly recited poetry from memory. Sometimes when I was bored during our journeys I asked him to recite something and with great feeling he would recite a long poem. Sometimes he would recite two poems.

4   For example, 70 percent of the inhabitants of the Korsakov Post are between twenty and forty-five years old. It was the former custom, though not the law, to assign newly arrived short-term convicts, who were considered to be lesser criminals and not incorrigible, to the South, where it is warmer. However, the necessary caution was not always exercised in allocating long- and short-term convicts according to prison lists. Thus the former island commandant, General Gintse, reading the list while on board a ship, himself decided to send the short-term convicts to the South. Among these fortunate ones there were later found twenty vagrants and those who were called "Not Remembering" —i.e., the very worst type of incorrigible and hopeless criminals. At the present time this custom has obviously been abandoned, since now long-term and even life-term convicts are also sent South, while I met short-term convicts in the terrifying Voyevodsk prison and in the mines.

5   The agronomist Mikhail Semenovich Mitsül was one of those who took part in the expedition of 1870 sent from Petersburg under the command of Vlasov. He was a man of rare ethical standards, industrious, an optimist and idealist, enthusiastic and possessing the ability to communicate his enthusiasm to others. He was then about thirty-five years old. He carried out his duties with exceptional exactitude. In investigating the Sakhalin soil, flora and fauna, he went on foot over all the land included in present day Alexandrovsk and Tymovsk, the western coast, and the entire southern part of the island. There were no roads on the island then. Occasionally he came upon miserable paths which vanished in the taiga and swamps, and every journey, whether on horseback or on foot, was like a martyrdom. The idea of a penal agricultural colony astonished and fascinated Mitsul. He devoted himself to it wholeheartedly, fell in love with Sakhalin, and just as a mother sees no wrong in a beloved child, he paid no attention to the frozen soil and mists of the island which became his second homeland. He thought of it as a flourishing oasis. Neither the meteorological data, practically nonexistent at the time, nor the bitter experiences of men who had come in previous years, which he obviously disbelieved, changed his opinion. Had he not seen the wild grapes, the bamboos, the giant grasses and the Japanese? Later in life he became a manager, and then a civilian adviser, always enthusiastic and indefatigably industrious. He died on Sakhalin from a severe nervous disorder at the age of 41. I saw his grave. He left a book: *An Outline on Sakhalin Island in Respect to Its Agriculture* (1873). This is a lengthy poem in praise of Sakhalin productivity.

6   A convict handed me a slip of paper resembling a petition, which bore the following title: "Confidential. Something about

Our Wretched Hole. To the Great-Hearted and Benevolent Litera-
teur Mr. Chekhov, Who Has Graced This Unworthy Island of
Sakhalin with His Presence. Post of Korsakov." In the petition I
found a poem entitled "Wolfsbane":

> Near the river proudly grows,
> In a swampy place, in a hollow,
> That blue leaf, so beautiful,
> In medicine called Aconite.
>
> This is the root of the wolfsbane,
> Planted by the hand of the Creator.
> Often it tempts people
> And sends them to the grave,
> Bestowing them on Abraham's bosom.

7 Those who select the sites of new settlements find that larches
indicate the presence of poor, swampy soil. The subsoil clay does
not drain water, but forms a peat bog. Marsh rosemary, cran-
berries and moss appear, the larch itself deteriorates, grows crook-
edly and is covered with Iceland moss. The larches here are ugly,
with thin trunks, and they soon wither away without reaching
maturity.

8 Cork trees and grapevines grow here, but they have degenerated and resemble their forebears as little as Sakhalin bamboo
cane resembles Ceylon bamboo.

9 In one of his orders General Kononovich testifies that "partly
because of its isolation and the difficulties of communication, and
partly because of private considerations and designs which in the
full sight of my predecessors had the effect of ruining all these
affairs and corroding everything touched by their rotten breath,
the Korsakov district was continuously ignored and unfairly treated,
and not one of its most pressing needs was examined, satisfied or
resolved" (Order No. 318, 1889).

10 One verst from Bolshoye Takoe, a mill was built on the river
by a German convict called Laks, by orders of General Kononovich. He also built a mill on the Tym near Derbinsk. At the
Takoe mill they charge one pound of flour and one kopeck for
milling a pood of grain. The settlers are satisfied, because formerly
they paid fifteen kopecks for a pood or milled the grain themselves on a homemade elm hand mill. A canal had to be dug and
a dam built for the mill.

11 I am not naming here the small tributaries where the Susui
and Naybuchi watershed settlements lie, because they all have

hard-to-pronounce Ainu or Japanese names such as Ekureki or Fufkasamanay.

12 Michman V. Vitgeft, "Two Words About Sakhalin Island," *Kronstadt News* (1872), Nos. 7, 17 and 34.

THE SISKA SETTLEMENT is situated at a place called the Tarayka, located on one of the southernmost tributaries of the Poronaya, which falls into Terpeniye Bay. All of the Tarayka belongs to the Southern district, although this affiliation is farfetched because it is some 400 versts from Korsakov and the climate is forbidding, worse than in Dué. The projected district mentioned in Chapter X will be called the Taraykinsky district. It will include all the settlements along the Poronaya, including Siska. In the meantime, only Southerners are being settled here. Government data show only 7 inhabitants, 6 males and 1 female. I did not visit Siska but quote an excerpt from someone's diary: "The settlement and the locality are desolate. First, there is no clear water or wood. The inhabitants use well water that turns red from tundra seepage during rainy periods. The sandy shore on which the settlement stands is surrounded by tundra. . . . The site is distressing and depressing."[1]

In order to finish with Southern Sakhalin, it remains to say a few words about those people who formerly lived and still live here independent of the penal colony. I will begin with the attempts at free colonization.

In 1868 one of the Eastern Siberian offices decided to settle twenty-five families in Southern Sakhalin. These were to be free peasants, immigrants who had already settled along the Amur. Their conditions were so miserable that one author calls their settlement lamentable and the settlers themselves wretched. These were Ukrainian peasants, natives of Chernigovsk *guberniya*, who, before living on the Amur, had settled in Tobolsk *guberniya*, also unsuccessfully. In proposing that they resettle on Sakhalin, the administration made tremendously enticing promises. They announced that they would provide each family with free flour and groats for two years, would supply all agricultural implements, cattle and seeds on credit, and would lend money, the debt being repayable in five years. They were also to be free of taxes for twenty years and excused from military service. Ten of the Amur families agreed to emigrate. These were joined by eleven families from Balagansk district, Irkutsk *guberniya*, a total of 101 people. In August of 1869 they were sent out on the transport *Mandzhur* to Muravyevsky Post. Thence they were to be taken around Cape Aniva via the Okhotsk Sea to Naybuchi Post, from which it was but thirty versts to the Takoyskaya valley, where it was proposed to found the free colony. However, autumn had come, no ship was available, and therefore the *Mandzhur* landed them and their possessions at Korsakov Post, from which they planned to travel overland to the Takoyskaya valley. At the time there was no road. According to Mitsul, Ensign Dyakonov "bestirred himself" and fifteen soldiers to cut a narrow road for them. He obviously bestirred himself very slowly, because sixteen of the families did not wait for the road to be completed and went off to the Takoyskaya valley, crossing the taiga in oxcarts. On the way they were caught by a heavy snowstorm and were obliged to abandon some of the carts and make runners for the rest. Upon reaching the valley, on November 20, they immediately set to work building barracks and dugouts to protect themselves from the freezing cold. The remaining six families arrived a week before Christmas, but since there was no room for them and it was too late to build houses for them, they left to find shelter in Naybuchi. They then went on the Kusunnay Post, where they wintered in the soldiers' barracks. They returned to Takoyskaya valley in the spring.

"At this point all the slovenliness and ignorance of the administration became evident," writes one author. They had been promised various agricultural articles costing 1,000 rubles and 4 heads of cattle for each family. But when the emigrants were put aboard the *Mandzhur* at Nikolayevsk, there were no grindstones, no working oxen, there was no place on the ship for the horses, and the plows had no plowshares. The plowshares were brought by dog sledge during the winter, but only nine were supplied. When the settlers at once sent requests for plowshares to the administration, their pleas "did not receive the proper attention." Oxen were delivered to Kusunnay in the fall of 1869, but they were exhausted and half dead. No hay had been prepared in Kusunnay and of the 41 oxen, 25 died during the winter. The horses remained to winter in Nikolayevsk but since feed was dear, they were auctioned off. The money was used to buy new horses in Zabaikal, but these proved to be even worse than the former ones and the peasants rejected several of them. Seed grains were all mixed up together, regardless of germination periods. Summer rye was delivered in the same bags with winter rye, with the result that the homesteaders came to lose all faith in the seeds and although they took them from the warehouse, they either fed them to the cattle or ate them themselves. Since there were no grindstones, the rye was not ground. They boiled it and ate it as porridge.

After a number of crop failures, they were hit by a flood in 1875 which finally destroyed the settlers' remaining ambition to farm on Sakhalin. Again they began migrating. A group of twenty houses for the exiles was built at Chibisani, on the banks of the Aniva, halfway between the Korsakov and Muravyevsky Posts. They later began to plead to be allowed to settle in the South Ussuriysky Kray. They waited impatiently for the permission, as for a special favor, for ten long years. Meanwhile they lived by hunting sable and fishing. It was not until 1886 that they reached the Ussuriysky Kray. A correspondent writes: "They are abandoning their homes; they are completely destitute; they are bringing only a part of their belongings, and each one has only one horse" (*Vladivostok,* 1886, No. 22). At the present time there still exists a burned-out area not too far from the road between Bolshoye and Maloye Takoe. This is the site of the former free settlement of Voskresenskoye. The huts abandoned by the settlers were burned down by vagrants. They say that even now the huts are standing in Chibisani, with the chapel and the school building. I did not visit it.

Only three free settlers remain on the island: Khomutov, whom I have already mentioned, and two women who were born in Chibisani. They say that Khomutov is "roaming around somewhere," and supposedly lives at the Muravyevsky Post. He is rarely seen. He hunts sable and catches sturgeon in Bussé Bay. As to the women, one—Sofya—is married to Baranovsky, a peasant-formerly-exiled, and lives in Mitsulka. The other, Anisya, is married to the settler Leonov and lives in Tretya Pad. Khomutov will soon die and Sofya and Anisya will leave for the mainland with their husbands and so there will soon be only a memory of the free settlers.

Free colonization on the southern part of Sakhalin must therefore be called unsuccessful. It is difficult to ascertain whether the fault lies with the natural conditions which were so grim and inimical to the settlers or whether the whole matter was ruined by the ignorance and negligence of the officials, since the experiment was short-lived. In addition, the experiment was made with people who were obviously nomadic, for they had acquired a taste for nomad life during their long rovings over Siberia. It is difficult to say whether the experiment might have proved successful if it had been repeated.[2]

Actually, the unsuccessful experiment can be educational for the penal colony in two respects. First, the free settlers did not farm for any length of time, and in the last ten years before returning to the mainland they lived only on fishing and hunting. At the present time, Khomutov, despite his debilitating age, finds it more advantageous and gainful to catch sturgeon and shoot sable than to sow wheat and plant cabbage. Second, it is impossible to hold a free healthy man, full of life, in Southern Sakhalin when he is told daily that only two days' distance from Korsakov there lies the warm and rich South Ussuriysky Kray.

When asked who they are, members of the native population of Southern Sakhalin, the local foreigners, do not respond with the name of a tribe or nation, but say simply, "Ainu," a word which means "a man." In Shrenk's ethnographic map the area inhabited by the Ainu, or Aynu, is indicated in yellow. This color completely covers Matsmay Island and the southern section of Sakhalin up to Terpeniye Bay. They also live on the Kurile Islands and are therefore called Kurils by the Russians. The number of Ainu living on Sakhalin is not known exactly, but there is no doubt that this tribe is dying out extremely rapidly.

Dr. Dobrotvorsky, who served in Southern Sakhalin[3] twenty-five years ago, states that there was a time when there were 8 large Ainu settlements having almost 200 inhabitants each year near Bussé Bay alone. Close to the Nayba he saw traces of many settlements. At the time he considered three census figures taken from various sources: 2,885, 2,418 and 2,050, but he felt the last one was the most authentic. According to one author who was his contemporary, Ainu settlements existed along the shore on both sides of Korsakov Post. However, I did not find even one settlement remaining, and I saw only a few Ainu yurts near Bolshoye Takoe and Siyantsy. The number of Ainu given in the *Record of the Number of Foreigners Living in the Korsakov District in 1889* is 581 males and 569 females.

The reasons for the extinction of the Ainu is given by Dobrotvorsky: he says they were devastated by wars which apparently took place some time ago on Sakhalin, and there was a low birth rate due to the infertility of the Ainu women, but the chief reason was that they suffered from disease. Syphilis and scurvy were always prevalent among them. They may also have suffered from smallpox.[4]

All of these reasons usually given for the chronic extinction of foreigners do not explain, however, why the Ainu are becoming extinct so rapidly, almost in front of your eyes. There has been no war within the last twenty-five or thirty years, nor any significant epidemic; nevertheless during that period the tribe decreased by more than half. It seems to me it would be more accurate to suppose that this swift extinction, their vanishing, is caused not only by their dying out but also by the migration of the Ainu to the neighboring islands.

Before Southern Sakhalin was occupied by the Russians, the Ainu were virtually Japanese serfs. It was so much the easier to subjugate them because they are meek and timid, and because they were hungry and could not live without rice.[5]

After occupying Southern Sakhalin, the Russians freed the Ainu and they have safeguarded their freedom up to the present day, and they have protected them from oppression and refrained from interfering in their private lives. In 1884 some escaped convicts murdered a few Ainu families. They also tell the story that an Ainu dog-sledge owner who refused to carry mail was beaten with birch rods, and there have been attempted rapes of Ainu women. However, they speak of similar oppressions and injuries as isolated cases and extremely rare occurrences.

Unfortunately, the Russians did not bring rice along with freedom. With the departure of the Japanese nobody fished any more, wages stopped and the Ainu began to starve. They were unable to survive on fish and meat, as do the Gilyaks. They needed rice. Hunger forced them to disregard their dislike of the Japanese, and they began migrating to Matsmay. I read in one correspondent's report in *Golos* [Voice] (1876), No. 16, that an Ainu delegation is said to have arrived at Korsakov Post and begged for work, or at least for potato seeds and lessons on how to cultivate the soil for potatoes. We learn that they were refused work, but promised the potato seeds; the promise was not kept. The suffering Ainu continued to move to Matsmay. Another report concerning 1885 (*Vladivostok,* No. 28) says the Ainu made some petitions which were obviously ignored and they desperately wanted to leave Sakhalin for Matsmay.

The Ainu are as dark as gypsies. They have tremendous beards and mustaches, and thick, wiry black hair.

Their eyes are dark, expressive and gentle. They are of medium height and have a strong, stocky physique. Their features are massive and coarse but, in the words of the sailor V. Rimsky-Korsakov, they have neither the flat faces of the Mongols nor the slit eyes of the Chinese. It would appear that the bearded Ainu closely resemble Russian peasants. Actually, when an Ainu dons his *khalat,* which is similar to our farmer's short coat, and belts it, he resembles a merchant's coachman.[6]

The Ainu's body is covered with dark hair which at times grows quite thick and in bunches on his chest, although it is far from being hirsute. This chest hair, and his heavy beard and thick wiry head of hair, is so rare in aboriginals that it astounded travelers, who returned home and spoke of "the hairy Ainu." Our Kazakhs who exacted tribute in furs from them on the Kurile Islands during the last century also called them "hairy ones."

The Ainu live close to other peoples whose facial growth is extremely sparse, therefore it is not difficult to understand why their tremendous beards cause ethnographers quite a problem. To this day science has still not discovered the Ainu's proper place in the racial scheme of things. The Ainu are categorized either as Mongols or as Caucasians. One Englishman said they were the descendants of Hebrews who had scattered over the Japanese Islands in ancient times. There are two opinions which may be fairly accurate: first, that the Ainu belong to a special race which formerly populated all the eastern Asiatic islands; second, according to our Shrenk, they were a paleo-Asiatic people which was squeezed out of Asia onto the neighboring islands by Mongolian tribes, the course of the migration from Asia to the islands being through Korea. At any rate, the Ainu moved from the south to the north, from a warm climate to a cold one, constantly changing their living conditions for the worse. They are not warlike and they despise violence. It was not difficult to conquer, enslave or expel them. They were forced out of Asia by the Mongols, from Nippon and Matsmay by the Japanese, on Sakhalin the Gilyaks did not permit them to live beyond the Tarayka, and on the Kurile Islands they came up against the Kazakhs, and so they finally found themselves in an intolerable situation. Now, usually hatless, barefoot, their trouser legs pulled up above their knees, the Ainu meet you on the road, bow low, while at the same time glancing at you cordially, mournfully and sorrowfully, as though they were complete failures, and wanted to apologize for having full-grown beards while unable to scratch a living for themselves.

Details on the Ainu can be obtained in Shrenk, Dobrotvorsky and A. Polonsky.[7] The information on Gilyak food and clothing also applies to the Ainu, with the addition that the lack of rice, for which they inherited their craving from ancestors who once lived on the southern islands, is a serious deprivation. They do not like Russian bread. Their food is more varied than that of the Gilyaks. In addition to meat and fish they eat various plants, mollusks and what lower-class Italians call *frutti di mare.* They eat very little, but often, almost every hour. Gluttony, a vice of all the northern savages, has not been found among them. Since breast-fed babies must make the transition from milk directly to fish and whale fat, they are weaned late. Rimsky-Korsakov saw an Ainu woman suckling a three-year-old boy who was quite capable of getting around by himself and even had a little knife stuck in his belt like a grown-up man.

Their clothing and housing show a strong southern influence—not that of Southern Sakhalin, but of the tropical south. In the summer the Ainu wear shirts woven of grass or inner bark. Formerly, when they were not so impoverished, they wore silk *khalats*. They do not wear hats, and walk barefoot in the summer and autumn until snowfall. Their yurts are smoky and smelly but are much lighter, cleaner and, as it were, more cultured than those of the Gilyaks. Racks for drying fish usually stand near the yurts, emitting a foul, stifling odor. Dogs howl and fight. Occasionally you can see a cage made of tree trunks with a young bear sitting in it. He will be butchered and eaten in the winter at the so-called Bear Festival. One morning I saw a little Ainu girl feeding a bear by thrusting in moistened dry fish on a little shovel.

The yurts are made of rough wood and planks, the roofs of thin poles covered with grass. Plank beds line the walls. Shelves mounted over them contain their belongings. In addition to hides, jars of fat, nets, kitchenware and the like, you find baskets, tinwear and even musical instruments. The master of the house can usually be found sitting on the plank bed, always smoking a small pipe, and when you ask him a question he answers unwillingly and tersely, although courteously.

In the middle of the yurt is a hearth with burning wood, the smoke escaping through an opening in the roof. A large black kettle hangs on a hook over the fire and contains a bubbling, sulphurous, foaming fish soup which I believe no European would eat for love or money. Monstrosities crouch around the kettle. In the same degree that the Ainu men are solid-looking and handsome, so are the Ainu wives and mothers repugnant. Some authors describe the appearance of Ainu women as hideous and even loathsome. Their coloring is a swarthy yellow, akin to parchment, their eyes are narrow, their features massive. Straight, wiry hair hangs over their faces in shaggy strands, like straw on an old barn. Their clothing is untidy and ugly. Together with all this they are extraordinarily thin and have a senile look about them. The married women use a blue coloring on their lips as a result of which their faces lose all semblance of humanity. When I had the opportunity to see them and observe the gravity, almost the grimness, with which they stirred the kettles with their spoons and removed the filthy foam, I felt I was seeing real witches. The younger and older girls do not give such a repulsive impression.[8]

The Ainu never wash, and they sleep in their clothing.

Almost all those who have described the Ainu refer to their characteristics in the best possible light. The consensus is that they are a gentle, modest, good-natured, trustworthy, loquacious, courteous people who respect property, are brave when out hunting, and according to Dr.

Rollen, the companion of La Pérouse, they are intelligent. Unselfishness, forthrightness, fidelity in friendship, and generosity are their customary traits. They are truthful and cannot countenance deceit. Krusenstern was enraptured with them. After enumerating their wonderful spiritual qualities, he concludes: "Such truly rare qualities, for which they are not beholden to an exalted culture but to nature alone, awoke in me the sentiment that they are better than all the others I have known up to this time."[9]

Rudanovsky writes: "There cannot be a more peaceful and modest people than those we encountered in the southern part of Sakhalin." All violence arouses disgust and fear in them. Polonsky describes the following grievous episode recorded in the archives: It happened long ago, in the past century. Cherny, the captain of the Cossack troop escorting the Ainu from the Kurile Islands into Russian subjugation, decided to beat some of them with birch rods. "When the Ainu saw the preparations for the beating they became terrified, and when the Cossacks began tying the hands of two Ainu women behind their backs in order to obtain satisfaction more conveniently, some of the Ainu escaped to an inaccessible cliff, while another fled out to sea in a canoe loaded with twenty women. The women who had not been able to escape were beaten. The Cossacks then took six men with them in a canoe, and in order to prevent them from escaping, they tied their hands behind their backs. This was done so brutally that one of them died. They tossed his body weighted down with a rock into the sea, his swollen hands looking as though they had been scalded, and Cherny exclaimed to his comrades in high elation: "That's the way we do it in Russian style!"

Finally, a few words about the Japanese, who played such a leading role in the history of Southern Sakhalin. It is a fact that the southern third of Sakhalin has belonged to Russia only since 1875. Previously it was subject to Japan. In *A Guide to Practical Navigation and Nautical Astronomy* by Prince Golitsyn, published in 1854, a book used by sailors even today, Northern Sakhalin, with the Capes of Maria and Elizaveta, is described as Japanese.

Many people, including Nevelskoy, doubted that Southern Sakhalin belonged to Japan. Even the Japanese themselves were not convinced about it until the Russians suggested it to them by their strange behavior.

The Japanese first appeared in Southern Sakhalin at the beginning of this century; not earlier. In 1853, N. V. Bussé recorded a conversation with some old Ainu men, who remembered the time when they were independent. They said, "Sakhalin is the land of the Ainu. There is no Japanese territory on Sakhalin." In 1806, the year of Khvostov's piratical expedition, there was only one Japanese settlement on the banks of the Aniva, and it was all built of new wooden boards. It was obvious that the Japanese had only recently settled there. Krusenstern was on the Aniva in April when the herring were running. The water seemed to boil with an amazing multitude of fish, whales and seals. The Japanese had no nets or seines and caught the fish in pails. This shows they had no conception of the wealth of fish to be found here; later, of course, large-scale fisheries were established. These first Japanese colonists were probably escaped convicts or men exiled from their homeland for having visited a foreign country.

Our diplomats first turned their attention to Sakhalin at the beginning of the century. Ambassador Rezanov[10] was authorized to conclude a trade alliance with Japan and "to acquire Sakhalin Island, which is independent of both the Japanese and the Chinese." He conducted himself with extreme stupidity. "Taking into consideration the Japanese intolerance of the Christian faith," he forbade the members of his party to cross themselves and ordered the confiscation without any exceptions of all crosses, holy pictures, prayerbooks and "everything that represents Christianity or bears a Christian symbol." If one is to believe Krusenstern, Rezanov was denied a chair during the audience, he was not permitted to wear his sword and, "bowing to the stiff-necked attitude of the Japanese," he walked barefoot. And this was an ambassador, a Russian nobleman! It would, I imagine, be difficult to demonstrate a greater lack of dignity.

Having suffered a complete fiasco, Rezanov decided to revenge himself upon the Japanese. He ordered the naval officer Khvostov to terrorize the Sakhalin Japanese. This order was not given in exactly the customary manner, but rather deviously; it came in a sealed envelope with the explicit instruction that it was to be opened and read only when he arrived at his destination.[11]

Thus Rezanov and Khvostov were the first to admit that Southern Sakhalin belonged to the Japanese. However, the Japanese did not take possession of their new property, but merely sent their surveyor Mamia-Rinzo to ascertain what kind of island it was. In general, although shrewd, hard-working and cunning, the Japanese conducted themselves sluggishly and indecisively thoughout the entire history of Sakhalin, and this can only be explained by the fact that they had as little faith in their own rights as the Russians had in theirs.

Apparently the Japanese, after getting to know the island, thought of establishing a colony, or perhaps an agricultural settlement, but experiments in this direction, if there were any, could only have resulted in disillusionment since, according to the engineer Lopatin, Japanese laborers suffered greatly and were quite unable to withstand the winter. Only Japanese traders, rarely accompanied by their wives, came to Sakhalin. They lived here in bivouacs, and only a small group, amounting to a score or two, remained to spend the winter. The rest returned home on junks. Those who remained did not sow anything, they did not have vegetable gardens or horned cattle, but they brought all necessary supplies with them from Japan. The only thing attracting them to Sakhalin was the fish. It brought them tremendous profits because it was caught in great abundance, while the Ainus who did all of the hard work cost them almost nothing. The profit from the fishing industry reached 50,000 and later 300,000 rubles a year. It is therefore not surprising that these Japanese overlords took to wearing seven silk kimonos, one on top of the other.

At first the Japanese had factories only on the banks of the Aniva and in Mauka, their main office being at the

Kusun-Kotan gap, where the Japanese consul now resides.[12]

Later they cut a road from the Aniva to the Takoyskaya valley. They maintained supply depòts near the place known today as Galkino-Vraskoye. The road has not yet overgrown and is called the Japanese Road. The Japanese also reached the Tarayka, where they caught migratory fish in the Poronaya River and established the Sitka settlement. Their boats sailed as far as Nyisky Bay. The boat with the beautiful rigging seen by Polyakov in 1881 on the Tro was Japanese.

The Japanese were interested in Sakhalin strictly for commercial reasons, just as the Americans were interested in Tyuleni [Seal] Island.[13] After the Russians founded the Muravyevsky Post in 1853, the Japanese began to show some political activity. Knowing that they might lose their large profits and free labor compelled them to look closely at the Russians and they attempted to strengthen their influence on the island in order to offset Russian influence. But again, probably from lack of confidence in their own rights, they carried on the struggle with the Russians in an almost ludicrously irresolute manner, and acted like children. They limited themselves merely to spreading gossip about the Russians among the Ainus, boasting that they could slaughter all the Russians at any time they pleased. Wherever the Russians built a post, a Japanese picket outpost was immediately stationed there, on the opposite side of the river. In spite of their desires to appear terrifying, the Japanese nevertheless remained peaceful and amiable. They sent sturgeon to the Russian soldiers, and when the Russians asked for nets, the Japanese gladly satisfied their requests.

A pact was concluded in 1867 whereby Sakhalin became the common possession of both countries with the right of joint domain. The Russians and Japanese recognized their equal rights to the island. In other words, neither of them considered the island to be their sole possession.[14]

By the treaty of 1875 Sakhalin definitely became a part of the Russian Empire and the Japanese were recompensed with the gift of all of our Kurile Islands.[15]

Alongside the mountain pass where the Korsakov Post is situated is another pass which has retained its name since the time when it was the Japanese settlement of Kusun-Kotan. No Japanese buildings remain. However, there is a shop run by a Japanese family which sells groceries and various trifles, where I purchased hard Japanese pears, but this was built later. On the best location in the pass there is a white house where from time to time a flag can be seen waving—a red circle on a white background. This is the Japanese consulate.

One morning during a northeaster when it was so cold in my quarters that I wrapped myself in a blanket, I was visited by the Japanese consul, Mr. Kuzé, and his secretary, Mr. Sugiama. I immediately began to apologize that it was so cold.

"Oh, no," my guests said. "It is very warm here!"

By their facial expressions and tones of voice they attempted to tell me not only that it was warm in my quarters, but that I was living in an absolute paradise on earth. Both are pure-blooded Japanese of medium height, with Mongoloid faces. The consul is about forty years old, he wears no beard, his mustache is barely visible, and he is of solid build. The secretary is about ten years younger and wears blue eyeglasses, obviously a consumptive—a victim of the Sakhalin climate. There is another secretary, Mr. Suzuki. He is below medium height, has a very large mustache which droops in Chinese fashion, and has narrow, slanting eyes—an irresistibly handsome man in the eyes of the Japanese. Once, when telling me about a Japanese minister, Mr. Kuzé said, "He is as handsome and manly as Suzuki." They wear European clothing outside their home and they speak Russian very well. When I visited the consulate I often found them reading Russian or French books. They had a bookcase full of books. They had had European education, were exquisitely courteous, considerate and cordial. The Japanese consulate was a warm and charming meeting place for the local officials. Here they could forget the prison, penal servitude and office squabbles, and relax.

The consul is the intermediary between the Japanese

who come to trade and the local administration. On the most solemn occasions he and his secretary, dressed in full regalia, drive from the Kusun-Kotan pass to the post to the District Commander and congratulate him on the holiday. Mr. Bely returns the compliment. Every year on December 1 he goes with his staff to Kusun-Kotan to congratulate the consul on the birthday of the Emperor of Japan, and drink champagne. When the consul visits naval vessels, he receives a seven-gun salute. During my visit there arrived the orders of Anna and Stanislav, both of the third degree, to be awarded to Kuzé and Suzuki. In full dress, Mr. Bely, Major S. and Mr. F., and the secretary of the police department, ceremoniously departed for Kusun-Kotan to present the Orders. I went with them. The Japanese were tremendously touched by both the orders and the solemnity of the occasion, for they greatly delighted in such things. They served champagne. Mr. Suzuki did not conceal his pleasure, and examined the order from all sides with sparkling eyes, like a child with a toy. I detected a struggle in his "handsome and manly" face. He wanted to dash to his quarters and show the order to his young wife (he had married recently), and at the same time politeness demanded that he remain with the guests.[16]

Now that I have completed the survey of the settled areas of Sakhalin, I will proceed to discuss various matters, some important and others unimportant, which comprise the contemporary life of the colony.

---

[1]   The settlement lies at a crossroads. Those traveling from Alexandrovsk to Korsakov in the winter or vice versa always stop here. A way station was built in 1869 near the present, formerly Japanese, settlement. Soldiers and their wives, and later convicts, lived here. A brisk trade flourished during the winter, spring, and at the end of summer. During the winter the Tungus, Yakuts and the Amur Gilyaks came to trade with the foreigners in the South, while during the spring and late summer the Japanese came to fish from their junks. The name of the way station, the Tikhmenevsky Post, has been retained to the present day.

[2]   This experiment applies only to Sakhalin. However, in his article "Banishment to Sakhalin" (*Vestnik Evropy,* 1879, V),

Professor D. G. Talberg considers it of general importance and, applying its results generally to our ineptitude in colonization, he comes to the following conclusion: "Is it not time for us to give up all our colonizing efforts in the East?" In their introduction to Professor Talberg's article the editors of *Vestnik Evropy* state that "we will scarcely find another such example of colonizing ability demonstrated by the Russian people in the past when they seized all of the European East and Siberia." Furthermore, the esteemed editors base their opinion on the work of the now deceased Professor Yeshevsky, who presented "an amazing picture of Russian colonization."

In 1869 a trader brought twenty Aleuts of both sexes to Southern Sakhalin from Kodiak Island to hunt game. They were settled near Muravyevsky Post and were supplied with provisions. They did absolutely nothing but eat and drink. In a year the trader moved them to one of the Kurile Islands. At approximately the same time two Chinese political exiles were settled in Korsakov Post. Since they expressed the desire to engage in farming, the governor-general of Eastern Siberia ordered each of them to be supplied with six oxen, a horse, a cow and enough seeds for two years. They received nothing, however, presumably because no stock was available, and finally they were sent to the mainland. Among the unsuccessful free colonists can also be included the Nikolayevsk town-dweller Semenov, a tiny, gaunt man, forty years old, who now wanders all over the Southern District searching for gold.

3   He left two serious works: *The Southern Section of Sakhalin Island* (an abstract from a military medical report), published by the Siberian Division of the Imperial Russian Geographic Society (1870), Vol. I, Nos. 2 and 3, and *An Ainu-Russian Dictionary*.

4   It is difficult to believe that this disease which devastated Northern Sakhalin and the Kurile Islands could have bypassed Southern Sakhalin. A. Polonsky writes that when a person died in a yurt, the Ainus abandoned it and built another one elsewhere. Such a custom obviously arose at the time when, fearing epidemics, the Ainus abandoned their infected dwellings and settled in other locations.

5   An Ainu told Rimsky-Korsakov: "The *sizam* sleeps while the Ainu works for him; he chops trees, catches fish; the Ainu doesn't want to work—but the *sizam* beats him."

6   In the book by Shrenk which I have already mentioned there is a picture of an Ainu. See also the book by Friedrich von Hellwald, *Natural History of Tribes and Peoples*, Vol. II, which depicts a mature Ainu dressed in a *khalat*.

7　A. Polonsky's research work "Kurily" [The Kurilians] was published in the *Reports of the Imperial Russian Geographic Society* (1871), Vol. 14.

8　N. V. Bussé, who rarely said anything good about anybody, stated the following about the Ainu women: "One evening a drunken Ainu came to me. I knew him to be a real tippler. He brought along his wife, so far as I could understand, with the aim of offering up her fidelity to the connubial couch and thus to wheedle fine gifts from me. It seemed that the Ainu woman, who was pretty in her own way, was ready to assist her husband in his plan, but I pretended not to understand their explanations. . . . On leaving my house, right before my own eyes and in full sight of the sentry, the husband and wife paid their debt to nature without any ceremony. This Ainu woman did not demonstrate any feminine modesty whatsoever. Her breasts were practically uncovered. The Ainu women wear the same garments as the men, consisting of several loose short *khalats* belted with a low sash. They do not wear shirts or underwear and therefore the slightest disarray of their clothing discloses all their hidden charms." But even this dour author admits that "among the young girls there were some who were pretty, with pleasant, soft features and ardent black eyes." Be it as it may, the Ainu woman is very retarded in her physical development. She ages and withers sooner than a man. This can be attributed perhaps to the fact that during the age-long migrations of the people the lion's share of privations, hard work and tears fell to the woman.

9　Here he tells of their great qualities: "When we visited an Ainu dwelling on the bank of Rumyantsev Bay, I noted the most delightful harmony in a family which comprised ten persons. One could almost say there was absolute equality among its members. After having spent several hours with them we were unable to determine who was the head of the family. The older members demonstrated no signs of authority over the younger. When gifts were distributed to them, not one showed the slightest sign of discontent that he had received less than another. They vied with each other to serve us in every possible way."

10　Nikolay Petrovich Rezanov (1764–1807), the founder and leading spirit of the Russian-American Company, was the Russian Ambassador to the court of Japan before his appointment as Governor of Kamchatka. The Russian-American Company set up its headquarters in Sitka in Alaska, and from there Rezanov made his famous journey to San Francisco, offering furs to the government of California in exchange for food. He became engaged to the beautiful daughter of the *Comandante* of San Francisco, but died shortly afterward of fever during a journey through Siberia. Chekhov's verdict on him is not borne out by serious historians. —TRANS.

11 Khvostov destroyed Japanese homes and barns on the banks of the Aniva and awarded one Ainu elder with a silver medal on a Vladimir ribbon. This piracy greatly alarmed the Japanese government, which began to take measures to defend itself. Shortly thereafter Captain Golovin and his companions were taken prisoner on the Kurile Islands, exactly as though they were in a state of war. When the governor of Matsmay later released the prisoners, he told them solemnly: "You were all captured because of Khvostov's raids, but we have now received from the Okhotsk administration the explanation that his raids were acts of piracy. This is clear to us, and therefore we are ordering your release."

12 Particulars may be obtained in Venyukov's "A General Survey of the Gradual Expansion of Russian Boundaries in Asia and Means for Their Defense. The First Region: Sakhalin Island," *Military Miscellany* (1872), No. 3.

13 Tyuleni Island lies in the Sea of Okhotsk, 11 miles off Cape Patience in Southern Sakhalin.—TRANS.

14 It was obviously because of the Japanese desire to legalize the servitude of the Ainu that a risky clause was included among others in the pact, in which foreigners who have fallen into debt can repay their debt through work or by offering services. However, there were no Ainus on Sakhalin whom the Japanese did not consider their debtor.

15 Nevelskoy always regarded Sakhalin as a Russian possession, basing this claim on the occupation of the island by our Tungus in the seventeenth century, the first description of which appeared in 1742, and the occupation of Southern Sakhalin by the Russians in 1806. He believed the Orochi tribe consisted of Russian Tungus, with which ethnographers disagree. It was in fact first described in writing not by the Russians but by the Dutch; and as for the occupation in 1806, the primacy of the Russian claim is refuted by the facts. Undoubtedly, the right of first exploration belongs to the Japanese, and the Japanese were the first to occupy Southern Sakhalin. However, it seems that we overreached ourselves in our generosity. "Out of respect," as the peasants say, we could have given the Japanese the 5 or 6 Kurile Islands closest to them, but instead we gave them 22 islands, which, if we are to believe the Japanese, bring in 1,000,000 rubles in profits annually.

16 Relations are splendid between the local administration and the Japanese, which is as it should be. They serve champagne to each other on solemn occasions, and they find other means to maintain good relations. I cite verbatim one of the letters received from the consul: "To the Honorable Commander of the Korsakov Post: With respect to Order No. 741, dated August 16 of this year, I have made arrangements to distribute supplies consisting of 4 barrels of salted fish and 5 bags of salt to the men who suffered an accident on the brig and on the junk. In addition, in the name of these poor fellows, I have the honor to express to you, gracious sir, the extremely sincere recognition of your friendly compassion and your gift to a neighboring nation, a gift which is so important to them and which, I feel absolutely certain, they will always remember with gratitude. Kuzé, Consul of the Japanese Empire." This letter gives some idea of the success achieved by the young Japanese secretaries in learning our language. German officers who have learned Russian, and foreigners who translate Russian literature, write our language in an incomparably worse fashion.

Japanese courtesy is not cloying, and I find it charming. No matter how often it is practiced, it is not obnoxious, in accordance with the proverb "Butter does not spoil the porridge." A Japanese wood-turner in Nagasaki from whom our naval officers bought various knickknacks always politely praised everything Russian. He would see an officer's trinket or wallet and go into raptures, saying, "How magnificent! How elegant!" Once one of the officers brought an extremely crudely fashioned wooden cigarette case from Sakhalin. "Won't I pull a fast one on him now," he thought. "Let us see what he'll say now." But when they showed the cigarette case to the Japanese, he did not falter for a moment. He shook it in the air and said in tones of wonder, "How strong it is!"

WHEN PUNISHMENT, in addition to its primary aims of vengeance, intimidation or correction, is combined with other aims, such as colonization, it should properly be adapted to the needs of the colony and yield to compromises. The prison is antagonistic to the colony; their interests are completely opposed to one another. Life in prison wards enslaves and eventually degenerates the convict. The instincts of a settled householder, of good management, of family life are stifled in him by habits acquired through a gregarious existence. He loses his health, grows old, becomes morally weak. The longer the time he spends in prison, the less likely will he become an energetic and useful member of the colony. Instead he will become a burden to it.

For this reason our colonizing system chiefly requires a reduction in the length of prison terms and of penal servitude. Our *Code on Convicts* makes significant compromises in this respect. For convicts who are regarded as on their way to reformation, ten months count as a year, and convicts in the second and third categories—i.e., those convicted for four to twelve years—find that when they are assigned to the mines each year of work is credited as a year and a half.[1]

Convicts regarded as on their way to reformation are

permitted by law to live outside the prison. They can build homes, get married, possess money. But the facts far surpass the *Code*. To ease the transition from convict status to one of greater independence, the Governor-General of the Amur region in 1888 permitted the freeing of industrious and well-behaved convicts before the end of their term. In announcing this order (No. 302), General Kononovich promised to free them from work two and even three years before completing the full term of penal servitude. Actually, without any legal clauses or orders but solely as a result of necessity (because it is good for the colony), all convict women without exception, many of them on probation and even those who have been sentenced to indefinite terms, and all those convicts who have families or are good draftsmen, surveyors, drivers of dog sleighs, etc., live outside the prison, in their own homes and in free men's quarters. Many are permitted to live outside the prison out of "common humanity," or because it is assumed that if X. lives in a hut rather than in prison no harm will result, or if it happens that Z., who has been sentenced to an unlimited term, is permitted to live in a free man's quarters because he arrived with his wife and children, then it would be absolutely unjust to refuse the same permission to N., who was sentenced to a short term.

As of January 1, 1890, there was a total of 5,905 convicts of both sexes in all three Sakhalin districts. Of these, 2,124 (36 percent) were sentenced to terms up to 8 years. There were 1,567 (26.5 percent) sentenced from 8 to 12 years, 747 (12.7 percent) from 12 to 15 years, 731 (12.3 percent), from 15 to 20 years. There were 386 (6.5 percent) sentenced to indefinite terms, and there were 175 (3 percent) who were regarded as incorrigibles and sentenced from 20 to 50 years. Those with short terms, with sentences of up to 12 years, comprise 62.5 percent, i.e., over half of the entire number. I do not know the average age of those recently sentenced, but judging from the present composition of the penal population, it should be not less than 35. If the average length of an 8-to-10-year term is added to this, and if we consider that a man ages much more rapidly in penal servitude than in ordinary circumstances, it is obvious that if the actual term is served and if the *Code* is observed with strict adherence to confinement in prison and work under the supervision of convoys, etc., not only the long-term convicts but over half of the short-term convicts will become a part of the colony after their colonizing abilities have been completely spent.

In my time there were 424 convict homesteaders of both sexes who had plots of land. I recorded 908 convicts of both sexes who lived in the colony, and among them were wives, cohabitants of both sexes, laborers, lodgers, etc. There was a total of 1,332 who lived outside the prison in their own huts and free men's quarters, which is 23 percent of the total number of convicts.[2]

There is almost no difference in homesteading between the convicts and the homesteading settlers in the colony. Convicts who are laborers on homesteads work exactly like our peasant workers. Releasing a prisoner to work for a good peasant homesteader, also a convict, is a unique penal measure developed from Russian experience, and it is undoubtedly more humane than the condition of Australian farmhands. Convict lodgers spend the night in their own quarters and must appear for labor assignments and work just like their comrades living inside the prison. Craftsmen such as cobblers and cabinet makers often serve their sentence in their own quarters.[3]

No particular disharmony is observed from the fact that a fourth of all the convicts live outside the prison, and I would enthusiastically admit that it is not easy to regulate our penal system precisely because the remaining three-fourths live inside the prison walls. We can naturally only speak of the advantages of huts over common wards as a probability, since absolutely no observations have so far been made on the subject. No one has yet proved that crimes and escapes occur less frequently among convicts living in huts than among those living in prison and that the work of the former is more productive than that of the latter. In all probability the prison statistics which eventually deal with this problem will decide in favor of the huts. One thing is certain. The colony will gain if every convict arriving on Sakhalin, regardless of his term, could immediately begin building a hut for himself and his family, and in this way his colonizing activities will begin very early while he is still comparatively young and healthy. Nor would justice suffer, for the criminal on the very first day of joining the colony would suffer his greatest trials before being transferred to settler status and not afterward.

When the convict's term is completed he is free from work and is transferred to settler status. There are no delays connected with this. If the new settler has money and administrative patronage, he remains in Alexandrovsk or settles in the settlement which is most desirable to him, and he either buys or builds a house unless he acquired one while in penal servitude. Even farming and labor are not obligatory for such a person. If he is a member of the ignorant masses which constitute the majority, he usually settles on a plot of land in the settlement where the administration orders him to go. If the settlement is crowded, and there is no suitable land available for a plot, he is placed on a homestead which is already established as a co-owner or half-owner, or he is made to settle on a new location.[4]

The selection of sites for new settlements, which demands experience and some specialized knowledge, is entrusted to the local administration—in other words, to the district supervisors, prison wardens and settlement supervisors. There are no specific laws or instructions controlling the selection of sites, and the whole matter finally depends on the caliber of the staff members, whether they have been in service for a long time and whether they are acquainted with convict population and the terrain. For example, Butakov knew the North, Bely and Yartsev were knowledgeable about the South. Then it was a question of whether they had come recently, whether they were philologists, law students and infantry lieutenants, or merely uneducated persons who had never served anywhere before. The majority were young townsfolk who knew nothing about life. I have already written about the official who refused to believe the settlers and the natives when they told him the site he had chosen would be under water in the spring and during heavy rains. During my stay an official with an escort rode some 15 to 20 versts to inspect a new site and returned the same day, having supposedly made a thorough inspection in the course of two or three hours. He approved the site and said he had had a most enjoyable trip.

Rarely and reluctantly do the older and more experienced officials go out in search of new sites, since they are always occupied with other matters, while the younger officials are inexperienced and careless. The administration is sluggish, affairs are always being delayed, and the result is the overcrowding of already existing settlements. Finally, help is sought from convicts and military guards, and according to the reports they have sometimes succeeded in selecting good sites. Because there was no more space for distributing plots in the Tymovsk or Alexandrovsk districts, and because at the same time the number of poverty-stricken people was rapidly increasing, General Kononovich proposed in his order (No. 280) of 1888 "to organize land-seeking parties composed of reliable convicts under the supervision of completely efficient and literate guards with experience of these affairs, or even officials, and to send them out to seek locations appropriate for settlements." These parties are wandering over unexplored territory untrodden by the mapmakers; they search for sites with no available data on their height above sea level, the composition of the soil, the water and so on. The administration can only guess at the suitability of these sites for settlement and farming, and so it happens that the final decision about the site is made haphazardly and at random. Moreover, they never seek the opinion of a doctor or of a topographer, who is nonexistent on Sakhalin, and the surveyor appears at the new site after the land has been cleared and is already populated.[5]

Recounting his impressions to me after his tour of the settlements, the Governor-General expressed himself as follows: "Penal servitude does not begin with penal servitude, but with colonization." If the severity of the punishment is measured by the amount of work done and the physical deprivations resulting from the work, then the settlers on Sakhalin often suffer far more severe punishment than the convicts. The settler arrives at a new place which is generally marshy and covered with trees, and he has only a carpenter's ax, a saw and a shovel. He fells trees, uproots stumps, digs canals in order to drain the site, and during the entire period of these preparatory labors he lives under the open sky, on the damp ground. The delights of the Sakhalin climate, with its gloom, almost daily rain and low temperature, are never felt so keenly as during this time when a man cannot escape even for a moment from the sensation of piercing dampness and shivering fits over many weeks. This is the true *febris sachalinensis*,[6] with headaches and rheumatic pains over the entire body caused not by infections but by climatic influences.

The settlement is built first and the road leading to it comes later, rather than the other way round. For this reason a tremendous amount of strength and health is involuntarily wasted on transporting heavy burdens from the post at a time when there are no footpaths to the new site. A settler loaded down with tools, provisions and so on walks through the dense taiga, either up to his knees in water, or scrambling over mountains of windfalls, or entangled in stiff clumps of marsh rose.

Clause 307 of the *Code on Convicts* states that people outside the prison must be supplied with lumber for building their homes. The clause is interpreted to mean that the settler must cut and prepare the lumber for himself. In the past convicts were assigned to help settlers, and money was provided for hiring carpenters and purchasing material; but this arrangement was abandoned when it was discovered, as one official told me, that "the plan resulted in idleness, and the convicts worked while the settlers played games of pitch-and-toss." Now the settlers do their own work, helping one another. A carpenter builds the frame, a stovemaker builds up the stove, sawyers cut the boards. Anyone who lacks the strength or the know-how but has some money can hire someone to do the work. Those who possess strength and endurance do the hardest work. Anyone who is weak or has lost the habit of hard peasant-like work in prison, if he is not playing cards or pitch-and-toss, or is not bundling himself up against the cold, takes on some comparatively light work. Many break down with fatigue, lose courage and abandon their unfinished homes. The Chinese and Caucasians who do not know how to construct Russian huts usually escape during the first year. Almost half of the homesteaders on Sakhalin have no homes, and the explanation seems to be that the settlers encounter great difficulties at the outset when they settle down. According to data I took from the report of the agricultural inspector, homesteaders in 1889 without homes constituted 50 percent of the total in the Tymovsk district, in the Korsakov district the figure was 42 percent, and in the Alexandrovsk district, where households are built with less difficulty and the settlers buy their homes more often than build them, it was only 20 percent.

When the frame is completed, window glass and ironware are given to the homesteader on credit. The island commandant speaks about this credit in one of his orders: "With extreme regret we inform you that this credit, together with many others, is a long time in coming, and this lack of credit paralyzes the will to settle down. . . . Last autumn during my tour of the Korsakov region, I saw houses which were waiting for glass, nails and iron stove bolts; today I again saw these houses in the same state of expectancy" (Order No. 318, 1889).[7]

They do not consider it necessary to investigate a new site even after it is settled. They send out fifty to a hundred homesteaders to the new site and add scores more every year. Meanwhile nobody knows how much arable land is available for how many people, which is the reason why extraordinarily soon after having settled the new area, the new settlement is beset by overcrowding and a surplus of people. This is not only evident at the Korsakov Post; every one of the posts and settlements of both the Northern districts is crammed with people. Even such an undoubtedly solicitous person as A. M. Butakov, the commander of the

Tymovsk district, settles people on plots haphazardly, without giving thought to the future, and in no other district are there so many co-owners and multi-cohomesteaders as in his. It seems that the administration itself has no faith in the agricultural colony and has little by little come to believe that the settler requires the land only for a short while, perhaps a period of six years, since as soon as he achieves peasant status he will immediately leave the island, and under such conditions the problem of plots has merely formal significance.

Of the 3,522 homesteaders whom I recorded, 638, or 18 percent, are co-owners. If we exclude the Korsakov district, where only one settler is assigned to a plot, this percentage will be significantly greater. In the Tymovsk district, the younger the settlement, the larger the percentage of half-owners. In Voskresenskoye, for instance, there are ninety-seven homesteaders, seventy-seven of whom are half-owners. This means that each year it becomes more difficult to find new sites and to divide up the plots for settlers.[8]

Organizing his homestead and running it properly becomes a permanent obligation on the settler. For laziness, negligence and reluctance to occupy himself with homesteading he is reverted to the communal labor, that is, to convict status. He is sentenced to penal servitude for one year, and is removed from his hut to prison.

Article 402 of the *Code* permits the Governor-General of the Amur "to maintain at government cost those Sakhalin settlers who are acknowledged by the local authorities to possess no private means." At present the majority of the Sakhalin settlers receive clothing and food allowances equal to prison rations from the government for the first two or three years after being released from penal labor. The administration renders such assistance to settlers on the grounds that it has a humane concern for their practical needs. In fact it would be difficult to see how a settler could build a hut, plow the land and earn his bread at the same time. Nevertheless, it is quite common to find an order showing that some settler is being deprived of his rations because of negligence, laziness and because "he did not begin building a house," etc.[9]

After ten years of settler status, the settlers are permitted to transfer to peasant status. This new term is accompanied by extensive rights. A peasant-formerly-a-convict can leave Sakhalin and settle anywhere he wishes in Siberia, with the exception of the Semirechensk, Akmolinsk and Semipalatinsk provinces. He is permitted to join peasant societies with their approval, and can live in cities, and engage in trade and industry. He is now subject to trial and punishment by civil courts and not by the *Code on Convicts*. He also receives and sends correspondence through the regular postal service without the preliminary censorship established for convicts and settlers. Nevertheless, the main element of exile still remains in this new status; he cannot return to his homeland.[10]

The grant of peasant rights in ten years is not conditioned by any special provisions in the *Code*. Except for the conditions provided in the clauses to Article 375, the condition requiring a ten-year period is not dependent upon whether the settler was a farming homesteader or an apprentice. When we talked about this, the Superintendent of Prisons of the Amur Kray, Mr. Kamorsky, confirmed that the administration does not have the right to retain an exile in his settler status for longer than ten years, or to place any conditions upon his receiving peasant rights. However, I did encounter some old folk on Sakhalin who had enjoyed settler status for more than ten years and had not as yet been awarded peasant status. I was unable to check their claims against the official list and therefore cannot judge as to their veracity. The old folk can make mistakes or even lie, although with the stupidity and confusion rampant among the clerks and the ignorance of the younger officials, all kinds of caprices can be expected from the Sakhalin offices.

The ten-year term can be cut to six years for those settlers who "behaved in the approved fashion, engaged in beneficial work and acquired settler characteristics." This privilege permitted by Article 377 is widely used by the island commandant and the district commandants. Almost all of the peasants with whom I became acquainted received this status in six years. Unfortunately, "beneficial labor" and "settler characteristics," which are the conditions enumerated in the *Code* for receiving the privilege, are understood differently in the three districts. For example, in the Tymovsk district a settler will not become a peasant so long as he is indebted to the government and his hut is not covered with boards. In Alexandrovsk a settler does not practice farming, does not need tools and seeds, and therefore incurs smaller debts. He therefore can obtain his rights more easily.

One unconditional requisite is imposed: the settler must become a homesteader. Penal convicts more than others are people who by nature are incapable of becoming homesteaders, and they feel comfortable only when they are working for somebody else. When I asked whether a settler who does not have his own homestead because he works as a cook for an official or is a bootmaker's apprentice can ever profit from the reduction and actually receive peasant rights, I was told that it was true in the Korsakov district; the answers were more vague in both the Northern districts. Under such conditions there can obviously be no talk of norms, and if a new district commandant demands iron roofs and the ability to sing in a choir, it will be difficult to convince him that his demands are arbitrary.

When I was in Siyantsy, the settlement inspector ordered twenty-five settlers to gather around the guardhouse and announced to them that by a decree of the island commandant they had been transferred to peasant status. The decree was signed by the general on January 27, and announced to the settlers on September 26. The joyful tidings were received in total silence by all twenty-five settlers. No one crossed himself or expressed gratitude; they all stood there with grave faces and were silent as though all of them had become homesick with the thought that everything on earth, even suffering, comes to an end. When Yartsev and I asked which of them would remain on Sakhalin and which would leave, not one of the twenty-five expressed the desire to remain. They all said they yearned to return to the mainland and would gladly leave immediately, but they had no money and would have to think it over. As they talked, they agreed that it is not sufficient to have money for the fare because they would also have to spend money on the mainland. They would have to plead for acceptance into society and entertain everyone, and they would have to buy land and build a house, and finally they would need about 150 rubles. And where could they get a sum as large as that?

In spite of its size, I found only 39 peasants in Rykovskoye, and they had no intention of putting down their roots here. They were all planning to leave for the mainland. A man called Bespalov was building a large two-story house with a balcony on his plot; it was rather like a country villa. They were all observing the building with perplexed looks on their faces, and they could not understand why he was building it. That a rich man with grown sons should remain in Rykovskoye forever when he had the means to settle anywhere outside of Sakhalin gave them the feeling that he was suffering from a strange whimsical extravagance. When I asked a cardsharp peasant in Dubky if he would go to the mainland, he stared proudly at the ceiling and answered, "I will make an effort to leave."[11]

The peasants are driven from Sakhalin by a feeling of insecurity, loneliness and constant fear for their children. The main reason is the peasant's passionate longing to live in freedom before he dies and to live a real life, not a prison existence. They speak of Ussuriysky Kray and the Amur, both of them nearby, as the promised land. You sail on a boat for three or four days, and then you come upon freedom, warmth, harvest. People who have moved to the mainland and settled there write to their Sakhalin friends saying that people shake hands with them and vodka costs only 50 kopecks a bottle.

Once when I was strolling along the pier in Alexandrovsk, I entered the cutter boathouse and saw an old man of sixty or seventy and an old woman. They were surrounded with bundles and bags and were obviously all ready to travel. We started to talk. The old man had recently received his peasant rights and was now leaving for the mainland with his wife; he would go to Vladivostok and then "wherever God sends us." They said they had no money. The boat was scheduled to depart in twenty-four hours but they had already come to the pier and were hiding in the cutter boathouse with their belongings and waiting for the boat, as though they were afraid they would be turned back. They spoke of the mainland with affection, with reverence and with the conviction that they would find a truly happy life.

At the Alexandrovsk cemetery I saw a black cross with a picture of the Mother of God and the following inscription: "Here lie the ashes of the maid Afimya Kurnikovaya, deceased May 21, 1888, 18 years of age. This cross was erected to honor her memory and the departure of her parents to the mainland in June, 1889."

A peasant is not permitted to leave for the mainland if he is not of trustworthy character and if he owes money to the government. If he is the cohabitant of a convict woman and has had children by her, his travel ticket is issued to him only if he has left sufficient property to provide for the future of his mistress and his illegitimate children (Order No. 92, 1889). On the mainland a peasant is registered at his preferred *volost*.[12] The governor in whose province the *volost* is situated then informs the island commandant, who in turn issues an order to the police administration to remove the peasant so-and-so and his family from the lists—and thus officially it comes about that there is one less "unfortunate." Baron Korf told me that if the peasant misbehaves on the mainland, he is returned by administrative order to Sakhalin for the rest of his life.

According to rumor, the people of Sakhalin live well on the mainland. I was able to read their letters but never saw how they live in their new locations. However, I saw one—not in a village, but in a city. One day the monk Irakly—the missionary and priest from Sakhalin—and I were leaving a shop together in Vladivostok, and a man in a white apron and high polished boots, probably a porter or a member of a cooperative, saw Father Irakly, was delighted and asked for his blessing. It appeared that he was once Father Irakly's spiritual charge, a peasant-formerly-a-convict. Father Irakly recognized him, and remembered his name and surname. "Well now, how are you getting on?" he asked. "Thank God, very well indeed!" the peasant said excitedly.

Those peasants who have not yet departed for the mainland live in posts or settlements and run their homesteads under the same miserable conditions as the settlers and convicts. They remain under the domination of the prison authorities and must remove their caps at fifty feet if they live in the South. The officials treat them a little better and do not beat them; however, they are not peasants in the true sense; they are still prisoners. They live near the prison and see it every day; and a happy coexistence between a penal servitude prison and peaceful farming is unthinkable. Some writers have described ring-dancing and singing in Rykovskoye and they say they heard the sounds of the accordion and distant singing. I neither saw nor heard anything of the sort and cannot imagine girls singing and dancing around a prison. Even if I had heard a distant song mingling with the clanging of chains and the shouting of the guards, I would have regarded the singing as an act of malice, for a kind and merciful man does not sing near a prison.

The peasants and the settlers, their wives and their children, are all oppressed by the prison regime. The prison regulations, which resemble military regulations with their extraordinary strictness and continual tyranny, keep them under constant tension and fear. The prison administration confiscates their meadows, their best fishing sites and their best forests. Escapees, prison usurers and thieves cause them injuries; the prison executioner as he strolls down the street intimidates them; the guards debauch their wives and daughters. The prison is a perpetual reminder of their past, telling them where they are and whom they belong to.

The local villagers do not yet comprise a society. There are still no mature native-born people of Sakhalin who regard the island as their motherland. There are very few old inhabitants. The majority are newcomers. The population changes annually; some arrive, others leave, and in many settlements, as I have already said, the inhabitants do not give the impression of a village community but of a rabble brought together by chance. They call themselves brothers because they suffer together, but they have very little in common and are strangers to one another. They do not share the same faith and they speak different languages. The old-timers despise this motley crew and ask disdainfully how there can possibly be a community if in the same settlement you find Russians, Ukrainians, Tatars, Poles, Jews, Finns, Kirghiz, Georgians and gypsies. I have already mentioned the disproportional distribution of the non-Russian elements in the settlements.[13]

A diversity of another kind reacts adversely on the growth of each settlement: the colony is augmented by many aged, physically weak and psychically ill criminals, people incapable of work and those who are unprepared for practical life, people who lived in cities in their homeland and knew nothing about farming. As of January 1, 1890, according to data which I extracted from the prison reports, on the whole of Sakhalin including the prisons and the entire colony there were ninety-one members of the nobility and 924 people from the towns—i.e., former respectable citizens, merchants, city dwellers and foreign nationals—totaling 10 percent of those in penal servitude.[14]

Each settlement has an elder chosen from among the homesteaders, always either a settler or a peasant, who is confirmed as the settlement supervisor. Elders are usually selected from among those who are sober, intelligent and educated. The extent of their responsibilities has not yet been completely established, but they attempt to conduct themselves in the manner of Russian elders. They decide various petty matters, assign horses and carts to people in turn, intercede for their own people whenever necessary, etc. The Rykovskoye elder even has his own seal. Some receive a salary.

A prison guard is always stationed in each settlement,

and most often he is an ignorant member of the lower echelon of the local command who always reports to visiting officials that everything is just fine. He oversees the conduct of the settlers and makes certain they do not absent themselves without permission and that they keep up with their farming. He is the settlement's nearest thing to an official, is often the sole judge, and his reports to the administration are actually documents which are quite important in evaluating the extent to which a settler has succeeded in achieving a proper behavior and a settled way of life as a homesteader. Here is an example of a guard's report:

LIST

of Inhabitants of Verkhny Armudan Who Have Misbehaved

	Surname and Name	Criminal Record
1	Izdugin, Anany	Thief
2	Kiselev, Petr Vasilyev	The same
3	Glybin, Ivan	The same
1	Galysky, Semen	Neglectful of his home, obstinate
2	Kazankin, Ivan	The same

1 Every office on Sakhalin contains a "Table for Calculating Sentences." It shows, for example, that a convict who has been sentenced for 17½ years will in actuality spend 15 years and 3 months in penal servitude. If he is fortunate enough to be eligible for an amnesty under an imperial edict, the term then is only 10 years and 4 months. A person sentenced to 6 years is freed in 5 years and 2 months, and in the event of an amnesty, in 3 years and 6 months.

2 I did not include those convicts who lived in the homes of the officials in the capacity of servants. I believe that 25 percent live outside the prison, which means that out of every four convicts, the prison yields one to the colony. This percentage will increase significantly when Clause 305 of the *Code,* which permits reformed convicts to live outside the prison, will also be applied in the Korsakov district, where, by order of Mr. Bely, all convicts without exception live within the prison.

3   In Alexandrovsk almost all homesteaders have lodgers, and this gives it an urban aspect. I noted seventeen persons in one hut. Such crowded quarters, however, differ little from common wards.

4   Sakhalin is comparable to the most remote places in Siberia. Probably because of the exceptionally rigorous climate, the only settlers were those who had served their sentence on Sakhalin and so, even if they were not accustomed to it, they could come to terms with it. It is obvious that attempts are being made to change this arrangement. While I was there, a certain Juda Gamberg, sentenced to exile in Siberia, was sent to Sakhalin as a settler by order of Baron Korf. He settled in Derbinskoye. Settler Simeon Saulat, who did not serve his sentence in Sakhalin but in Siberia, now lives in Dubky. There are exiles serving in the administration here.

5   In time to come, the selection of new sites will be made by a commission composed of Prison Department officials, a topographer, an agronomist and a doctor. It will then be fairly clear from the reports of the commission why each site was chosen. At present, the usual idea is to settle people along river valleys and near existing or projected roads, and this has some justification. But it is more a matter of routine than a definite system. If they select a particular river valley it is not because it has been investigated more thoroughly than others and is best for farming, but because it is close to headquarters. The southwestern shore is distinguished by its comparatively mild climate, but it is farther from Dué or Alexandrovsk than the Arkovskaya valley or the Armudan River valley, and therefore the latter are preferred. When they settle people on sites along the projected road, they are not considering the well-being of the people in the new settlement, but instead they are thinking of the officials and the drivers of dog sleighs who will eventually travel along the road. If it were not for this simple plan to settle the barren road with human beings, to guard the road and provide shelter for travelers, it would be difficult to understand the need for the projected settlements on the road running the whole length of the Tym from the upper sources of the river all the way to Nyisky Bay. The people will probably receive money and food supplies from the government for guarding and looking after the road. If those settlements become a continuation of the present agricultural colony, and if the administration is dependent on rye and wheat, Sakhalin will acquire a few more thousand starving, underprivileged paupers fed by nobody knows what.

6   Sakhalin fever (Lat.).

[7] This is where the money which should have been received during his term of penal servitude as wages would have come in useful for the settler. According to the law, the prisoner sentenced to convict labor is entitled to receive 10 percent of the customary wage. For example, if road work is valued at the customary wage of 50 kopecks a day, a convict is supposed to receive 5 kopecks. During the period of his incarceration the prisoner is permitted to spend not less than half of his earnings. The remaining sum is to be given him upon his release. The money he has earned is not supposed to be applied to the payment of any civil penalties or court costs. In the event of the convict's death, it is to be given to his heirs. Prince Shakhovskoy, who was the commandant of the Dué prison in the seventies, expresses his ideas in a report, *The Problem of Organizing Sakhalin Island,* written in 1878, which should be adopted by the present administration as being fully informative and a guide to action. "Remunerating convicts for their work at least provides the prisoner with some private possessions, and private property tends to attach him to a place. By mutual agreement, this remuneration permits the prisoner to obtain better food and to keep his clothing and quarters cleaner; and the greater the sum of things which accustom him to conveniences, the greater the suffering when he is deprived of them. The complete absence of these conveniences and the continually melancholy and unfriendly atmosphere in which he lives produce in the prisoner a callous attitude to life, and all the more toward punishment. So it happens that when the number of men flogged reaches 80 percent of the total, we were forced to doubt the advantages of flogging for punishing men who are prepared to be flogged simply because they have acquired some necessities of life. Remuneration evokes independence among convicts, prevents bargaining of clothes, helps them in their homesteading and significantly decreases government expenditure with respect to attaching them to the soil after they are transferred to settler status."

Tools are given on credit for 5 years with the condition that the settler pay a fifth of the price annually. At the Korsakov post a carpenter's ax costs 4 rubles, a ripping saw 13 rubles, a shovel 1 ruble 80 kopecks, a rasp 44 kopecks, nails 10 kopecks per pound. A woodsman's ax is issued on credit at 3 rubles 50 kopecks only in the event that the settler did not take care of his carpenter's ax.

[8] The homesteader and the co-owner live in one hut and sleep on one stove. Neither religion nor sex is a deterrent to co-ownership. I recall that the co-owner of settler Golybev in Rykovskoye was the Jew Lyubarsky. In the same settlement, settler Ivan Khavriyevich had a female cohomesteader, Marya Brodyaga.

9 I have already spoken of the poverty in which the local peasant inhabitants live, regardless of the many loans and assistance received from the government. Here is a scene depicting this beggarly existence which came from the pen of an official: "In the village of Lyutoga I entered the very poorest hovel. It was owned by settler Zerich, an inept tailor by trade, who has been in the process of settling himself for four years. The poverty and want are appalling. There is absolutely no furniture except for a decrepit table and a tree stump which serves as a chair. Except for a tin tea kettle made from a kerosene can, there is no evidence of any dishes or kitchenware. Instead of a bed, there is a small pile of straw covered with a sheepskin coat and an extra shirt. He has none of the tools of his trade except for a few needles, a few gray threads, several buttons and a copper thimble which he also uses as a pipe for smoking tobacco. The tailor perforated a hole in it, and whenever he so desires, he inserts a thin mouthpiece made of a local reed. His total supply of tobacco could fill half the thimble" (Order No. 318, 1889).

10 Before 1888 those who received peasant rights were forbidden to leave Sakhalin. This prohibition destroyed all hope in a settler for a better life and instilled in him a hatred for Sakhalin. Since it was a repressive measure, it would only increase the number of escapes, crimes and suicides. Justice herself became the victim of its practicality, since the Sakhalin convicts were prohibited the same things which were permitted to Siberian convicts. This measure was evoked by the consideration that if the peasants should leave the island, Sakhalin would eventually become merely a place for penal servitude and not a colony. How could convicts living out their lives on Sakhalin make a second Australia out of the island? The vitality and growth of a colony does not derive from prohibitions or orders but from the presence of conditions which will guarantee a peaceful and secure life at least for their children and grandchildren if not for the convicts themselves.

11 I met only one man who expressed the desire to remain on Sakhalin for the rest of his life. He is an unfortunate man, a farmer from Chernigov, condemned for raping his own daughter. He does not like his homeland because he left a bad reputation. He never writes to his grown-up children, hoping they will forget him. He will not leave for the mainland because he is too old.

12 A small administrative district which generally includes only a few villages.—TRANS.

13 In answer to the question "What *guberniya* do you come from?" I received replies from 5,791 persons. These were: Tam-

bov 260, Samara 230, Chernigov 201, Kiev 201, Poltava 199, Voronezh 198, Donskoya Oblast 168, Saratov 153, Kursk 151, Perm 148, Nizhegorod 146, Penzen 142, Moscow 133, Tver 133, Kherson 131, Ekaterinoslav 125, Novgorod 122, Kharkov 117, Orel 115. Figures for the remaining *guberniyas* were less than one hundred. All the Caucasian *guberniyas* were included to a total of 213, or 3.6 percent. There is a larger percentage of Caucasians in prison than in the colony, which means that they are unable to endure their sentences with fortitude, and very few become settlers. The explanation is given by their frequent escapes and perhaps their high death rate. The *guberniyas* of the Kingdom of Poland include a total of 455 convicts, or 8 percent. Finland and the Ostzeyskiye *guberniyas* include 167, or 2.8 percent. These figures give only an approximate idea of the population according to places of birth, but would anyone dare to draw the conclusion that Tambov *guberniya* is the most criminal and that the Ukrainians, of whom there are actually very many on Sakhalin, are more criminal than the Russians?

14 The nobles and the privileged class in general know nothing about tilling the soil and felling timber for making huts. They must work and bear the same punishments as the others, but they lack the strength. Of necessity they seek light work and they often do nothing. They live in constant fear that their fate will be changed, that they will be sent to work in the mines, physically punished or put in chains, etc. In the majority of cases these people are already weary of life, humble and melancholy, and when you see them you find it impossible to regard them as criminals. You also find vicious and insolent persons who finally become utterly depraved, suffer from "moral insanity" and give the impression of being criminal adventurers; their manner of speech, smile, gait, cringing servility are all in a discordant and common key. No matter what happens, it would be terrible to be in their place. One convict, a former officer, as he was being transported in a prison van to Odessa, gazed through the window and observed "the poetic fishing with the aid of torches and blazing branches dipped in tar. . . . The fields of the Ukraine were already green. In the oak and linden forests violets and lilies of the valley were visible along the roadway; and so the aroma of flowers and of lost freedom were intermingled" (*Vladivostok,* 1888, No. 14).

A former nobleman, a murderer, telling me how his friends saw him off, said: "I awoke to reality. I only wanted one thing— to vanish, to sink into the ground—but my friends did not understand this and they continuously tried to cheer me up and shower me with all kinds of attention." Nothing is more unpleasant for criminals of the privileged class, when they are being led along the street or transported in a prison van, than to find themselves the butt of the curiosity of free men, especially of their friends. If someone attempts to identify a prisoner in a crowd of convicts, shouting his name in a loud voice, he suffers untold agony. It is unfortunate that criminals of the privileged class are often jeered at in prison, on the street and in the press. I read in a newspaper about a former commercial councillor who was invited to breakfast while at a prisoner way station somewhere in Siberia, and when the gang was moved on, the hosts were minus one spoon: the commercial councillor had stolen it! This former Gentleman of the Imperial Bedchamber was described as a man who was thoroughly enjoying himself, wallowing in seas of champagne and the company of as many gypsies as he pleased. This is brutal.

XVI *Composition of the Convict Population According to Sex - The Female Problem - Convict Women and Female Settlers - Male and Female Cohabitants - Free Women*

THERE ARE 53 women to 100 men in the penal colony.[1] This ratio properly applies only to the population living in huts. There are also men who sleep in prison and bachelor soldiers for whom, as one local official explained, all the convict women and all the women in contact with convicts serve as "a requisite source for satisfying natural needs." However, if this category of people is included in determining the composition of the colony's population, it should be done with reservations. While living in prison or barracks they merely regard the colony as a means for satisfying their needs. Their visits to the colony are but harmful external influences which decrease the birth rate and increase morbidity. These influences can be greater or lesser depending on how close or far the prison or barracks is from the settlement. Life in a Russian village is similarly affected by roughnecks building a railroad which passes in the neighborhood. If we combine all the men, including those in prison and in the barracks, the figure of 53 will be cut in half, and we will have a ratio of 100:25.

Although the figures of 53 and 25 are low, they must not be regarded as unusually low for a new penal colony, which is developing under most unfavorable conditions. In Siberia, women represent only 10 percent of the population of convicts and settlers. If we examine deportation practices as they affect non-Russians, we will find respectable farmer colonists who have been so deprived that they joyfully welcomed prostitutes from the cities and paid the procurers 100 pounds of tobacco for each one. The so-called female problem is handled infamously on Sakhalin, but it is less disgusting than it was during the early development of penal colonies in Western Europe.

Not only convict women and prostitutes come to Sakhalin. Thanks to the prison administration headquarters and to the Voluntary Fleet, which has succeeded in establishing speedy and convenient communication between European Russia and Sakhalin, the problem of wives and daughters who wanted to follow their husbands and parents into exile became greatly simplified. Not too long ago the ratio was only 1 woman voluntarily accompanying her husband to 30 convicts. Today the presence of free women is characteristic of the colony, and it is now difficult to imagine Rykovskoye or Novo-Mikhaylovka without these tragic figures who "came to remedy their husbands' lives and lost their own." This may be one of the indications that our Sakhalin will not be last in the history of penal servitude.

I will begin with the convict women. As of January 1, 1890, women represented 11.5 percent of the total number of convicts in all three districts.[2]

With regard to colonization, these women have one important advantage: they join the colony at a comparatively early age. Mostly they are neurotic women who have been sentenced for crimes of passion or crimes connected with their families. "I came because of my husband." "I came because of my mother-in-law. . . ." Most of them are murderers, the victims of love and family despotism. Even those who are sent out here for arson and for counterfeiting are being punished for their love affairs, since they were enticed into crime by their lovers.

The love element plays a fateful part in their sorrowful existence before and after their trials. While they are being transported by ship to penal servitude, they hear the rumor that they will be forced to marry on Sakhalin. This frightens them. On one occasion they begged the court to intercede for them, so that they would not be forced into marriage.

Some fifteen to twenty years ago convict women were

immediately dispatched to a brothel when they reached Sakhalin. Vlasov wrote in his report: "Because of the lack of separate quarters, the women in Southern Sakhalin are housed in the bakery. . . . The island commandant Depreradovich ordered that the women's section of the prison be turned into a house of prostitution." There was no question of any work being available for them, since "only those guilty of a misdemeanor or who had not earned the favor of men were forced to work in the kitchen." The remainder served men's "needs" and were blind drunk. Finally, according to Vlasov, the women became so depraved that while stupefied "they sold their own children for a pint of alcohol."

When a party of women reach Alexandrovsk today, they are accompanied ceremoniously from the prison to the pier. The women, bent under the weight of bundles and knapsacks hanging fore and aft, stagger along the road, pale from seasickness, while mobs of women, men, children and office workers follow behind, like the troops of people who follow comedians at a fair. The scene brings to mind a run of herring on the Aniva River, when the fish are followed by whole schools of whales, seals and dolphins determined to feast on the spawning herring. The peasant settlers follow the crowd with obvious and honorable intentions: they need housewives. The women look to see whether they can find fellow countrywomen. The clerks and guards need "girls." This usually happens in the early evening. The women are locked up in wards which have been prepared for them, and then all night long the talk goes on in the prison and at the post about the new arrivals, about the joys of family life, about the impossibility of homesteading without women, etc.

During the first twenty-four hours, before the boat has left for Korsakov, the women are assigned to districts. This distribution is made by Alexandrovsk officials, and therefore this district receives the lion's share as to quantity and quality. The nearest district, Tymovsky, receives slightly fewer and less qualified women. The North makes a careful selection. Here, as though they have been filtered out, remain the youngest and prettiest, so that the good fortune of living in the Southern district falls only to the lot of those who are getting old or those who "did not earn the favor of men." No thought is given to the agricultural colony during this distribution, and so, as I have already stated, women in Sakhalin are assigned to districts with no thought of a fair distribution. Furthermore, the worse the district, the less hope for success in colonization, and the more women there are. In the worst district, Alexandrovsk, there are 69 women to 100 men; in the second worst, Tymovsky, 47, and in the best, Korsakov, only 36.[3]

One party of women chosen for the Alexandrovsk district are designated as servants of the officials. After their experiences in prisons, the prison vans and the ship's hold, the well-lit rooms of an official must seem to these women to be an enchanting palace, and the lord of the palace appears as a good or evil genius with unlimited power over her. However, she soon becomes accustomed to her new circumstances, while the prison and the ship's hold can long be heard in her speech: "I don't know"; "Eat, your worship"; "Exactly so."

A second batch of women enter the harems of the clerks and the guards. The third batch, the majority, go to live in the settlers' huts. Only the richer settlers and those with influence get these women. A convict, even a convict on probation, can get a woman if he has some money and influence within the prison hierarchy.

At the Korsakov Post the newly arrived women are again housed in separate barracks. The district commander and the settlement supervisor decide which of the settlers and peasants is worthy of having a woman. Preference is given to those who have settled down, are good homebodies and are well behaved. These few chosen ones are ordered to appear on such and such a day at the post, in the prison, to receive a woman.

So it happens that on the designated day, along the whole length of the long road from Naybuchi to the post, there can be seen travelers making their way to the south; these are the suitors or bridegrooms, as they are called, not without irony. They all have a peculiar look about them; they actually look like bridegrooms. One has donned a red bunting shirt, another wears a curious planter's hat, a third sports shining new high-heeled boots, though nobody knows where he bought them and under what circumstances. When they arrive at the post they are permitted to enter the women's barracks and they are left there with the women. The suitors wander around the plank beds, silently and seriously eyeing the women; the latter sit with downcast eyes. Each man makes his choice. Without any ugly grimaces, without any sneers, very seriously, they act with humanity toward the ugly, the old and those with criminal features. They study the women and try to guess which of them will make good housekeepers by looking into their faces. If some younger or older woman "reveals herself" to a man, he sits down beside her and begins a sincere conversation. She asks if he owns a samovar, and whether his hut is covered with planks or straw. He answers that he has a samovar, a horse, a two-year-old heifer, and his hut is covered with planks. Only after the housekeeping examination has been completed, when both feel that a deal has been made, does she venture to say:

"You won't hurt me in any way, will you?"

The conversation comes to an end. The woman signs herself over to such and such a settler, to such and such a settlement—and the civil marriage is completed. The settler leaves for his home with his cohabitant, and as a final act, to make a good impression, he hires a horse and cart, and frequently it happens that this costs him his last penny. At home, the first thing she does is set up the samovar, and all the neighbors, seeing the smoke, jealously comment that so-and-so has finally got a woman.

There is no penal labor for women on the island. True, the women sometimes scrub the floors in offices, or work the gardens, or sew bags, but there is no systematic or clearly defined work in the sense of hard compulsory labor, and probably there never will be.

In this way the prison yields all the convict women to the colony. While they are being transported to the island, the officials do not think in terms of punishment or reform but only of their ability to bear children and work homesteads. Convict women are assigned to settlers as laborers, according to Article 345 of the *Code on Convicts,* which permits unmarried women convicts "to earn their living by working in the nearest settlements of older inhabitants until they get married." This article, however, exists only as a screen for the law which prohibits fornication and adultery, since a convict woman or a woman settler who lives with a settler is not primarily a female farmhand but his cohabitant, an illegal wife who has achieved her status with the knowledge and consent of the administration. In the government departments and in the orders issued by them, a woman living under the same roof with a settler is recorded as existing in "the joint organization of a homestead" or in "joint housekeeping."[4] The man and the woman are described as "a free family."

We can say definitely that with the exception of a small number of women from the privileged class and women who arrive on the island with their husbands, all convict females become cohabitants. This may be regarded as a rule. I was told that when one woman in Vladimirovka refused to become a cohabitant and announced that she had come here to serve a sentence of penal servitude, to work and to do nothing else, her words caused great consternation.[5]

Local practice has developed a peculiar view of the convict woman, and this probably exists in all penal colonies. She is regarded as being neither a person, nor a homemaker, nor a creature lower than a domestic animal. The settlers in the Siska settlement presented the following petition to the regional supervisor: "We humbly beg your worship to release to us one head of horned cattle for milking in the above-mentioned locality and one of the female sex for keeping house." The island commandant, speaking in my presence with a settler from the Uskovo settlement and making various promises, said among others:

"As to women, I will see that you get what you want."

One official said to me: "It's very bad that women are

sent here from Russia in the autumn rather than in the spring. In the winter the woman has nothing to do, she is not a helpmate to the peasant, but only another mouth to feed. That is the reason why good homesteaders receive them reluctantly in the autumn."

This is exactly the way they discuss working horses when feed is expected to be expensive during the winter. Human dignity, the femininity and modesty of convict women, are never taken into account. It seems to be implied that all of a woman's virtues were burned out of her in her disgrace, or they were lost by her during her incarceration in prison and at convict way stations. When they punish her corporally, they are not constrained by the consideration that she might be suffering overwhelming shame. But degradation of her person never reached the point where she was forced into marriage or coerced into cohabitation. Rumors of compulsion in this respect are the same idle tales as gallows on the seashore or being forced to work underground.[6]

Neither a woman's age, nor differences of religion, nor vagrancy are deterrents to cohabitation. I have met female cohabitants fifty years old and more, living with young settlers and even with guards who have barely passed twenty-five. Sometimes an old mother and her grown daughter arrive together in penal servitude. Both become cohabitants with settlers and both begin to bear children as if running a race. Catholics, Lutherans and even Tatars and Jews often live with Russians. In one hut in Alexandrovsk I found a Russian woman with a large company of Kirghiz and Caucasians whom she was serving at table and I recorded her as the cohabitant of a Tatar, or, as she called him, a Chechenets. In Alexandrovsk, the Tatar Kerbalay, who is known here to everyone, lives with the Russian Lopushina and has had three children by her.[7]

Vagrants also attempt to live a family life and one of them in Derbinskoye, named Vagrant Ivan 35 Years, even announced to me with a smirk that he has two cohabitants: "One is here; the other is billeted in Nikolayevsk." Another settler has been living for the past ten years with a woman named Not Remembering Her Kin as though she were his wife, and he still does not know her real name or birthplace.

In answer to the question How are they getting along, the settler and his cohabitant usually answer, "We live well." Some of the convict women told me that at home in Russia they had suffered from the insolence and beatings of their husbands, and rebukes for each piece of bread eaten, while here, in penal servitude, they learned to enjoy the world for the first time. "Thank God! I am now living with a fine man; he feels compassion for me." Those in penal servitude sympathize with their cohabitants and treasure them.

Baron Korf told me: "Here, because of the scarcity of women, a peasant must plow, cook, milk the cow and wash his laundry, and if he is fortunate enough to obtain a woman, he really holds on to her. Take a look how he clothes her. A woman is honored by the convicts."

"Which, by the way, doesn't prevent her from going around with black-and-blue marks," added General Kononovich, who participated in the conversation.

There are quarrels and brawls, and black-and-blue marks result, but the settler still chastises his cohabitant cautiously, since she has the upper hand. He knows that she is an illegal wife and can leave him any time and go to somebody else. Understandably the convicts do not feel for their women only because they know they may be abandoned. No matter how simple the composition of illegal marriages on Sakhalin, even here love in its purest and loveliest form is not a stranger. In Dué I saw an insane convict woman suffering from epilepsy who lives in her cohabitant's hut. He is a convict, and nurses her very carefully, and when I said it must be difficult for him to live in one room with the woman, he said joyfully, "Not at all, your worship; it's a question of having compassion for her!" In Novo-Mikhaylovka the cohabitant of one settler has long been unable to walk and lies day and night on rags in the middle of the room while he takes care of her. When I tried to convince him that it would be more convenient to take her to a hospital, he spoke of his pity for her.

With these good and commonplace families, there also exists a type of free family, which partly accounts for the bad reputation of the "female problem" among convicts. From the very first moment of coming in touch with them, you find something nauseating in their artificiality and hypocrisy. They give you the feeling that they have been corrupted by prison life and slavery, and the family has long since rotted away and something which is not a family has taken its place. Many men and women live together, because they feel this is the way it should be, this is the custom in penal servitude. Cohabitation has become traditional in the colony, and these people, possessing sick and weak-willed natures, have submitted to the arrangement although nobody has forced them into it.

A fifty-year-old Ukrainian peasant woman in Novo-Mikhaylovka came here with her son, also a convict. Her daughter-in-law had been found dead in the well, and so she left her husband and children and lives here with a cohabitant. Obviously all this is most repugnant to her, and she is ashamed to speak about it before a stranger. She despises her cohabitant, and at the same time she lives with him and sleeps with him; that's the way it has to be in penal servitude. The members of similar families are so alien to each other that no matter how long they live together under one roof, even five or ten years, they do not know how old the others are, from which *guberniya* they came, or their patronymic. Asked the age of her cohabitant, a woman looks aside wanly and lazily, and usually answers, "Who the devil knows!" While the cohabitant is working or playing cards somewhere, the female cohabitant lolls in bed, lazy and hungry. If one of the neighbors enters the hut, she gets up unwillingly and says with a yawn that she "came because of her husband," and she is innocent of the crime for which she has been made to suffer. "The boys killed the devil, but they sent me to penal servitude." Her cohabitant returns home; there is nothing to do, there's nothing to talk about with the woman; the samovar should be lit, but there's no sugar or tea. Seeing his lazy cohabitant, a feeling of boredom and lassitude overwhelms him, but he never mentions his hunger or vexation. Instead he sighs, and falls into bed.

When women in these families engage in prostitution, their cohabitants usually encourage them. A cohabitant regards a prostitute who earns a piece of bread as a beneficial domestic animal and respects her; that is, he himself prepares the samovar and is silent when she argues with him. She changes cohabitants frequently, selecting the one who is richer, or has vodka, or she changes them out of sheer boredom, for the sake of variety.

A convict woman receives prison rations which she shares with her cohabitant; sometimes this woman's ration is the only source of food for the family. Since the female cohabitant is formally listed as a worker, the settler recompenses the government for her as for a worker. He pledges to deliver 20 poods of freight from one district to another or to deliver scores of logs to the post. This formality, however, is only obligatory for peasant settlers and does not apply to convicts who live on posts and do nothing.

Having completed her term, the convict woman is transferred to settler status and stops receiving food and clothing allowances. Thus transfer to settler status does not ease her lot on Sakhalin. Convict women who receive rations from the treasury live better than settler women, and the longer the prison term, the better it is for the woman. If she has an unlimited term, this means that she is assured her piece of bread for an unlimited time. Settler women usually achieve peasant rights on favorable terms, that is, in six years.

At the present time there are more free women in the colony who voluntarily followed their husbands than there are convict women. Their ratio to the total number of convict women is 2:3. I recorded 697 free women. There was a total of 1,041 convict, settler and peasant women, which means that the free women represent 40 percent of all the adult women.[8]

Many impulses work on the women who forsake their

homeland and follow their criminal husbands into exile. Some do so out of love and sympathy; some from a firm conviction that only God can separate a husband and wife; some leave home out of a feeling of shame. In an obscure village the stigma of a husband's crimes still falls upon the wife. For example, when the wife of a criminal is rinsing her laundry in the river, the other women call her a jailbird. Some of the women are lured to Sakhalin by their husbands, and they fall into the trap.

While still in the ship's hold, such prisoners write letters home, saying it is warm on Sakhalin, there is much land, the bread is cheap and the administration is wonderful. They write in the same manner from the prison, sometimes for several years at a stretch, always fabricating new allurements. They rely on the ignorance and gullibility of their women, and this reliance was frequently justified, as shown by the facts.[9]

Finally, there are women who go to Sakhalin because they are under the strong moral influence of their husbands. Such women probably participated in the husbands' crimes or enjoyed the fruits of crime. They were not arrested, only because there was insufficient evidence to bring them to court. The majority of the women who come to Sakhalin are moved by compassion and pity leading to self-sacrifice, and the unshakable force of conviction. In addition to the Russian women who voluntarily follow their husbands, there are also Tatars, Jewesses, gypsies, Poles and Germans.[10]

When free wives arrive on Sakhalin they do not receive any great welcome. Here is a characteristic episode: On October 19, 1889, 300 free wives, teen-agers and children arrived in Alexandrovsk on the Voluntary Fleet ship *Vladivostok*. They sailed from Vladivostok for three to four days in cold weather without any hot food. Among them, so I was informed by the doctor, there were 26 who suffered from scarlet fever, smallpox or measles. The ship arrived late at night. The commander, who evidently feared bad weather, ordered the passengers and freight to be disembarked that same night. They unloaded from midnight to

2 A.M. They locked the women and children on the pier in the cutter shed and in the warehouse built for storing merchandise; the sick were put in a quarantine shed specially built for the purpose, and their possessions were thrown helter-skelter into a barge. Toward morning the rumor spread that waves had torn the barge loose during the night and carried it out to sea. The women went into hysterics. In addition to all her possessions, one woman lost 300 rubles. The officials recorded the disaster and blamed the storm, but on the next day they began to find the lost articles in the possession of criminals in the prison.

On arriving on Sakhalin, a free woman at first looks stunned. She is dismayed by the appearance of the island and the conditions of penal servitude. She tells herself in despair that she was not deluding herself when she came to join her husband and she expected the worst, but the reality proved even worse than her expectations. After speaking a few words to the women who arrived before her and after seeing their living conditions, she is thoroughly convinced that she and her children are doomed. Although more than ten or fifteen years remain of her husband's term, she dreams hopelessly about Russia and has no desire to hear about local farming, which she regards as insignificant and beneath contempt. She cries day and night and is full of lamentations as she remembers the relatives she left behind, as though they were dead. Her husband, acknowledging the enormity of his guilt before her, remains sullenly silent, but finally, coming out of his shell, he begins to beat and berate her for having come to him.

If the free wife arrived without money or brought so little that it was only sufficient to buy a hut and if she and her husband do not receive anything from home, they soon begin to suffer hunger. There is no way to earn money, there is no place to ask for charity, and she and the children must be fed on the prisoner's rations which the convict husband receives from the prison and which is scarcely enough to feed one adult.[11]

Here daily thoughts move in only one direction: what can I eat and how can I feed my children? In time her soul hardens from constant hunger, the mutual reproaches over a piece of bread, the conviction that it will never get any better. She comes to the conclusion that on Sakhalin no one ever fed well on delicate feelings, and so she goes out to earn five or ten kopecks, as one woman expressed herself, "with her own body." The husband also becomes hardened, he cares nothing for cleanliness, everything seems unimportant to him. At the age of fourteen or fifteen the daughters, too, are sent out on the merry-go-round. The mothers haggle over them and arrange for them to live as cohabitants with rich settlers or guards. And all this takes place all the more easily because a free woman passes her time in complete idleness. There is absolutely nothing to do in the posts; in the settlements, especially those in the Northern districts, the amount of farming that goes on is insignificant.

In addition to indigence and idleness, the free woman has yet a third source of misfortune—her husband. He may squander his rations and even the wife's and children's clothing on drink or cards. He may commit another crime or try to escape. The settler Byshevets of the Tymovsky district was being held in a cell in Dué while I was there. He was accused of planning a murder. His wife and children lived nearby in the barracks, his house and homestead had been abandoned. In Malo-Tymovo, the settler Kucherenko escaped, leaving his wife and children behind. Even if the husband is not included among those who murder or escape, the wife lives in daily dread, hoping against hope that he will not be punished, that he will not be accused unjustly, that he does not overstrain himself, or get sick, or die.

The years pass, old age approaches. The husband has served out his term of penal servitude and his term as a settler and is petitioning for his peasant rights. The past is buried in oblivion, and he bids farewell to it, while there gleams before him, as he leaves for the mainland, the thought of a new, sensible, happy life far away. But it does not always happen in this way. The wife dies of consumption and the old husband leaves for the mainland alone.

Or else she becomes a widow and does not know what to do, or where to go.

In Derbinskoye, a free woman, Alexandra Timofeyeva, left her husband, a milker, for the shepherd Akim. They live in a tiny, filthy hovel and she has already given him a daughter, while the husband took another woman as a co-habitant. In Alexandrovsk, the free women Shulikina and Fedina also left their husbands and became cohabitants. Nenila Karpenko became a widow and is now living with a settler. Convict Altukhov became a vagrant and his wife Ekaterina, a free woman, is now illegally married.[12]

1 According to the tenth census, there were 104.8 women to 100 men in the Russian *guberniyas* (1857–60).

2 This figure only indicates the composition of convicts by sex, and is useless if it is interpreted as an index of sexual morality. Women are more rarely sentenced to penal servitude, not because they are more moral than men but because, as a result of the social order and to a lesser degree because of the peculiarities of their nature, they are less exposed to external influences and to the risk of committing serious crimes. They do not work in offices or join the armed forces, they do not leave home for seasonal work, they do not labor in forests, in mines or at sea, and therefore they do not commit criminal breaches of trust or of military discipline or crimes which require masculine strength, such as looting the mails, highway robbery, etc. The laws concerning crimes against chastity, rape, seduction and unnatural vice are only applicable to men. On the other hand, women commit murder, torture, cause severe crippling and conceal murder more frequently than men. Among the men, 47 percent are murderers; among the women convicts, 57 percent. As to those sentenced for poisoning, the number is not only relatively greater, but forms an absolute majority. In 1889, there were more female poisoners than men in all three districts, almost three times as many, but the relative proportions were 23 to 1. Nevertheless, fewer women than men arrive at the colony, and, regardless of the annual quota of free women, men still constitute an overwhelming majority. Such an unequal division of sexes is inevitable in a penal colony, and a balance will be achieved only when penal servitude comes to an end, or immigrants flood the island and merge with the convicts, or when our own Mistress Frey appears, energetically propagating the idea that wholesome young women from poor families should

be transported to Sakhalin so that some kind of family life can be developed.

For information on Western European and Russian penal servitude, and for some partial observations on the female problem, see the well-known book by Professor I. L. Foynitsky, *A Study of Punishment in Relation to the Prison System.*

3 In one of his articles Dr. A. V. Shcherbak writes: "The debarkation was only completed during the morning. All that remained was to embark the convicts who had been designated for the Korsakov Post and to receive the various delivery receipts. The first batch, 50 men and 20 women, were sent without delay. The itemized list of men did not indicate any trades, while the women were very old. They were sending out the worst" ("With Penal Prisoners," *New Times,* No. 5381).

4 For example, there is this order: "In accordance with the petition made to the commander of the Alexandrovsk district, presented in the report of January 5, No. 75, the convict Akulina Kuznetsova of the Alexandrovsk prison is moving to the Tymovsky district for joint housekeeping with settler Alexey Sharapov" (No. 25, 1889).

5 It is difficult to understand where women would live if they refused to become cohabitants. There are no separate quarters for them in penal servitude. In his report of 1889, the chief of the Medical Department writes: "Upon arrival in Sakhalin, they themselves must worry about living quarters . . . some of them cannot neglect any means whatsoever for obtaining funds to pay for them."

6 I personally was doubtful about these rumors. Nevertheless, I verified them on the spot and collected all instances which could serve as a basis for them. They say that three or four years ago, when General Gintse was the island commandant, a foreign convict woman was forcibly married to a former police officer. The convict Yagelskaya of the Korsakov district received thirty lashes because she wanted to leave her cohabitant, the settler Kotlyarov. It was in this place, too, that the settler Yarovaty complained that his woman refused to live with him. The following disposition was made: "NN. beat her." "How many?" "Seventy." The woman was beaten, but she still insisted on her own way and she moved in with settler Malovechkin who could not praise her enough. The settler Rezvetsov, an old man, caught his cohabitant with a certain Rodin and went to make a complaint. The following order was issued: "She is to be brought to the prison." The woman came. "You so-and-so, so you don't want to live with

Rezvetsov? Birch rods!" And Rezvetsov was ordered to beat his cohabitant himself, which he did with gusto. In the end she won out, and I have recorded her not as Rezvetsov's cohabitant, but as Rodin's. And this is the sum of all the cases remembered by the people here. If due to her quarrelsome nature or debauchery a woman often changes cohabitants, she is beaten; but even such cases are rare and crop up only when settlers complain.

7   In Verkhny Armudan I recorded cohabitant Ekaterina Petrova living with the Tatar Tukhvatuli. He has children by her. This family's hired hand is a Muhammadan, as are the boarders. In Rykovskoye, settler Mahomet Uste-Nor lives with Avdotya Medvedeva. In Nizhny Armudan the cohabitant of the Lutheran settler Peretsky is the Jewess Leya Permut Prokha, while in Bolshoye Takoe the peasant-formerly-convict Kalevsky cohabits with an Ainu woman.

8   In the first ten years of transportation by ships, from 1879 to 1889, the ships of the Voluntary Fleet carried 8,430 convict men and women and 1,146 members of their families following them into exile.

9   One prisoner even bragged in a letter that he had a foreign silver coin. The tone of these letters is cheerful and jocular.

10 Sometimes husbands voluntarily follow their wives into exile. There are three on Sakhalin: the retired soldiers Andrey Naydush and Andrey Ganin in Alexandrovsk, and the peasant Zhigulin in Derbinskoye. Zhigulin, who followed his wife and children, is an old man and behaves very oddly; he appears to be perpetually drunk and is the laughingstock of the whole street. One old German came with his wife to be with his son Gottlieb. He does not speak a word of Russian. Among other things, I asked him how old he is.

"I was born in 1832," he answered in German. Later he wrote 1890 with a piece of chalk and subtracted 1832.

A convict, a former merchant, was accompanied by his steward, who, incidentally, remained only one month in Alexandrovsk and then returned to Russia. According to Article 264 of the *Code on Convicts,* Jewish husbands cannot follow their convicted wives into exile and the latter are only permitted to bring the babies they are suckling, and then only with the husband's consent.

11 Here one is struck by the difference between the circumstances of this free woman, a legal wife, and her convict woman neighbor, a cohabitant, who daily receives three pounds of bread from the prison. In Vladimirovka one free woman is suspected of kill-

ing her husband. If she is convicted and sentenced to penal servitude, she will begin receiving rations; this means that she will be in better circumstances than before the trial.

[12] The *Code on Convicts* also covers free women. In Article 85 we read: "Women who go voluntarily should not be separated from their husbands during the entire journey and are not subject to strict supervision." In European Russia or on a ship of the Voluntary Fleet they are free of all supervision. However, when the prison party is walking across Siberia or is being conveyed in carts, the convoy guards do not have time to distinguish in the crowd who is a convict and who is free. In Zabaikal I happened to see men, women and children bathing together in the river. The guards, standing in a semicircle, did not permit anyone to pass their cordon, not even children. According to Articles 173 and 153, women who voluntarily accompany their husbands "receive clothing, shoes and food money during the trip until the designated place is reached"; they receive what amounts to a prisoner's ration. But the *Code* does not state how the free women are supposed to cross Siberia—by foot or by cart. According to Article 407 they are permitted temporary leaves of absence from their place of exile and may travel into the interior provinces if they receive their husbands' permission. If the husband dies in exile or if the marriage is dissolved as a result of a new crime, according to Article 408, the wife may return to her homeland at government expense.

Describing the circumstances of criminals' wives and their children, who are only guilty because fate has decreed that they should be related to criminals, Vlasov states in his report that this "is probably the darkest page in our entire deportation system." I have already spoken of the disproportionate number of free women distributed in the districts and settlements, and how little they are respected by the local administration. Let the reader recall the Dué barracks for families. The fact that free women and their children are kept in common wards, as in prison, under disgusting circumstances, together with prison cardsharps, with their mistresses and their pigs, that they are kept in Dué, in the most horrible and hopeless place on the island, paints a sufficient picture of the colonizing and farming policies of the local authorities.

XVII
Composition of the Population by Age - Family Status of Convicts - Marriages - Birth Rate - Sakhalin Children

EVEN if the figures referring to the age groups of the convicts were distinguished by an ideal exactitude and were incomparably more complete than mine, they would still be practically useless. First, they are irrelevant, because they are not based on natural or economic conditions but on juridical theories which have come into existence as a result of the *Code on Convicts* and the arbitrary actions of the people in the Prison Administration Headquarters. The age groups of the population will change only when a change occurs in their attitude to penal servitude in general and to Sakhalin in particular. This will happen when they begin to send twice as many women to the colony, or when free immigration commences with the completion of the Trans-Siberian railroad. Second, figures pertaining to a penal servitude island with its peculiar living conditions cannot be compared to figures relating to normal conditions in the Cherepovets or Moscow districts. So we find that the very small percentage of old people on Sakhalin does not indicate that there are any unusually grave conditions bringing about a high mortality, but merely that in most cases the convicts serve their sentences and leave for the mainland before reaching old age.

At present the age groups with the highest percentage are those between 25 to 35 (24.3 percent) and 35 to 45 (24.1 percent).[1] The ages between 20 and 55, which Dr. Gryaznov calls the work-producing ages, constitute 64.6 percent of the colony, which is one and a half times as much as in Russia generally.[2]

Alas, the high percentage and the surplus of able-bodied persons do not serve as an index of economic prosperity. They only indicate a labor-force surplus, and with their help cities and wonderful roads are being built on Sakhalin notwithstanding the enormous number of starving, idle and incapable people. The costly building program when set beside the poverty of the working-age groups reminds you of the ancient days when temples and circuses were being built, and there was an artificial labor surplus, while people of working age were starving.

Children up to fifteen years of age are prominent in the statistics: they comprise 24.9 percent of the population. In comparison with similar statistics in Russia,[3] this percentage is small, but it is large for a penal servitude colony, where family life exists under such unfavorable conditions. As the reader will be able to observe, the fecundity of the Sakhalin women and the low mortality of children will raise the percentage of children still further, perhaps as high as the Russian norm. This is all to the good because, notwithstanding all the consequences of colonization, the proximity of children serves as a moral support to the exiles, and more than anything else reminds them of their native Russian villages. Looking after their children saves the exiled women from idleness. There is also a harmful aspect, because the unproductive ages demand large expenditures by the population and contribute nothing materially to their lives, and so increase the economic pressure. They intensify the poverty, and so the colony is placed in an even more unfavorable circumstance than a Russian village. When the Sakhalin children become adolescents or reach maturity, they leave for the mainland, and thus the expenses borne by the colony are not reimbursed.

The ages which provide the foundation and hope for a growing colony, if not a real colony, constitute only a small percentage on Sakhalin. There are only 185 persons in the entire colony between the ages of 15 and 20, 89 males and 96 females, which is 2 percent of the total population. Of these only 27 are natives of the colony born on Sakhalin or along the road to exile; the remainder are newcomers. But even those born on Sakhalin are only waiting for the time when their parents or husbands depart for the mainland in order to leave with them. Nearly all the 27 are the children of prosperous peasants who have completed their sentences and remain on the island in order to have more capital. Such, for example, is the Rachkov family in the Alexandrovsk settlement. Even Mariya Baranovskaya, the daughter of a free settler, who was born in Chibisani and is now 18 years old, will not remain on Sakhalin, and she will leave for the mainland with her husband. Of those who were born on Sakhalin 20 years ago and are now nearly 21 years of age, not one has remained on Sakhalin. On Sakhalin there are now 27 persons who are 20 years of age. Of these 13 were sentenced to penal servitude, 7 arrived voluntarily with their husbands, and 7 are the sons of convicts, young people who have already become acquainted with the roads to Vladivostok and the Amur.[4]

On Sakhalin there are 860 legally married families and 782 illegal families. These figures sufficiently define the family status of exiles living in the colony. In general, almost half of the adult population enjoys the blessings of family life. The women in the colony are all taken. It follows that the remaining half of the colony, consisting of about 3,000 persons, must be made up only of men. This fortuitous ratio, however, is constantly changing. So it happens that when a royal edict announces that a thousand new settlers will be released from prison and settled on homesteads, the percentage of single men in the colony is increased. When Sakhalin settlers were permitted to work on the Ussuriysky section of the Siberian railroad —and this happened soon after my departure—the percentage decreased. Be it as it may, the development of family bonds is considered to be extremely feeble among the exiles, and the main reason why the colony has been unsuccessful up to the present time is that there is a large number of single men.[5] The question arises: why has illegal or free cohabitation become so widespread in the colony? Why, when we examine the figures referring to the family status of the convicts, do we have the impression that the convicts obstinately refrain from legal marriage? If it were not for the free women who voluntarily followed their husbands, there would be four times as many illegitimate families as legitimate ones.[6]

While dictating information for my notebook, the Governor-General called this a "crying state of affairs" and naturally did not blame the convicts for it. Since the people are mostly deeply religious and patriarchal, the convicts prefer legal marriage. Illegally married partners often ask the administration for permission to remarry, but the majority of such requests must be denied for reasons which depend neither on the local administration nor upon the convicts themselves. The fact of the matter is that together with the loss of all his rights, the convict is deprived of all marital rights and no longer exists for his family; it is as though he were dead. Nevertheless, his right to marry in exile is not determined by circumstances resulting from his subsequent life, but by his legally married partner who remained in the homeland. It is imperative that the spouse consent to the dissolution of the marriage and grant a divorce, for only then can the convict be married again.

Usually the spouses at home do not give consent, some from the religious conviction that divorce is sinful, others because they consider the dissolution of the marriage as being unnecessary, an idle gesture, a whim, and this is especially true when both partners are approaching forty. "Does he still think he's of marriageable age?" the wife asks herself, when she gets a letter from her husband demanding a divorce. "The old dog should be thinking of his soul." A third group of partners refuse because they are afraid of getting involved in such an extremely complicated, troublesome and expensive matter as a divorce, or simply because they do not know where and how to begin applying for a divorce.

The reason convicts do not marry is often due to a deficiency in the official records which in each case creates a whole series of tiresome formalities in the bureaucratic manner, which only lead to a situation where the convict who spends a considerable sum on stamps, telegrams and getting letters written for him finally gives up in despair and decides he will never have a legal family. Many convicts have no official records. Some records contain no reference to the marital status of the convict, or else the data is not clear or it is incorrect. Except for the official records, the convict has no other documents to prove his claims should he need them.[7]

Information on the number of marriages in the colony can be obtained from the church record books. However, since legal marriage is actually a luxury here, and is not accessible to just anybody, this information can scarcely serve as a determination of the real yearning for married life among the population. They do not get married here when they want to, but when they can. The average age of those getting married is a completely meaningless figure. It is impossible to ascertain the predominance of late or early marriages from the statistics or to draw any conclusions, since family life among the convicts begins long before the church marriage rite and usually the couples who get married already have children.

From the church records it is evident that during the past ten years the greatest number of marriages have taken place in January. Almost a third of the marriages take place in that month. The increase of marriages in autumn is so insignificant in comparison to January that no similarity can be drawn with our farming districts. Under normal conditions marriages of the free children of exiles always took place at an early age: the grooms were between 18 and 20 and the brides between 15 and 19. However, there are usually more young women between the ages of 15 and 20 than men, the latter having left the island before marriageable age. Perhaps because of the scarcity of young men and to a lesser extent because of economic deprivation, an excessive number of ill-matched marriages have occurred. Free young girls, still almost children, were married off by their parents to older settlers and peasants. Noncommissioned officers, corporals, military medical corpsmen, clerks and guards frequently got married, but the objects of their felicity were only 15 and 16 years old.[8]

Weddings are modest and dull. They say that in the Tymovsk district weddings are sometimes merry and noisy, and the Ukrainians are especially boisterous. In Alexandrovsk, where there is a printing press, it is customary among the convicts to send printed invitations before the wedding. The convict typesetters are weary of printing prison orders and are eager to demonstrate their art. In appearance and text these invitations differ little from those in Moscow. The government donates a bottle of vodka for each wedding.

The convicts themselves consider the fecundity in the colony to be exceedingly high, and this leads to constant ridicule of the women and to various profound observations. They say that on Sakhalin the very climate disposes the women to pregnancy. Old women give birth, even those who were barren in Russia and had given up hope of ever having children. The women are hastening to increase the population of Sakhalin and often give birth to twins. One woman in childbed in Vladimirovka, a middle-aged woman with a grown daughter, was certain she would have twins when she heard about frequent births of twins. She was most distressed when she bore only one child. "Look some more," she begged the midwife. The birth of twins, however, is no more frequent here than in Russia. In the ten-year period to January 1, 1890, 2,275 children of both sexes were born in the colony. There were only 26 so-called multiple births.[9]

All the somewhat exaggerated rumors on the excessive fertility of women, twins, etc., indicate that the convict population has a high interest in the birth rate and this is considered of great importance in Sakhalin.

Because the numerical composition of the population is subject to fluctuation as the result of the constant coming and going, and is at the mercy of chance like the coming and going on the marketplace, a determination of the coefficient of the general birth rate in the colony for several years must be considered an unattainable luxury. It is all the more difficult to ascertain because the statistics gathered by myself and others are extremely limited in scope. Population figures of former years are unknown, and when I became acquainted with the office records I recognized that the task of digging them out would be like the labor of slaves in Egypt, and would have the most dubious results. Only approximate coefficients can be determined and these will apply only to the present time.

In 1889, 352 children of both sexes were born in all four parishes. Under ordinary circumstances in Russia an equal number of children is born annually in localities with a population of seven thousand.[10] In 1889 the population of the colony was 7,000 plus several more hundreds. Obviously the local birth-rate coefficient is only slightly higher than in Russia generally (49.8) and in the Russian districts, as for example in the Cherepovets district (45.4). It may be accepted that the 1889 birth rate on Sakhalin was as large as that of Russia, and if there is a difference in coefficients, it will be quite small and probably of little consequence. Since out of two places with the same birth-rate coefficient the fertility of the women is greater in the place where there are comparatively less women, we may conclude that the fertility of women on Sakhalin is significantly greater than in Russia.

Hunger, yearning for the homeland, tendencies to depravity, slavery—the entire sum of unfavorable conditions in penal servitude—do not deprive the convicts of their reproductive capacity. But the high birth rate does not signify prosperity.

The reasons for the women's increased fertility and the high birth rate are: first, the indolence of the convicts, the compulsory housekeeping of husbands and cohabitants owing to the lack of seasonal trades and earnings, and the monotony of life with the satisfying of the sexual instincts often serving as the only means of diversion; and, second, the fact that the majority of women here are of reproductive age. There are probably other remote causes in addition to these proximate ones, but up to the present time they have been inaccessible to direct observation. Perhaps the high fertility should be viewed as a means which nature bestows on the population in order to fight against harmful and destructive influences and against such enemies of the natural order as the small numbers of inhabitants and especially the scarcity of women. The greater the danger to the population, the more children are born, and in this sense the high birth rate may be explained by the unpropitious state of affairs.[11]

Of the 2,275 births in the ten-year period, the greater number were born in the autumn (29.2 percent) and a lesser number in the spring (20.8 percent). More were born in winter (26.2 percent) than in summer (23.6 percent). The greater number of pregnancies and births to date have occurred between August and February, and evidently the short days and long nights were more favorable to reproduction than the gloomy and rainy spring and summer.

At present there are 2,122 children on Sakhalin, including adolescents who became fifteen years of age in 1890. Of these, 644 came from Russia with their parents, while 1,473 children were born on Sakhalin and on the way to penal servitude. There are five children whose place of birth I do not know. The first group is almost one-third as large as the second. Most of them arrived on the island at an age when they were aware of their surroundings. They remember and love their homeland. The second group, those born on Sakhalin, never saw anything better than Sakhalin, which remains their burdensome native land. Both groups differ significantly from each other. Thus, in the first group only 1.7 percent are illegitimate; in the second group, 37.2 percent.[12]

The representatives of the first group call themselves free persons. The overwhelming majority were either born or conceived prior to the trial and therefore retain all their status rights. The children born in penal servitude fit into no category. In time they will be registered into the common class and will call themselves either peasants or inhabitants of the towns. At present their social status is determined as follows: illegal son of a convict woman, daughter of a male settler, illegal daughter of a female settler, etc. They say that when a noblewoman, the wife of a convict, learned that her child was recorded in the parish register as the son of a settler, she burst into bitter tears.

There are almost no babies or children below 4 years of age in the first group; there is a preponderance of school-age children. In the second group, those born on Sakhalin, it is the exact opposite; the very youngest ages predominate. Moreover, the older the children, the fewer there are of the same age. If we were to make a graph of the children's ages in this group, we would obtain an extremely sharply declining curve. In this group there are 203 children less than a year old; of those who are 9 or 10 years old there are 45, of those from 15 to 16 there are only 11. As I have already mentioned, not one of the children born on Sakhalin who reached 20 years of age remained there. Thus the shortage of adolescents and young people is made up from the newcomers, who are the only ones from whose midst young brides and grooms are drawn.

The low percentage of older children born on Sakhalin is explained by the high child mortality and because there were fewer women on the island in the past years and, therefore, fewer children were born. But the greatest fault lies with the emigration. Those who leave for the mainland do not abandon their children on the island but take them along with them. The parents of a Sakhalin-born child usually begin serving their sentence long before he arrives, or before he is born, grows up and reaches the age of 10 years, and then most of them succeed in achieving peasant rights and depart for the mainland.

The position of a newcomer is completely different. When his parents are sent to Sakhalin, he is between 5 and 10 years old. While they are serving their sentence and then passing the years in settler status, he matures. While the parents are later petitioning for peasant rights, he has already become a laborer, and prior to the family's leaving for the mainland, he has already held several jobs in Vladivostok and Nikolayevsk. At any rate, neither the newcomers nor the native-born inhabitants of Sakhalin remain in the colony, and therefore all the Sakhalin posts and settlements should more properly be called temporary settlements rather than a colony.

The birth of a new child in a family is not accepted joyfully. Lullabies are not sung over the cradle. They complain ominously when a child is born. The fathers and mothers say they cannot feed the children, that they will not learn anything good on Sakhalin, and "the best possible fate for them will be if the good Lord takes them away as soon as possible." If a child cries or is naughty, they scream at him maliciously, "Shut up; why don't you croak!"

But no matter how they speak and how they complain, the most useful, the most necessary and the most pleasant people on Sakhalin are the children, and the convicts themselves understand this well and regard them highly. They bring an element of tenderness, cleanliness, gentleness and joy into the most calloused, morally depraved Sakhalin family. Notwithstanding their own purity, they love their impure mothers and criminal fathers more than anything else in the world, and if a convict who has become unaccustomed to tenderness in prison is touched by a dog's affection, how much more must he value the love of a child!

I have already said that the presence of children gives moral support to the convicts. I will now add that often children are the only tie that binds men and women to life, saving them from despair and a final disintegration.

Once I recorded two free women who voluntarily followed their husbands and were living together in one house. One of them, who was childless, continuously bemoaned her fate while I was in the hut. She disparaged herself, saying she was damned and foolish to have come to Sakhalin. She kept squeezing her hands convulsively. All this took place in the presence of her husband, who gazed at me with a guilty expression. The other woman, who had several children, was a "childbearer"—so they are called here— and as she remained silent, it occurred to me that the predicament of a childless woman must indeed be horrible. I remember that in one hut, as I was recording a three-year-old Tatar boy in a skullcap, his eyes wide apart, I said a few kind words to the child. Suddenly the languid face of the boy's father, a Kazan Tatar, brightened and he nodded his head merrily as if he agreed with me that his son was a very nice little fellow, and I had the feeling that this Tatar was a fortunate man.

The influences under which the Sakhalin children are reared and the impressions which determine their spiritual activity must be obvious to the reader from what I have already said. What is terrifying in the cities and villages of Russia is commonplace here. Children look apathetically at groups of prisoners in chains. When children see chained convicts dragging a wheelbarrow full of sand, they hang onto the back of the barrow and laugh uproariously. They play at being soldiers and prisoners. A little boy goes out on the street and yells to his playmates, "Fall in! As you were!" Or he will throw his playthings and a piece of bread in a sack and say to his mother, "I'm going away to become a vagrant." "Be careful, or a soldier might shoot you," his mother answers jokingly. He goes out on the street and wanders about. His playmates, disguised as soldiers, capture him. Sakhalin children talk about vagrants, birch rods and lashes; they know the exact meaning of "executioner," "prisoners in chains" and "cohabitant."

While making the rounds of the huts in Verkhny Armudan I did not find any adults in one hut. Only a ten-year-old boy was at home, a towhead, round-shouldered and barefoot. His pale face was covered with large freckles and seemed mottled.

"What is your father's name?" I asked him.

"I don't know," he answered.

"How so? You are living with your father and don't know his name? That's disgraceful."

"He's not my real father."

"What do you mean, he's not your real father?"

"He's my mother's cohabitant."

"Is your mother married or a widow?"

"A widow. She came because of her husband."

"What do you mean, she came because of her husband?"

"She killed him."

"Do you remember your father?"

"I don't remember him. I'm illegitimate. My mother gave birth to me in Kara."

Sakhalin children are pale, thin and flabby. They wear rags and are always hungry. As the reader will observe from what I have written below, they die nearly always from diseases of the alimentary canal. Their half-starved existence; their food, consisting only of turnips for months on end, the more prosperous among them eating salted fish; the low temperature and the humidity, all these waste away a child's organism slowly through emaciation; his tissues gradually degenerate. If it were not for the immigration, then within two or three generations the colony would probably be beset by all kinds of diseases arising from the extremely unbalanced diet.

At present the children of the poorest settlers and convicts receive a so-called food allowance from the government. Children from 1 to 15 years of age are given one and a half rubles per month, while orphans, cripples, twins and the deformed receive three rubles per month. A child's right to this assistance is determined at the personal discretion of the officials, and each of them understands the word "poorest" in his own way.[13]

The one-and-a-half- and three-ruble food allowances are spent at the discretion of the mothers and fathers. This monetary aid, which depends on so many considerations and which rarely achieves its purpose because of the poverty and unscrupulousness of the parents, should have been abolished a long time ago. It does not decrease the poverty; it merely masks it. It gives uninformed people the impression that provision has been made for the children on Sakhalin.

1 Herewith is a table of age groups compiled by me:

Years			
From	*To*	*Males*	*Females*
0	5	493	473
5	10	319	314
10	15	215	234
15	20	89	96
20	25	134	136
25	35	1,419	680
35	45	1,405	578
45	55	724	236
55	65	318	56
65	75	90	12
75	85	17	1
85	95	—	1

Of unknown age: males 142; females 35.

2 In the Cherepovets district, people of working age constitute 44.9 percent of the population; in the Moscow district, 45.4 percent; in the Tambov, 42.7 percent. See the book by V. I. Nikolsky, *The Tambov District. Statistics on Population and Morbidity* (1885).

3 In the Cherepovets district this figure is 37.3 percent; in Tambov, about 39 percent.

4 The table shows that in the children's ages the sexes are divided almost equally, while in the 15-to-20-year age group and from 20 to 25 there is even a slight surplus of women. In the 25-to-35 age group there are almost twice as many men, while in the older age groups this preponderance may be called overwhelming. The small number of aged men and the almost complete absence of aged women indicate a lack of family experience and tradition on Sakhalin. Every time I visited the prisons I had the feeling that they harbored more old men than the colony.

5 Stable conditions in a colony do not depend principally on the development of families. Virginia's prosperity was established before women settled in the colony.

6 Judging by the figures, we may conclude that marriage in church is most unsuitable for Russian convicts. We know from the government statistics of 1887 that there were 211 convict women in the Alexandrovsk district. Of these only 24 were legally married, while 136 were cohabitants with convicts and settlers. In the same year, out of 194 convict women in the Tymovsk district, 11 had legal husbands and 161 were cohabitants. In the Korsakov district not one convict woman was living with a husband; 115 were living in illegitimate unions. Of the 21 female settlers, only four were married.

7 In his *The Problem of Organizing Sakhalin Island,* Prince Shakhovskoy wrote: "A good deal of the difficulty in arranging marriages without let or hindrance lies with the family records, which often do not give the religion or the family status, and no one knows whether a divorce was obtained from the marriage partner who remained in Russia. It is almost impossible to find out, and it is even more difficult to petition for a divorce through the consistory from the island of Sakhalin."

8 Noncommissioned officers, especially guards, are considered excellent catches on Sakhalin. They are well aware of their value and conduct themselves with unbridled hauteur toward their brides and the brides' parents; N. S. Leskov despised such men and described them as "insatiable bishop-like beasts." [Nikolay Semenovich Leskov (1831–95), the novelist, was an enemy of ecclesiastical bureaucracy; the phrase was used in his book *Spiritual Regulations of Peter I.*] During the past ten years there were a number of mésalliances. A college registrar married a convict's daughter, a court councillor married a settler's daughter, a captain married a settler's daughter, a merchant married a peasant-formerly-a-convict, and a noblewoman married a settler. The rare cases when a member of the intelligentsia marries the daughter of a convict are extraordinarily appealing and probably have a good influence on the colony. In January, 1880, a convict married a Gilyak woman in the Dué church. In Rykovskoye I recorded Grigory Sivokobylka, eleven years old, whose mother was a Gilyak. Marriages between Russians and foreigners are rare. I was told of a guard who was living with a Gilyak woman who had given him a son, and now wants to become a Christian so that they can get married. Father Irakly knew a Yakut convict who married a Georgian woman. They knew very little Russian. As for Muhammadans, they do not renounce polygamy even in exile, and some of them have two wives. Thus, in Alexandrovsk, Dzhaksanbetov has two wives —Batyma and Sasena—and in Korsakov, Abubakirov also has two wives—Ganosta and Verkhonisa. In Andreye-Ivanovskoye I saw an extraordinarily beautiful fifteen-year-old Tatar girl whose husband bought her from her father for a hundred rubles. When her husband is not at home she sits on the bed. The settlers gaze at her through the open door and ogle her.

The *Code on Convicts* permits convicts of both sexes to marry one to three years after they have achieved a reformed status. Obviously a woman who enters the colony but is still on probation can only become a cohabitant, not a wife. Convict men are permitted to marry felons, but until they have achieved peasant status females who have been deprived of all rights can only marry convicts. A free woman receives 50 rubles from the government when she marries a convict in Siberia, if it is his first marriage. A settler in Siberia who is getting married for the first time with a convict woman is given 15 rubles outright and a loan of a similar sum.

The *Code* contains no provisions for marriages between vagrants. I do not know which documents determine their family status and their age at marriage. I first learned they were being married on Sakhalin from the following note written in the form of a petition. "To his Excellency the commander of Sakhalin Island. The certification of a settler of the Tymovsk district, settlement of Rykovskoye, Not-Remembering-His-Family Ivan 35 Years. I, Not-Remembering, was legally married to the settler Bereznikova Maria last year on November 12." Two settlers were responsible for this illiterate statement.

9 These figures which I extracted from church baptismal records apply only to the Orthodox population.

10 According to Yanson, 49.8 or almost 50 births per thousand.

11 Such severe and impermanent catastrophes as crop failures, war, etc., decrease the birth rate; chronic afflictions like high infant mortality and perhaps also imprisonment, bondage, penal servitude, etc., increase it. In some families a higher birth rate goes hand in hand with mental degeneration.

12 The illegitimate children in the first group are the offspring of convict women, the majority born in prison after the trial. There are no illegitimate children in the families which voluntarily followed their mates and parents into exile.

13 The amount of assistance also depends on whether the official interprets "crippled and deformed children" to mean only the lame, the hunchbacks and those without arms, or whether it includes children suffering from tuberculosis, imbecility and blindness.

How can the Sakhalin children be helped? First of all, it seems to me that the right to assistance should not depend on such conditions as "poorest," "cripple," etc. Assistance should be given to all who request it and there should be no fear of fraud. It is better to be deceived than to deceive oneself. The kind of assistance is determined by local conditions. If it were up to me, I would use the money now distributed in "food allowances" to build teahouses at the posts and in the settlements for the use of all the women and children. I would distribute food and clothing rations to all pregnant women and nursing mothers without exception, and I would only reserve the "food allowances" of one and one-half and three rubles a month for distribution to girls from thirteen years old and until they are married, and I would have this money given to them directly.

Every year philanthropists in St. Petersburg send sheepskin coats, aprons, felt boots, caps, accordions, pious books and pens to be distributed to children here. When these gifts are received, the island commandant invites the local ladies to take charge of distributing and apportioning them. They tell you that all these things are drunk up and gambled away by the fathers, that it would be better to send bread rather than accordions, etc. Such remarks should not disturb generous people. The children are usually delighted with their gifts, and the fathers and mothers are everlastingly grateful. It would be altogether proper if the philanthropists who are interested in the fate of the convicts' children could receive detailed information every year—as much information as possible—about the children of Sakhalin. This information would give their numbers, their ages and sexes, the number of those who can read and write, the non-Christians, etc. If, for example, a philanthropist knows how many children can read and write, he will then know how many books or pencils to send so that no one would feel hurt by being left out. He could ascertain the number of toys and the amount of clothing necessary if he knew their sexes, ages and nationalities. It is imperative that philanthropy on Sakhalin be removed from the jurisdiction of the police administration, which is overwhelmed with work without all this added responsibility, and the organizing of assistance should be left in the hands of the local intelligentsia. There are many people who would be glad to take on the responsibility of this benevolent activity. Amateur productions are sometimes presented in Alexandrovsk, the proceeds going to the children. Not long ago the officials of the Korsakov Post collected subscriptions and bought various kinds of sewing materials. Their wives sewed clothing and underwear and distributed them to the children.

Children are an economic burden, and they are God's punishment for sin. This does not prevent the childless convicts from taking and adopting someone else's children. Families with children hope their children will die, while childless families take orphans and raise them as their own. It sometimes happens that convicts adopt orphans and poor children because they receive a food allowance and all kinds of assistance, or because an adopted child can be sent out on the street to beg. Yet most of the convicts are probably motivated by good intentions. Not only children, but even adults and the aged, become "adopted children." Thus the settler Ivan Novikov the First, sixty years of age, is the adopted son of settler Evgeny Yefimov, forty-two years old. In Rykovskoye, Elisey Maklakov, seventy years old, agreed formally to become the adopted son of Ilya Minayev.

According to the *Code on Convicts,* minor children who accompany their convict or resettled parents to Siberia are supposed to travel by horse-drawn cart. One cart is assigned to every five persons. The *Code* does not state which children are deemed to be minors. Children who accompany their parents receive clothing, footwear and food allowances during the entire trip. If a family voluntarily accompanies a prisoner into penal servitude, fourteen-year-old children are sent along only at their own request. Children who attain seventeen years of age can leave the penal servitude location and return to their homeland without their parents' approval.

XVIII
Occupations of Convicts - Agriculture - Hunting - Fishing - Migratory Fish: Whales and Herring - Prison Fishing - Craftsmanship

AS I SAID BEFORE, the idea of adapting convict and settler labor to agriculture arose at the beginning of penal servitude on Sakhalin. The idea is a very appealing one. Agricultural work obviously has the advantage of keeping the convict occupied, attaching him to the land and reforming him. The work is suitable for the great majority of the convicts, for prisoners sentenced to penal servitude are chiefly recruited from the peasants, and only a tenth of the convict and settler population do not come from the agricultural class. The idea was successful; and up to the present time agriculture has been the chief occupation of the exiles on Sakhalin, and the colony has continued to call itself an agricultural colony.

The soil has been tilled, and grains have been sown annually during the entire existence of the Sakhalin colony. There was no interruption, and with the growth of the population the arable land annually increased. The labor of the local farmer was compulsory, and it was also hard labor. If compulsion and the taxing of physical strength are considered the basic criteria for penal labor, i.e., forced labor, it would be difficult to find a more suitable occupation for criminals than agriculture on Sakhalin. The sternest punitive aims have been satisfied.

But is it productive? Does it fulfill the aims of colonization? From the beginning of Sakhalin penal servitude to the present day, the most varied and extreme opinions have been expressed. Some regarded Sakhalin as a fertile island and so described it in their reports and correspondence. I was told that they even sent excited telegrams to the effect that the convicts were at last in a position to feed themselves, no longer requiring government assistance. Others were skeptical about agriculture on the island and stated flatly that agriculture was impossible. Such differences of opinion arose because Sakhalin agriculture was nearly always judged by people who knew nothing about actual conditions.

The colony was founded on an island which had never been explored. It was *terra incognita* from the scientific point of view, and the natural conditions and the possibility of farming were judged by such indications as geographic latitude, the close proximity to Japan, and the fact that there were bamboos, cork trees, etc. Occasional correspondents frequently passed judgments based on first impressions, depending on whether they saw the island in good or bad weather, depending on the bread and butter they were served in the huts, or depending on whether they first arrived in a foggy place like Dué or in a cheerful place like Siyantsy. The great majority of the officials placed in charge of the agricultural colony were neither landowners nor peasants before entering the service and they knew absolutely nothing about agriculture. In their reports they used the information obtained for them by inspectors. The local agronomists were ill-trained and did nothing, or their reports were distinguished by conscious prejudices, or, having come to the colony straight from the school bench, they limited themselves merely to the theoretical and formal aspects of the matter and their reports always relied on information which had been gathered for the office by the lower echelons.[1]

It would appear that the best information might be obtained from the people who plow and sow the land, but even this source proved unreliable. Fearing that their relief allotments would be stopped, and that seeds would no longer be provided on credit, and that they would be forced to remain on Sakhalin for the rest of their lives, the exiles usually said they had less land under cultivation and a smaller yield than was actually the case. The more prosperous exiles, who did not need relief allowances, also did not tell the truth; they did not tell lies because they were afraid, but from the same motive which compelled Polonius to agree that a cloud simultaneously resembled a camel and a weasel. They carefully watched the prevailing weather of ideas and if the local administration did not believe in agriculture, they, too, did not believe in it; but if a contrary position became fashionable in the administration, they found themselves agreeing, glory to God, that it was possible to live on Sakhalin, the crop yields were good, and there was but one problem—the people were becoming hopelessly spoiled, etc.—and to please the administration they told the most whopping lies and employed every conceivable kind of stratagem. So they picked the largest ears of grain from the field and brought them to Mitsul, who good-naturedly believed them and drew the proper conclusion about the excellent harvest. Newcomers were shown potatoes as large as a head, watermelons, radishes weighing half a pood, and the newcomers who viewed these monsters found themselves believing in a fortyfold yield of wheat on Sakhalin.[2]

During my stay the agricultural question on Sakhalin had reached a stage where it was difficult to understand anything. The Governor-General, the island commandant and the district officials had no faith in the productivity of Sakhalin farmers. They were in no doubt that the attempt to adapt prisoners sentenced to penal servitude to agriculture was a complete failure and at the same time they insisted that if the colony should remain an agricultural colony, at whatever the cost, then government funds would be spent unproductively and the people would continue to be subjected to useless torture. This is what the Governor-General dictated to me:

"A prisoners' agricultural colony is quite impracticable on the island. The people must be given the means of earning a living; agriculture can only be an additional form of revenue."

The younger officials expressed the same opinion and fearlessly criticized the island's past in the presence of their superiors. When asked how things were going, the exiles themselves answered nervously, hopelessly, with bitter grimaces. And regardless of their definite and unanimous attitude concerning agriculture, the exiles continue to plow and sow, the administration continues to give seeds on credit, and the island commandant, who has less belief than anyone in the future of farming in Sakhalin, issues orders in which "for the sake of getting the exiles interested in agriculture," he affirms that the achievement of peasant status by settlers who show no prospect of success in their farm work on the plots assigned to them "can never occur" (Order No. 276, 1890).

Up to the present, the amount of cultivated land has been shown by inflated and carefully selected figures (Order No. 366, 1888), and nobody can say exactly what the average amount of land is per homesteader. The agricultural inspector says the average amount of land per plot is 1,555 square sazhens, or about two-thirds of a desyatin, and in a better district, i.e., Korsakov, the average is 935 square sazhens. These figures are probably incorrect, and they have minimal significance because the land is apportioned extremely unequally among the homesteaders. People who arrived from Russia with money or profited as rich peasants have three to five and even eight desyatins of arable land, and there are many homesteaders, especially in the Korsakov district, who have only a few square sazhens. Obviously the quantity of arable land increases each year, but the average area of the plots does not increase and threatens to remain constant.[3]

They sow government seeds which are always obtained on credit. In the best district, that is, in Korsakov, "the entire proportion of sown grain amounting to 2,060 poods contained only 165 poods raised by the homesteaders themselves, and of the 610 persons who sowed the grain, only 56 men had their own seeds" (Order No. 318, 1889.) According to the agricultural inspector's data, an average of only 3 poods, 18 pounds of grain is sown per adult in the Southern section. It is interesting to note that in the district with the best climatic conditions agriculture is less successful than in the Northern districts, but this does not prevent it from being the best district.

In the two Northern districts not once was a sufficient amount of warm weather observed for the full ripening of oats and wheat, and there were only two years when it was warm enough for the barley to ripen.[4]

Spring and the beginning of summer are nearly always cold. In 1889 there were frosts in July and August, and bad autumn weather began on July 24 and continued to the end of October. One may combat the cold, and the acclimatization of grains on Sakhalin would be a very worthwhile endeavor if it were not for the exceptionally high humidity, and there may never be any effective way of combating humidity. During the period when the shoots are growing, flowering and ripening, and especially during the time of ripening, the number of foggy days on the island is disproportionally large, and for this reason the earth yields insufficiently ripened, watery, wrinkled and lightweight seeds. Or else, because of the numerous rains the grain perishes, rots or germinates on the sheaves in the field. The time for harvesting grains, especially summer wheat, always coincides with the rainy season and sometimes the entire harvest remains in the field because of the constant rains from August deep into the autumn. The report of the agricultural inspector contains a table of crops for the past five years based on data which the island commandant calls "mere invention." From this table we may conclude that the average grain harvest is approximately threefold, a fact which may be corroborated by another figure: in 1889 the harvested grains averaged some 11 poods per adult person, being a threefold yield of grain. The harvested grain was poor. One day while examining samples of the grain brought by settlers to be exchanged for flour, the island commandant found that some of them were completely unfit for sowing and the other grain samples contained a significant number of unripened and frost-killed grain (Order No. 41, 1889).

In view of such poor yields, the Sakhalin homesteader, if he is to be well fed, must have no less than four desyatins of fertile land, must not stint in his own efforts, and must not pay any money to workers. In the not too distant future when the one-field system without fallow land and without fertilization will bring about the exhaustion of the soil and the exiles "recognize the necessity for changing to a more rational method of working the fields and to a new system of crop rotation," more land and more labor will be required, and the growing of grains will perforce be abandoned as being unproductive and unprofitable.

Vegetable-raising, the branch of agriculture whose success does not depend so much on natural conditions as on the individual efforts and knowledge of the homesteader himself, obviously produces good results on Sakhalin. The success of local gardening is evident in that sometimes entire families live on turnips during the entire winter. In July a woman in Alexandrovsk complained to me that her flowers had not yet bloomed, while in one Korsakov hut I saw a bucket full of cucumbers.

From the agricultural inspector's report it appears that the 1889 harvest in the Tymovsk district yielded four and one-tenths poods of cabbage and about two poods of various root vegetables per adult; in Korsakov the yield was four poods of cabbage and four and one-eighth poods of root vegetables. That same year the potato yield per adult in Alexandrovsk was about 50 poods, in Tymovsk it was 16 poods and in Korsakov it was 34 poods. Potatoes generally give abundant yields and this is not only corroborated by statistics but by personal impressions. I did not see bins or bags of grain: I did not see settlers eating wheat bread although more wheat is sown here than rye; but I did see potatoes in every hut and heard complaints that many potatoes rotted during the winter.

With the development of city life on Sakhalin there is a slowly increasing need for marketplaces. An area has already been set aside in Alexandrovsk where women sell vegetables, and it is not rare to meet exiles on the streets selling cucumbers and various greens. In some Southern areas, as in First Drop, truck gardening has already become a serious business.[5]

Agriculture is considered the main occupation of the exiles. Secondary occupations, which provide additional earnings, are hunting and fishing. From a hunter's point of view, vertebrates are plentiful on Sakhalin. Sable, fox and bear are the animals most valuable to merchants, and they inhabit the island in especially large numbers.[6] Sable overrun the entire island. I was told that recently, as a result of forest fires and the cutting down of timber, the sable have abandoned the populated areas for more distant forests. I do not know how true this is. In my presence an inspector fired his revolver at a sable crossing a log over a stream just outside the Vladimirovka settlement, and the exile hunters with whom I was able to talk usually hunt quite close to the settlements. In former times bears did not attack people or domestic animals and were considered rather meek animals, but when the exiles began settling along the headwaters of the rivers, cutting down the forests and barring their access to the fish which were their chief food, the Sakhalin church records and the official reports began to record a new cause of death: "Clawed by a bear." The bear is now regarded as a dangerous natural phenomenon, and the war against bears is not regarded as a sport. They also find deer and musk deer, otter, wolverine and lynx, rarely a wolf, and even more rarely an ermine or a tiger.[7] In spite of this wealth of game, hunting as a commercial endeavor is virtually nonexistent in the colony.

The exiled kulaks who are making a fortune in trade deal in furs which they obtain from the natives for a pittance, in exchange for alcohol. This has nothing to do with hunting, however, but with another kind of industry. There are so few hunters that they can be counted. The majority are not professional hunters but men who have a passion for hunting, sportsmen who hunt with inferior weapons and without dogs merely for the pleasure of it. They dispose of their game at an absurdly low price or squander it on alcohol. One settler in Korsakov who tried to sell me a dead swan asked for "three rubles or a bottle of vodka."

We must assume that hunting in the exile colony will

never become a commercial venture, just because it is an exile colony. In order to hunt professionally a person must be free, courageous and healthy, but the overwhelming majority of convicts are people of weak characters, neurotic and indecisive. They were not hunters in their homeland, and they do not know how to handle guns. This free undertaking is so alien to their depressed souls that a settler would rather butcher a calf taken on credit from the government, even though he is then threatened with dire punishment, than go out and shoot wood grouse or rabbits. Then there is the question whether the widespread development of hunting is desirable in a colony where the majority of the people sent here for correction are murderers. A former murderer should not be permitted to kill animals frequently, nor should he be permitted to do the bestial things which are very nearly necessities in hunting, like stabbing a wounded deer, or cutting the throat of a downed partridge, etc.

Sakhalin's chief wealth and its hope for the future, which may perhaps become auspicious and enviable, lies with the migratory fish, not the game animals, nor the coal, as some think. Some or perhaps all of the fry carried by the rivers into the ocean return annually to the mainland as migratory fish. The keta, a fish of the salmon family which in size, color and taste resembles our own salmon and inhabits the northern Pacific Ocean, enters the Siberian and North American rivers at a certain period of its development and with irrepressible strength, in absolutely incalculable numbers, swims upstream against the current, reaching the very highest mountain streams. On Sakhalin this occurs at the end of July or in the first third of August. The mass of fish observed at this time is so great and its run is so precipitous and so extraordinary that anyone who has not seen this magnificent phenomenon cannot actually understand it. The swiftness and density of the run can be judged by the surface of the river, which seems to be seething. The water has a fishy taste, the oars are jammed, and the blades propel the obstructing fish into the air.

The keta (Siberian salmon) are healthy and strong when they enter the mouth of the river, but the constant struggle against the fierce current, the compact throng of fish, hunger, friction, collisions with bushes and rocks, all these exhaust them; they become gaunt, their bodies are covered with bruises, the meat becomes white and flaccid, and the teeth protrude. The keta so completely change their characteristics that the uninitiated assume they have become another fish, and they call it not keta but lancet fish. The keta slowly weaken and can no longer battle against the current. They submerge or hide behind bushes with their mouths buried in the soil. At such times you can pick them up with your hands; even a bear can reach them with his paw. Finally, exhausted by their sexual cravings and by their hunger, they die. By this time many dead fish can be seen halfway along the stream, but the banks of the upper reaches of the rivers are covered with dead fish exuding a foul stench. All the sufferings endured by the fish during their erotic journey culminate in "a nomadic thrust toward death," for they always lead to death, and not a single fish returns to the ocean; all perish in the rivers. Hillendorf says: "The irresistible impulse of an erotic craving for death is the basic concept of nomadism; such indeed are the ideas of these stupid cold fish!"

The herring runs which periodically occur along the seacoast in the spring, usually in the second half of April, are no less extraordinary. The herring arrive in enormous shoals, "in absolutely unbelievable quantities," in the words of one observer. The approach of the herring can always be detected: a circular band of white foam covering a tremendous stretch of sea, flocks of gulls and albatrosses, whales spouting, herds of sea lions. The scene is magnificent! The number of whales following the herring into the Aniva is so great that Krusenstern's ship was encircled by them, and it was only "with extreme caution" that they could reach the bank. During the herring run the sea appears to be boiling over.[8]

It is impossible to give an approximate figure to the amount of fish which can be caught here whenever there is a run in the Sakhalin rivers or along the shore. Only maximum figures would be appropriate.

At all events it may be said without exaggeration that fishing on Sakhalin during the runs, properly organized on a broad foundation for the markets which have long existed in Japan and China, would produce untold profits. When the Japanese controlled Southern Sakhalin and their fishing had barely begun to develop, they were already earning half a million rubles profit annually. According to Mitsul, blubber oil from Southern Sakhalin filled 611 caldrons and up to 15,000 sazhens of wood were burned in order to render the blubber, while the herring alone brought 295,806 rubles annually.

With Russia's occupation of Southern Sakhalin, fishing went into the decline which continues to the present day. L. Deyter[9] wrote in 1880: "Where life recently seethed, providing food for the native Ainus and substantial profits for the entrepreneurs, there is now a wilderness." The fishing by our exiles in both Northern districts is insignificant; it cannot be described in any other way. I was on the Tym when the keta run had already arrived at the upper reaches, and here and there on the green banks I saw occasional fishermen pulling out half-dead fish with pothooks attached to long poles.

Seeking means of providing earnings for the settlers, the administration in recent years has begun to order salted fish from them. The settlers obtain salt at reduced prices and on credit; the prison then purchases the fish from them at high prices in order to encourage them. I mention these insignificant earnings only because the prisoners say the prison soup cooked with fish cured by the local settlers is noted for its particularly repulsive taste and unbearable stench. The settlers do not know how to fish or how to cure the fish, and nobody teaches them. According to the present custom the prison takes over the best fishing grounds and the settlers are left with rapids and shallows, where their cheap homemade nets are torn to pieces by bushes and rocks. When I was in Derbinskoye the convicts were catching fish for the prison.

274

The island commandant, General Kononovich, ordered the settlers to appear before him. In his speech he reproached them for having sold unedible fish to the prison last year. He stated, "The convicts are your brothers and my sons. In cheating the prison you harm your brothers and my sons." The settlers agreed with him, but their faces showed that next year their brothers and his sons would again be eating stinking fish. Even if the settlers learn to preserve the fish properly, the new earnings will still be meaningless to the settlers since sooner or later the sanitation authorities will be forced to forbid the consumption of fish caught in the upper sources of rivers.

I visited the prison fishery in Derbinskoye on August 25. The interminable rain brought misery to all nature. It was difficult to walk along the slippery shore. We first entered the shed, where sixteen convicts were salting fish under the supervision of Vasilenko, a former Taganrog fisherman. They had already salted 150 barrels, some two thousand poods. It would seem that if Vasilenko had not happened to be convicted, nobody would know how to handle the fish. There was a slope leading down from the shed to the shore, and on this six convicts were cleaning fish with sharp knives; the water was red and turbid. There is a strong stench of fish and mire mixed with fish blood. A bit farther on, a group of convicts, soaking wet and barefoot, were casting a small seine. They pulled it out twice while I was there, and both times the seine was full. All the keta looked extremely suspect. They all had protruding teeth, their spines were humped and their bodies were covered with bruises. The bellies of almost all the fish were stained brown or green, and a water excrement was being secreted. The fish cast on shore died very quickly, if they were not already dead in the water or had not died while struggling in the net. The few fish which remained unblemished were called *serebryanka* [silver fish]. These were carefully set aside. They were not meant for the prison kettle, but would be especially "cured."

They do not know very much here about the natural history of the fish which enter the rivers periodically. They are not yet convinced that they should be caught at the mouth of the rivers and in their lower waters. The fish become unfit for consumption farther upriver.

While sailing on the Amur, I heard complaints from old inhabitants that at the mouth of the river real keta can be caught, but they only get lancet fish. On the boat I also heard people saying it was about time the fishing was regulated; they meant that it should be forbidden in the lower reaches.[10]

While the prisoners and the settlers were catching gaunt, half-dead fish in the upper reaches of the Tym, the Japanese were illegally fishing at the mouth of the river after blocking it with palings, while in the lower reaches the Gilyaks were catching fish for their dogs, and these fish were incomparably healthier and tastier than those which were being salted in the Tymov district for the people. The Japanese were loading junks and even larger ships, and the beautiful ship which Polyakov met at the mouth of the Tym in 1881 probably came again this summer.

For fishing to become a serious enterprise, the colony must be moved closer to the mouth of the Tym or the Poronaya. But this is not the only thing that has to be done. It is imperative that the free inhabitants not be allowed to compete with the exiles, because wherever there is a conflict of interests the free will always have the advantage over the exiles.

Moreover, the settlers are faced with competition from the Japanese, who are either fishing illegally or paying export taxes, and from the officials who have acquired the best fishing grounds for fishing by the prisoners. The time is drawing near for the completion of the Trans-Siberian railroad and the large-scale development of shipping, and then people will hear about the incredible abundance of fish and game, and free people will be attracted to the island. Immigration will begin, and regular fishing enterprises will be organized; in these the exiles will participate not as owner-entrepreneurs but merely as hired hands. And then it will happen, if we can judge by past occurrences, that complaints will be raised that the labor of the exiles is yielding place to the labor of free people, perhaps the Chinese and Koreans. The exiles will be regarded as an economic burden on the island, and with the increase in immigration and the development of a settled industrial life the government will find it more equitable and advantageous to be on the side of the free population, and penal servitude will be discontinued. In this way fish becomes the foundation of Sakhalin prosperity, but that has nothing to do with the penal colony.[11]

I have already referred to the harvesting of sea cabbage when I was describing the Mauka settlement. From March 1 to August 1 a settler earns from 150 to 200 rubles during the harvesting. A third of his earnings are spent on food and he brings two-thirds home. These are good wages; unfortunately they are only possible for settlers in the Korsakov district. The workers are paid according to their capacities, and their earnings reflect their experience, diligence and conscientiousness—qualities which are far from being common among the exiles. It follows that not everyone goes to Mauka.[12]

There are many carpenters, cabinetmakers, tailors and so on among the exiles, but most of them do nothing or they are farmers. One convict locksmith makes Berdan rifles and he has already sold four on the mainland. Another makes unusual steel watch chains, while another sculptures on gesso. These rifles, chains and expensive gesso boxes throw no more light on the colony's economic status than the information that there is a settler in the South who gathers whalebone along the coast and another who digs for mollusks. All of this is incidental. Those elegant and expensive wooden articles which were shown at the prison exhibition demonstrate only that sometimes fine cabinetmakers are sentenced to penal servitude. They have no connection with the prison, since it is not the prison which finds a market for them and it is not the prison which teaches craftsmanship to the convicts. The prison has profited from the work of these skilled craftsmen, but the supply of their work is considerably greater than the demand. One convict told me, "You can't even sell forged documents here!" Carpenters work for 20 kopecks a day and pay for their own food, while tailors sew for vodka.[13]

If we add up the average income of the settler from selling grain to the government, from hunting, fishing, etc., we obtain the pitiful figure of 29 rubles, 21 kopecks.[14] Moreover, the average debt of each homesteader to the government is 31 rubles, 51 kopecks. Since the total income includes fodder and the government allowance and sums of money received through the mail, and since the exile's income chiefly consists of earnings received from the government, which occasionally pays inflated prices, a good half of his income is purely fictitious and the debt he owes the government is in fact larger than the figures suggest.

1   In a resolution based on the agricultural inspector's report of 1890, the island commandant wrote: "At last there exists a document which is perhaps far from being perfect, but is firmly based on observed data gathered by a specialist and offered without the desire to please any special interests." He calls this report "the first step in the right direction." The implication is that all the reports prior to 1890 were written with the desire to please special interests. General Kononovich adds that "idle fabrications" were the sole source of information on agriculture in Sakhalin before 1890.

The official agronomist on Sakhalin is given the title of Inspector of Agriculture. It is a Class IV position with a good salary. The present inspector made his report after spending two years on the island. This is a short work which does not contain the author's personal observations, and his conclusions are not distinguished by their clarity. The report does, however, supply some brief information about meteorology and flora, and presents an adequate picture of natural conditions in the popoulated parts of the island. This report has been published and will probably be included in the literature relating to Sakhalin. As for the agronomists who served earlier, they were all very unfortunate. I have already mentioned M. S. Mitsul several times. He had been an agronomist, later he became a director, and he finally died of angina pectoris before the age of forty-five. I was told that another agronomist attempted to prove that agriculture was impossible on Sakhalin, and sent out a flood of documents and telegrams, and it appears that he suffered a severe nervous disorder. People now recall him as having been an honest and knowledgeable person, but insane. The third director of the Agronomy Department was a Pole: he was discharged by the island commandant and there was a scandal rare in official annals. By an official order his travel expenses were allowed only on condition that "he produce an agreement with the driver of a sleigh taking him to Nikolayevsk." Obviously the administration feared that after receiving his travel expenses the agronomist would continue to remain on the island (Order No. 349, 1888). Father Irakly told me about the fourth agronomist, a German, who did nothing and knew hardly anything at all about agronomy. Once, after an August frost which killed off the grain, he drove to Rykovskoye, called a meeting and pompously demanded, "What for did you have a frost?" A most intelligent man stepped out of the crowd and said, "We do not know, your excellency; probably it was brought about by God's grace." The agronomist was completely satisfied with this answer, mounted his carriage and departed for home, conscious that he had performed his duty.

2   A correspondent writes in *Vladivostok* (1886), No. 43: "A newly arrived agronomist on Sakhalin (a Prussian subject) organized and opened a Sakhalin agricultural exhibition on October 1 in his own honor, the exhibitors being the settlers of the Alexandrovsk and Tymovsk districts, as well as the prison gardens. . . . The grain seeds exhibited by the settlers were not exceptional unless you include among the *yakova* seeds grown on Sakhalin other seeds mixed with them which have been ordered from the famous Grachev [Yefim Andreyevich Grachev, 1826–77, a renowned agronomist] for sowing. Settler Sychov of the Tymovsk district exhibited wheat with a certificate from the Tymovsk administration that he has a current harvest of seventy poods. He was charged with perpetrating a fraud for exhibiting only carefully selected kernels of wheat." Issue No. 50 of the same newspaper also describes the exhibition: "Everyone was astonished by the extraordinary vegetables: for example, a head of cabbage weighing twenty-two and a half pounds, radishes weighing thirteen pounds, potatoes weighing three pounds, etc. It can safely be said that Central Europe cannot boast of better vegetables."

3   With the increase in population it becomes all the more difficult to find suitable land. Riparian valleys covered with deciduous forests—elms, hawthorn, elders, etc.—where the topsoil is deep and fertile are rare oases among the tundras, bogs, mountains covered with burning forests, and lowlands with coniferous forests and poorly draining subsoil. On the southern portion of the island these valleys, or *yelans,* alternate with mountains and bogs on which the sparse vegetation differs little from the polar. Thus the vast region between the Takoye valley and Mauka, which are cultivated areas, is covered with absolutely unusable marshlands. Perhaps it will be possible to build roads through these marshes, but it is not within human power to change the grim climate. As

great as the area of Southern Sakhalin obviously is, until the present time only 405 desyatins of land suitable for grain fields, gardens and farmsteads have been discovered (Order No. 318, 1889). But the commission headed by Vlasov and Mitsul, which had studied the problem of the suitability of Sakhalin for an agricultural penal colony, found that in the central section of the island "there should be considerably more than 200,000 desyatins of land" capable of being brought under cultivation and that "extends to 220,000" in the southern section.

[4]   Details are recorded in *Report on the Status of Agriculture on Sakhalin Island in 1889* by Von Friken.

[5]   For some reason only onions have been difficult to raise up to the present time. The scarcity of this vegetable in the exile's diet has been compensated for by wild ramson [bear garlic]. This onion-type plant with a strong garlic odor was once considered by soldiers and exiles an excellent remedy for scurvy, and we can judge the prevalence of the disease by the hundreds of poods which the military and prison commands kept in stock every winter. They say that ramson is tasty and nutritious, but not everyone likes its odor. I felt suffocated when a man came near me in a room or even in the open after eating ramson.

The amount of land devoted to hayfields on Sakhalin is still unknown, although the agricultural inspector's report does cite figures. No matter what figures are quoted, however, it is indisputable that few homesteaders know in the spring where they will mow in summer, and it is indisputable that there is insufficient hay, and that by the end of winter the cattle become emaciated from lack of feed. The best hayfields are taken by the strongest—i.e., the prison and the military commands. The meadows remaining for the use of settlers are either very distant or they cannot be harvested with a scythe but must be cut with a sickle. Because of the poor permeability of the subsoil, the majority of the meadows are marshy, and are always wet, thus producing sour grass and sedge; this makes for a coarse hay, containing little nourishment. The agricultural inspector says that the local hay in terms of nutrition can scarcely be compared with half the same amount of ordinary hay. The exiles find the hay poor, and they do not feed it to their animals without adding flour or potatoes. I will not make a judgment about whether the giant grasses in the forest valleys, of which so much is spoken, can be regarded as good fodder. I note that the seeds of one of these grasses, known as Sakhalin buckwheat, are now available to consumers in Russia. The report of the agricultural inspector does not even mention whether grass-sowing is necessary or even possible on Sakhalin.

Now, as to cattle-raising. In 1889 there was one milk cow for every two and a half homesteads in the Alexandrovsk and Korsakov districts, and one for every three and a third in the Tymovsk. Practically the same figures apply to draft animals, that is, horses and oxen; in addition, the lower figures in this case apply to the best district, the Korsakov. These figures do not denote the actual conditions, however, since all the Sakhalin cattle are distributed very unequally among the homesteaders. The ownership of all the cattle is concentrated in the hands of the rich homesteaders who have large plots of land or else are engaged in trade.

6 Details may be found in A. M. Nikolsky, *Sakhalin Island and Its Vertebrate Fauna.*

7 Wolves keep far away from dwellings because they fear domestic animals. As this may appear incredible, I cite a further example: Bussé writes that when the Ainus saw a pig for the first time, they were terrified. Millendorf informs us that when sheep were first raised along the Amur, the wolves did not bother them. Wild deer are especially numerous on the western shore of the northern part of the island. During the winter they gather on the tundra, but in the spring, according to Glen, when they go down to the sea to lick salt, they can be seen in vast herds on the broad plains in this part of the island. As to birds, there are limitless numbers of geese, various species of ducks, white grouse, wood grouse, hazel grouse, curlews and woodcocks. The migration lasts until June. I arrived on Sakhalin in July, when there was deathly silence in the taiga. The island seemed lifeless, and I had to take the word of observers that the Kamchatka nightingale, the titmouse, the thrush and the siskin may be found here. There are many black ravens, but no magpies or starlings. Polyakov saw only one country swallow on Sakhalin, and in his opinion it arrived on the island by accident after losing its way. One day I thought I saw a quail in the grass, but upon looking more closely I saw a pretty tiny animal which they call a chipmunk. This is the smallest mammal in the northern districts. According to A. M. Nikolsky there are no house mice. Reports relating to the early days of the colony mention "food particles, sawdust and mouse holes."

8 One writer describes a Japanese seine which "spanned an area of three versts in the sea and, being strongly anchored to the shore, resembled a funnel through which herring were systematically extracted." Bussé says in his notes: "The Japanese sweep-seines are often seen and extremely large. One seine encircled an area of 70 sazhens offshore. I was amazed when, having pulled the seine to ten sazhens from shore, the Japanese left it in the water because at ten sazhens the seine was so full of herring that even with the combined labor of 60 workmen, they were unable to pull the seine any closer to shore. . . . When placing their oars in the

oarlocks, the rowers threw a number of herring out of the boat, complaining that the herring made it difficult to row." The herring run and the catch by the Japanese is described in detail by Bussé and Mitsul.

9 *Marine Gazette* (1880), No. 3.

10 The fishing industry is very poorly organized on the Amur, although there is a vast wealth of fish. The reason would seem to be that the fishing entrepreneurs are too miserly to import specialists from Russia. For example, they catch huge quantities of sturgeon but are completely unable to prepare the roe so that it resembles Russian caviar, at least in outward appearance. The art of the local entrepreneur stops with curing the keta and goes no further. General L. Deyter wrote in the *Marine Gazette* (1880), No. 6, that it was believed that a fishing enterprise was formed at one time on the Amur by a group of capitalists, and the business was built on a large scale, and the owners served caviar to each other at a cost, according to his informant, of 200 to 300 rubles per pound, paid in silver.

11 Fishing can be a supplement to homesteading and can provide some profits for the exiles now living at the mouths of small rivers and by the sea. Good nets must be provided, and only those who lived by the sea in their homeland should be settled on the seacoast.

At present, the Japanese boats which arrive in Southern Sakhalin for fishing pay a duty of seven kopecks in gold per pood. All products of fish are similarly taxed—e.g., manure fertilizer, herring oil and cod liver oil—but the profits from all these taxes do not amount to 20,000 rubles. This is almost the only profit we obtain for the exploitation of the wealth of Sakhalin.

In addition to keta, other species related to the salmon run periodically in the Sakhalin rivers, such as the humpbacked salmon and fish locally known as *kundzha, goy* and *chevitsa.* Trout, pike, bream, carp, gudgeon and the smelt, which is called *ogurechnik* [cucumber fish] because it has the strong odor of a fresh cucumber, are always found in the fresh waters of Sakhalin. Besides herring, the salt-water fish caught here are cod, plaice, sturgeon and the goby, which is so big here that it swallows a smelt whole. In Alexandrovsk one convict deals in delicious long-tailed crustaceans which are locally called *chirims* or shrimps.

The sea mammals existing in large quantities in Sakhalin waters are whales, sea lions, seals and sea bears. When we were approaching Alexandrovsk on the *Baikal* I saw many whales swimming and frolicking in pairs in the strait. Near Sakhalin's western bank a lone crag called Danger Rock rises above the sea.

An eyewitness on the schooner *Yermak* wanted to examine the rock, and wrote: "One and a half miles before reaching the rock we saw that the crag was occupied by some exceptionally large sea lions. The roaring of this enormous wild herd astounded us. The animals had grown to such a fabulous size that from the distance they seemed to be crags themselves. The sea lions were two sazhens large and greater. . . . In addition to the sea lions, the crag and the sea around it teemed with sea bears" (*Vladivostok*, 1886, No. 29).

The possible dimensions of the whaling and seal-hunting business in our northern seas are demonstrated in figures quoted by one of our writers. He says that according to the calculations of American owners of whalers in the fourteen years previous to 1861, sperm oil and whalebone worth two hundred million rubles were shipped from the Okhotsk Sea (V. Zbyshevsky, "Observations on the Whaling Industry in the Okhotsk Sea," *Marine Miscellany*, 1863, No. 4). It should be noted that in spite of their brilliant future, these industries will not bring additional wealth to the penal colony just because it is a penal colony.

According to Brem's testimony, "seal-hunting is a vast, merciless slaughter carried out with vulgarity and extreme insensibility. This is the reason why they do not 'hunt seals,' but use the expression 'to beat seals.' The most savage tribes hunt in a far more humane manner than a civilized European." When they slaughter the sea bears with cudgels, their brains splatter on all sides and the eyes of the poor creatures jump out of their sockets. The exiles, especially those sent here for murder, should not be permitted to participate in similar spectacles.

12 On account of the sea cabbage and the comparatively mild climate, I consider the southwestern shore to be the only area on Sakhalin where a penal colony is possible. In 1885 an interesting paper relating to the sea cabbage was read at one of the meetings of the Society for the Study of the Amur Region. This was written by the present owner of the business, Y. L. Semenov, and published in *Vladivostok* (1885), Nos. 47 and 48.

13 At the present time these craftsmen can earn money only by working for the officials and the rich exiles at the posts. The local intelligentsia deserves an accolade for always paying generously for services rendered by the craftsmen. Stories are told about the doctor who kept the shoemaker in the infirmary, pretending that he was ill so that he could make boots for his son, and about the official who assigned himself a dressmaker to sew clothes for his wife and children free of charge, but these stories are regarded as unhappy exceptions to the rule.

14 According to information given by the agricultural inspector.

XIX
Convicts' Food - What and How the Prisoners Eat - Clothing - Church - School - Literacy

WHILE THE SAKHALIN CONVICT is on prison rations he receives daily 3 pounds[1] of baked bread, 40 *zolotniks* of meat, about 15 *zolotniks* of groats, and various additional rations worth 1 kopeck. On a fast day 1 pound of fish is substituted for the meat.

The accepted departmental method is most inadequate to determine how far this ration satisfies the convict's actual needs, if only because it draws conclusions from comparative as well as purely external evaluations of statistics which apply to the food rations of various groups of populations both abroad and in Russia. If prisoners in Saxon and Prussian prisons receive meat only three times a week, always to the extent of less than one-fifth of a pound, and if the Tambovsky peasant eats four pounds of bread a day, this does not mean that the Sakhalin convict receives a large amount of meat and little bread; it only means that the German prison officials are afraid of being accused of misguided philanthropy and that the Tambovsky peasant's diet differs in that it contains more bread. From the practical point of view, it is very important that the evaluation of the rations of any given group begin with a qualitative, not with a quantitative, analysis. This would permit a simultaneous study of the natural and living conditions in which the group lives. If a strict individuality is not adhered to, the solution of the problem will be one-sided, and I imagine it will be regarded as conclusive only by dry-as-dust formalists.

One day the agricultural inspector, Mr. Von Friken, and

I were returning to Alexandrovsk from Krasny Yar, I in a *tarantass*[2] and he on horseback. It was hot and the taiga was sweltering. Prisoners were working hatless on the road between the post and Krasny Yar, their shirts drenched with perspiration; they probably thought I was an official when I drove up beside them unexpectedly. They stopped my horses and complained to me that they were being given bread which was impossible to eat. When I told them to appeal to the authorities, they answered:

"We told the senior guard Davydov, and he called us mutineers."

The bread actually was terrible. When broken open, it glistened in the sun with minute drops of water, stuck to the fingers and looked like a dirty, slimy mass, repulsive to hold in the hands. Several pieces of bread were brought to me, and it was all underbaked and made from badly milled flour. Quite obviously there was a vast difference in the weight of the flour which reached the baker and the bread made from it. It was baked in Novo-Mikhaylovka under the supervision of senior guard Davydov.

The three pounds of bread which are included in their rations contain much less flour than the regulations require,[3] owing to the misuse of the weight differential between the flour and the bread. The convict bakers in the above-mentioned Novo-Mikhaylovka sold their own portions of bread and gorged themselves on the surplus. In the Alexandrovsk prison the people who are fed from the common kettle receive decent bread; those living in their own quarters are issued inferior bread, and those who work outside the post receive even worse bread. In other words, the only bread that is fairly good is that which might be seen by the island commandant or the inspector.

In order to increase the amount of bread obtained from the flour, the bakers and the guards connected with food rationing use various devices which had been improved upon by Siberian practices, with the scalding of flour being one of the least harmful. At one time the flour was mixed with sifted clay in the Tymovsk district, to increase the weight of the bread.

Similar abuses are all the easier because the officials cannot sit in the bakery all day and inspect and keep watch over every loaf of bread. Furthermore, almost no complaints are voiced by the prisoners.[4]

Whether the bread is good or bad, not all of it is eaten by the prisoners. They ration themselves prudently, because it has long been the custom among exiles and in our prisons to use government bread as small change. The prisoner pays bread to the person who cleans his cell, to the man who substitutes for him at work, to the sharer of his frailties. He pays with bread for needles, thread and soap. To vary his dull, extremely monotonous and perpetually salty diet, he saves his bread and then exchanges it at the maidan for milk, a white roll, sugar, vodka. . . . The majority of people born in the Caucasus become ill from the black bread and so they attempt to barter it. Thus, if the three pounds of bread listed in the regulations seem completely adequate quantitatively, when we realize the quality of the bread and the living conditions in prison, the value of the food allotment is seen to be a delusion and the statistics lose their meaning. Only salted meat is provided; the fish, too, is salted.[5] They are served boiled, in a soup.

The prison soup looks like a semiliquid porridge made of groats and potatoes cooked to a pulp, with little red pieces of meat or fish floating in it. Some of the officials praise it, but they do not dare to eat it themselves. The soup, even when it is prepared for the sick convicts, is extremely salty. If visitors are expected in the prison, if the smoke of a ship is visible on the horizon, or if the guards and cooks have been having an argument in the kitchen—all these things have their effect on the taste, color and odor of the soup. It is disgusting stuff, and not even pepper and bay leaf could improve it. The salted fish soup is regarded as exceptionally bad, and it is easy to understand why. First, it spoils quickly, and so they try to make use of the already decaying fish as quickly as possible. Second, the polluted fish which the exiles catch at the headwaters is also thrown into the kettle. At one time the convicts in the Korsakov prison were fed with a soup made

286

of salted herring. According to the physician in charge of the medical department, this was supremely tasteless; the cooked herring quickly disintegrated into tiny pieces, while the presence of small bones made swallowing difficult and caused inflammation of the alimentary canal. No one knows how often the prisoners throw the soup away because it is unpalatable, but it is known that they do so.[6]

How do the prisoners eat? There is no mess hall. The prisoners line up at noon in the barracks or at the lean-to where the kitchen is located, as though they were at a railroad ticket office. Each one holds some sort of receptacle. By this time the soup is usually ready and being overcooked: it is kept "steeping" in the covered kettles. The cook has a long pole with a scoop attached to it, and with this he ladles the stew from the caldron and gives each person his portion. He can scoop up two portions of meat at a time, or no meat, exactly as he pleases. By the time the people at the end of the line reach him, the soup is no longer soup, but a thick tepid mass at the bottom of the kettle. This weak stew is then diluted with water.[7]

After receiving their portions the prisoners leave. Some eat while walking, others eat sitting on the ground, and still others eat on their plank beds. There is no supervision to make certain that they eat everything, and that they refrain from selling and exchanging their portions. Nobody asks whether everyone has eaten, or whether anyone fell asleep before ration time. And if you tell the people in charge of the kitchen that among the depressed and mentally ill people serving terms of penal servitude there are many who must be supervised to make certain they eat and must even be force fed, such an observation only evokes a perplexed expression on their faces and the answer: "How could I know, your worship?"

Of those receiving government rations, only 25 to 40 percent[8] are fed from the prison kettle; the remainder obtain provisions where they are. This majority is divided into two categories: some consume their rations in their own quarters with their families or with their co-owners; others, who have been commandeered for work far from

287

the prison, eat where they are working. After finishing his work quota each worker of the second category cooks his own meal separately in a tin pot unless it is raining and unless he falls asleep after his hard labor. He is fatigued and hungry, and to save himself trouble he will often eat the meat and fish raw. The guard does not care whether he falls asleep during the meal, or whether he sold his rations, or squandered them in card-playing, or whether the food was spoiled or the bread sodden with rain. Sometimes they will eat three to four days' rations in one day, and then they eat bread or starve. The supervisor of the medical department says that when they are working by the seashore or on the riverbanks they are not squeamish about eating mussels or fish, while the taiga provides roots of various kinds if they are famished. According to the mining engineer Keppen, workers in the mines have been known to eat tallow candles.[9]

For two and perhaps three years after being released from hard labor the settler receives an allowance from the treasury. After this he must feed himself at his own expense and his own risk. There are no figures or documented data either in the existing literature or in the official files regarding the nutrition of settlers. If one may judge from personal impressions and from the fragmentary accounts which can be gathered on the spot, potatoes are the main food of the colony. Potatoes and root vegetables, such as turnips and rutabagas, are often the only food a family has for a very long while. They eat fresh fish only during the runs, and because of its price, salt fish can be obtained only by the more prosperous.[10]

There is nothing that can be said about the meat. Those who have cows prefer to sell the milk rather than drink it themselves. They do not store it in crocks but in bottles, which signifies that it is for sale. In general, the settler sells the food produce of his homestead very eagerly, even at the expense of his own health, because he considers money more necessary to him than health. If you do not save enough money, you will not be able to leave for the mainland, where you can eat your fill and recover your health while living in freedom.

The uncultivated plants used as food are ramson and various berries such as the cloudberry, bog whortleberry, cranberry, moss berry and others. It can be said that the exiles living in the colony eat vegetables exclusively, and this is true at least of the overwhelming majority. At any rate, their food is characterized by its low fat content, and it is questionable whether this is better than the food rationed from the prison kettles.[11]

The prisoners obviously receive sufficient clothing and footwear. Both men and women prisoners are issued an overcoat and a sheepskin coat each year. Soldiers, who work just like the prisoners on Sakhalin, receive a uniform every three years and a heavy coat every two years. A prisoner uses up four pairs of shoes and two pairs of work boots a year; a soldier wears out one pair of leggings and two and a half pairs of leather soles. But the soldier has better sanitary conditions. He has a bed and a place where he can dry his clothes during bad weather. The convict has of necessity to wear bedraggled clothes and footwear, because he does not have a bed, sleeps on his overcoat, all his rotten rags foul the air with their evil-smelling emanations, and he has no place where he can dry his wet clothes. Until such time as they provide more humane living conditions for the convicts, the question as to the adequacy of the quantity of clothing and footwear must remain open. As to the quality, history repeats itself here; the same history applies to the issue of bread. Whoever lives in sight of the officials receives better clothing; whoever is commandeered for distant work receives worse clothing.[12]

Now, as to the spiritual life and the satisfaction of needs of a higher order. The colony is called a reform colony, but it contains no institutions or persons who specialize in reforming criminals. There are no instructions or articles in the *Code on Convicts* regarding religion unless we include the few instructions to convoy officers or non-commissioned officers on whether to use weapons against convicts, or how the priest should "edify them with teachings on their duties to their faith and to morality," and explaining to the convicts "the importance of the commutations of their sentences," etc.

No definite opinions are ever expressed on this subject. It is accepted that the primary responsibility for reform belongs to the church and to the schools, and then to the members of the free population, who through their authority, tact and personal example contribute significantly to ameliorating the condition of the prisoners.

In church affairs Sakhalin belongs to the diocese of the Bishop of Kamchatka, the Kurile Islands and Blagoveshchensk.[13] Bishops repeatedly visited Sakhalin, traveling as simply and suffering the same discomforts and privations as the ordinary priest. During their visits, while organizing churches, blessing various edifices,[14] and making the rounds of prisons, they spoke words of solace and hope to the convicts. The character of their guidance can be judged by the following excerpt from a resolution by the Most Reverend Gury in one of the letters which has been kept by the Korsakov Church. "If not all of them [i.e., the convicts] have faith and contrition, then, at any rate, many whom I personally saw do have. Nothing else but the very feeling of contrition and faith made them weep bitterly when I delivered a sermon to them in 1887 and 1888. In addition to punishing their crimes, the task of the prison is to arouse morally sound sentiments in the prisoners, and especially to prevent them from falling into complete despair during their imprisonment." This point of view was also inherent in the younger representatives of the Church. The Sakhalin priests always keep themselves aloof from punishment and conduct themselves with the convicts not as with criminals but as with people, and in this respect they demonstrate more tact and understanding of their duties than the doctors or agronomists, who often interfere in what is none of their business.

The most prominent place in the history of the Sakhalin Church is held by Father Simeon Kazansky, or, as he is called by the people, Papa Simeon, who was the pastor of the Aniva or Korsakov church in the seventies. He was active during those "prehistoric" times when there were no roads in Southern Sakhalin and the Russian population, especially the military, was scattered in small groups over the entire South. Pop Simeon spent almost all his time in the wilderness, traveling from one group to another by dog sleigh or reindeer sleigh, and in the summer by sailboat or by walking through the taiga. He was frozen, was snowbound, was stricken by illness, was tormented by mosquitoes and bears, his boats were overturned in the swift rivers and he had to swim in the cold water, but he endured all this with unusual grace, delighted in the beauty of the wilderness, and never complained of his harsh existence. He behaved like an excellent friend in his relations with officials and officers, never refused to join in a party, and during gay discussions always knew how to interpolate an apt biblical text. His opinion of convicts was: "To the Creator of the world all men are equal," and so he wrote in an official letter.[15]

During his tenure the Sakhalin churches were very poorly furnished. Once when blessing the iconostas in the Aniva church he spoke of its poverty in this way: "We have no bell, we have no books of divine worship, but what is important is—God is here!" I mentioned him previously when I described Popovskiye Yurty. Through soldiers and exiles his fame has spread all over Siberia and now Pop Simeon is a legend in Sakhalin and far beyond.

At the present time there are four parish churches on Sakhalin: in Alexandrovsk, Dué, Rykovskoye and Korsakov.[16] The churches are not poor. The priests receive a salary of 1,000 rubles a year. Each parish has a choir of singers who read music and are dressed in appropriate kaftans. Services are held only on Sundays and on great holy days. Matins and lauds are sung first, and then at nine o'clock in the morning Mass is celebrated. There are no vespers. The local priests do not have any special obligations arising from the exceptional composition of the population and they behave exactly like our village priests—that is, they confine themselves to church services on holy days, to religious ceremonies and to school duties. I did not hear of any conferences, admonitions, etc.[17]

During Lent the convicts prepare for Holy Communion. They are allowed three days to accommodate all the convicts. When the chained convicts or those living in the Voyevodsk and Dué prisons prepare for the Sacrament, the church is encircled by sentries. They say this produces a dispiriting impression. The unskilled laborers among the convicts usually do not attend church because they take advantage of the holy days to rest, make repairs or go berrypicking. The local churches are small, and somehow it has become customary only for those who are dressed in the garb of free men to go to church. Only the "clean" people go there.

When I was at Alexandrovsk the front half of the church at Mass was occupied by officials and their families. Then followed a mixed row of soldiers' and guards' wives and free women with their children. Then came guards and soldiers, and behind all these along the walls were the settlers dressed in city clothes and the convict clerks. Can a convict with a shaved head and one or more stripes down his back, wearing shackles or with a ball and chain around his feet, go to church if he so desires? I asked one of the priests and he answered, "I don't know."

The settlers prepare for the Sacrament, get married and baptize their children in churches if they are living close enough to a church. Priests visit distant settlements to see that the exiles keep the fast and perform other duties. Father Irakly had "vicars" in Verkhny Armudan and in Malo-Tymovo; these were the convicts Voronin and Yakovenko, who read the lauds on Sundays. When Father Irakly arrived at a settlement to conduct services, a peasant went up and down the street shouting at the top of his voice, "Come for prayers!" When there is no church or chapel, services are held in cells or in huts.

One evening while I was living in Alexandrovsk the local priest, Father Yegor, visited me and after staying a short while he left to conduct a marriage ceremony at the church. And I accompanied him. The candelabrum was already being lit and the choristers were standing in the choir, their faces expressing indifference as they waited for the bridal couple. There were many women, both convict and free, and they kept glancing impatiently at the door. A whisper was heard. Somebody at the door waved his hand and whispered excitedly, "They're driving up!" The singers began to clear their throats. A wave of people were pushed back to clear the door, someone yelled, and finally the bridal couple entered. He was a convict typesetter, twenty-five years old, wearing a jacket with a hard collar bent at the edges and a white tie. The convict woman, three or four years older, wore a blue dress with white lace and a flower in her hair. They laid a kerchief on the rug. The groom stepped on it first. The best men, who were type-setters, also wore white ties. Father Yegor came down from the altar and leafed through the book on the lectern for a long time. "Blessed be our God . . ." he sang, and the marriage ceremony started.

When the priest placed wreaths on the groom and bride and begged God to wed them in glory and honor, the faces of all the women who were present expressed tenderness and joy, and it seemed that they had forgotten that the ceremony was taking place in a prison church, in penal servitude, far, far from home. The priest said to the bridegroom, "Exalt yourself, bridegroom, as did Abraham. . . ." The church emptied after the wedding and the air was filled with the scent of burning candles, and the guard hastened to extinguish them, and melancholy set in. We went out on the steps. Rain! Near the church a crowd of people stood in the darkness and two springless carriages waited outside the church. In one sat the bride and bridegroom, the second was empty.

"Father, please!" voices were calling, and scores of hands stretched out toward Father Yegor as if to seize him.

"Please! Honor us!"

Father Yegor settled down in the carriage and they drove him to the home of the bride and groom.

On September 8, a holy day, I was leaving the church after Mass with a young official, and just then a corpse was brought in on a stretcher. It was carried by four ragged convicts with coarse, livid faces resembling our own city beggars. They were followed by two more ragged men, who formed the reserve, and by a woman with two children and a gloomy Georgian, Kelbokiani, who was dressed in a free man's clothing (he was a clerk and they called him Prince). They were all obviously in a hurry, afraid of missing the priest at church. We learned from Kelbokiani that the deceased was a free woman named Lyalikova whose husband, a settler, had gone to Nikolayevsk. She had two children, and now Kelbokiani, who had been living in Lyalikova's quarters, did not know what to do with the children.

My companion and I had nothing to do, so we went ahead to the cemetery, not waiting for the funeral service to end. The cemetery is a verst from the church, behind the Slobodka and close to the sea on a high steep hill. When we were climbing the hill the funeral cortege was already catching up with us. Obviously only two or three minutes were required to sing the service. From the summit we could see the coffin jogging on the stretcher, and the little boy, who was being led by the woman, was holding back and pulling away from her.

From one side there is a broad view of the post and the surrounding country, from the other side the sea, calm and shimmering in the sunlight. There are many graves and crosses on the hill. Here you will find two large crosses side by side. They are the graves of Mitsul and the guard Selivanov, who was killed by a prisoner. The small crosses standing over the graves of convicts are all exactly the same and all are silent. They will remember Mitsul for a while, but nobody will find it necessary to remember all the dead who are lying under the little crosses, those who have murdered, who tried to escape, who clanged their chains. Perhaps only somewhere in the Russian steppe around a campfire or in the forest will an old wagon driver begin telling a story out of boredom about the crimes committed by so-and-so in their village. The listener, staring into the darkness, shudders, a night bird will suddenly shriek—and this is the only way he will be remembered. The cross which indicates where a convict medical assistant lies buried bears the verses:

Passer-by! May this verse remind you
That all in time under the sky, etc.

And at the end there is the line:

Forgive me, my friend, until that joyful morning!
                                        Y. Fedorov

The newly dug grave was one quarter filled with water. The convicts, puffing and panting, their faces perspiring, loudly discussed something which had nothing to do with the funeral. Finally they carried up the coffin to the edge of the grave. The coffin was made of boards hastily nailed together and unpainted.

"Well?" said one.

They quickly dropped the coffin, which plopped into the water. Clods of clay knocked against the lid, the coffin shuddered, water splashed, and the convicts working with their shovels continued their own discussions. Kelbokiani looked at us perplexedly, stretching out his hands and complaining helplessly.

"What shall I do with the children? I'm saddled with them! I went to the warden and begged him to give me a woman, but he won't give me one!"

The woman was leading the little boy, Aleshka, three or four years old, by the hand, and he stood there, gazing down at the grave. He wore a woman's blouse with long sleeves many sizes too large for him, and faded blue trousers. His knees were covered with bright-blue patches.

"Aleshka, where is your mother?" asked my companion.

"They b-b-buried her!" said Aleshka as he laughed and then he waved his hand toward the grave.[18]

There are five schools on Sakhalin, not counting Derbinskoye, where there were no classes for lack of a teacher.

From 1889 to 1890 they had 222 students: 144 boys and 78 girls, with an average of 44 pupils at each school. I visited the island during the school vacations. No classes were being held during my stay and therefore the conduct and behavior in the schools, no doubt very original and interesting, remain unknown to me. They say that Sakhalin schools are poor, miserably furnished, not compulsory, living out a haphazard existence, and their status completely indefinite because nobody knows whether they will continue to exist or not. They are supervised by one of the functionaries in the office of the island commandant. He is an educated young man; nevertheless he is a king who reigns but does not rule, for in fact the schools are supervised by the district commandants and the prison wardens who select and assign the teachers. The schoolteachers are convicts who were not teachers in the homeland. They have little knowledge of teaching and have not been trained for it. They receive ten rubles a month. The administration finds it impossible to pay more and does not invite free persons to act as teachers because it would have to pay them at least 25 rubles. Teaching school is considered a very mean occupation, for the guards hired among the exiles, whose duties are vague and who act as errand boys for the officials, receive 40 and sometimes 50 rubles a month.[19]

The literate male population, counting both adults and children, comprises 29 percent; the literate female population is 9 percent. And even this 9 percent refers exclusively to those of school age, and so it can be said of the adult Sakhalin woman that she can neither read nor write; enlightenment has not touched her; she embarrasses you with her crude illiteracy, and it seems to me that nowhere else have I seen such stupid and dull women as I found among the criminal and oppressed population of Sakhalin. Among the children who came from Russia 25 percent are literate, but only 9 percent of those born on Sakhalin are literate.[20]

---

[1]   A Russian pound is about 9/10 of the American pound; a *zolotnik* is 1/96 of a pound.—TRANS.

2   A large, low, half-covered, four-wheeled carriage without springs.—TRANS.

3   "A Table of Food Rations for Convict Men and Women" was composed on the basis of *Regulations on Provisions and Additional Food Rations for the Armies,* as approved by His Imperial Majesty on July 31, 1871.

4   The weight differential between flour and bread is a seductive demon whose wiles, it appears, are very difficult to resist, and as a result many people have lost their scruples and even their lives. The guard Selivanov, whom I have already mentioned, became a victim of the weight differential when he was killed by a convict baker, while giving a tongue-lashing to the convict for having obtained a low weight differential. This is really worth being disturbed about. Let us suppose that bread is baked for 2,870 persons in the Alexandrovsk prison. If they hold back only 10 zolotniks from each ration, that amounts to 300 pounds a day. These tricks with bread are generally very profitable. Thus, in order to embezzle 10,000 poods of flour, it would take only 2 to 3 years to conceal this amount with flour taken in small amounts from prisoners' rations.

Polyakov wrote: "The bread was so bad in the Malo-Tymovskoye settlement that not even the dogs could bring themselves to eat it. It contained a great deal of unground whole grain, chaff and straw. One of my associates, who accompanied me during my bread inspection, said rightly: 'With this bread it is just as easy to tie up all your teeth with straw as to find a toothpick to clean them.' "

5   Soup is occasionally cooked with fresh meat in the prison. This only happens when a bear has killed a cow, or some accident has happened to an ox or cow belonging to the government. But the prisoners often consider this butchered meat to be carrion and refuse to eat it. Here are some lines from Polyakov: "The local corned beef was always very bad. It was prepared from the meat of government oxen which had grown exhausted by work on poor and difficult roads. They were butchered the day before they would have expired, unless it happened that their throats were cut when they were already half dead." During the run of migratory fish the prisoners are fed fresh fish at the rate of one pound per person.

6   The administration knows all about this. At any rate, here is the opinion of the island commandant himself: "In the local operations of distributing food rations to convicts, circumstances exist which unwittingly cast a suspicious shadow" (Order No. 314, 1888). If an official says he has been eating prison food for

a week or a month and still feels well, this means that his food has been especially cooked for him in the prison.

7 From the quantities which are placed in the caldron one can see how easily the cooks can make mistakes and prepare a volume of soup which is greater or lesser than the required number of portions. On May 3, 1890, 1,279 prisoners were fed from the caldron, which contained 13½ poods of meat, 5 poods of rice, 1½ poods of flour for thickening, 1 pood of salt, 24 poods of potatoes, ⅓ pound of bay leaf and ⅔ pounds of pepper. On September 29, for 675 persons in the same prison the caldron contained 17 poods of fish, 3 poods of groats, 1 pood of flour, ½ pood of salt, 12½ poods of potatoes, ⅙ pound of bay leaf and ⅓ pound of pepper.

8 On May 3, of the 2,870 persons in the Alexandrovsk prison, 1,279 were fed from the common caldron; on September 29, of the 2,432 prisoners, only 675 were fed from it.

9 The administration and the local doctors have found the prison rations to be quantitatively inadequate. According to data which I obtained from a medical report, the rations measured in grams are as follows: albumen–142.9; fats–37.4; carbohydrates–659.9 on meat days and 164.3, 40.0 and 671.4 on fast days. According to Erisman, the diet of our factory workers on meat days contains 79.3 grams of fat, and on fast days, 67.4. Hygienic rules demand that the more a man works, the greater and more prolonged the physical strain he undergoes, the more fat and carbohydrates must be taken in. The reader can judge by the foregoing how little trust can be placed in the nourishment obtained from the bread and the soup. Prisoners working in mines receive increased rations during the four summer months—i.e., 4 pounds of bread and 1 pound of meat and 24 *zolotniks* of groats. Through the intercession of the local administration the same rations were ordered for the laborers working on roads.

In 1887, at the suggestion of the Director of the Prison Administrative Headquarters, questions were raised about "the possibility of changing the existing regulations in Sakhalin in order to decrease the cost of provisioning convicts without impairing nutrition," and experiments were conducted in a manner recommended by Dobroslavin. As can be seen from his report, the late professor found it inconvenient "to limit the amount of food which has been issued for so many years to the convicts without entering into a more detailed study of the working and prison conditions into which the prisoners have been placed, since it is very difficult to form an exact opinion here on the quality of the meat and bread which are issued locally." Nevertheless, he still found it possible to limit the use of expensive meat rations during the year and proposed three sets of regulations: two for meat days and one for fast days.

On Sakhalin these tables were proposed for consideration by a commission appointed under the chairmanship of the director of the medical department. The Sakhalin physicians who participated in the commission proved to be at the height of their calling. Without equivocation they asserted that in light of the working conditions on Sakhalin, the severe climate and the intense physical exertion during all seasons of the year and in all types of weather, the present rations were insufficient and that the provisions proposed by Professor Dobroslavin's tables, notwithstanding the reduction in meat portions, would be far more expensive than those now being issued according to the existing tables.

Answering the main point of the problem with regard to decreasing the cost of the rations, they proposed their own tables, which failed to bring about the savings demanded by the prison administration. "There will be no material savings," they wrote. "Rather there can be expectations of improvement in the quantity and quality of prison labor, a decrease in the number of the sick and infirm; the general health of the prisoners will be improved, and this will reflect favorably on the colonization of Sakhalin by providing vigorous and healthy settlers to achieve this goal." This "Statement from the Office of the Commandant of Sakhalin Island" refers to changes in the tables brought about in order to decrease costs, and contains twenty different reports, ratios and laws. It deserves close study by persons interested in prison hygiene.

[10] Smoked keta is sold in stores at 30 kopecks each.

[11] As I have already said, the local natives use a great deal of fat in their food, which undoubtedly aids them in combating the low temperatures and the excessive humidity. I was told that in some places along the eastern shore and on our neighboring islands the Russian traders are slowly beginning to use whale blubber in their diet.

[12] When Captain Mashinsky was cutting a road along the Poronaya for the telegraph line, his convict laborers were sent short shirts which could only fit children. The prison clothing is made according to a routine, clumsy pattern which does not permit ease of movement by a working man and therefore you will never see a convict wearing his long overcoat or *khalat* when shipping cargo or doing roadwork. However, discomforts arising from the cut of the clothing are easily remedied by selling or exchanging it. Since the most comfortable clothing for work and life in general is the usual peasant garb, the majority of the exiles wear the same clothing as free men.

13 Since the Kurile Islands went to Japan, the Bishop should now properly be called Bishop of Sakhalin.

14 Regarding the blessing of the Krilon lighthouse by Bishop Martimian, see *Vladivostok* (1883), No. 28.

15 The tone of his letters is very original. Requesting the administration to provide him with a convict assistant to act as a lay reader, he wrote: "As to the reason why I do not have a reader, this is explained by the fact that the Consistory has no trained readers and even if there was one, a psalmist would be unable to exist under the living conditions of the local clergy. The past has come to an end. It seems that I will soon have to depart from Korsakov into my beautiful wilderness, saying unto you: 'I am leaving your house empty.'"

16 There is another church in the Rykovskoye region, located in Malo-Tymovo, where a service is held only on the feast day of Anthony the Great. In the Korsakov region there are three chapels: in Vladimirovka, Kresty and Galkino-Vraskoye. All the Sakhalin churches and chapels were built by convict labor on prison time. Only the Korsakov church was built by funds donated by the *Vsadnik* and *Vostok* commands and by the military living at the post.

17 Professor Vladimirov says in his *Textbook on Criminal Law* that when a convict joins the ranks of the reformed, a ceremony takes place. He probably had Article 301 of the *Code on Convicts* in mind. According to this article the convict is to be informed of his transfer to the designated category in the presence of higher prison officials and the invited priest, who . . . etc. In practice, however, this article is impracticable, because the priest would have to be invited daily, and such ceremonies do not coincide with working conditions. The law which permits prisoners to be excused from work on holy days is also disregarded. According to this law, convicts in the reformed category should be excused more frequently than those on probation. Differentiation of this kind would require a great deal of time and trouble.

The only usual activity of the local priests is connected with their missionary obligations. While I was on the island, the priest-monk Irakly was still living there. A Buriat by birth, clean-shaven, he had come from the Posolsky Monastery in Zabaikal. He has spent eight years on Sakhalin and in recent years he was the pastor of the Rykovskoye parish. His missionary duties obliged him to travel to Nyisky Bay once or twice a year and along the Poronaya to baptize, hold services and preside at the marriages of natives. He instructed some of the 300 Orochi tribesmen. He could scarcely expect any comforts in his travels over the taiga, especially in winter. At night Father Irakly customarily crawled into a sheepskin sleeping bag with his watch and tobacco. His traveling companions built a fire two or three times a night and warmed themselves with hot tea while he slept in his sleeping bag.

[18] According to the records, the Orthodox comprise 86.5 percent, Catholics and Lutherans combined 9 percent, Muhammadans 2.7 percent, the remainder being Hebrews and Armenians of the Gregorian [Latin] rite. A Catholic priest comes once a year from Vladivostok and then the Catholic convicts are "herded" down from the northern districts to Alexandrovsk, and this occurs during the spring season when the roads are terrible. The Catholics complained to me that their priest comes very seldom. Their children remain unbaptized for a long time, and many parents turn to the Orthodox priest so that their children may not die unbaptized. I actually encountered Orthodox children whose fathers and mothers were Catholics. When Catholics die, because they have no priest of their own, they invite a Russian priest to sing the "Holy God, have mercy upon us."

In Alexandrovsk I was visited by a Lutheran who was sentenced in St. Petersburg for arson. He said that the Lutherans on Sakhalin have a society and as proof showed me a seal on which there had been carved: "The Seal of the Lutheran Society on Sakhalin." The Lutherans gather at his home for prayers and for exchanging ideas.

The Tatars choose a mullah from among themselves, the Hebrews choose a rabbi, but they do this unofficially. A mosque is being built in Alexandrovsk. Mullah Vas-Khasan-Mamet, a handsome dark-haired man of thirty-eight who was born in Dagestan, is erecting it at his own expense. In the Peysikovskaya Slobodka in Alexandrovsk there is a windmill which is utterly neglected. They say a Tatar and his wife chopped down the trees themselves, dragged the logs to the site and made the boards. Nobody helped them and they continued to work for three years. On obtaining peasant status the Tatar moved to the mainland, donating the mill to the government rather than to his own Tatars, because he was angry at them for not having selected him as mullah.

[19] After fulfilling the island commandant's order to seek settlers or reliable persons of free status who could be substituted for the convicts presently carrying out the obligations of teachers in the village schools, the commandant of the Alexandrovsk district states in his report of February 22, 1890, that in the district under his jurisdiction there is nobody either among the free people or among the settlers who could qualify as a teacher. He writes: "Since I have encountered insurmountable difficulties in selecting people

who by education would be eligible to some extent for teaching, I do not presume to designate anybody from among the settlers or peasants-formerly-exiles living under my jurisdiction who could be entrusted with teaching duties." Although the honorable commandant of the district does not presume to entrust teaching duties to convicts, they still continue as teachers with his knowledge and by his appointment. To avoid similar contradictions it would seem that the simplest solution would be to invite qualified teachers from Russia or Siberia and to specify the same salary as that received by jailers. This would require a radical change of attitude to teaching, making it at least as important as guard duty.

[20] If we are to judge by fragmentary records and suggestions made on the spot, literate persons bear their punishment better than the illiterate. Apparently there are more habitual criminals among the latter, while the former obtain their peasant rights more readily. In Siyantsy I recorded 18 literate males, of whom 13—that is, almost all the literate adults—have achieved peasant status. As yet it is not customary to teach reading and writing to adults although there are days in the winter when the prisoners sit helplessly in the prison because of the bad weather and languish there with nothing to do. On such days they would eagerly study reading and writing.

Because so many convicts are illiterate, letters home are usually written for them by the more literate convicts, who act as scribes. They describe the sad local life, their poverty and misfortune, they beg their wives for divorces, etc., but in such a way that they seem to be describing yesterday's drunken revels: "Well, finally I am writing a little bit of a letter to you. . . . Free me from marriage ties," etc., or else they wax philosophical and it is difficult to understand what they mean. One such scribe in the Tymovskoye district was named Baccalaureate by the other scribes because of his florid style.

SOLDIERS are called "Sakhalin pioneers" because they lived here before the establishment of penal servitude.[1] Beginning with the fifties, when Sakhalin was first occupied, and almost to the eighties, the soldiers performed all the work now being done by the convicts in addition to their military duties. The island was a wilderness. It had no dwellings, no roads, no cattle, and the soldiers were obliged to build barracks and houses, cut roads through the forest and carry burdens on their shoulders. If an official engineer or scientist arrived on Sakhalin, he was assigned several soldiers who were used in place of pack horses. The mining engineer Lopatin wrote: "Planning to go into the interior of the Sakhalin taiga, I couldn't even think of riding horseback and transporting my baggage by pack horse. Even on foot I encountered great difficulties in climbing over the steep Sakhalin mountains, which are covered either with dense windfalls or by the local bamboo. In this manner I traveled over 1,600 versts on foot.[2] And following him walked soldiers lugging his heavy baggage on their backs.

The entire small force of soldiers was scattered over the western, southern and southeastern shores. The sites where they lived were called posts. Abandoned and forgotten today, at that time they played the same role as the settlements of today and were regarded as the nuclei of a future colony. A company of riflemen was stationed at the Muravyevsky Post; three companies of the Fourth Siberian Battalion and a mining battery platoon were at the Korsakov

Post. The remaining posts, such as, for example, Manuisky and Sortunaisky, contained only six soldiers. The six men, separated from their company by a distance of several hundred versts and under the command of a corporal or even a civilian, lived like real Robinson Crusoes. Life was primitive, extremely monotonous and boring. If the post was situated on the seashore, a boat arrived in the summer with provisions and departed. In the winter a priest came to supervise the fast. Dressed in fur trousers and jacket, he looked more like a Gilyak than a priest. Misfortune brought the only variety into their life: a soldier was carried out to sea on a hay raft, or he was clawed by a bear, or he was snowbound, or he was attacked by escaped convicts, or scurvy insidiously crept upon him. Or, getting bored with sitting in the snow-covered shack or with walking around the taiga, he began manifesting "uproariousness, drunkenness, impertinence," or was caught stealing or embezzling ammunition, or was court-martialed for disrespect rendered to somebody's convict mistress.[3]

Due to the diversity of his labors, the soldier did not have the time to improve his military training and forgot what he had been taught. The officers also became careless, while the drill unit was in a truly deplorable state. Reviews were always accompanied by misunderstandings and expressions of dissatisfaction by the authorities.[4]

The service was harsh. People coming off sentry duty immediately went out on a convoy, from the convoy back to sentry duty or to the hayfields or to unload government cargo. There was no rest day or night. They lived in tight, cold and dirty quarters which differed little from the prisons. Until 1875 the Korsakov Post sentry lived in the penal prison. The military guardhouse was also situated there; it was nothing more than a dark and wretched hovel. "Perhaps such crowding is permissible for convicts as a punitive measure," writes Dr. Sintsovsky. "But a sentry is something else again and nobody knows why he should be made to suffer similar punishment."[5]

They ate the same wretched food as the prisoners, and were dressed in tatters because no clothing could have withstood the wear and tear resulting from their work. The soldiers who chased escaped convicts over the taiga tore their clothing and shoes so much that on one occasion in Southern Sakhalin they themselves were mistaken for escaped convicts and shot at.

At the present time the island's military defense consists of four commands: Alexandrovsk, Dué, Tymovsky and Korsakov. As of January, 1890, there were 1,548 men in the lower ranks of all four commands. As before, the soldiers carry a heavy burden of work incommensurate with their strength, their intelligence and the requirements of military regulations. True, they no longer cut roads through the forest nor build barracks, but, as in former times, a soldier who returns from sentry duty or from drill can never depend on getting any rest; he may immediately be ordered out on a convoy, or sent to mow hay, or commanded to capture escaped convicts. Supply requirements divert a significant number of soldiers, and this results in a constant shortage of men for convoy duty, and the sentries cannot be scheduled in three shifts. When I was in Dué at the beginning of August, 60 men of the Dué command were out mowing hay, half of them having marched out to hayfields 109 versts distant.

The Sakhalin soldier is meek, taciturn, obedient and sober. The only drunken soldiers who acted boisterously on the streets were those I saw at the Korsakov Post. They sing rarely, and it is always the same song: "Ten girls, and only one man. Where the girls go, there go I. . . . The girls go into the forest, I'm right behind them. . . ." This is a gay song they sing with such ennui, such boredom that when you hear them you begin pining for your homeland and you feel all the wretchedness of the Sakhalin countryside. They humbly bear all privations, and they are indifferent to the dangers which so often threaten their lives and their health. But they are coarse, backward and confused, and from lack of opportunity they never come to be inspired with any military skills and have no conception of honor, and therefore they are continually committing the same mistakes as those enemies of order whom they are called upon to guard and to pursue.[6] They disclose their limitations in sharp relief when they find themselves unable to fulfill those obligations which demand some intelligence, as happens when they become prison guards.

In compliance with Article 27 of the *Code on Convicts,* prison surveillance in Sakhalin is maintained "by senior and junior guards, based on one senior guard for each 40 persons and 1 junior guard for each 20 prisoners, these being appointed yearly by the Main Prison Administration." There are in fact 3 guards, 1 senior and 2 juniors, for 40 persons, that is, 1 to 13. If you imagine 13 men working, eating and passing their time in prison under the constant supervision of one conscientious and experienced man, and that over him in turn there is a superior officer in the person of the warden, and over the warden there is the district commandant, and so on, then you can rest content with the thought that everything is wonderfully under control. But in fact supervision is the worst aspect of the penal system in Sakhalin.

At present there are some 150 senior guards on Sakhalin and twice as many junior guards. The senior guards are literate noncommissioned officers and privates who completed their terms of service in local regiments, and included among them are a few intellectuals who do not belong to the privileged classes. Lower ranks in service constitute 6 percent of the total number of senior guards, but the functions of these junior guards is almost exclusively carried out by privates who have been detached from local regiments. When there is not a full complement of guards, the *Code* permits appointments from the lower ranks of the local regiments to perform guard duty. Thus young Siberians regarded as being incapable of convoy duty are ordered to perform guard duty. This is a "temporary measure" and "within the limits of dire necessity," but this "temporary measure" has been dragging on for dozens of years and "the limits of dire necessity" are constantly expanding so that the lower ranks of the local military detachments already comprise 73 percent of the junior guards and nobody can guarantee that within two to three years this figure will not grow to 100 percent.[7]

There are many guards in prison but there is no order, and the guards are a constant drag on the administration, as the island commandant himself has said. He penalizes them nearly every day in his daily orders, decreases their salary or discharges them. He will discharge one for unreliability and nonperformance of duties, a second for immorality, unlawful behavior and stupidity, a third for stealing government supplies entrusted to him, a fourth for hiding them. A fifth, who was assigned to a barge, not only did not keep the prisoners in order but set them a bad example by stealing Greek nuts; a sixth is under judicial examination for selling government oxen and nails; a seventh has more than once been observed in the illegal use of forage for the government cattle; an eighth for reprehensible behavior toward convicts.

We learn from the daily orders that one senior guard from the ranks who was on duty in the prison took the liberty of entering the women's barracks through the window after bending back the bars, the aim being a romantic alliance. Another guard on night duty allowed a private, also a guard, to enter the quarters where unmarried women prisoners were being held.

The guards' amorous adventures are not only limited to the cramped area of the women's barracks and their private quarters. I found adolescent girls in the guards' quarters, and when I asked them who they were, they said, "I am a cohabitant." You enter the quarters occupied by a guard, and you find a man who is thick-set, well-fed and fleshy, his waistcoat unbuttoned and wearing squeaky new boots; he is sitting at a table and drinking tea. A pale fourteen-year-old girl with a weary face sits at the window. He usually calls himself a noncommissioned officer, a senior guard, and says that the girl is the daughter of one of the convicts, that she is sixteen years old, and is his cohabitant.

While on duty at the prison the guards permit the prisoners to play cards and they join in themselves. In the daily orders we hear of violent behavior, insubordination, extremely impertinent behavior toward superiors in the presence of convicts, and we also hear of prisoners being beaten over the head with canes, which cause head wounds.

These guards are callous and backward; they are drunkards and play cards with the convicts, eagerly accept love and liquor from the female convicts, are undisciplined and unscrupulous and thus can exert only a negative type of authority. The exile population does not respect them and acts with contemptuous indifference toward them. They call them *sukharniki* [dried biscuits] to their faces and address them with the familiar second person singular. The administration does nothing to raise their prestige, probably because it feels that such attempts would be useless. The officials address the guards familiarly and revile them in front of the convicts. In this way we often hear: "What are you looking at, you idiot?" or "You don't understand anything, you blockhead!" How little the guards are respected is demonstrated by the fact that many are assigned "tasks which do not conform with their status," meaning that they act as flunkeys and errand boys for the officials. As though ashamed of their duties, the guards belonging to the privileged class attempt to distinguish themselves from the rest, and so you find one wearing wider braid on his shoulders, another wears an officer's cockade, and a third, the college registrar, does not refer to himself as a guard in official documents, but as a "director of labor and laborers."

Since the Sakhalin guards never had any idea of the meaning of surveillance, it followed inevitably that the very purposes of surveillance degenerated slowly, over a period of time, to their present low status. Surveillance deteriorated to such a degree that all the guard does now is to sit in a ward, see that "they don't raise a hullabaloo," and complain to the authorities. While on duty he is armed with a revolver, which he fortunately does not know how to use, and a sabre, which he has difficulty in drawing from its rusty sheath. He hovers around, watches them at their work without participating in it, smokes and feels bored. In the prison he is merely a servant who opens and closes doors, and when the prisoners are out on a job he is superfluous.

Although 3 guards are supposed to be assigned to every 40 prisoners, 1 senior and 2 junior guards, nevertheless you always encounter 40 to 50 men working under the supervision of one guard, or with no guard at all. If 1 of the 3 guards is out at work, the second stands at the government store and salutes passing officials, and the third languishes in somebody's vestibule or, although it is not required of him, he stands at attention in the infirmary waiting room.[8]

Very little can be said about the intellectuals. To have to punish your fellowmen because you are under oath and in duty bound to do so, constantly violating your feelings of repugnance and horror, knowing that you are far away from anywhere, ill-paid and bored, in continual proximity with shaved heads, chains, executioners, bribes, fights, and with the knowledge of your complete helplessness to combat the encompassing evil—all these things make service in the penal administration exceptionally difficult and forbidding. There was a time when these civil servants were slovenly, negligent and slothful, and it made no difference to them where they served so long as they could eat, drink, sleep and play cards. Then, of necessity, respectable people were employed, but they left their posts at the first opportunity or else they became confirmed drunkards, or went insane, or committed suicide. Slowly they were engulfed in the poisonous atmosphere, as by an eight-armed octopus, and they, too, began stealing and beating prisoners savagely.

If we are to judge by official reports and correspondence, the Sakhalin intelligentsia in the '60s and '70s was distinguished by its nihilism. Under the officials then in charge the prisons became nests of corruption and gambling dens. Debauched, hardened and unrepentant people were sometimes beaten to death. The most extraordinary administrator was a certain Major Nikolayev, who was the warden of the Dué prison for seven years. His name is often mentioned in the correspondence.[9] He had been a serf recruit. There is no information concerning those abilities which smoothed the road for this gross, uncouth

309

man, and so enabled him to attain the rank of major. When one correspondent asked him if he had ever visited the interior of the island and what he saw there, the major answered, "A mountain and a valley—a valley and again a mountain; obviously the soil is volcanic, and it erupts." When asked to describe something called ramson, he answered, "First of all, it is not a thing, it is a plant, and secondly, it is most beneficial and tasty; it is true it produces wind in the belly, but we don't care a rap about that; after all, we don't go into the company of ladies."

He substituted barrels for wheelbarrows as a means of transporting coal, so that it would be easier to roll them along gangways. He also placed convict offenders in barrels and ordered them to be rolled along the shore. "You know, when they roll that sweetheart around for an hour, the fellow becomes as gentle as silk." Desiring to teach the soldiers their numbers, he resorted to playing lotto. "When a number is called, whoever cannot cover it himself must pay a *grivennik* [ten-kopeck silver coin]. He'll pay once or twice, and then he'll understand that it isn't profitable. The next time you'll find him laboriously studying his numbers and he learns them in a week." Similar absurdities reacted unfavorably on the Dué soldiers; at times they sold their weapons to the convicts. When the major was about to give a thrashing to a convict, he announced that the man would not come out of it alive and, in fact, the offender died immediately after the beating. Following this incident Major Nikolayev was tried and sentenced to penal servitude.

When you ask an old settler if there have ever been any good people on the island in his time, he remains silent for a while, as if remembering, and finally he says, "There were all kinds." Nowhere are past times so quickly forgotten as on Sakhalin, and this is because of the extraordinary turnover in the convict population, which changes basically every five years, and partly because of the lack of accurate archives in the local offices. What transpired twenty to twenty-five years ago is considered to belong to a dark antiquity, already forgotten, lost to history. What survived consists only of a few buildings, Mikryukov, about a score of anecdotes, and also some figures which cannot be trusted because there was not even one department which knew how many prisoners there were on the island, how many had escaped, died and so on.

"Prehistoric" times continued on Sakhalin until 1878, when Prince Nikolay Shakhovskoy, a distinguished administrator and an intelligent and honorable man,[10] was appointed the leading authority over the penal convicts in the Primorskaya oblast. He left a work which is exemplary on many accounts. A copy of *The Problem of Organizing Sakhalin Island* is to be found in the office of the island commandant. By preference the Prince was a man who kept to his desk. Under him the prisoners were no better off than they were before, but the observations which he shared with the administration and his staff, and his book, which was thoroughly candid and quite uninfluenced by outside sources, served as the forerunner of new and more beneficent ideas.

In 1879 the Voluntary Fleet began to function and slowly positions on Sakhalin began to be filled by natives of European Russia. In 1884 a new order was instituted on Sakhalin which stimulated an intensified influx, or as they say here, an infusion of new people.[11]

At the present time we have three district towns in which officials and officers reside with their families. Society is already so varied and well-educated that in Alexandrovsk, for example, they were able to present an amateur production of *Zhenitba* [The Wedding] in 1888. For the usual entertainments offered by officials and military officers on the great feast days in Alexandrovsk, they have now substituted gifts of money to poor convict families and poor children. The subscription list usually contains about forty signatures.

Sakhalin society makes a favorable impression on a visitor. It is cordial and hospitable, and can stand comparison with our own social communities in all respects. It considers itself the most vivacious and interesting on the eastern shore. At any rate, officials here are reluctant to transfer to Nikolayevsk or De Kastri. But just as violent storms occur in the Tatar Strait and the sailors proclaim that these are the aftermath of a cyclone raging in the Chinese or Japanese seas, so in the same way the recent past and the proximity of Siberia reverberate on this society's life.

The type of rascals who came to work here after the reforms of 1884 can be seen from the dismissal notices, from accounts of trials, and from official reports on acts of disorderly conduct which reached the point of "insolent corruption" (Order No. 87, 1890). These are also evident from anecdotes told about them, like the one about the wealthy convict Zolotarev, who associated with officials, caroused and played cards with them. When this man's wife found him in the company of the officials, she took to rebuking him for associating with people who could be a bad influence on his morals.

Even now we find officials who think nothing of beating a convict over the face, even when he belongs to the privileged class, and when a convict has failed to remove his cap quickly enough, he is told "to go to the guard and tell him to give you thirty lashes." Even today we hear of such irregularities as the fact that two prisoners were believed to be absent at some unknown place for a year when they were actually receiving rations and being assigned to work (Order No. 87, 1890).

Not every warden knows exactly how many prisoners live in the prison at any particular time, exactly how many are fed from the common kettle, how many escaped and so on. The island commandant himself declares: "The general condition of affairs in all branches of administration in the Alexandrovsk district leaves a distressing impression and requires many serious improvements." Concerning the actual conduct of affairs, it was left too much to the discretion of the clerks, who "run things without any control over them, judging by some accidentally discovered forgeries" (Order No. 314, 1888).[12]

I will speak in an appropriate place of the grievous plight in which the department of investigation finds itself in Sakhalin.

At the post and telegraph office the officials are rude and ill-disposed to their clients. Mail is distributed four or five days after its receipt. The telegraph men are ignorant; telegraph secrecy is not maintained. I did not receive even one telegram which was not mutilated in the most barbaric fashion. Once when a piece of someone else's telegram was somehow included in mine, and I asked that the error be rectified so that I could find out the meaning of both telegrams, they told me it could only be done at my expense.

An obvious role is being played in Sakhalin's new history by representatives of the late administrative structure of the island, mixtures of Derzhimorda[13] and Iago—men who in their dealings with inferiors recognize nothing but fists, lashes and abusive language, while they propitiate their superiors by their intellectualism and even by their liberalism.

Nevertheless, the "House of the Dead" no longer exists. Among the intellectuals working in office positions on Sakhalin I met intelligent, good and honorable people whose presence is sufficient guarantee that the past cannot come back again. They no longer roll convicts in barrels and a prisoner can no longer be beaten to death or driven to suicide without shocking the local community and without its being discussed along the Amur and all over Siberia. Every evil action comes to the surface sooner or later, and becomes notorious; the proof of this lies in the grim past, when, in spite of all efforts to conceal them, these crimes aroused a good deal of talk and reached the newspapers, thanks to the intelligentsia of Sakhalin. Good people and good deeds are no longer a rarity. Recently a woman who had been a doctor's assistant died in Rykovskoye. She had served many years on Sakhalin because of her desire to devote her life to the suffering. One day while I was in Korsakov a convict was carried out to sea on a hay raft. The prison warden, Major S., went out on the sea in a cutter and, although caught in a storm which threatened his life, he spent the night until two o'clock in the morning at sea until he was able to locate the hay raft and rescue the convict.[14]

The reforms of 1884 demonstrated that the more numerous the administration in the penal colony, the better. The complexity and dispersion of affairs demand a complex mechanism and the participation of many people. It is important that minor matters should not distract officials from their main duties. Furthermore, because the island commandant has no secretary or government employee always available, he has to spend the greater part of the day issuing orders and preparing documents, and this complicated and tedious office work takes up almost all the time which should be spent in visiting prisons and making the rounds of settlements.

In addition to being in charge of the police departments, the district commanders must distribute food rations to the women, participate in all kinds of commissions, inspections, etc. The prison wardens and their assistants are charged with the duties of investigation and policing. Under such conditions the Sakhalin official must either work beyond the limits of his strength and, as the saying goes, until he goes insane, or he can throw up his hands and place the entire burden on his convict clerks, as most often happens. In local offices the convict clerks are not only kept busy copying, but they also have to write out important documents. Since they are often more experienced and more energetic than the officials, and this is true especially of novices, the convict or settler sometimes has to do all the work of the office, writing up all the account books, and doing all the necessary investigation. Then, after working for many years, the clerk, through either ignorance or malice, mixes up all the documents, and since he is the only one who can make head or tail of the mess, he becomes indispensable and irreplaceable; the result is that the administration cannot do without his services. There is only one way to get rid of such a clerk—by replacing him with one or two honest officials.

Where there exists a large number of educated people, a public opinion inevitably arises; and then there is no question of anyone, even a Major Nikolayev, setting himself up with impunity against the moral law and customary ethical behavior. And as community life develops, so government service slowly begins to lost its forbidding character, and the number of insane, drunkards and suicides decreases.[15]

1 See N. V. Bussé, *Sakhalin Island and the Expedition of 1853–1854.*

2 Lopatin, "Report to the Governor-General of Eastern Siberia," *Mining Journal* (1870), No. 10.

3 At the Korsakov Police Department I saw the following pertaining to 1870:

List for the lower ranks stationed in the Post at the Putyatinsky coal mines on the Sortunay River.

Vasily Vedernikov—as the senior, he is a bootmaker, and serves as the baker and cook.

Luka Pylkov—demoted from senior for negligence and arrested for drunkenness and impertinence.

Khariton Mylnikov—was not caught at anything, but is lazy.

Evgraf Raspopov—an idiot and incapable of any work.

Fedor Cheglokov ⎱ Were caught stealing money and in my
Grigory Ivanov ⎰ presence were observed behaving violently, being drunk and insubordinate.

—The Post Commandant at the
Putyatinsky coal mine on Sakhalin Island,
DISTRICT SECRETARY F. LITKE

4 N. Sm——iy tells the story that not so long ago, in 1885, a general who was reviewing the Sakhalin army asked a soldier prison guard:

"Why are you carrying a revolver?"
"To intimidate the penal convicts, your worship!"
"Then shoot at that tree stump," the general commanded.

Great confusion followed. The soldier was unable to withdraw the revolver from his holster no matter how he tried, and he succeeded only when someone came to his assistance. He raised the revolver and was handling it so inexpertly that the order was countermanded. Instead of hitting the tree stump he could easily have sent a bullet into an onlooker.

—*Kronstadt News* (1890), No. 23

5 Sintsovsky, "Hygienic Conditions of the Convicts," *Health* (1875), No. 16.

6   In the Voyevodsk prison I was shown a convict, a former convoy soldier, who had aided vagrants to escape in Khabarovka and had escaped with them. In the summer of 1890 a free woman accused of arson was being held in the Rykovskoye prison. The prisoner Andreyev, who was in the neighboring cell, complained that he could not sleep nights because the convoy guards were visiting this woman and carousing. The district commandant solved the problem by replacing the lock on her cell and taking the key with him. The guards found another key to fit the lock, and the district commandant could no longer control them. The nightly orgies continued.

7   This gives rise to an obvious injustice: The better soldiers who remain with their regiments receive only their soldiers' rations, while the less skilled soldiers serving at the prison receive both their rations and a salary. Prince Shakhovskoy complained in his book *The Problem of Organizing Sakhalin Island:* "The main contingent of the guards (66 percent) consists of privates from local regiments who receive a government salary of twelve rubles and 50 kopecks per month. Their illiteracy, low level of intelligence, and their complaisant attitude toward the bribes which fall within the scope of their activity, and also their complete lack of military discipline and their incomparably greater freedom of action result not infrequently in unlawful arbitrary treatment of the prisoners or in undue degradation before them." The present commandant of the island is of the opinion that "many years of experience have demonstrated the utter unreliability of guards detached from the local regiments."

8   The senior guards receive 480 rubles and the junior guards 216 rubles annually. After some time this salary is increased by one-third and then by two-thirds, and is sometimes even doubled. Such a salary is considered excellent, and minor officials such as telegraph operators are tempted to leave their posts to become guards at the first opportunity. It is feared that if schoolteachers are eventually assigned to Sakhalin and paid the customary 20 to 25 rubles per month, they will definitely leave their positions to become guards.

Because it was impossible to find free people locally who would take on guard duty and equally impossible to recruit more men from the local regiments without seriously diminishing their ranks, the island commandant in 1888 decided to enlist settlers and peasants who were formerly convicts into guard duty, if they were found to be reliable and could pass the tests. But this measure was unsuccessful.

9   See Lukashevich, "My Acquaintances in Dué on Sakhalin," *Kronstadt News* (1868), Nos. 47 and 49.

[10] Prior to 1875, penal servitude on Northern Sakhalin was under the direction of the supervisor of the Dué Post, an officer whose superior lived in Nikolayevsk. After 1875 Sakhalin was divided into two districts: Northern Sakhalin and Southern Sakhalin. Both districts, which were part of the Primorskaya Oblast, were subject to the military governor in civil affairs and to the commander of the army of the Primorskaya Oblast in military affairs. Local administration was entrusted to district commandants. The title of Commandant of Northern Sakhalin was given to the supervisor of convicts on Sakhalin Island and Primorskaya Oblast, who resided in Dué, and the title Commandant of the Southern District was given to the officer in command of the 4th East Siberian Line Battalion, who resided in Korsakov. The local government, both military and civil, was concentrated in the hands of the district commandants. The administration was entirely military.

[11] According to this new state of affairs the chief governing power over Sakhalin was entrusted to the Governor-General of the Priamur region, and the local government was entrusted to the island commandant, who was appointed from among the military generals. The island was divided into three districts. The prisons and settlements in each district were under the authority of district commandants, who correspond to our district police captains. They were in charge of the police administration. Each prison and the nearby settlements were administered by a prison warden. When settlements are administered by a special official, he is called the supervisor of settlements. Both of these positions correspond to our district police officer. Working under the island commandant is an office manager, a bookkeeper and treasurer, an agricultural inspector, a land surveyor, an architect, a translator of the Ainu and Gilyak languages, the supervisor of the central warehouses and the chief of the medical department. Each of the four military commands must have a staff officer, two officers, and a physician. In addition there is an adjutant for administering the armed forces on Sakhalin Island, his aide and an auditor. There are also four priests and those other employees who are not directly connected with the prison, such as the manager of the post and telegraph office, his assistant, the telegraph operators and two lighthouse keepers.

[12] One day of rummaging through office materials is sufficient to drive one to despair over the inflated figures, false totals and the "idle fabrications" of the various assistants to the wardens, senior guards and clerks. I was completely unable to find any reports on the year 1886. I find penciled annotations in the reports reading: "Obviously this is untrue." Particularly extensive fabrications

317

were noted in sections dealing with the convicts' family status, children and the lists of crimes committed by the convicts. The island commandant told me that one day when he wanted to know how many prisoners arrived yearly from Russia on the ships of the Voluntary Fleet, beginning with 1879, he was forced to request this information from Prison Administrative Headquarters because the local offices did not have the requisite figures. The island commandant complains in one of his reports: "Regardless of repeated requests, no information on 1886 has been produced. I am placed at an even greater disadvantage because it is impossible for me to establish the exact information because of the lack of data. No data was collected in former years. Thus, at present it is extremely difficult to learn the number of personnel as of January 1, 1887, as well as of settlers and peasants."

13 The obscene police captain in Gogol's play *Revizor.*—TRANS.

14 In fulfilling their duties the local officials are often exposed to serious dangers. When he traveled on foot along the entire length of the Poronaya River and back, Butakov, the commander of the Tymovsky district, contracted dysentery and almost perished. One day Bely, the commander of the Korsakov district, was traveling by whaleboat from Korsakov to Mayka. A storm rose, and they were forced out to sea. The boat was battered by waves for almost forty-eight hours, and Mr. Bely himself, his rower, who was a convict, and a soldier who found himself on the whaleboat by chance decided that the end had come. They were cast ashore near the Krilon lighthouse. When Bely met the lighthouse keeper and saw himself in a mirror, he found gray hairs where there were none before. The soldier fell asleep and could not be awakened for forty hours.

15 Today such diversions as amateur plays, picnics and evening parties are becoming frequent. Formerly it was difficult even to organize a game of preference. Intellectual interests are also being increasingly cared for. Journals, newspapers and books are on order. Telegrams come daily from eastern agencies. There are pianos in many homes. Local poets find readers and audiences. At one time a handwritten journal, *Butonchik* [Little Bud], was published in Alexandrovsk, but it stopped with the seventh issue. Senior officials are provided by the government with warm and spacious accommodation; they have chefs and horses. Minor officials rent quarters from the settlers, taking either an entire house or furnished rooms with all the necessary appurtenances. The young official, a poet, whom I mentioned at the beginning rented a room decorated with numerous paintings, a fancy bed with a canopy, and there was even a tapestry on the wall depicting a horseman shooting a tiger.

The island commandant receives 7,000 rubles, the director of the medical department 4,000, the agricultural inspector 3,500, the architect 3,100, and the district commanders 3,500 rubles each. Every three years an official is granted six months' leave of absence, his position remaining secure. In five years he gets a 25 percent raise in salary. In ten years he goes on pension. Two years is counted as three years of service. Travel allowances are also not skimpy. A prison warden's assistant who has no rank receives a travel allowance from Alexandrovsk to Petersburg in the amount of 1,945 rubles, 68¾ kopecks. This is a sum which would be sufficient to make a trip around the world in complete comfort (Orders No. 302 and 305, 1889). Travel allowances are also issued on retirement and to those who take a leave of absence, both five and ten years after entering the service. They do not have to take a leave of absence, and these travel allowances serve as additional compensation. Priests receive travel allowances for all the members of their families. An official going into retirement usually requests a travel allowance during the winter to Petropavlovsk, which is some 8,500 miles away, or to Kholmogorsky Uyezd, which is 7,000 miles away. Simultaneously while applying for retirement he sends a telegram to the Prison Administrative Headquarters with a request for passage for himself and his family to Odessa on a ship belonging to the Voluntary Fleet. It should be added that while an official serves on Sakhalin, his children are educated at government expense.

Nevertheless, the local officials are dissatisfied with life. They are irritable, argue among themselves over trifles, and are bored. A predisposition to consumption, and nervous and psychic disorders can be observed among them and among members of their families. During my stay in Alexandrovsk one young official, a kindly man, always carried a tremendous revolver, even in daytime. When I asked him why he carried such a cumbersome weapon in his pocket, he said seriously:

"Two officials are planning to beat me and have already attacked me once."

"And what can you do with the revolver?"

"It's very simple. I won't stand on ceremony, and I'll kill them like dogs."

XXI   *The Morality of the Exile*
Population - Crimes - Investigation and Trial -
Punishment - Birch Rods and Lashes - The
Death Penalty

SOME CONVICTS bear their punishment with fortitude, readily admit their guilt, and when you ask them why they came to Sakhalin, they usually answer, "They do not send anyone here for their good deeds." Others astonish you with their cowardice and the melancholy face they show to the world. They grumble, they weep, are driven to despair, and swear they are innocent. One considers his punishment a blessing because, he says, only in penal servitude did he find God. Another attempts to escape at the first opportunity, and when they catch up with him, he turns on his captors and clubs them. Accidental transgressors, "unfortunates," and those innocently sentenced[1] live under one roof with inveterate and incorrigible criminals and outcasts.

When the general question of morality is discussed, we must admit that the exile population produces an extremely mixed and confusing impression, and with the existing means of research it is scarcely possible to form any serious generalizations. The morality of a population is usually judged by statistics of crimes, but even this normal and simple method is useless in a penal colony. The strictly nominal infractions of the law, the self-imposed rules and the transgressions of the convict population living under abnormal and exceptional conditions—all these things which we consider petty violations are regarded as serious crimes in Sakhalin, and conversely a large number of serious crimes committed here are not regarded as crimes at all, because they are considered perfectly normal and inevitable phenomena in the atmosphere of the prison.[2]

The vices and perversions which may be observed among the exiles are those which are peculiar to enslaved, subjected, hungry and frightened people. Lying, cunning, cowardice, meanness, informing, robbery, every kind of secret vice—such is the arsenal which these slavelike people, or at least the majority of them, employ against the officials and guards they despise, fear and regard as their enemies. The exile resorts to deceit in order to evade hard labor or corporal punishment and to secure a piece of bread, a pinch of tea, salt or tobacco, because experience has proved to him that deceit is the best and most dependable strategy in the struggle for existence. Thievery is common and is regarded as a legitimate business.

The prisoners grab up everything that is not well hidden with the tenacity and avarice of hungry locusts, and they give preference to edibles and clothing. They steal from each other in the prison; they steal from settlers, and at their work, and when loading ships. The virtuosity of their dexterous thieving may be judged by the frequency with which they practice their art. One day they stole a live ram and a whole tub of sour dough from a ship in Dué. The barge had not yet left the ship, but the loot could not be found. On another occasion they robbed the commander of a ship, unscrewing the lamps and the ship's compass. On still another occasion they entered the cabin of a foreign ship and stole the silverware. During the unloading of cargo whole bales and barrels vanish.[3]

A convict takes his recreation secretly and furtively. In order to obtain a glass of vodka, which under ordinary circumstances costs only five kopecks, he must surreptitiously approach a smuggler and if he has no money he must pay in bread or clothing. His sole mental diversion—card-playing—can only be enjoyed at night in the light of candle stubs or in the taiga. All secret amusements, when repeated, slowly develop into passions. The extreme imitativeness among the convicts causes one prisoner to infect another and finally such seeming inanities as contraband vodka and card-playing lead to unbelievable lawlessness. As I have already said, kulaks among the convicts often amass fortunes. This means that alongside convicts who possess 30,000 to 50,000 rubles, you find people who systematically squander their food and clothing.

Card-playing has infected all the prisons like an epidemic. The prisons are large gambling houses, while the settlements and posts are their branches. Gambling is exceptionally widespread. They say that during a chance search the organizers of the local card games were found to be in possession of hundreds and thousands of rubles, and they are in direct communication with the Siberian prisons, notably the prison at Irkutsk, where, so the prisoners say, they play "real" cards.

There are several gambling houses in Alexandrovsk. There was even a scandal in a gambling house on Second Kirpichnaya Street, which is characteristic of similar haunts. A guard lost everything and shot himself. Playing faro dulls the brain and acts like a narcotic. The convict loses his food and clothing, feels neither hunger nor cold, and suffers no pain when he is beaten. And how strange it is that even when they are loading a ship, and the coal barge is bumping broadside against the ship, and the waves are smashing against it and they are growing green with seasickness, even then they play cards on the barge and casual everyday expressions are mingled with words which arise purely from card-playing: "Push off!" "Two on the side!" "I've got it!"

Furthermore, the subservient status of the woman, her poverty and degradation, are conducive to the development of prostitution. When I asked in Alexandrovsk if there were any prostitutes there, they answered, "As many as you want."[4] Because of the tremendous demand, neither old age, nor ugliness, nor even tertiary syphilis is an impediment. Even extreme youth is no hindrance. I met a sixteen-year-old girl on a street in Alexandrovsk, and they say she has been engaged in prostitution since she was nine years old. The girl has a mother, but a family background on Sakhalin does not always save a young girl from disaster. They talk about a gypsy who sells his daughters and even haggles over them. One free woman in Alexandrovsk has an "establishment," in which only her own daughters operate. In Alexandrovsk corruption is generally of an urban character. There are "family baths" run by a Jew, and the names of the professional panderers are known.

According to government data, incorrigible criminals, those who have been resentenced by the district court, comprise 8 percent of the convicts as of January 1, 1890. Among the incorrigibles were some who have been sentenced three, four, five and even six times. There are 175 persons who through their incorrigibility have spent twenty to fifty years in penal servitude—i.e., 3 percent of the total. But these are exaggerated figures for incorrigibles, since the majority of them were shown to have been resentenced for attempts to escape. And these figures are inaccurate with regard to attempted escapes, because those who have been caught are not always brought to trial but are most frequently punished in the usual fashion. The extent to which the exile population is delinquent or, in other words, criminally inclined is presently unknown.

True, they do try people here for crimes, but many cases are dismissed because the culprits cannot be found, many are returned for additional information or clarification of jurisdiction, or the trial remains at a standstill because the necessary information has not been received from the various Siberian offices. Finally, after a great deal of red tape, the documents go into the archives upon the death of the accused, or if nothing more is heard of him after his escape. Credence is attached to evidence by young people who have received no education, while the Khabarovsk court tries people from Sakhalin *in absentia,* basing its verdict only on documents.

During 1889, 243 convicts were under juridical investigation or on trial, that is, one defendant for every 25 convicts. There were 69 settlers under investigation and on trial, i.e., one in 55. Only 4 peasants were under investigation, i.e., one in 115. From these ratios it is evident that with the easing of his lot and with the transition of the convict to a status giving him more freedom, the chances of being brought to trial are decreased by half each time. All these figures pertain to persons on trial and under investigation, but do not necessarily represent crimes committed in 1889, because the files dealing with these crimes refer to trials begun many years ago and not yet completed. These figures give the reader some idea of the tremendous number of people on Sakhalin who languish year after year in the courts and under investigation, because their cases have been drawn out over a period of years. The reader can well imagine how destructively this system reacts on the economy and on the spirit of the people.[5]

Investigation is usually entrusted to the prison warden's assistant or to the secretary of the police department. According to the island commandant, "investigations are begun on insufficient information, they are conducted sluggishly and clumsily, and the prisoners are detained without any reason." A suspect or an accused person is arrested and put in a cell. When a settler was killed at Goly Mys, four men were suspected and arrested.[6] They were placed in dark cold cells. In a few days three were released, and only one was detained. He was put in chains and orders were issued to give him hot food only every third day. Then, by order of the warden, he was given 100 lashes. A hungry, frightened man, he was kept in a dark cell until he confessed. The free woman Garanina was detained in the prison at the same time on suspicion of having murdered her husband. She was also placed in a dark cell and received hot food every third day. When one official questioned her in my presence, she said that she had been ill for a long time and that for some reason they would not permit a doctor to see her. When the official asked the guard in charge of the cells why they had not troubled to get a doctor for her, he answered, "I went to the honorable warden, but he only said, 'Let her croak.' "

This incapacity to differentiate imprisonment before trial from punitive imprisonment (and this in a dark cell of a convict prison), the incapacity to differentiate between free people and convicts amazed me especially because the local district commander is a law-school graduate and the prison warden was at one time a member of the Petersburg Police Department.

I visited the cells a second time early in the morning in the company of the island commandant. Four convicts suspected of murder were released from their cells; they were shivering with cold. Garanina, in stockings and without shoes, was shivering and blinking in the light. The commandant ordered her transferred to a room with good light. I saw a Georgian flitting like a shadow around the entrance to the cells. He has been held for five months in the dark hallway on suspicion of poisoning and is awaiting investigation. The assistant prosecutor does not live on Sakhalin and there is nobody to supervise an investigation. The direction and speed of an investigation are totally dependent on various circumstances which had no reference to the case itself. I read in one report that the murder of a certain Yakovleva was committed "with the intent of robbery with a preliminary attempt at rape, which is evidenced by the rumpled bedding and fresh scratches and impressions of heel spikes on the backboard of the bed." Such a consideration predetermines the outcome of the trial; an autopsy is not considered necessary in such cases. In 1888 an escaped convict murdered Private Khromatykh and the autopsy was only conducted in 1889 on the demand of the prosecutor when the investigation had been completed and the case brought to trial.[7]

Article 469 of the *Code* permits the local administration to specify and carry out punishment without any formal police investigation for such crimes and offenses by criminals for which punishment is due according to the general criminal laws, not excluding the loss of all personal rights and privileges in imprisonment. Generally the petty cases on Sakhalin are judged by a formal police court which is under the authority of the police department. Notwithstanding the broad scope of this local court, which has jurisdiction over all petty crimes as well as over a multitude of cases which are only nominally regarded as petty, the local community does not enjoy justice and lacks a court of law. Where an official has the right, according to law, to flog and incarcerate people without trial and without investigation and even to send them to hard labor in the mines, the existence of a court of law has merely formal significance.[8]

Punishment for serious crimes is decided by the Primorskaya district court, which settles cases only on documentary evidence without questioning the defendants or witnesses. The decision of a district court is always presented for approval to the island commandant, who, if he disagrees with the verdict, settles the case on his own authority. If the sentence is changed, the fact is reported to the ruling senate. If the administration considers a crime as being more serious than it appears to be on the official record, and if it regards the punishment as insufficient according to the *Code on Convicts,* then it petitions for arraignment of the defendant before a court-martial.

The punishment usually inflicted upon convicts and settlers is distinguished by extraordinary severity. Our *Code on Convicts* is at odds with the spirit of the times and of the laws, and this is especially evident in the sections concerning punishment. Punishments which humiliate the offender, embitter him and contribute to his moral degradation, those punishments which have long since been regarded as intolerable among free men, are still being used here against settlers and convicts. It is as though exiles were less subject to the dangers of becoming bitter and callous, and losing their human dignity. Birch rods, whips, chains, iron balls, punishments which shame the victim and cause pain and torment to his body, are used extensively. Floggings with birch rods and whips are habitual for all kinds of transgressions, whether small or large. It is the indispensable mainstay of all punishment, sometimes supplementing other forms of chastisement, or used alone.

The most frequently used punishment is flogging with birch rods.[9] As shown in the official report, this punishment was imposed on 282 convicts and settlers in Alexandrovsk in 1889 by orders of the administration: corporal punishment, i.e., with birch rods, was inflicted on 265, while 17 were punished in other ways. The administration used birch rods in 94 out of 100 cases. In fact, the number of criminals suffering corporal punishment is far from being accurately recorded in the reports. The reports of the Tymovsky district for 1889 show that only 57 convicts were beaten with birch rods and only 3 are recorded in Korsakov; although the truth is that they flog several people every day in both districts, and sometimes there are 10 a day in Korsakov.

All sort of transgressions my result in a man's getting thirty to a hundred strokes with birch rods: nonperformance of the daily work quota (for example, if the shoemaker did not sew his required three pairs of shoes), drunkenness, vulgarity, insubordination. . . . If 20 to 30 men fail to complete their work quota, all 20 to 30 are beaten. One official told me:

> The prisoners, especially those in irons, like to present absurd petitions. When I was appointed here, I toured the prison and received 50 petitions. I accepted them, and then announced that those whose petitions do not deserve attention would be punished. Only 2 of the petitions proved to be worthwhile, the remainder were nonsense. I ordered 48 men to be flogged. The next time 25 were flogged, and later fewer and fewer, and now they no longer send me petitions. I cured them of the habit.

In the South, as a result of a convict's denunciation, a search was made of another convict's possessions and a diary was found which was presumed to contain drafts of correspondence carried on with friends at home. They gave him fifty strokes with birch rods and kept him 15 days in a dark cell on bread and water. With the knowledge of the district commander, the inspector in Lyutoga gave corporal punishment to nearly everyone. Here is how the island commandant describes it:

> The commander of the Korsakov district informed me about the extremely serious instances of excessive authority used by X., who ordered some settlers to receive corporal punishment far beyond the limits set by the law. This in-

stance, shocking in itself, is even more shocking when the circumstances which provoked the punishment are analyzed. There had been a quite commonplace and futile brawl between exiled settlers; and it made no difference to him whether he punished the innocent or the guilty, or pregnant women. [Order No. 258, 1888.]

Usually an offender receives 30 to 100 strokes with birch rods. This depends on who gave the order to punish him, the district commander or the warden. The former has the right to order up to 100, the latter up to 30. One warden always gave 30. Once when he was required to take the place of the district commander, he immediately raised his customary allotment to 100, as though this hundred strokes with birch rods was an indispensable mark of his new authority. He did not change the number until the district commander returned, and then in the same conscientious manner he resumed the old figure of 30. Because of its very frequent application, flogging with birch rods has become debased. It no longer causes abhorrence or fear among many prisoners. They tell me that there are quite a number of prisoners who do not feel any pain when they are being flogged with birch rods.

Lashes are used far less frequently and only after a sentence passed by the district courts. From a report of the director of the medical department it appears that in 1889, "in order to determine the ability to endure corporal punishment ordered by the courts," 67 prisoners were examined by the doctors. Of all the punishments exacted on Sakhalin this punitive measure is the most abominable in its cruelty and abhorrent circumstances, and the jurists of European Russia who sentence vagrants and incorrigible criminals to be flogged would have renounced this mode of punishment long ago had it been carried out in their presence. But these floggings are prevented from being a scandalous and outrageously sensational spectacle by Article 478 of the *Code,* which specifies that the sentences of the Russian and Siberian courts must be executed in the place where the prisoner is confined.

I saw how they flog prisoners in Dué. Vagrant Pro-

khorov, whose real name was Mylnikov, a man thirty-five
to forty years of age, escaped from the Voyevodsk prison,
and after building a small raft, he took off for the mainland.
On shore they noticed him in time, and sent a cutter to
intercept him. The investigation of his escape began. They
took a look at the official records and then they made a discovery: this Prokhorov was actually Mylnikov, who had
been sentenced last year by the Khabarovsk district court to
90 lashes and the ball and chain for murdering a Cossack and his two grandchildren. Owing to an oversight the
sentence had not yet been carried out. If Prokhorov had
not taken it into his head to escape, they might never have
noticed their error and he would have been spared a flogging and being chained to an iron ball. Now, however, the
execution of the sentence was inevitable.

On the morning of the appointed day, August 13, the
warden, the physician and I leisurely approached the prison
office. Prokhorov, whose presence in the office had been
ordered the previous evening, was sitting on the porch
with a guard. He did not know what awaited him. Seeing
us, he got up. He may have understood then what was
going to happen, because he blanched.

"Into the office!" the warden ordered.

We entered the office. They led Prokhorov in. The doctor, a young German, ordered him to strip and listened to
his heart to ascertain how many lashes the prisoner could
endure. He decides this question in a minute and then in a
businesslike fashion sits down to write his examination
report.

"Oh, the poor fellow!" he says sorrowfully in a thick
German accent, dipping the pen into the ink. "The chains
must weigh upon you! Plead with the honorable warden
and he will order them removed."

Prokhorov remains silent. His lips are pale and trembling.

"Your hope is in vain," the doctor continues. "You all
have vain hopes. Such suspicious people in Russia! Oh,
poor fellow, poor fellow!"

The report is ready. They include it with the documents

on the investigation of the escape. Then follows utter silence. The clerk writes, the doctor and the warden write. Prokhorov does not yet know exactly why he was brought here. Is it only because he escaped, or because of the escape and the old question as well? The uncertainty depresses him.

"What did you dream of last night?" the warden asks finally.

"I forgot, your worship."

"Now listen," says the warden, glancing at the official documents. "On such and such a date you were sentenced to 90 lashes by the Khabarovsk district court for murdering a Cossack. . . . And today is the day you are to get them."

Then he smacks the prisoner on his forehead with the flat of his hand and admonishes him:

"Why did all this have to happen? It's because your head needs to be smarter than it is. You all try to escape and think you will be better off, but it turns out worse."

We all enter the "guardhouse," which is a gray barracks-type building. The military medical assistant, who stands at the door, says in a wheedling voice as though asking a favor:

"Your worship, please let me see how they punish a prisoner."

In the middle of the guardroom there is a sloping bench with apertures for binding the hands and feet. The executioner is a tall, solid man, built like an acrobat. His name is Tolstykh.[10] He wears no coat, and his waistcoat is unbuttoned. He nods at Prokhorov, who silently lies down. Tolstykh, taking his time, silently pulls down the prisoner's trousers to the knees and slowly ties his hands and feet to the bench. The warden looks callously out the window, the doctor strolls around the room. He is carrying a vial of medicinal drops in his hands.

"Would you like a glass of water?" he asks.

"For God's sake, yes, your worship."

At last Prokhorov is tied up. The executioner picks up the lash with three leather thongs and slowly straightens it.

330

"Brace yourself!" he says softly, and without any excessive motion, as though measuring himself to the task, he applies the first stroke.

"One-ne," says the warden in his chanting voice of a cantor.

For a moment Prokhorov is silent and his facial expression does not change, but then a spasm of pain runs along his body, and there follows not a scream but a piercing shriek.

"Two," shouts the warden.

The executioner stands to one side and strikes in such a way that the lash falls across the body. After every five strokes he goes to the other side and the prisoner is permitted a half-minute rest. Prokhorov's hair is matted to his forehead, his neck is swollen. After the first five or ten strokes his body, covered by scars from previous beatings, turns blue and purple, and his skin bursts at each stroke.

Through the shrieks and cries there can be heard the words: "Your worship! Your worship! Mercy, your worship!"

And later, after 20 or 30 strokes, he complains like a drunken man or like someone in delirium:

"Poor me, poor me, you are murdering me. . . . Why are you punishing me?"

Then follows a peculiar stretching of the neck, the noise of vomiting. Prokhorov says nothing; only shrieks and wheezes. A whole eternity seems to have passed since the beginning of the punishment. The warden cries, "Forty-two! Forty-three!" It is a long way to 90.

I go outside. The street is quite silent, and it seems to me that the heartrending sounds from the guardhouse can be heard all over Dué. A convict wearing the clothing of a free man passes by and throws a fleeting glance in the direction of the guardhouse, terror written on his face and on his way of walking. I return to the guardhouse, and then go out again, and still the warden keeps counting.

Finally, 90! Prokhorov's hands and feet are quickly released and he is lifted up. The flesh where he was beaten is black and blue with bruises and it is bleeding. His teeth are chattering, his face yellow and damp, and his eyes are wandering. When they give him the medicinal drops in a glass of water, he convulsively bites the glass. . . . They soak his head with water and lead him off to the infirmary.

"That was for the murder. He'll get another one for escaping," I was told as we went home.

"I love to see how they execute punishment!" the military medical assistant exclaims joyfully, extremely pleased with himself because he was satiated with the abominable spectacle. "I love it! They are such scum, such scoundrels. They should be hanged!"

Not only do the prisoners become hardened and brutalized from corporal punishment, but those who inflict the punishment become hardened, and so do the spectators. Educated people are no exception. At any rate, I observed that officials with university training reacted in exactly the same way as the military medical assistants or those who had completed a course in a military school or an ecclesiastical seminary. Others become so accustomed to birch rods and lashes and so brutalized that in the end they come to enjoy the floggings.

They tell a story about one prison warden who whistled when a flogging was being administered in his presence. Another warden, an old man, spoke to the prisoner with happy malice, saying, "God be with you! Why are you screaming? It's nothing, nothing at all! Brace yourself! Beat him, beat him! Scourge him!" A third warden ordered the prisoner to be tied to the bench by his neck so that he would choke. He administered five or ten strokes and then went out somewhere for an hour or two. Then he came back and gave him the rest.[11]

The courts-martial are composed of local officers appointed by the island commandant. The documents on the case and the court's verdict are sent to the Governor-General for confirmation. In the old days prisoners languished in their cells for two and three years while awaiting confirmation of the sentence; now their fate is decided by telegraph. The usual sentence of the courts-martial is death by hanging. Sometimes the Governor-General reduces the

sentence to a hundred lashes, the ball and chain and deten-
tion for those on probation with an indefinite term. If a
murderer is sentenced to death, the sentence is very seldom
commuted. "I hang murderers!" the Governor-General told
me.

On the day before an execution, during the evening and
throughout the entire night, the prisoner is prepared for his
last journey by a priest. The preparation consists of confession and conversation. One priest told me:

At the beginning of my priestly career, when I was
only twenty-five, I was ordered to prepare two convicts for
death at the Voyevodsk prison. They were to be hanged for
murdering a settler for 1 ruble 40 kopecks. I went into
their cell. The task was a new one for me, and I was
frightened. I asked the sentry not to close the door and to
stand outside. They said, "Don't be afraid, little father. We
won't kill you. Sit down."

I asked where I should sit and they pointed to the plank
bed. I sat down on a water barrel and then gaining courage,
I sat on the plank bed between the two criminals. I asked
what *guberniya* they came from and other questions, and
then I began to prepare them for death. While they were
confessing I looked up and saw the men carrying the beams
and all the other necessities for the gallows. They were
passing just below the window.

"What is that?" the prisoners asked.

"They're probably building something for the warden,"
I said.

"No, little father, they're going to hang us. What do
you say, little father, do you think we could have some
vodka?"

"I don't know," I said. "I'll go and ask."

I went to Colonel L. and told him the prisoners wanted
a drink. The colonel gave me a bottle, and so that no one
should know about it, he ordered the turnkey to remove the
sentry. I obtained a whiskey glass from a guard and returned to the cell. I poured out a glass of vodka.

"No, little father," they said. "You drink first, or we
won't have any."

I had to drink a jigger, but there was no snack to go
with it.

"Well," they said, "the vodka brightened our thoughts."

After this I continued their preparation. I spoke with

333

them an hour, and then another. Suddenly there was the command: "Bring them out!"

After they were hanged, I was afraid to enter a dark room for a long time.

The fear of death and the conditions under which execution are carried out have an oppressive effect on those sentenced to death. On Sakhalin there has not been a single case where the condemned man went to his death courageously. When the convict Chernosheya, the murderer of the shopkeeper Nikitin, was being taken from Alexandrovsk to Dué before execution, he suffered bladder spasms. He would suffer a spasm and have to stop. One of the accessories in the crime, Kinzhalov, went mad. Before the execution they were clothed in a shroud and the death sentence was read out. One of the condemned men fainted when the death sentence was being read out. After Pazhukin, the youngest murderer, had been dressed in his shroud and the death sentence was read out, it was announced that his sentence had been commuted. How much this man lived through during that brief space of time! The long conversation with the priests at night, the ceremony of confession, the half-jigger of vodka at dawn, the words "Bring them out," and then the shroud, and then listening to the death sentence, and all this followed by the joy of commutation. Immediately after his friends were executed, he received a hundred lashes, and after the fifth stroke he fell in a dead faint, and then he was chained to an iron ball.

Eleven men were sentenced to death for the murder of some Ainus in the Korsakov district. None of the officers and officials slept on the night before the execution; they visited each other and drank tea. There was a general feeling of exhaustion; nobody found a comfortable place to rest in. Two of the condemned men poisoned themselves with wolfsbane—a tremendous embarrassment to the military officials responsible for the execution of the sentences. The district commander heard a tumult during the night and was then informed that the two prisoners had poisoned themselves. When everyone had gathered around the scaffold just before the execution, the district commander found himself saying to the officer in charge:

"Eleven were sentenced to death, but I see only nine here. Where are the other two?"

Instead of replying in the same official manner, the officer in charge said in a low, nervous voice:

"Why don't you hang me! Hang me. . . ."

It was an early October morning, gray, cold and dark. The faces of the prisoners were yellow with fear and their hair was waving lightly. An official read out the death sentence, trembling with nervousness and stuttering because he could not see well. The priest, dressed in black vestments, presented the Cross for all nine to kiss, and then turned to the district commander, whispering:

"For God's sake, let me go, I can't. . . ."

The procedure is a long one. Each man must be dressed in a shroud and led to the scaffold. When they finally hanged the nine men, there was "an entire bouquet" hanging in the air—these were the words of the district commander as he described the execution to me. When the bodies were lifted down the doctors found that one was still alive.

This incident had a peculiar significance. Everyone in the prison, all those who knew the innermost secrets of the crimes committed by the inmates, the hangman and his assistants—all of them knew he was alive because he was innocent of the crime for which he was being hanged.

"They hanged him a second time," the district commander concluded his story. "Later I could not sleep for a whole month."

---

1 Mr. Komarsky, the prison inspector under the local Governor-General, told me: "In the final analysis, if fifteen or twenty out of a hundred convicts turn out to be decent people, this is not due to the liberal measures we practice so much as to our Russian courts, which send these upstanding and reliable people to us."

2 A natural and unquenchable yearning for the supreme blessing of freedom is here regarded as an indication of criminal tendencies, and an attempt at escape is a serious criminal offense punished by

penal servitude and flogging. A settler who is prompted by pure compassion, in the name of Christ, to offer shelter for the night to an escapee is punished with penal servitude. If a settler is lazy and fails to live a sober life, the island commandant may sentence him to hard labor in the mines for a year. On Sakhalin even indebtedness is considered a criminal offense. Settlers may not be transferred to peasant status as a punishment for indebtedness. The island commandant permitted the police to sentence a settler to hard labor for a year on the grounds of his laziness and negligence in maintaining his homestead and deliberately evading the payment of debts due the government, for which the settler may be assigned immediately to the "Sakhalin Company" in order to earn the money to pay his debts (Order No. 45, 1890). In brief, an exile is often sentenced to penal servitude and flogging for offenses which in ordinary circumstances would only necessitate a reprimand, arrest or imprisonment. On the other hand, robbery, which is so often committed in the prisons and settlements, is rarely punished, and if one may judge by the official statistics, we arrive at the completely false deduction that exiles are more respectful of other people's property than free men.

3 The convicts throw bags of flour into the water and probably retrieve them from the bottom at night. An assistant officer on one of the ships told me: "You turn your back and find the place stripped. When they are unloading barrels of salted fish, they all try to stuff fish into their pockets, their shirts, their pants. . . . When we find them, we go to work on them! We take the fish by the tail and then smack them over the mouth, and we keep on smacking them. . . ."

4 The police administration, however, gave me a list that contained the names of only thirty prostitutes. They are examined weekly by the physician.

5 There were 171 convicts on trial and under investigation in 1889 for attempting to escape. The case of a certain Kolosovsky was begun in July of 1886 and remained at a standstill because the witnesses did not appear for interrogation. Some cases concerning prison escapes were started in September, 1883, and were given by the public prosecutor for disposition at the Primorskaya Regional Court in July, 1889. The case of Lesnikov was begun in March, 1885, and was concluded in February, 1889, etc. The largest number of cases in 1889 involved escapes—70 percent. After this came murder and implication in murder—14 percent. If cases involving escape were omitted, half the total would be connected with murder, which is probably the most frequent crime committed on Sakhalin. Half the convicts have been sentenced for

336

murder, and the local murderers commit murder with singular ease. When I was in Rykovskoye one convict slit another convict's throat with a knife while working the government garden. He explained that he murdered the man because he would not have to work, since persons under investigation sit in their cells and do nothing. In Goly Mys the young carpenter Plaksin killed his friend for a few silver coins. In 1885 escaping convicts attacked an Ainu village and then, for no better reason than that their own strong passions were aroused, they tortured the men and women, then raped the women, and hanged the children on the crossbeams. Most murders are shocking in their senselessness and brutality. Murder cases are extremely prolonged. Thus, one case begun in September, 1881, was completed only in April, 1888. Another case was begun in April, 1882, and completed in August, 1889. The trial of the murderers of the Ainu families has still not been completed. "The case of the Ainu murders was decided by the military field court and eleven of the accused convicts were sentenced to death. The verdict of the military field court with respect to the remaining five prisoners of the police department is not known. Presentations of documents were made in reports to the island commandant dated June 13 and October 23, 1889."

Cases on "changing given names and surnames" are especially prolonged. One case was begun in March, 1880, and is still continuing, because information has not yet been received from the Yakutsk Regional Government. Another case was begun in 1881, a third in 1882. Eight convicts are on trial and under investigation "for forging and selling counterfeit banknotes." They say that counterfeit money is printed on Sakhalin itself. When prisoners unload cargo from foreign ships, they buy tobacco and vodka from the barmen and usually pay with counterfeit bills. The Jew from whom 56,000 rubles were stolen on Sakhalin was sent here for counterfeiting money. He has completed his sentence and wanders around Alexandrovsk in a hat, a coat and a gold chain. He always speaks sotto voce or in a whisper to officials and guards. This disgusting fellow denounced a peasant with a large family, who was also a Jew, and the peasant was arrested and put in chains. He had previously been sentenced to an undetermined term by a military court "for sedition," but on his way across Siberia the term was reduced to four years. This was done by forging official records. A case "involving stealing from the armory of the Korsakov Local Command Post" is also described in "Information Concerning Men Being Investigated and Placed on Trial During the Year 1889." The case of the accused has been dragging on since 1884 but "there is no information on the beginning and conclusion of the investigation in the reports of the former commander of the Southern Sakhalin district and it is unknown when the case was brought to trial." By order of the island commandant the case was referred to the district court in 1889. And it seems that the accused will be tried for a second time.

6 According to the *Code on Convicts* the administration is not bound by the regulations contained in the *Laws of Legal Procedure* when arresting a convict. A convict can be arrested at any time when suspected of a crime (Article 484).

7 In former days case histories sometimes secretly vanished or cases were dismissed "for a mysterious reason" (see *Vladivostok* [1885], No. 43). They even stole one case history which had been ruled upon by a field court. In his report Mr. Vlasov mentions Ayzik Shapiro, a convict sentenced to an unlimited term of imprisonment. This convict lived in Dué and dealt in vodka. In 1870 he was accused of seducing a five-year-old girl, but the affair was hushed up despite the existence of the corpus delicti. The investigation of this case was conducted by an officer of the post command who had pawned his rifle to Shapiro and owed him money. When the case was taken away from the officer, no documents accusing Shapiro were found. The latter enjoyed great respect in Dué. When the post commander asked one day where Shapiro was, they replied, "They've gone off to drink tea," using the honorific "they" to describe him.

8 In the Andreye-Ivanovskoye settlement a pig was stolen at night from C. Suspicion fell on Z., whose trousers were stained with pig excrement. They searched his homestead, but did not find the pig. Nevertheless, the village commune passed a verdict to confiscate a pig belonging to his tenant A., who could have been an accessory in concealing the pig. The district commander sanctioned this verdict, although he felt it was unjust. He told me, "If we do not sanction the verdicts of the village, Sakhalin will simply have no courts of justice."

9 The mark on the back of the convict's coat, the shaving of half of the head, and the fetters once used to prevent escape and to facilitate the recognition of convicts have lost their former significance, and are now retained only as minor punitive measures. The mark, a four-cornered diamond about two vershoks square, is required by the *Code* to be of a different color from the cloth of the prisoner's coat. Until recently it was yellow, but since this is the color of the Amur and Zabaikal Cossacks, Baron Korf ordered it to be made of black cloth. On Sakhalin these marks have long since lost their significance: the people have grown accustomed to them and are not even aware of them. The same can be said of shaved heads. On Sakhalin heads are rarely shaved, with the exception of those who have been returned to prison after attempting

escape, those under investigation and those chained to an iron ball, while in the Korsakov district the practice has been abandoned. According to the *Code* concerning those under arrest, the weight of the fetters must be between five and five and a half pounds. The only woman in chains in my time was one who was given the name of "The Golden Hand": her hands were in irons. Irons are mandatory for those on probation, but the *Code* permits them to be removed if it is necessary for the performance of work, and since chains are a hindrance in nearly every kind of work, most of the convicts have been freed of them. Today large numbers of convicts with unlimited sentences are not chained, although the *Code* demands that they be chained hand and foot. No matter how light the irons, they still hamper movement to a certain degree. Some prisoners grow accustomed to them, many others do not. I had occasion to see older prisoners who covered their chains with their *khalat* skirts when they saw visitors. I have a photograph which shows a crowd of Dué and Voyevodsk convicts in a work detachment, most of them attempting to stand in such a way that their irons would not be visible in the photograph. Obviously, as an ignominious punishment, these irons often achieve their aim, but the feeling of degradation which they evoke in a criminal has scarcely anything in common with the feeling of shame.

10 He was sentenced to penal servitude for hacking off his wife's head.

11 Yadrintsev tells the story of a certain Demidov who wanted to discover all the details of a murder and had the wife of the murderer beaten, although she was a free woman. She had followed her husband voluntarily to Siberia and was therefore not liable to corporal punishment. He then had the eleven-year-old daughter of the murderer beaten. They held the little girl in the air and she was beaten with birch rods from head to foot. After she had received a number of strokes, she begged for a drink and they gave her a salty salmon. They might have gone on to beat her again and again, but the executioner himself refused to go on. Yadrintsev wrote: "Demidov's brutality is the natural result of the training inevitable to a man who has been in charge of large numbers of convicts" ("The Condition of Convicts in Siberia," *Vestnik Evropy* [News of Europe], 1875, XI, XII). Vlasov's report contains an account of Lieutenant Yevfonov, whose two weaknesses consisted of "turning the convict prison into a public gambling den and a feeding house for crime, and being so brutal that he bred violence in the convicts. One prisoner who had been ordered to receive an excessive number of birch rods killed the guard before the flogging could begin."

The present island commandant, General Kononovich, has always opposed corporal punishment. When the sentences handed down by the police administration and the Khabarovsk court are shown to him, he usually writes: "Agreed, except in the matter of corporal punishment." Unfortunately he has rarely enough time to visit the prisons and does not know how frequently the convicts are beaten with birch rods. This may be happening 200 or 300 yards from his headquarters, and the number of corporal punishments inflicted can be judged only by the reports on his desk. One day when we were sitting in his drawing room, he told me in the presence of some officials and a visiting mining engineer: "Here on Sakhalin corporal punishment is almost never inflicted; it is astonishingly rare."

XXII

Escapees on Sakhalin - Reasons for Escapes - Composition of Escapees by Origin, Class and Others

A FAMOUS COMMITTEE of 1868 pointed out that one of the more important advantages of Sakhalin lay in the fact that it was an island. There appeared to be no particular difficulty in establishing a large prison on an island separated from the mainland by a stormy sea on the principle of "water surrounding a center of adversity." Penal servitude on the Roman model could therefore be instituted in such a way that thoughts of escape would be nothing but idle fantasies. In reality, from the very beginning of Sakhalin as a prison center, the island proved to be a peninsula. The strait separating the island from the mainland freezes over during the winter months, and the water which serves as a prison wall during the summer becomes smooth and level like a field in winter. Anyone can then make his way across on foot or by dog sleigh. And it is not impossible to cross the strait in summer. The width is only six or seven versts in the narrows between Capes Pogobi and Lazarev. On calm bright days it is not difficult to make a journey of one hundred versts in a dilapidated Gilyak boat. The people on Sakhalin are able to see the mainland shore quite clearly even where the strait is at its widest. Every day the convict is fascinated and tempted by the hazy strip of shore with its lovely mountain peaks, which gives promise of freedom and the homeland. In addition to these physical conditions, the committee either did not foresee or overlooked the possibility of escaping into the interior of the island rather than to the mainland. The two kinds of escape were equally disturbing to the authorities, and therefore Sakhalin's position far from justified the committee's hopes.

But it still retains certain advantages. It is not easy to escape from Sakhalin. Vagrants, who may be regarded as specialists in this activity, tell you candidly that it is more difficult to escape from Sakhalin than from Kariysky or Nerchinsky penal servitude. In spite of the illimitable debauchery and indifference which existed under the old administration, the prisons were full and the prisoners did not escape as often as the guards might have desired, since they had much to gain from escapes. Nowadays the officials admit that in view of the inadequate surveillance and the wide area over which convict labor is carried on, if it were not for the fear of the physical difficulties of escaping, the only people who would remain on the island would be those who liked to live on it, and that means nobody.

The sea is not the most fearful of the impediments which prevent people from escaping. The impassable Sakhalin taiga, the mountains, the everlasting humidity, fogs, desolation, bears, hunger, gnats, severe frosts and snowstorms—all these immeasurably assist official surveillance. Even well-fed men who are not prisoners can make no more than eight versts a day in the Sakhalin taiga. At every step he confronts huge windfalls, and thick tangles of marsh rosemary or bamboo must be surmounted. He finds himself sinking up to the waist in marshes and streams, and he must keep shielding himself from the gnats. A man who has grown emaciated in prison, whose food on the taiga consists of rotten wood sprinkled with salt, and who does not know north from south, can make no more than three to five versts a day. He is forced to travel in a wide circle to avoid the cordon. His escape lasts for a week or two, rarely for a month, and then, exhausted with hunger, dysentery and fever, bitten by gnats, his feet bruised and swollen, wet, filthy, ragged, he either perishes in the taiga, or else he summons up the last vestiges of his strength and turns around and staggers back, praying that God may grant him the supreme good fortune of meeting a soldier or a Gilyak who will send him back to prison.

The main reason why a criminal finds salvation in escape rather than in repentance and work lies in his unending awareness of life. Unless he is a philosopher who can live anywhere and under any conditions, he simply cannot prevent himself from desiring to escape and he is not obliged to do so.

The convict's passionate love for his homeland is the chief impulse which drives him from Sakhalin. To hear the convicts talk, living in one's homeland is an endless joy! They speak with contemptuous derision, aversion and malice about Sakhalin, of the local earth, the people, the trees and the climate, but in Russia everything is wonderful and delightful. The most audacious imagination cannot tolerate the idea that there may be unfortunate people in Russia. To be living in Tulsk or Kursk *guberniya,* seeing the native huts every day and breathing the Russian air are for them the greatest happiness. May I be visited with poverty, sickness, blindness, deafness and slander, but, O God, let me die in my native land! One old convict woman who was my servant for a while was enchanted with my luggage, my books and my blanket because they did not come from Sakhalin but from the homeland. When priests were my guests, she never asked them for a blessing but glared at them with a sneer on her lips because in her view there would be no authentic priests on Sakhalin. Their longing for the homeland is expressed in the form of continual melancholy and sorrowful reminiscences intermingled with laments and bitter tears, or in the form of unrealizable expectations astonishing in their absurdity and resembling lunacy, or else they are demonstrated in a form of insanity.[1]

The aspiration for freedom, which under normal circumstances is one of the most noble attributes of man, sometimes drives convicts from Sakhalin. A strong young convict will attempt to escape as far as possible into Siberia or to Russia. He is usually captured, tried and returned to penal servitude, but this is not so terrifying. There is a certain poetry in the slow halting march back across Siberia, in the constant change of prisons and companions and convoy guards, and in the adventures he enjoys on the way. This is more like freedom than being in the Voyevodsk prison or working in a road gang. His strength sapped by age, and with no faith in his powers of walking, he escapes to some nearby place: the Amur River or the taiga or the mountains, going as far as he possibly can from the prison, and so he avoids seeing the same walls and the same people, or hearing the same clattering of chains and the same conversations of the convicts.

The old convict Altukhov, who lives at the Korsakov Post, a man of sixty or more, escapes in the following way. He takes a piece of bread, closes up his hut and, going no more than half a verst from the post, he sits on the side of a mountain and gazes at the taiga, the sea and the sky. After sitting there for three days he goes home, brings out more supplies and again returns to the mountain. There was a time when they used to beat him, but now they only laugh at his escapes.

Some escape to enjoy freedom for a month or a week; there are some who find even one day sufficient. One day, but it is mine! The yearning for freedom seizes some people periodically and resembles drinking bouts and fits of epilepsy. They say it appears at certain times of the year or month, and reliable convicts who feel an attack coming on always inform the officials of a forthcoming escape. All escapees without exception are flogged with birch rods or lashes. These escapes are often quite astonishing in their incongruity and absurdity. It happens that a sensible, discreet family man will escape without clothing, without bread, without any aim or purpose, in the knowledge that he will eventually be captured, and he does this at the risk of his health, at the risk of losing the trust of the administration, his comparative freedom and sometimes his pay, at the risk of freezing to death or of being shot. These absurd results should convince the Sakhalin doctors who decide whether a convict is to be beaten that in many cases they are not dealing with a crime but with a disease.

Life terms should also be numbered among the reasons for escape. It is well known that our system of penal servitude goes hand in hand with the colonization of Siberia. A person sentenced to penal servitude in Siberia is removed from normal human environment without any hope of ever

344

returning; he is dead to the society in which he was born and bred. So the convicts say, "The dead never return from the grave!" It is this absolute despondency and despair which prompt the convict to decide on escape and to change his fate—it cannot be worse! And this is the expression they use when a man escapes: "He wants to change his fate!" If he is captured and brought back, they say that fortune did not favor him—he was unlucky. Escapes and vagrancy are inevitable and indispensable evils connected with penal servitude for life, and they serve as a kind of safety valve. If a convict were deprived of his hope of escaping as the only means of changing his fate, if he thought he would never return from the dead, then without this outlet for his despair, he would probably give vent to despair in some more brutal and more horrible way.

There is still another common reason for escapes. The convicts have a curious belief in the legality of escape, and they regard it as easy, and imagine they will not suffer for it. In fact escapes are difficult, they are cruelly punished and they are regarded as serious crimes. These strange beliefs have been bred in the people for generations and their beginnings are lost in the mists of those ancient days when escapes could easily be made and they were even encouraged by the authorities. A work manager or a prison warden thought he had been punished by God if his prisoners did not escape, and he was overjoyed when large numbers of prisoners left him. If 30 or 40 men escaped before October 1, the day when winter clothing was issued, this meant a profit of 30 to 40 sheepskin coats for the warden.

According to Yadrintsev, one work manager was heard to greet a new party: "Whoever wants to stay, go get your clothes. Whoever wants to escape gets nothing!" The administration appeared to approve of escapes, and no one in the entire population of Siberia had any feeling that there was any sin in escaping. The convicts tell about their escapes with a smile or with an air of regret because the escape was unsuccessful; it would be useless to expect repentance or pangs of conscience. Of all the escapees with whom I spoke there was only one sick old man, fettered to a ball and chain for numerous escape attempts, who passionately reproached himself, regarding his attempts at escape stupid rather than criminal. "When I was younger I did stupid things," he said, "and now I must suffer for them."

There are many reasons for escaping. Among these I include dissatisfaction with the prison regimen, the abominable food, the brutality of some officials, idleness, inaptitude for work, illness, lack of will power, a tendency toward imitativeness, love of adventure. Sometimes entire groups of convicts escaped in order to "have a good time" on the island, this good time being accompanied by murders and various kinds of barbarism which caused panic and utterly infuriated the people.

Permit me to tell a story about an escape which was made for the sake of vengeance. Private Belov wounded convict Klimenko when capturing him and brought him to the Alexandrovsk prison. After recovering, Klimenko again escaped, this time with the sole purpose of exacting vengeance on Belov. He went directly to the guard post, where he was captured and detained. "Lead your adventurer back again," his companions told Belov. "It's your hard luck." And so he did. On the way the guard and the prisoner struck up a conversation. It was autumn, windy and cold. They stopped to have a smoke. When the soldier drew his collar up in order to light his pipe, Klimenko grabbed his gun and killed him on the spot. He then returned to Alexandrovsk as though nothing had happened. He was arrested and hanged soon afterward.

And here is another story about a man who escaped for love. Convict Artem, whose surname I do not recall, twenty years old, a guard at the government house in Naybuchi, was in love with an Ainu woman who lived in a yurt on the Nayba River, and it is said that his love was reciprocated. For some reason he was suspected of theft and he was punished by being transferred to Korsakov prison, ninety versts away from the Ainu woman. He escaped from the post to Naybuchi in order to visit his beloved and he kept on escaping until they shot him in the leg.

Escapes are sometimes sheer speculation. I shall describe one kind of speculative venture which combines greed with the basest treachery. A vagrant, grown old with his many escapes and subsequent imprisonments and chains, seeks out a more affluent convict among some newly arrived prisoners (the new ones always have money) and suggests that they should escape together. He has no great difficulty in convincing him. The novice escapes and the vagrant kills him somewhere in the taiga and then returns to the prison.

A more prevalent kind of speculation is based on the three rubles which the government pays for capturing a fugitive. After making a preliminary agreement with a soldier or a Gilyak, several convicts escape from the prison and meet with their escort at an appointed place in the taiga or by the seashore. The escort returns them to the prison as captured convicts and obtains three rubles for each. Later, naturally, there is a division of the spoils. It was sometimes ludicrous to see a small, puny Gilyak, armed with only a stick, leading back six or seven broad-shouldered, impressive-looking vagrants. One day I saw the soldier L., who was not particularly well built, leading back 11 men.

Prison statistics scarcely touch on the question of escapees. It may be said that the convicts who escape most frequently are those who feel the difference in climate between Sakhalin and their homeland most keenly. They are primarily natives of the Caucasus, the Crimea, Bessarabia and the Ukraine. Lists of escapees or of men captured sometimes contain the names of 50 or 60 men with not a single Russian surname among them; they are all Oglis, Suleymans and Hasans. There is no doubt that convicts with long or indefinite sentences escape more frequently than convicts of the third category, while those living in prison escape more frequently than those quartered outside. Young men and novices escape more frequently than older men.

Women escape incomparably less frequently than men,

347

and this is explained by the hardships which accompany escape for a woman and partially because in servitude she soon becomes preoccupied with a lasting attachment. Responsibilities toward wife and children restrain men from escaping, but there are instances when married men have escaped. Legally married wives escape less often than illegal spouses. When I was making the rounds of the huts and asked women convicts the whereabouts of their cohabitants, they often answered, "Who knows? Go and find him!"

Convicts of the privileged class escape side by side with convicts of the common class. Leafing through the alphabetical list at the Korsakov Police Department I came across a former nobleman who had escaped, had been tried for a murder committed during his escape, and received 80 or 90 lashes. The notorious Lagiyev, sent to Sakhalin for murdering the rector of the Tiflis Seminary, was a former Korsakov teacher and escaped on Easter night in 1890 with the convict Nikolsky, a priest's son, together with three vagrants. Not long afterward there came the rumor that three vagrants in "civilian" clothing had been seen making their way along the shore toward the Muravyevsky Post, but Lagiyev and Nikolsky were no longer with them. The vagrants had probably convinced young Lagiyev and his friend to escape with them and had murdered them for their money and clothing.

Archpriest K.'s son, who was sentenced for murder, succeeded in escaping to Russia, committed another murder and was sent back to Sakhalin. I saw him one morning in a crowd of convicts near a mine. Extraordinarily emaciated, round-shouldered, with lackluster eyes, wearing an old summer coat and hopelessly ragged trousers, still sleepy-eyed and shivering in the morning frost, he approached a guard who was standing beside me, took off his cap and, baring his bald head, began to beg.

Here are a few figures I was able to find which have some bearing on the time of year when escapes most frequently take place. In 1877, 1878, 1885, 1887, 1888 and 1889, 1,501 convicts escaped. The monthly distribution follows:

January	. . .	117	July	. . .	283
February	. . .	64	August	. . .	231
March	. . .	20	September	. . .	150
April	. . .	20	October	. . .	44
May	. . .	147	November	. . .	35
June	. . .	290	December	. . .	100

If a graph is drawn, its highest points indicate the summer and winter months, with the months of sharpest frosts being the most popular. Obviously the most auspicious conditions for escaping are warm weather, when they work outside the prison and the migratory fish run and the berries ripen in the taiga and the settlers have their potato crop; and in winter when the sea is covered with ice and Sakhalin ceases to be an island. The arrival of new convict groups in spring and autumn also present favorable conditions of escape. Escapes are least frequent in March and April, for these are the months when the rivers thaw and it is impossible to obtain food either in the taiga or from the settlers, who are usually without bread in the spring.

At Alexandrovsk in 1889, 15.33 percent of the average number of inmates escaped. In the same year 6.4 percent escaped from the Dué and Voyevodsk prisons, where prisoners are guarded by armed sentries as well as by guards, and 9 percent escaped from the prisons of Tymovsk district. These figures represent escapes in a single year, but if we consider the total number of convicts from the very beginning of their arrival on the island, then the ratio of escapes to the total would be less than 60 percent—i.e., of every five persons you see in prison, three have already attempted to escape. From conversations with convicts I derived the impression that everyone tried to escape. It was a very rare convict who did not take a holiday during his term of penal servitude.[2]

An escape is usually planned when the convicts are still in the ship's hold or on an Amur barge while being transported to Sakhalin. During the journey old vagrants who have already attempted to escape from penal servitude tell young convicts about the geography of the island, about regulations and surveillance, and all the other blessings and misfortunes to be expected in escaping from Sakhalin. If they kept vagrants separated from new convicts in temporary prisons and ships' holds, perhaps they would not be in such a hurry to escape. Novices usually escape quite early, not long after they have disembarked. In 1879, 60 men escaped shortly after their arrival, first killing their guards.

There is absolutely no need for escapees to take those careful precautions which have been described so well by Vladimir Korolenko in his collection of stories called *Sokolinets*.[3] Escapes are strictly forbidden, and they are no longer encouraged by the administration, but the conditions of local prison life, surveillance and penal servitude, and even the very nature of the land, are such that an overwhelming majority of escapes cannot be prevented. If it were impossible to leave the prison today through the open gates, then tomorrow it would be possible to escape while working in the taiga, where 20 or 30 men go out to work with only one soldier guarding them. A man who has failed to escape while working in the taiga waits for a month or two until he is assigned to work as some official's servant or as a laborer working for a settler. Careful precautions, deliberately deceiving officials, breakouts, the digging of tunnels, etc., are needed only by the few who are in chains, in cells and the Voyevodsk prison, and by those who work in the mines, where the sentries stand guard and are on the march along the entire prison line from Voyevodsk prison to Dué. Here an escape attempt is fraught with danger; nevertheless, opportunities present themselves almost daily. Trackers and adventure-lovers offer assistance in the form of changes of clothing and every kind of subterfuge, and sometimes these subterfuges go too far, as in the case of Zolota Ruchka, who changed into a soldier's uniform in order to escape.

In most cases the escapees head north to the narrows which lie between Capes Pogobi and Lazarev, or a little farther north. The land is uninhabited, it is easy to hide from the cordon of guard posts and a boat may be obtained from the Gilyaks or a raft may be built by the convict and a crossing made to the other side. If it is already winter, it takes only two hours to walk across in good weather. The farther north the crossing, the closer it is to the mouth of the Amur, which means less danger of perishing from hunger and cold. There are many Gilyak hamlets at the mouth of the Amur, the city of Nikolayevsk is close by, then come Mariinsk, Sofiysk and the Cossack villages, where a man can hire himself out for work during the winter and where, as they say, even among the officials there are people who will give shelter and a piece of bread to the miserable. Since they have no way of knowing the true north, escapees sometimes make a full circle and return to the place they started from.[4]

Escapees often attempt to cross the strait somewhere close by the prison. This requires exceptional courage and favorable circumstances, and also—and most important—a good deal of previous experience of the enormous difficulties and risks involved in escaping in a northerly direction through the taiga. Incorrigible vagrants escaping from Voyevodsk or Dué prison go to sea on the first or second day after their escape. There is no question of storms and peril. They suffer from a panic-stricken fear of pursuit and a great longing for freedom; even if they drown, it will be in freedom. They usually travel 5 or 10 versts south of Dué, to Agnevo, where they build a raft and hurry over to the misty shore, which is 60 to 70 miles away over a cold and stormy sea. During my visit the same method was used by the vagrant Prokhorov in his escape from Voyevodsk prison. He is the same person as Mylnikov, whom I described in the previous chapter.[5]

They also escape on lighters and hay rafts, but the sea always smashes them unmercifully and throws them up on the shore. Once convicts escaped on a cutter belonging to the mining administration.[6]

Sometimes convicts escape on the ships they are loading. In 1883 the convict Franz Kits escaped on the *Triumph,* having dug himself into the coal. When he was discovered and removed from the coal bunker, he answered all questions by saying, "Give me water. I haven't had a drink in five days."

Having reached the mainland in one way or another, the escapee heads west, begging food in Christ's name, getting work wherever possible, and stealing anything he can lay his hands on. They steal domestic animals, vegetables, clothing—in other words, everything that can be eaten, worn or sold. They are captured, held in prison for long periods of time, put on trial, and returned to Sakhalin with a terrible mark on their records. As the reader knows from reading about court trials, many of them reach the Khitrov market in Moscow,[7] and some return to their own villages.

In Palevo the baker Goryachy, a simple, openhearted and obviously good man, told me how he returned to his own village, visited his wife and children, and was then sent to Sakhalin, where he is now completing his second term.

People say that escapees are being picked up by American whaleboats and taken to America,[8] and this has been discussed in the press. It is possible, of course, but I never heard of a single case. American whaleboats working the Okhotsk Sea rarely approach Sakhalin and rarer still would they be standing close by when the escapees were on the desolate eastern shore. According to Mr. Kurbsky (*Golos*, 1875, No. 312), whole colonies of vaqueros composed of Sakhalin convicts live in Indian territory on the right bank of the Mississippi. These vaqueros, if they actually exist, did not reach America on whaleboats, but probably through Japan. It does happen very rarely that people escape out of Russia altogether. Back in the 1820's we hear of some convicts escaping from the Okhotsk salt works to the "warm islands," meaning the Sandwich Islands.[9]

There is tremendous fear of the escapees, and this explains why the punishment for escaping is so severe and so astonishing in its brutality. When a notorious vagrant escapes from the Voyevodsk prison or from a cell, the reports not only terrify the people on Sakhalin, but even residents on the mainland are afraid. They say that when Blokha escaped, the rumor of his escape so terrified the residents of

Nikolayevsk that the local police captain was compelled to send a telegram: "Is it true that Blokha escaped?"[10]

Escaping is dangerous to society in the first place because it encourages and supports vagrancy, and in the second place because the fugitive occupies an illegal position by the fact that in the overwhelming majority of cases he cannot help but commit new crimes. The largest contingent of incorrigible criminals is made up of escapees. Up to the present time the most horrible and brutal crimes on Sakhalin have been committed by them.

Escapes are now mainly forestalled by repressive measures. These measures decrease the number of escapes, but only to a certain extent, and if repression were brought to the peak of perfection it would still not exclude the possibility of escapes. There is a limit after which repressive measures lose their effectiveness. It is well known that a convict continues to try to escape even when a sentry is taking aim at him. He is deterred from escaping neither by a storm nor by the conviction that he will drown. There is also a limit beyond which the repressive measures themselves are conducive to escape. Thus the terrible punishment for escaping consists of an extra term of years of penal servitude, and this has the effect of increasing the number of long-term prisoners and those with indefinite sentences while increasing the number of escapes. Generally speaking, repressive measures have no future in the struggle against escapes. They have nothing in common with the ideals of our legislation, which views punishment primarily as a measure of reform. When all the energy and resourcefulness of a jailer is spent day by day in placing the prisoner in a physical condition which makes escape impossible, then it is no longer a question of reforming him, and there is in fact only the question of transforming him into a wild beast and making the prison his cage. These measures are also impractical. First, they are a heavy weight on the population innocent of escaping, while, secondly, imprisonment in a strongly built prison, with the usual chains, cells, dark holes and iron balls, makes a person incapable of working.

The so-called humanitarian measures, with improvements in the prisoner's living conditions, whether they consist of an extra piece of bread or in giving him some hope in the future, also significantly decrease the number of escapes. I will cite one example: in 1885, 25 settlers escaped, but in 1887, after the 1886 harvest, only 7 escaped. Settlers escape far less frequently than convicts, while peasants-formerly-convicts scarcely ever escape. The Korsakov district has the least number of escapes because the crops are better, short-term convicts predominate, the climate is milder and it is easier to obtain peasant rights than on Northern Sakhalin, and on completing their sentence there is no need for them to return to the mines to earn a piece of bread. The easier the prisoner's lot, the less danger of escaping. In this respect great expectations can be held for such measures as the improvement of prison conditions, the construction of churches, the founding of schools and hospitals, and providing for the needs of the convicts' families, earnings, etc.

As I have already said, for each captured escapee who is returned to the prison, the soldiers, Gilyaks and others who are engaged in capturing fugitives receive a monetary reward from the government amounting to three rubles per head. There is no doubt that the monetary reward, so tempting to a hungry man, offers an inducement to them and increases the number of those who are "captured, found dead or killed." This inducement, of course, is not worth the ill effects which are inevitably visited on the island population as a result of the evil instincts aroused by the three-ruble reward. Whoever is forced to capture escapees, whether he is a soldier or a settler who has been robbed, will capture them without the reward of three rubles. Whoever captures them when it is not his duty to do so, not from necessity but simply because it is a profitable affair, such a man is merely taking part in a miserable enterprise, and the three rubles are nothing more than an expression of his connivance at the basest possible alliance of interests.

According to my data, out of 1,501 escapees, 1,010

convicts were captured or returned voluntarily; 40 were found dead or were killed in pursuit; 451 were missing. In spite of being an island, Sakhalin loses one-third of all its escapees.

In the reports from which I gathered these figures, those who returned voluntarily and those who were captured are included in one figure, those found dead or killed while being pursued are also listed together, and no one knows how many must be credited to captors and what percentage of the fugitives perished from soldier's bullets.[11]

---

[1] Nostalgia is commonly found among our officials and sailors in Vladivostok. I myself saw two insane officials—a lawyer and a bandmaster. Such cases are not rare among free people living under comparatively healthy conditions, and it is quite understandable that they occur frequently on Sakhalin.

[2] I remember when I was once approaching a ship by cutter I saw a barge filled to overflowing with escapees pulling away. Some of the escapees were gloomy, others were laughing uproariously, and one had no feet—they had been frozen off. They were being returned from Nikolayevsk. Looking at this barge teeming with people, I could imagine how many more convicts there were wandering on the mainland and the island.

[3] Vladimir Galaktionovich Korolenko (1853–1921). The stories recounted escapes by prisoners from Sakhalin.—TRANS.

[4] One day some escapees stole a compass in Dué to help them find their way north and to bypass the cordon of guard posts at Cape Pogobi, but the compass led them straight into the cordon. I heard that in order to avoid the guarded western shore, the convicts have recently begun to escape along a route eastward to Nyisky Bay, then northward along the shores of the Okhotsk Sea to Capes Maria and Yelizaveta, then southward to enable them to cross the strait opposite Cape Pronge. They told me this was the route chosen by the notorious Bogdanov, who escaped just before my arrival, but this may not be accurate. There are Gilyak pathways along the Tym River, and there are a few yurts, but the journey from Nyisky Bay is long, tortuous and arduous. The great privations suffered by Polyakov when he traveled south from Nyisky Bay should be remembered if one wishes to judge the risk of traveling north from the bay.

I have already described the terrible experiences suffered by escapees. Escapees, especially the incorrigible ones, gradually grow accustomed to the tundra and the taiga, their feet become calloused, and it is not surprising that some of them have been known to sleep while walking. I was told that Chinese vagrants, the *khun-khuzy,* who are sent to Sakhalin from the Primorskaya district, can remain at large longer than others because they seem to be able to subsist on roots and grasses for months at a time.

5 ˙ On June 29, 1886, the naval vessel *Tungus* observed a black speck on the sea some 20 miles from Dué. When they approached closer they saw two men sitting on a platform of bark atop four lashed logs, and they were obviously heading somewhere. Next to them on the raft was a bucket of fresh water, a loaf and a half of bread, an ax, about a pood of flour, some rice, two tallow candles, a bar of soap and two bricks of tea. When they were taken aboard and questioned about their identity, it was learned that they were prisoners from the Dué prison who had escaped on June 17 (12 days earlier), and they were traveling "that way, to Russia." A violent storm struck two hours later and the ship was unable to reach the Sakhalin shore. The question is, what would have happened to the escapees in such weather if they had not been picked up by this ship? See *Vladivostok* (1886), No. 31, with reference to this.

6 In June, 1887, coal was being loaded aboard the ship *Tira* in Dué waters. Usually the coal was brought up on barges towed by a steam cutter, and the barges came alongside the ship. Toward evening the wind freshened and a storm rose. The anchors could not hold the *Tira,* so it sailed to De Kastri. The coal barge was cast up on shore near Dué, while the cutter sailed to the Alexandrovsk Post and sheltered itself in the river. At night, when the weather grew somewhat calmer, the workmen on the cutter, all of them convicts, gave the guard in charge of the cutter a forged telegram from Dué ordering him to proceed immediately to sea to save people supposed to have been carried out to sea on a barge during the storm. The guard had no idea a trick was being played on him, and he unmoored the cutter from the dock. Instead of going south to Dué, the cutter turned north. There were seven men and three women on board. Toward morning the weather grew worse. The engine of the cutter was swamped near Cape Khoe. Nine were drowned and their bodies were cast ashore; only one man, the pilot, saved himself by floating on a board. This sole survivor, Kuznetsov, is now working for the mining engineer at the mine in Alexandrovsk Post. He served tea. He is a strong, swarthy, handsome man, about forty years old, obviously proud and ferocious. He reminded me of Thomas Ayrton in *The Children of Captain Grant* [by Jules Verne].

7   Khitrov market was a disreputable square in Moscow.—TRANS.

8   An old resident of Nerchinsk says: "American whaleboats have given sanctuary to escapees from Botany Bay, and they will do the same for escapees from Sakhalin" (*Moscow News,* 1875, No. 67).

9   This is described in "Penal Convicts in Okhotsk," *Russian Antiquity,* XXII, where an interesting incident is related. In 1885 the Japanese newspapers carried the story that nine foreigners had been shipwrecked near Sapporo. The authorities sent officials to assist them. As well as they could, the foreigners explained that they were Germans, their schooner had been shipwrecked, and they had saved themselves in a lifeboat. They were taken from Sapporo to Khokodate. When addressed in English and Russian they failed to understand what was being said; they went on repeating, "German, German." Somehow the Japanese found out which of them was the captain of the ship, and showed him an atlas, asking him to indicate the exact position of the shipwreck. For a long time his finger moved over the map, but he could not find Sapporo. The replies of all the shipwrecked men were vague. At that time one of our cruisers was in dock at Khokodate. The Governor-General asked the captain of the cruiser to provide a German interpreter. The captain sent a senior officer. Recognizing them to be Sakhalin convicts, the same escapees who had recently attacked the Krilon lighthouse, this officer resorted to a ruse; he made them line up in single file and then gave the command in Russian: "To the left in a circle, march!" One of the convicts forgot his role and immediately executed the command. In this way it was possible to learn what country these clever Odyssean travelers belonged to. See *Vladivostok* (1885), Nos. 33 and 38.

10 Blokha is famous for his escapes and for having murdered many Gilyak families. Recently he has been held in "The Irons," chained hand and foot. When the Governor-General was visiting "The Irons" with the island commandant, the latter ordered the chains to be removed, and ordered him to give his word of honor not to escape any more. It would be interesting to learn what honor means to Blokha. When he is being flogged, he screams, "For what I have done, your worship! For what I have done! I really deserve this!" It is quite conceivable that he will keep his word. The convicts enjoy the reputation of being honorable men.

11 The *Code on Convicts* designates degrees of punishment for an escape, for absence, for escaping in Siberia, for escaping outside Siberia, for the first, second, third, fourth and subsequent escapes. A convict is considered to have been absent and not to have escaped if he is caught within less than 3 days or if he voluntarily

returns within less than 7 days from the time of his escape. For settlers the period of absence is increased in the first instance to 7 days and in the second to 14. Escape beyond the boundaries of Siberia is considered a more serious crime than escape within Siberia. This difference in the punishments is probably based on the idea that an escape to European Russia requires a far greater intensity of deliberate evil than an escape into some Siberian *guberniya*. The mildest punishment for escape is usually 40 lashes and an increase in the sentence of 4 years of penal servitude; the severest punishment is 100 lashes, an unlimited term of penal servitude, being chained to a ball for 3 years and being retained in the reform category for 20 years. See Articles 445 and 446 of the *Code on Convicts,* edition of 1890.

XXIII   *Diseases and Mortality of the*
Convict Population - The Medical Organization -
The Hospital in Alexandrovsk

IN 1889 THE THREE DISTRICTS had a combined total
of 632 feeble and incapacitated convicts of both sexes,
which is 10.6 percent of the total. Thus there is one feeble
and incapacitated convict for every ten persons. Even the
population which is capable of working does not look completely healthy. You will not find well-fed, stout and red-
cheeked people among the convicts. Even the settlers who
do nothing are gaunt and pale. Of the 131 convicts working on the road in the Tarayka in the summer of 1889,
37 were ill, while the remainder as described by the visiting island commandant "presented a horrifying appearance:
they were in rags, many had no shirts, they were full of
mosquito bites and scratches from twigs, but nobody complained" (Order No. 318, 1889).

There were 11,309 cases requiring medical assistance in
1889. The medical report from which I obtained this figure
does not differentiate between convicts and free men but
the writer of the report notes that the penal convicts constituted the largest group of patients. Since soldiers are
treated by their own army doctors, while officials and their
families receive medical treatment at home, it can be presumed that the 11,309 consisted only of convicts and their
families, the convicts being in the majority, and that therefore every convict and everyone connected with the convicts requested medical assistance at least once that year.[1]

I can only judge the illnesses of the convict population
by the Report of 1889. Unfortunately it is based on data
contained in the "True Books" of the infirmaries, which are

maintained in a most slovenly fashion, and therefore I was forced to seek assistance from church records and to extract therefrom the causes of death for the past ten years. The causes of death are almost always registered by the priests in accordance with the reports of doctors and medical assistants, and they contain many fantasies,[2] but in general this material is essentially the same as that in the "True Books," and is neither better nor worse. It is understandable that both these sources were far from adequate and everything the reader finds below concerning sicknesses and mortality is not a true picture but merely a meager sketch.

The infectious and epidemic diseases, which are recorded in the report under separate groupings, have not been widespread on Sakhalin to date. Thus, in 1889 measles was recorded three times, while there is no record of scarlet fever, diphtheria or croup. Death from these diseases, which usually attack children, is recorded only 45 times in the church books of the past 10 years. This number included "tonsillitis" and "inflammation of the throat," which are of an infectious and epidemic character and always indicate that a number of children will die within a short period of time.

The epidemics usually began in September or October, when the sick children arrived in the colony on the ships of the Voluntary Fleet. The course of the epidemics was prolonged, but they were not very serious. Thus, in 1880, tonsillitis began to occur in the Korsakov parish in October and ended in April of the following year, causing death to only ten children. The diphtheria epidemic of 1888 began in the Rykovskoye parish in the fall and continued through the entire winter; it then jumped to the Alexandrovsk and Dué parishes and finally ended in November, 1889—i.e., it prevailed for an entire year; 20 children died. Smallpox is recorded once; 18 persons died of it in 10 years. There were two epidemics in the Alexandrovsk district, the first in 1886 from December to June and the second in the fall of 1889. Those terrible smallpox epidemics which once ran rampant over all the Japanese islands and the Okhotsk Sea, including Kamchatka, and occasionally annihilated whole tribes, such as the Ainus, no longer occur here, at least there is no report on them. Pockmarked faces are frequently seen among the Gilyaks but this is due to chicken pox (varicella), which in all probability is not infectious among foreigners.[3]

As to types of typhus, 23 cases of typhoid fever were recorded, with a 30 percent mortality, and three cases of relapsing typhoid and typhus occurred. There were no deaths. The church records reveal 50 deaths from various forms of typhus and fevers, but these are individual cases scattered throughout the books of all four parishes during a ten-year period. I did not see any indication of the various forms of the typhus epidemics in the correspondence and in all probability there were none. According to reports, typhoid fever was observed only in the two northern districts. The causes were found to be the lack of clean drinking water, contamination of the soil near prisons and rivers, as well as the crowded and congested conditions. I myself did not see even one case of typhoid fever on Northern Sakhalin, although I vsited all the huts and was in the infirmaries. Some physicians assured me that this form of typhus is nonexistent on the island and I am myself inclined to believe it. I relate all cases of relapsing fever and typhus on Sakhalin to incursions of scarlet fever and diphtheria. The supposition is that serious infectious diseases have so far found unfavorable ground for their development.

"Inexactly definable feverish illnesses" are recorded in seventeen cases. The report describes this type of illness as follows: "It appeared chiefly during the winter months with symptoms of a remittent type of fever, sometimes with the appearance of roseola[4] and a general depression of the brain centers. In a short time, within five to seven days, the fever passed and complete recovery occurred rapidly." This form of typhoid is very prevalent here especially in the northern districts, but not even a hundredth of the cases are recorded, because the sick are not usually treated; they suffer on their feet or lie on their stoves at home. I became convinced during my short visit to the island that colds play the main role in the etiology of this illness, those who are stricken being people who work in the taiga in cold and raw weather and who sleep under the open sky. People suffering with this illness are most frequently seen on roadwork and on new settlement sites. This is veritable *febris sachalinensis*.

In 1889, 27 became ill with croupous pneumonia; a third of them died. This illness was evidently just as dangerous to the convicts as to the people who were free. Church records for the ten-year period give croupous pneumonia as the cause of 125 deaths; 28 percent of these were recorded in May and June with the start of the bad, changeable weather, when convicts were sent to work far from the prison. Forty-six percent died in December, January, February and March, i.e., during the winter.[5] The main causes of illness from croupous pneumonia are the extreme cold in the winter, sharp changes in the weather and hard labor during inclement weather. The report of March 24, 1889, by Dr. Perlin, the physician of the district infirmary, says: "I was constantly dismayed by the tremendous morbidity of penal servitude workers suffering from severe inflammation of the lungs." These were the causes, in Dr. Perlin's opinion: "Logs 6 to 8 vershoks in diameter and 4 sazhens long being hauled 8 versts by 3 workers, the approximate weight of the log being 25 to 35 poods, the snow-covered roads, the warm clothing, the accelerated activity of the respiratory and circulatory systems," etc.[6]

Dysentery or bloody diarrhea is recorded only five times. There were known epidemics of dysentery in Dué in 1880 and in Alexandrovsk in 1887, but the church records show a total of eight deaths due to this illness during the ten-year period. Old correspondence and reports often mention dysentery, which in former days was probably as common as scurvy. Convicts, soldiers and foreigners suffered from it and there are further indications that suggest it was caused by the vile food and the abominable living conditions.[7]

There was no case of Asiatic cholera on Sakhalin. I

observed erysipelas and military hospital gangrene myself, and apparently both these illnesses are not infectious in the local infirmaries. There was no whooping cough in 1889. Intermittent fever was recorded 428 times, more than half of the cases occurring in the Alexandrovsk district. The report names the causes as the warmth of the habitations, which lack sufficient fresh air, contamination of the soil near habitations, work in localities which undergo periodic flooding, and the construction of settlements in such localities. All of these unhealthy conditions do exist; nevertheless the island does not give the impression of being a malarial location. During my visit to the island I never saw anyone suffering from malaria and I do not recall even one settlement where men complained of this disease. It is possible that many of the recorded examples were contracted when they were still in Russia and they arrived on the island with an already enlarged spleen.

Death from malignant anthrax was mentioned only once in the church records. Neither glanders nor hydrophobia has been observed on the island.

Diseases of the respiratory organs cause one-third of the deaths, tuberculosis in particular being responsible for 15 percent. The church records only contain data on Christians, but if we added the number of Moslems who die from tuberculosis there would be an impressive percentage. In any case, adults on Sakhalin are susceptible to tuberculosis to a high degree. Here it is a most frequent and most dangerous disease. Deaths occur most often in December, when it is extremely cold on Sakhalin, and in March and April. The lowest incidence of death is in September and October. Herewith is a breakdown of deaths from tuberculosis by ages:

From	0 to 20 years of age	.	.	.	3%
From	20 to 25 years of age	.	.	.	6%
From	25 to 35 years of age	.	.	.	43%
From	35 to 45 years of age	.	.	.	27%
From	45 to 55 years of age	.	.	.	12%
From	55 to 65 years of age	.	.	.	6%
From	65 to 76 years of age	.	.	.	2%

Consequently, those in the 25–35 and 35–45 age brackets, workers in the prime of life,[8] are most subject to the peril of dying from tuberculosis. The majority of those who died of tuberculosis are convicts (66 percent). This predominance of working-age convicts gives us the right to conclude that the significant mortality from tuberculosis in the penal colony is produced by the adverse living conditions in the prison wards and the oppressiveness of penal labor, which exacts more energy from the worker than prison fare can give him. The raw climate, all the deprivations suffered during work, escapes, and imprisonment in cells, the turbulent life in the prison wards, the insufficiency of fats in the food, longing for the homeland—these are the causes of Sakhalin tuberculosis.

Syphilis was recorded in 246 cases, with five deaths. All of these, as stated in the report, were old syphilitics in secondary and tertiary stages of the disease. The syphilitics whom I saw were pathetic. These neglected, chronic cases indicated a complete lack of medical inspection, which in effect should have been ideally thorough in view of the scant convict population. Thus in Rykovskoye I saw a Jew with syphilitic consumption. He had not been treated for a long time and was slowly wasting away while his family impatiently awaited his death. And this occurred about half a verst from the hospital. The church records indicate 13 deaths from syphilis.[9]

There were 271 cases of scurvy recorded in 1889, with 6 deaths. The church records show 19 deaths from scurvy. Some twenty to twenty-five years ago this disease was incomparably more prevalent on the island than within the past decade, and many soldiers and prisoners perished from it. Some of the old writers who favored the founding of the penal colony on the island completely denied the existence of scurvy, while they simultaneously praised wild garlic as a marvelous preventive of scurvy. They wrote that the people stored hundreds of poods of this preventive for the winter. The scurvy which raged on the Tatar shore would scarcely have spared Sakhalin, where living conditions at the posts were hardly any better. At present this disease is most frequently imported by prisoners arriving on the ships of the Voluntary Fleet. This is also stated in the medical reports. The district commander and the prison doctor in Alexandrovsk told me that on May 2, 1890, the *Petersburg* landed 500 prisoners, 100 of whom were suffering from scurvy; 51 of these were put into the infirmary and the clinic by the doctor. One of these sufferers from scurvy, a Ukrainian from Poltava whom I found in bed in the infirmary, told me he had contracted scurvy in the Kharkov central prison.[10]

Of the common illnesses due to the bad diet I especially recall marasmus, from which people of working age, not old people, die on Sakhalin. One died at 27, another at 30, others at 35, 43, 46, 47, 48 years of age. Could it be a priest's or a medical assistant's slip of the pen when "senile marasmus" is recorded as the cause of 45 deaths of people who were still young and had not yet reached the age of sixty? The average life expectancy of the Russian penal convict is not yet known, but judging by appearance, people in Sakhalin age and grow senile very early in life, and in the majority of cases a forty-year-old convict or settler is already an old man.

The exiles do not usually request treatment at the infirmary for nervous disorders. Thus, only 16 cases[11] of neuralgia and convulsions were recorded in 1889. Obviously only those who are ill with nervous disorders who have come on foot or in some conveyance to the infirmary are treated. Meningitis, apoplexy and paralysis caused 24 cases, with 10 deaths; epilepsy is recorded in 31 cases, and mental aberrations in 25. As I stated previously, people with mental illnesses are not treated in a separate institution on Sakhalin. During my visit to the Korsakov settlement a mental case was found living among syphilitics, and I was told that another became infected with syphilis. Others living in freedom worked together with healthy persons. They were cohabitants, they escaped and were put on trial. I personally met a number of insane persons in the posts and settlements.

I recall that in Dué a former soldier constantly talked

about the oceans of air and sea, his daughter Nadezhda and the Persian Shah, and of his killing the Kristovosdvizhensky church deacon. One day in my presence in Vladimirovka a certain Vetryakov, who had spent five years in penal servitude, approached the settlement inspector, Mr. Y., with a stupid and idiotic expression and extended his hand in a friendly manner. "Are you greeting me?" said the astonished inspector. It appeared that Vetryakov had come to ask if he could have a carpenter's ax from the government warehouse. "I'll build myself a shack and later I'll build a hut," he said. He had long been recognized as a lunatic, had been examined by a physician and found to be a paranoiac. I asked his father's name. He answered, "I don't know." Nevertheless they gave him an ax.

I cannot even discuss the cases of mental disorders, of the onset of progressive paralysis and the like, where a greater or lesser specialized diagnosis is required. All these people are working and are considered healthy. Some arrive here already ill or they bring the germination of illnesses with them. Thus the church records describe convict Gorodov as having died from progressive paralysis. He had been sentenced for premeditated murder, which he had probably committed after having already been stricken with the disease. There are many on the island whose sufferings every day and every hour offer a sufficient reason for a weak man with broken nerves to go insane.[12]

There were 1,760 cases of gastrointestinal disorder recorded in 1889. In ten years 338 died; of these 66 percent were children. July and August are the most dangerous months—a third of the total of children's deaths occur in those months. Adults also die most frequently from gastrointestinal disorders in August. This is probably because August is the month of the migratory fish runs and they gorge themselves on fish. Gastric catarrh is a common illness. Natives of the Caucasus always complain that their "heart hurts," and vomit after eating rye bread and prison cabbage soup.

Cases of female illnesses were infrequent in 1889. Only 105 were recorded. There are almost no healthy women in the colony. One of the commissions which inquired into the provisioning of convicts—the director of the medical department was one of those who sat on the commission—declared *inter alia* that "about 70 percent of the convict women suffer from chronic female illnesses." Sometimes there was not one single healthy woman in a group of female prisoners arriving on the island.

The most prevalent eye disease is conjunctivitis. Its epidemic form is not contagious among foreigners.[13] I can say nothing about more severe eye afflictions because all disorders of the eye are included in the figure of 211 cases. In the huts I saw people who had only one eye, with cataracts, completely blind. I also saw blind children.

There were 1,217 persons who requested medical aid for traumatic injuries, for dislocations, fractures, contusions and all types of wounds. All these injuries were suffered at work, in a variety of unfortunate accidents, in escapes (shotgun wounds) and in fights. This group contains four infirmary cases of women who had been beaten by their cohabitants.[14] Rigor was recorded in 290 cases.

In ten years there were 170 cases of unnatural death amid the Orthodox population. Of this number 20 were sentenced to death by hanging, 2 were hanged by unknown persons, 27 committed suicide—in Northern Sakhalin they shot themselves (1 shot himself on sentry duty), and in Southern Sakhalin they poisoned themselves with wolfsbane. Many were drowned, frozen to death, crushed by trees; one was torn to bits by a bear. In addition to such causes of death as stroke, heart attack, apoplexy, general paralysis of the body, etc., the church records show 17 cases of "sudden death." More than half of these were between the ages of 22 to 40, and only 1 was over 50.

This is all that I can say about morbidity in the penal colony. Despite the exceptionally weak development of infectious diseases, I still cannot fail to acknowledge their significance on the basis of the above figures. There were 11,309 patients requesting medical aid in 1889. During the summer most of the convicts work and live at a considerable distance from the prison and even in the prison a medical assistant is assigned only to large groups. Since the majority of the settlers cannot walk or ride to the infirmary because of the great distances and the terrible weather, this figure applies chiefly to that portion of the population which lives close to the medical stations at the posts.

According to data in the report, there were 194 deaths in 1889, or 12.5 percent, for every thousand persons. This percentage might serve as the basis for a magnificent illusion and suggest that Sakhalin is the healthiest place in the world. However, it is necessary to weigh the following facts. Under ordinary conditions half of the deceased are usually children, and somewhat less than a quarter are the aged. But there are very few children on Sakhalin and there are almost no aged, so that in actuality the coefficient of 12.5 percent refers only to those of working age. Since it is shown to be lower than the facts warrant, and since it was calculated in relation to a population of 15,000, the death rate is at least half again as large as that indicated here.

At present Sakhalin has three medical centers, one in each district: in Alexandrovsk, Rykovskoye and Korsakov. Hospitals are called district infirmaries in the old-fashioned way, and those huts or wards where patients with minor illnesses are treated are called clinics. Each district is assigned one physician, and all medical matters are headed by the director of the medical department, a physician. The military have their own infirmaries and doctors, and the military doctors often substitute temporarily for prison doctors. During my visit, because of the absence of the director of the medical department, who had left to attend a prison exhibition, while the prison doctor had taken a leave of absence, the military doctor was in charge of the Alexandrovsk infirmary. During my presence in Dué the military doctor substituted for the prison doctor during the executions. The local infirmaries are guided by civilian hospital regulations and are supported by prison funds.

I will say a few words about the Alexandrovsk infirmary. It consists of several buildings resembling barracks,[15] with 180 beds. When I approached the infirmary, the new barracks with their heavy round logs glistened in the sun and exuded a coniferous odor. In the dispensary everything was new, everything was shiny and there was even a bust of Botkin[16] sculptured by a convict from a photograph. "It's not a very good likeness," said the medical assistant, glancing at the bust. As usual there were large boxes of medicinal bark and roots, from which a good half had already been dispensed. As I proceeded farther into the barracks, I found the floor between the two rows of beds has been covered with fir twigs. The beds were of wood. On one lay a convict from Dué with his throat cut. The wound is over half a vershok long, dry and gaping. You can hear the air escaping. The patient complains that he had been hit by a falling tree which injured his side. He requested admittance to the surgery, but was refused by a medical assistant. Feeling deeply insulted, he attempted suicide—he cut his throat. There is no bandage on his neck; the wound is left to heal itself. Some three to four arshins to the right of this patient is a Chinese with gangrene, to the left a convict with erysipelas. In the corner lies another with erysipelas. . . . The dressings of the surgical patients are filthy; the marine cord is suspicious, looking exactly as though it has been walked on. The medical assistant and the infirmary workers are undisciplined, do not understand questions, and look unpleasant. A convict called Sozin, who had been a medical assistant when he was free, is the only one who obviously knows the proper regimen in a Russian hospital, and it seems to me that he is the only person in the entire hospital staff who will not offend the god Aesculapius by his attitude toward his duties.

Later I visited the ambulatory patients. The receiving room next to the dispensary was new; it smelled of fresh wood and varnish. The desk where the doctor sits is enclosed with a wooden lattice like a banker's office, so that during his examination the patient never comes close to the doctor, who in the majority of cases examines him from a distance. Next to the doctor there is a student medical assistant who plays silently with a pencil. It looks as though the assistant is undergoing an examination.

Some men and women are scurrying about while a guard with a revolver stands at the door. This strange circumstance disturbs the patients, and I feel that there are no syphilitics or women who will willingly discuss their illnesses in the presence of the guard with the revolver and of other men. There are few patients. They are all suffering either from *febris sachalinensis,* from eczema, or their "hearts hurt," or they are malingerers. Convict patients keep begging to be released from work.

A young boy was brought in with an abscess on his neck. I must incise it. I ask for a scalpel. The medical assistant and two men jump up from their seats and run off; they return in a little while and hand me a scalpel. The instrument is blunt, but they tell me this is impossible because the blacksmith sharpened it recently. Again the assistant and the men jump up and after two or three minutes they bring me another scalpel. I begin to cut, and this scalpel also proves to be dull. I ask for carbolic acid; they bring it to me but they take their time. It is obvious that carbolic acid is seldom used. There is no basin, no cotton balls, no probes, no good scissors, and not even enough water.

The average daily number of ambulatory patients is 11, the average yearly number (for 5 years) 2,581. The average number of bed patients is 138. The infirmary has 1 senior,[17] 1 junior physician and 2 medical assistants, a midwife (1 for 2 districts) and, terrible to relate, there are 68 workers, 48 men and 20 women. In 1889, this infirmary cost 27,832 rubles, 96 kopecks.[18]

The 1889 report states that there were 21 forensic examinations and autopsies in all 3 districts. Injuries required 7 examinations, pregnant women 58, and 67 examinations were conducted to determine the ability to withstand corporal punishment according to the sentences of the court.

I add here excerpts from this report which cover the

hospital inventory. In all three infirmaries the total inventory was as follows:

Gynecological set, 1; laryngoscopic set, 1; maximum thermometers, 2, both broken; thermometers "for taking body temperatures," 9, 2 broken; thermometers "for taking high temperatures," 1; trocar, 1; injectors, 3, the needle broken in 1; pewter syringes, 29; scissors, 9, 2 broken; enema tubes, 34; drainage tubes, 1; large mortar and pestle, 1, with cracks; razor strop, 1; cupping glasses, 14.

It is clear from *Information on Receipt and Expenditure of Medications in the Governmental Medical Institutions on Sakhalin Island* that in all three districts the following were expended during the reported year: 36½ poods of hydrochloric acid and 26 poods of chlorated lime; carbolic acid, 18½ pounds; aluminum crudum, 56 pounds; and more than a pood of camphor. Camomile, one pood, nine pounds. Quinine, 1 pood, 8 pounds, and 5½ pounds of red cayenne pepper. (The report does not contain the amounts of alcohol used.) Oak bark, 1 pound; mint, 1½ poods; arnica, ½ pood; marshmallow, 3 poods; turpentine, 3½ poods; olive oil, 3 poods; another type of olive oil, 1 pood, 10 pounds; iodoform, ½ pood. . . . According to the data in the *Information,* not including the lime, 63½ poods of all sorts of medications, hydrochloric acid, alcohol, disinfecting and dressing materials were used. Consequently the Sakhalin population can pride itself that in 1889 it was given a tremendous dosage.

I will cite two articles of the law pertaining to the convicts' health: (1) Work which is harmful to people's health is not permitted even if chosen by the prisoners themselves ("Supreme Affirmation of the Opinion of the Government Council," January 6, 1886, p. 11). (2) Pregnant women are excused from work until their delivery and after delivery for forty days. Afterward women who are breast-feeding their babies are assigned lighter tasks to the extent required to prevent harm to the mother or the breast-fed baby. Convict women are usually permitted one and a half years to breast-feed their children. (*Code on Convicts,* Article 297, 1890 edition.)

¹ In 1874 the ratio of the sick to the total population in the Korsakov district was 227.2:100 (Sintsovsky, "Hygienic Conditions of the Convicts," *Health*, 1875, No. 16).

² Incidentally, I came across such diagnoses as excessive suckling of the breast, lack of development toward life, psychical heart disease, inflammation of the body, inner exhaustion, curious pneumonias, growth, etc.

³ See Vasilyev, "A Journey to Sakhalin Island," *Archives of Forensic Medicine* (1870), No. 2, for information on this epidemic disease, which extended all over Sakhalin in 1868, and on the vaccination of foreigners in 1858.

⁴ Rash (*Lat.*).

⁵ There was not a single case in July, August and September of 1889. Only one death has occurred from croupous pneumonia in October during the past ten years. This month can be considered the healthiest on Sakhalin.

⁶ Incidentally I found the following in this report: "The convicts are subjected to brutal beatings with birch rods and are brought to the infirmary in an unconscious state after the beating."

⁷ Dr. Vasilyev often met Gilyaks on Sakhalin who were suffering from dysentery.

⁸ I remind the reader that these age groups refer to 24.3 percent and 24.1 percent of the entire convict population.

⁹ Syphilis is most frequently observed in the Alexandrovsk Post. This concentration of the disease is explained in the report as being due to the significant number of newly arrived prisoners and their families, the soldiers, the artisans, and the entire incoming population, the arrival of ships in the Alexandrovsk and Dué waters, and summer seasonal work. The report also contains measures used against syphilis: (1) examination of convicts on the first and fifteenth of every month; (2) examination of newly arrived convict groups to the island; (3) weekly examination of women of questionable character; (4) inspection of those formerly afflicted with syphilis. Despite all these examinations and inspections, "a significant percentage of syphilitics are not included in the records." Dr. Vasilyev, who was assigned to Sakhalin in 1869 to render medical aid to foreigners, found no Gilyaks suffering from syphilis. The Ainus call syphilis a Japanese disease. The

Japanese who come to work in the fishing industries are obliged to present a medical certificate to the consul certifying that they are not suffering from syphilis.

10 The prolonged incarceration in central prisons and ships' holds is conducive to scurvy and sometimes whole groups of prisoners became afflicted with it soon after arriving on the island. One correspondent writes: "The last transport of prisoners from the *Kostrom* arrived in good health, but now everyone has scurvy" (*Vladivostok*, 1885, No. 30).

11 A convict complaining of migraine or sciatica is often suspected of malingering and denied access to the infirmary. One day I saw a large group of convicts begging the prison warden to send them to the infirmary. He refused because he did not want to be bothered sorting out the sick from the well.

12 For example, pangs of conscience, longing for the homeland, pride, constant abuse, loneliness and the various quarrels among convicts.

13 Dr. Vasilyev says: "Among the Gilyaks the continuous contemplation of fields of snow is tremendously influential in causing diseases of the eyes. I know through experience that a few days after continuous contemplation of snow fields blennorrheal inflammation of the mucous membrane of the eyes can take place." Convicts are very prone to night blindness (nyctalopia). Sometimes it attacks entire groups of prisoners, who can only grope in the darkness, holding on to one another.

14 The writer of the report comments on these cases as follows: "The distribution of convict women as cohabitants for convict settlers is of a coercive nature." To avoid being sent out to work, some convicts maim themselves by chopping off the fingers of their right hand, or in other ways. Malingerers are especially ingenious. They apply red-hot five-kopeck pieces to their flesh, purposely get frostbitten feet, use some sort of Caucasian pulverized drug which when applied to a small wound or even an abrasion produces a foul ulcer with a putrid excretion. One inserted snuff into his urethra, etc. The *manzy* [Chinese], who are sent here from the Primorskaya district, malinger more than any others.

15 The infirmary covers an area of 8,574 square sazhens, consists of 11 buildings and is divided into 3 sections: (1) The administrative building, which includes the drug dispensary, surgery, receiving office, 4 barracks, a kitchen with the woman's section next to it, and the chapel. The entire complex is called the infirmary.

(2) Two buildings for male and female syphilitics, a kitchen and guardroom. (3) Two buildings housing patients suffering from epidemic diseases.

16 Sergey Petrovich Botkin, 1832–89. Renowned clinical physician. First to build an experimental medical research laboratory in Russia. Author, lecturer and medical innovator.—TRANS.

17 He is the director of the medical department.

18 Clothing and linen cost 1,795 rubles, 60 kopecks; food, 12,832 rubles, 94 kopecks; medicines, surgical instruments and apparatus, 2,309 rubles, 60 kopecks; the commissariat, office and other expenses, 2,500 rubles, 16 kopecks; the medical personnel, 8,300 rubles. Repairs were made at prison cost; the workers were free. Now I invite you to make a comparison. The Zemstvo Hospital in Serpukhov, Moskovskaya *guberniya,* was built luxuriously and furnished according to modern scientific requirements. In 1893 there was a daily average of 43 bed patients, an average of 36.2 ambulatory patients (13,278 yearly), and the doctor operated daily on serious cases, was on the alert for epidemics, maintained complicated records, etc. This, the best hospital in the district, cost the Zemstvo 12,803 rubles, 17 kopecks in 1893; insurance and building repairs amounted to 1,298 rubles and the workers' wages of 1,260 rubles were included in the total. (See *Survey of the Serpukhovskoye Zemstvo Sanitary-Medical Organizations for 1892–93.*) Medicine is very expensive on Sakhalin; in addition the infirmary is disinfected "by fumigation with chlorine," there is no ventilation, and the soup which I saw prepared in Alexandrovsk for the patients was extremely salty, because it was made from corned beef. Until recently, supposedly "due to an insufficient supply of kitchenware and disorganization in the kitchen," the patients were fed from the common prison kettle (Order No. 66, 1890).

ABOUT THE AUTHOR

Anton Pavlovich Chekhov, outstanding nineteenth-century Russian short-story writer and world-famous dramatist, when asked for an autobiography by the editor of a magazine, wrote:

"You want my autobiography? Here it is. I was born in Taganrog in 1860. I graduated from the gymnasium. I got an M.D. from Moscow University. I received the Pushkin Prize. I began to write in 1879. I took a trip to Sakhalin in 1890. I took a trip to Europe, where I drank excellent wine and ate oysters. . . . I sinned a little in the drama, but moderately. My works were translated into all languages, except foreign. . . .

"With my colleagues, the doctors, as well as my fellow writers, I have excellent relations. . . . I would love to get a pension. But it is all nonsense. Write whatever you wish . . . if you run out of facts, replace them with lyrics."

ABOUT THE TRANSLATORS

Luba and Michael Terpak, an American husband-and-wife translating team, received their training in Slavonic languages at Columbia University. They have translated poetry from the Russian, Ukrainian, and Belorussian, have written articles about travel in the USSR and on the Soviet theater, and have had a great deal of experience in simultaneous translation from the Russian and the Ukrainian.